GOD, BOMBS & VIET NAM

Based on the Diary of a 20-year-old Navy Enlisted Man
in the Vietnam Air War – 1967

Gerald MacLennon

USS Oriskany WestPac Cruise 50th Anniversary Edition
February 16, 2017

GOD, BOMBS & VIET NAM:
Based on the Diary of a 20-Year-Old US Navy Enlisted Man in the Vietnam Air War – 1967

Author: Gerald MacLennon
Photo collages and cover designs by Gerald MacLennon

Executive Producer – Jeris Logan Haney

© Copyright 2012, Gerald MacLennon USA
© Copyright 2017, Gerald MacLennon USA

US Copyright Office Registered 2017
Permissions: geraldmaclennon@hotmail.com – Subject Line: GB&VN

Front Cover Photography
#1 Crusader F-8 Fighter Jet unleashing its missiles over North Vietnam
[photo by LTjg Charles Rudd, VFP-63, US Navy Aviator]
#2 The USS Forrestal ablaze on 29 July 1967, Gulf of Tonkin, Vietnam
[photo by PHAN Ernest Lewis, USN]

Back Cover Photography
#1 On the USS Oriskany (CVA-34) flight deck, pilot LTjg Dave Beam and Plane Captain Jackson approach their RF-8G Crusader aircraft.
[by PH3 Logan USN]
#2 On liberty, USS Oriskany tied up at Army Pier, Sasebo, Japan
[by PH3 Logan USN]
#3 Three Navy Destroyers escort the USS Oriskany in the Gulf of Tonkin as a typhoon nears Yankee Station.
[by PH3 Logan USN]

A Special Thank You to:
David Beam CDR USN-ret [VFP-63]
Harry Sampson CDR USN-ret [VFP-63]
Ronald G Sonniksen CDR USN-ret [VFP-63]
Harry W Hebb PHC USN-ret [VFP-63]

ISBN-13: 978-1975633332
ISBN-10: 1975633334

DISCLAIMER

Although this account is largely autobiographical, certain artistic liberties have been taken with people, places and events depicted. Some material is fiction based on non-fictional circumstances. I have altered names, personalities and otherwise disguised some men for purposes of sparing embarrassment or added sorrow to individuals and families involved. It is not my intention to dishonor the memory of any Vietnam Veteran alive or dead; for all provided noble service to our nation. Any derogatory comments uttered by these very young men (my 20-year-old self especially) were for the most part mere opinion, scuttlebutt, joking, ranting or playful harassment – the type born out of the human tendency for men to squabble, develop pet peeves and just plain bitch and moan when confined to one mission, in one base of operations for long, stressful periods of time.

Today I look back and realize that all of these men were my brothers – and most readers will understand that brothers certainly can have their differences. The officers and public figures in this narrative, such as John McCain III, are accurately represented and need not be cloaked with pseudonyms. No attempt has been made to create comprehensive or balanced characterizations. A few of the main players in this production are composite characters. for example, Petty Officer Craig Danko is a composite of several leading petty officers I encountered during my hitch, including my boot camp company commander, a man whom at first I swore must have been born a sadist but after twelve weeks of misery, I realized the guy's job was to make men out of spoiled, rebellious teenage boys, an extremely difficult task. In this book, I portray the characters as our lives related to participation in President Johnson's Operation Rolling Thunder and also to reveries of family and acquaintances back home in the States.

Any similarity of a fictional character to an actual, living person is coincidental; and should not be construed as intentional malice. To my knowledge, I have not misrepresented the atmosphere of the circumstances as I knew them in 1967-68. If you believe that I have, this old veteran offers his most sincere apologies. I will make amends in my next printing.

Gerald Logan MacLennon

*To S. Without your persistent
encouragement this book would
not have been published.*

PREFACE

This is not another Vietnam memoir penned by a retired officer. It is the story of a 20-year-old U.S. Navy Enlisted man trying to make sense of life in general and his own life in particular as he obediently participated in what was called a justifiable police action by our nation's leaders. The entirety of the original diary was written from the O-2 level of the attack aircraft carrier, U.S.S. Oriskany (CVA-34). It's a story of a young man seeking an identity and a sense of purpose amidst bombs, rockets and sordid temptations of port cities abroad.

This was my reality – my culture's reality in the year 1967. And, it was the U.S. Navy culture of that time. True to form, the dialogue is salted with an excess of crude and obscene language, bigotry and misogyny. If I had cleaned-up those aspects it would not have been an honest representation.

Gerald MacLennon is not the same man today that he was fifty years ago. I've been tried and tested thousands of times. As a result, I've learned invaluable lessons with each experience. My older and wiser self is not condoning the behaviors and attitudes of who I was at twenty. I believe the value of this account comes by recognizing that many of the struggles Petty Officer 3rd Class MacLennon encountered are common to young men then and now. And that, if the reader fits this category, he may know and understand that there is indeed safe mooring just beyond the horizon. Through perseverance, let him rest assured eventually his true identity and purpose will be revealed.

Additionally, the reader will soon recognize that the style of writing in this book, especially the free flow of emotional expression, is not typical of a young man with military training. Most of us male animals can attest to the fact that peer pressure often demands we project an image of toughness and heartlessness, especially in our early adulthood, as in, "We take no shit, show no compassion and feel no pain."

I emphasize that the book is based on my Vietnam cruise diary. During my off-and-on, two decade writing process, I employed regression techniques that allowed me to return to the mind of Gerald MacLennon, United States Navy 1967 and, more importantly, return to what I was feeling on the inside at that time. It was a tedious process and in some cases painful but I believe it was worthwhile because it has resulted in personal healing and a heartfelt account that I want to pass on to future generations long after this old body is rotting in the grave and my soul joins those poor bastards who came home from 'Nam in black body bags.

For this edition, I *am* pleased to say one retired officer, pilot and friend, CDR Harry B. Sampson, USN has consented to including two of his accounts of the Vietnam War in the Epilogue of this book.

Gerald Logan MacLennon

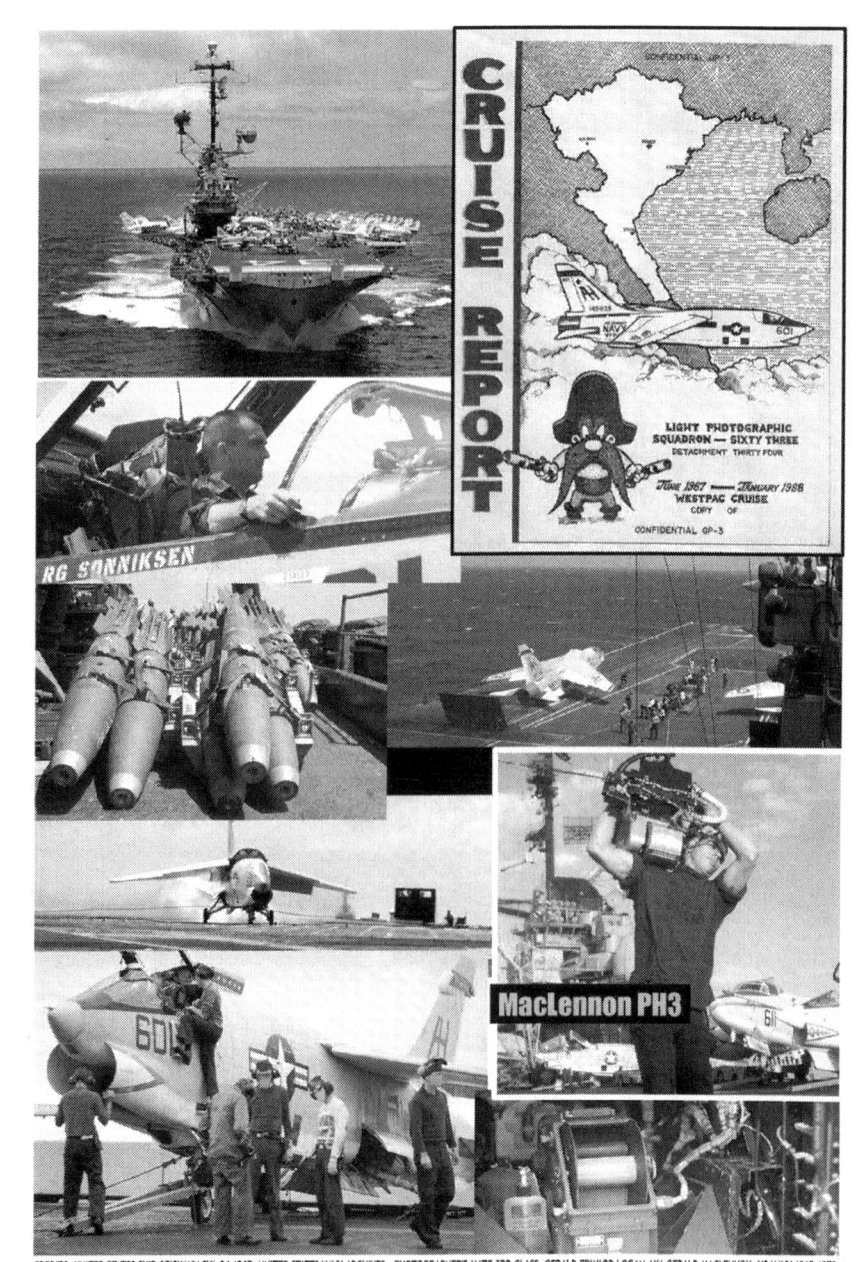

CREDITS: UNITED STATES SHIP ORISKANY CVA-34 1967, UNITED STATES NAVY ARCHIVES; PHOTOGRAPHER'S MATE 3RD CLASS GERALD EDWARD LOGAN AKA GERALD MACLENNON, US NAVY 1965-1970

DEDICATION

I dedicate this book to the memory of my shipmate and friend, Big Ern; it is also dedicated to Master Chief William Leon Logan, US Navy; to my step-father, Chief Neal Cady, US Navy-retired who honorably served his country for thirty years during World War II, Korea and Vietnam; to my biological father, Navy Chief Engineer Harry Dean Salisbury, who likewise served in all three wars; to my cousin, Captain Gary Hilding, US Army, Huey pilot and a time-delayed victim of Agent Orange... and Mister Rudd. May your memories be for blessing. I dedicate it to all the dead and MIA's, to the PTSD's and all who participated in the Vietnam War, in all wars, including those who went to early graves here at home because of the ghosts that continued to haunt them even as they sought to reclaim a semblance of sanity. Thanks men. *All gave some. Some gave all.*

I'd be remise not to add a word of appreciation for the wives, fiancés and sweethearts back in the States who waited and worried for their men in 'Nam; for the mothers, fathers and other family members who likewise lived with a chronic subliminal apprehension. These dear people also bore an additional burden because of the unpopularity of the Vietnam War. They unjustly suffered alienation from their own society; a cruel estrangement from fellow citizens for whom their servicemen (and women, too) placed their lives on the line. May such callousness, on such a large scale, never, never occur again in this, the greatest of all nations on earth, the United States of America.

A special thank you to my detachment commanding officer, Commander Ronald G. Sonniksen, U.S. Navy—retired, who on 12 September 2012 ordered me, by telephone from San Diego, to "Grow some balls and get that book published!"

I proceeded as ordered. His son had told me by email that the Old Man was not in the best of health. Unaware of the extent of his illness, I was saddened when I learned that Mr. Sonniksen had taken permanent leave from this world three months later on December 7th, 2012. God bless your soul, Sir.

Gerald MacLennon
16 February 2013

NEWSLETTER

LIGHT PHOTOGRAPHIC SQUADRON 63
DETACHMENT THIRTY-FOUR
5 NOVEMBER-17 DECEMBER
MCMLXVII

CREDITS: CVA-34 UNITED STATES NAVY ARCHIVES; GERALD MACLENNON PH3 USN 1967; PEOPLES REPUBLIC OF VIETNAM PROPAGANDA LITERATURE 1967, KOWLOON, HONG KONG
OFFICERS OF PHOTO RECON SQUADRON-63 Det 34: (L-R) LTJG CHARLES H RUDD, LT HARRY B SAMPSON, LCDR RONALD G SONNIKSEN, UNIDENTIFIED, UNIDENTIFIED, LTJG DAVID M BEAM

CONTENTS

A Crashing Halt To Civility 1
Kicked Out By The Mouse 5
U.S.S. Oriskany (Cva-34) 9
Photo Recon Squadron 13
Steaming Across The Pacific 19
Olongapo City 27
Russian Bears Approaching 33
Back In The Philippines 37
Entering The War Zone 39
Reminiscing On My Sister'S Birthday 51
Eluding The Dogs Of North Vietnam 61
Meeting Michael Goldberg 67
Back To The Bombing 77
Down Time Off The Line 97
The Tonkin Gulf Yacht Club 107
Second Conversation With Michael 119
From Silly Sacred To Dead Serious 123
Fight To Win Or Get Out 125
Peggy Lee 131
The Micky Mouse Club 134
The Devil Within 137
First Period Finals 141
The Land Of The Rising Sun 145
Back To The Carnage 155
Tokyo Calling 195
The Great Buddha 200
Typhoon Gilda 205
From Tempest To Madness 209
Lesser Men Die; Presidents Don't 213
Music To Sooth The Savage 228
Rolling Thunder 231
Philippine Beauty & Debauchery 239
Christmas In Hong Kong 257
Last Chance To Die 271
Lieutenant Goldberg'S Omen 275
The Last Week Of War 285
Farewell To Pepé 291
Homebound 303
Epilogue 316
Distinguished Flying Cross (DFC) for Heroism at Thanh
    Hoa Bridge, 10/1967. *by CDR H. Sampson, USN-ret* 322
Remembering the USS Oriskany Fire, on Yankee Station,
    Tonkin Gulf, North Vietnam. *by CDR H. Sampson, USN-ret* ... 330
Navy Lingo Glossary 333

CHAPTER I
A CRASHING HALT TO CIVILITY

I write songs that nobody sings.

Aye, the devil, they say, still rides the waves in the soul of a seafarin' man. / Now, back in the States, I left there ashore a pretty young whore who swallowed my bore and was beggin' for more. / Gentlemen once, now pirates we be, raising hell from our ship on the South China Sea. / Aye, we'll sink all their boats and whatever floats; we'll kidnap their women and slit the men's throats. / Alas to our port, let the bar maids beware; when our demons come stalking, we'll strip you down bare, because... The devil, they say, still rides the waves in the soul of a seafarin' man.

A crude song about a crude war. Is it out-of-line? Maybe... but sometimes it seems the devil does stow away in the mind of a sailor. Sequestered out here on the briny blue, I share company with about thirty-five hundred swinging dicks, and not one tender breast to be seen. Three thousand, five hundred... that's one hell of a lot of horny dogs.

Cruising out here on the Tonkin Gulf, we are spared the despair of seeing the scenes of horror that our bombs inflict on men, women and children in North Vietnam.

Now on my third year away from my Lutheran household, I have learned some lessons of life. I now know for sure that power, lust, greed and the acquisition of money tend to trump any spring of innocent civility that the enlightened and wise, time and again, have attempted to endow on the race of man.

But here am I, riding this steel behemoth – the most ominous killing machine ever conceived; a weapon of war with the innocuous name of carrier. It transports our crew and air wing personnel to the Oriental dens of sin. It takes us to the blood-soaked terrain of the Vietnamese. It is, in a single thought, one of the most obscene but amazingly brilliant products of human ingenuity.

Far removed from family I am, and it wasn't all that long ago – a couple of years – that I sat there observing the Family MacLennon gathered at the river's shore in Omaha. Intently, I listened to my father's father and his two eldest sons singing songs to Jesus Christ in three-part harmony immediately followed by Rastus and Liza and

Abie jokes. Aye, 'tis wonderful to be Scots-Irish American – king of the hill and top of the heap. Be it not? Near my departure I was told on the long-distance phone, "Good luck over there. 'Hope your air wing kills a lot of them gooks."

What a heritage! And, that's the torch I was told would be passed on to me as I entered the age of maturity. Bullshit! I refused then and I still do now. I am moving forward in time; not backwards. Put the white sheets and the hood back in the trunk, Uncle Jed. That, among several good reasons, is why I left the placid Midwest and joined the Navy while yet just a boy of seventeen years. But y'know, matey, I never counted on being where I am right now. Holy Mother of God, I'm in a world of shit.

* * * * * * *

29 July 1967 – Gulf of Tonkin, North Vietnam

Our forty-third day at sea started out just like the others. No one, but God, could have foretold that by the end of this day one-hundred thirty-two Americans at sea would be dead, with just as many wounded. It's hard to believe that only six weeks ago we sailed out of San Francisco Bay and now this. Damn, things can change quickly.

Earlier this morning, we saw several junks and sampans originating out of coastal villages. They were using our sector of the Gulf of Tonkin for fishing. Dumb shits. It was another one of those heavy, damp summer mornings when the humidity was so thick our Flight Deck jerseys were soaked in sweat.

At 1045, Big Ern, Ray Hines, Harry Hedge and I were on deck giving Photo Bird 602 a pre-flight inspection. After cleaning the camera-bay windows on the RF-8G Crusader, we stood by for the arrival of Lieutenant JG David Beam, today's target for the Vietnamese Surface-to-Air Missiles... the SAM's. At 1100, Beam was in the cockpit, grinning and listening for orders from the Air Boss on the loud speakers tower.

Before we received word to start engines, I heard a booming noise in the distance somewhere across the blue. I thought nothing of it at first. Probably just a destroyer firing off a practice round.

Five seconds later... two, three, four, the percussions popped off like fireworks. I ran portside and saw a column of black smoke rising on the horizon. I couldn't see what was exploding. It was too far away. Maybe, I thought, a plane had blown-up in the ocean. No, there was too much smoke. The base of the smoke column was black and billowing and, as I watched, an orange fireball shot up, followed by another horrific explosion. A plane director in his yellow jersey came running over. "It's the Forrestal. She's blowin' up!"

Damn, I didn't even know the USS Forrestal was operating on the line with us. She's the first of what are called the super-carriers, with about 5,000 personnel onboard.

CHAPTER II
KICKED OUT BY THE MOUSE

For me, high school was a bust. Sitting at my desk at Lincoln Northeast, in our neatly aligned rows, I daydreamed about what I could be doing if only I was out there in the real world. My home life, although not ideal, was the common Midwestern variety. My father drank too much beer for his own good and fought with Mom too much. Friction was growing between Dad and I because I was nearing manhood and beginning to demand territorial rights in what was undeniably Neal MacLennon's little castle.

Junior High School had been different, not as much distress at home or in school. Yet there were embarrassments typically adolescent in nature. From age fourteen on, my skin was a zit-ridden disaster. And the zits weren't just your normal blackheads and pimples, they became infected and turned into what the dermatologist called pustulates. For two years, I made weekly trips to the skin doctor's office where his gorgeous, young assistant – much to my humiliation – had to lance and squeeze the disgusting little devils. Nothing seemed to slow the profusion of my facial blemishes not even X-ray treatments. When I left the office every Wednesday, my face looked like someone had set it on fire and tried to extinguish the blaze with a hatchet. With head lowered, I walked home as fast as possible, hoping no one would stare at me.

At school the next day, and every day, my fertile imagination and hypersensitivity had me convinced that groups of girls in the hallway were whispering about my Frankenstein face as I walked by. The laughter I heard after I passed them was always about me, of course, and all my physical imperfections: my mutated face, my gangly little body, my overgrown butt and my lop-sided head.

In high school, I strived to become just the opposite of that younger, nerdier Mac. I was running with the hoods and buying into whatever I thought was cool and rebellious. The flat top haircut that my father had forced on me since I was twelve was replaced by a greased down, slicked-back Duck's Ass. My dad, after much begging and bargaining on my part, bought me a black '56 Chevy Convertible with white rag top and chrome wheels. It was cherry. To round off the new persona, by age sixteen, I was smoking Lucky Strikes, drinking Schlitz beer, shoplifting, and cussing like a sailor.

I took off my glasses in the school halls so no one would call me four-eyes. Practicing in front of the bathroom mirror, I perfected my Marlon Brando leer.

In high school, I became two people. While I was trying to be a bad ass rebel, I was also president, vice-president and treasurer of the Luther League, our church's youth group. I held those positions alternatively with my best friend, Nathan Haus, a nice Christian kid who later went to seminary and became a Lutheran pastor. I was even sent to Midland Lutheran College one summer for Leadership School but got myself in trouble for passing around my drawings of naked women. The other boys enjoyed them but Janet Mainquist, upon intercepting the forbidden renderings, did not. She turned me in to the counselors and I got my ass royally chewed – in Christian love, of course.

The pop culture scene of 1963 was that period just before the British Invasion of the Beatles. Elvis and all his greased-back clones still ruled the airwaves. The Righteous Brothers were still righteous. Del Shannon still boss. We liked the Beach Boys as long as they stuck to songs about fast cars and California girls. Surfing wasn't too popular in Nebraska.

Three months after President Kennedy's assassination, I was expelled from Lincoln Northeast High School, the reason, permanently inscribed on my high school record, was indifference. I remember Egbert Shumacher, Dean of Students, escorting me to the front door. I had been his nemesis for several months: absent, tardy, lethargic and sassy but the day he kicked me out, it seemed to me that he was basking in his glory. I was finally out of his hair. Eggy the Mouse had won the game. Looking back, I can't really say if the assassination had anything to do with my attitude or if it merely took a prevailing attitude and made it worse.

I drifted for most of 1964. Our family moved to Fort Collins, Colorado where I re-entered high school as a FCHS Lambkin, and again as a sophomore, but I did not adapt to the new school environment as my parents had hoped. Soon I was skipping classes again. One afternoon in mid-October, parked in my Chevy at the local burger joint instead of in my desk at school, I was more uncaring, unscathed than ever before. By that time, I had refined indifference to a fine art. My cool was only slightly rattled when a familiar car pulled up alongside. It was Dad, but he wasn't angry. He got out and walked over to my open car window. He didn't shout or lecture me this time. Instead, he just looked me in the eye and in a firm but unusually gentle tone said to me, "Son, you have two choices: either stay in school or join the Navy. If you want to join the Navy, I'll take you down to the recruiter tomorrow. I want you to think about it, and give me your answer tonight."

On October 27, 1964, I was sworn in to the United States Navy in Denver, Colorado. On the morning of October 28th, I was jolted out of my bunk at 5:00 AM to begin twelve weeks of hell on earth as a Seaman Recruit at the United States Naval Training Center, San Diego, California. Boot camp proved to be a lifesaver for me. Suffice it to say, I learned self-discipline, self-esteem and respect for authority. For a spoiled brat from the comfortable American suburbs, boot camp was a radical culture shock. I hated every minute of it but, by the same token, it was the best thing that ever happened to me. I cursed my father right up to the day I graduated, but, thereafter, have respected him immensely for having the wisdom to know exactly what I needed.

Because I received high scores on my boot camp tests, I was allowed to choose my favorite job rating. Photography was the closest to art I could find, so I applied for Aviation Photographer's Mate and was granted the Naval School of Photography in Pensacola, Florida. The Navy has also administered GED tests which will grant me a Certificate of High School Equivalency from the State of Nebraska when I'm released from active service. The G.I. Bill will give me bucks for college.

Prior to this Vietnam Cruise, I was stationed in the Philippines for eighteen months working at the Fleet Intelligence Center Pacific Facility at Subic Bay. We handled all the significant photo reconnaissance film shot over Southeast Asia. We'd process film, make select prints, run it through the photo interpreters, package and send it to Fleet Intelligence in Hawaii, or to Defense Intelligence, the CIA or one of the other agencies in Washington, D.C.

As for recreation, millions of old fleet sailors can tell you about the liberty call at Subic Bay and the sinful pleasures of Olongapo City – anything your heart's desire, for a price – and they all do it with wry smiles on their faces.

CHAPTER III
U.S.S. ORISKANY (CVA-34)

15 July 1967
Alameda Naval Station, San Francisco Bay, California.

The United States Ship Oriskany (CVA-34) is a small Aircraft Carrier – small compared to the majority of carriers in the U.S. Fleet. She is approximately one-fifth of a mile long but I won't bother with boring technicalities. I'll just mention that she's big enough to accommodate about sixty aircraft. She is an attack carrier, a CVA. The bird farm, as we call her, can travel in excess of thirty knots. We have a handful of pet names for her: The Mighty-O, The Big O, the O-Boat, the Old Risky, and one that I prefer: The Big Zero.

The Oriskany is a mountainous mass of steel and iron: steel bulkheads, decks, overheads; steel pipes, vents, sinks, even steel commodes. The overheads are low, a constant hazard to anyone taller than 5-feet-10. The hatches throughout the ship are a hazard to everyone's shins. One must step up from 10-to-20 inches to clear the hatchways which range, on the average, about thirty feet apart. Negotiating long distances at moderate speed is like running hurdles. Being heat-conductive metal, the ship can become extremely warm on these sunny, summer days. The ventilation system is a life-saver. Many compartments would be like sauna baths if not for the vents and blowers. For the virgins onboard, the ship is a hopeless maze; Levitt discovered that. The Oriskany's Flight Deck is heavy steel girders and plating, covered with tight rows of wood, similar to railroad ties, and then coated with asphalt and non-skid surfacing. The forward section accommodates two steam catapults and the Number One Elevator, which lowers to the Hangar Deck. The rear section is the angle deck with four arresting cables for snaring the landing aircraft. There is one elevator on the mid-port side and another on the rear starboard making a total of three for transporting planes from the Flight Deck to the 3-sector Hangar Bay maintenance and repair facility and vice-versa.

While on cruise, about 35-hundred men occupy the Oriskany. There's Ship's Company, permanently stationed personnel who take care of normal shipboard operations and then there's us, the

Carrier Air Group – Navy Pilots and Airdales. We handle the aviation operations. The Carrier Air Group (CAG) is comprised of several detachments from shore-based squadrons in California. The Attack Squadrons all use A-4 Skyhawk aircraft. The Fighter Squadrons are all F-8 Crusaders, with one exception, the antiquated A-1 Spad propeller-driven planes flown by Attack Squadron-152. I often use the word "Bombers" when referring to the Attack jets even though they are not US military bombers in the true sense of the word... but they do carry bombs and they do drop them. So, why not? It would be weird to call them "Attackers." There are also smaller specialized detachments such as Early Warning Aircraft, known affectionately as Willie Fudds. These craft are prop-driven, with radar domes, radomes, mounted on top of the fuselage. My squadron, Photographic Reconnaissance Squadron-63 (VFP-63), known as The Eyes of the Fleet, performs an essential service to CAG. We find the targets for the bombing missions and assess the damage after the raids. We fly Crusaders with no assault capability, just cameras. Our protection comes from a Fighter escort. Flight operations on the Old Risky are an exercise in precision timing. To launch all aircraft, re-spot the planes, and recover incoming craft requires a keen awareness of fuel capacity and flight times for all planes as well as efficient Flight Deck maneuvering. Safety is preached to us constantly especially in regard to Flight Deck operations. A jet's rotary turbine engine with its intake suction and exhaust blast can kill a guy in seconds. You definitely can't have your head up your ass. Flight crew has to always remain vigilant as dozens of planes are on the move. Our Hazardous Duty Pay is well-earned.

In addition to housing the navigational center of the Captain's Bridge, the superstructure (or island) of the carrier is the brain of the ship. Here, standard tasks, flight coordination, radar tracking, meteorology, and radio communication take place. On the Hangar Deck, facilities are provided for squadrons to work on aircraft. It is possible to completely tear down and rebuild a plane onboard ship.

Now consider the noise, the sounds of the carrier: the metal hull reverberates the chisels and hammers of painters. On the 1MC, the ship's public address system, we hear the shrill whistle of the Boatswain's pipe followed by an announcement from a gravelly voice. Atop the ship, mechanics test their aircraft engines creating a roar similar to Nebraska tornadoes coursing over the prairie. Then add to that the noise of flight quarters when dozens of jets turn up simultaneously, vibrating the ship in preparation for launch from the catapults. Then there's the awful booming noise of aircraft recovery. When a bird catches the arresting cable or wire, as we call it, a piercing screech ricochets off the bulkheads of the Hangar Deck because the activated mechanism runs down to that level. It's a very shrill metal-on-metal noise. Ever present is the hum of the ship's engines. So, too, the rushing sound of the ventilation system blowers in every compartment.

Drills aboard ship are essential for keeping the crew primed and ready for action. Fire and General Quarters are the main drills. Ship's Company wants no repeat of last year's disaster. On the morning of October 26, 1966, fire broke out in the ordnance storage pit of the Oriskany's Hangar Bay One due to careless handling of flares. The flame and smoke were significant, the heat very intense. Officers' Country is just above Bay One. Most of the forty-three fatalities were Officers. As their steel compartments transformed into ovens, they succumbed to extreme heat and smoke inhalation. Too damaged to continue missions over North Vietnam, the Oriskany steamed back to Subic Bay, Philippines for preliminary patch-up, then home to Naval Station Alameda, California, for major repairs. As a result of last year's disaster, Captain Billy Holder has become fanatically fire conscious. 'Can't blame him. Most of Ship's Company were required to attend Fire Fighting School prior to deployment. Several fire drills are held weekly while at sea and in-port.

CHAPTER IV
PHOTO RECON SQUADRON

Whenever a few planes detach from our main squadron at Naval Air Station Miramar, California for temporary assignment to an Aircraft Carrier, they receive a letter designation such as Alpha (A), Bravo (B), Charlie (C), and so on. We are Photographic Reconnaissance Squadron-63, detachment G, or in military lingo, VFP-63, Det Golf. Our Oriskany detachment constitutes three RF-8G Crusader aircraft; four Navy Pilots and thirty-five Enlisted Men.

Our Officer-in-Charge is pilot Lieutenant Commander Ronald G. Sonniksen, a seasoned air-combat veteran. The Old Man is in his mid-thirties. He's tough in a good way – a guy you like to dislike – but, at the same time, one you respect. If a Hollywood casting director was looking for a man to play the role of a hardened Naval Aviator, Ron would fit the bill perfectly. Standing about 6-foot, Mr. Sonniksen carries himself with dignity. His facial features are rugged: thick black eyebrows; square jaw; high-chiseled cheekbones; a beard so thick that a couple of hours after his morning shave, he has five o'clock shadow. When he barks commands with his deep baritone voice, we jump. I'm in awe of the guy but, of course, I'd never admit that to anyone.

The other five Officers are in their early to mid-twenties.

This is the second Vietnam tour for pilot Lieutenant Harry Sampson. Standing 5-foot-10, Sampson is a reserved, no-nonsense type of fellow. If he displays any humor, it's usually in the form of sarcasm. His hair is a light, sandy brown. All the Officers have short military crew cuts, that's a given. The pilots call him "Dirty Harry"... we grunts just call him Lieutenant Sam. Contemplative but congenial, he's an "I love to fly" aviator, who could very well end up as a NASA Astronaut someday.

Lieutenants Junior Grade Charles Rudd and David Beam are the virgin fly boys. This is their first experience in a bona fide combat zone and even though they try to mask it, I can tell they're apprehensive. I don't know much about his background but Mr. Rudd reminds me of a handsome, intellectual man-around-campus. Not only is he a pilot but he serves as the detachment's Administrative Officer. Even-tempered and amiable, Mr. Rudd doesn't flaunt his superiority in rank over us Airdales. He treats us respectfully, like fellow humans, and we return the favor. We have nicknamed LTJG Beam, "Beamer" because when he smiles, the corners of his mouth extend from ear to ear, and he literally beams. He's the joker of the Officers – hands down, the most well-liked Officer among the grunts. It's to a pilot's advantage to be extra good to his support team because the integrity of his aircraft and photo recon equipment and often his very life, depend on our efficiency.

Our Photographic Intelligence Officers are Lieutenant Junior Grade James Norville Muffley and Ensign Kenneth Alan Kanker. Sometimes, I refer to them respectively as Merkin Muffley – after the president in "Dr. Strangelove" – and Kanker Sore. Not to their faces of course. Anyway, the two photo intel officers are not aviators on this cruise but are ultimately responsible for making damned sure the aerial photo images our pilots shoot are correctly read and interpreted. Supervising the three Photo Intelligencemen, Muffley and Kanker must be reasonably sure of their targeting suggestions before passing them on to the bomber and fighter Squadrons. Additionally, they bear the burden of locating as many Anti-Aircraft Artillery (AAA) and Surface-to-Air Missile (SAM) sites around proposed targets as they possibly can. Rocket-bearing fighter aircraft attempt to take out AAA and SAM sites prior to the bombing runs. If the bomber pilots encounter unexpected heavy flak, Muffley and Kanker may also encounter unexpected heavy flak from the pilots... if they make it back alive. Lieutenant JG Merkin Muffley is a product of proud parentage and a Harvard education. In his mid-twenties, his boyish face doesn't match the Officer's countenance that he tries so hard to project. Ensign Kenny Kanker is an O-1. That's the bottom of the totem pole for Commissioned Officers. As the low-ranker, poor Kanker Sore catches a raft of shit, some of it deserved; some of it just plain mean-spirited. He will toughen up eventually.

The thirty-five Enlisted Men are divided into four divisions: Maintenance, Plane Captains, Photo and Photo Intelligence. The leading Chief Petty Officer (CPO) is Aviation Mechanic Chief O'Brian. He is a tough, dedicated career man with over twenty years of service. I work in Photo Division. I am one of the five Aviation Photographer's Mates (PH) that work together on the Flight Deck and in the Camera Repair Shop. I just call it the Photo

Shop. Our job is to maintain operation of the photographic systems aboard our aircraft. Each plane is capable of carrying six aerial cameras that when combined can photographically cover 180-degrees, horizon to horizon. The larger cameras are capable of taking 600 exposures on one mission. The cameras are electronically operated and require a very complicated system of computers, servo-power and exposure-control units.

Our Crusaders fly over North Vietnam and photograph the terrain. Upon returning to the ship, we unload the film on the Flight Deck and then rush it to the Flash Lab, the cramped little processing laboratory on the 02 level. From there, it goes to Photo Intelligence (PI) for interpretation. The elapsed time from touch-down to photo interpretation is about 25 minutes. The PI department staffed by the two Officers I already mentioned and three Enlisted Photographic Intelligencemen: Chapin PTAN, Duncan PT3, and Lehmann PT3, view the film. They sight and plot strategic targets for bombing, such as airfields, bridges, railroad lines, petroleum storage (POL) sights, power plants, communications sites, and ammo storage buildings. This information is conveyed to the other squadrons and launches are made to bomb and destroy.

So far in this war, the Navy's Photo Reconnaissance Squadrons have suffered three times the loss rate of other squadrons because the aircraft are forced to fly straight on a constant course to get the best imagery. This makes them highly vulnerable to anti-aircraft ground fire, surface-to-air missile strikes, and the occasional Russian MIG aircraft.

My little Aviation Photo Team is an eclectic mixture of personalities.

Petty Officer in Charge is Photographer's Mate First Class (PH1) Harry Hedge, age 25. At home in San Diego, he and his wife reside in off-base housing, with two kids. He's a straight arrow sort of guy, definitely all-military. Standing about 5-foot-10, he's even-featured and handsome. Harry routinely marches down to the barbershop every week for his regulation Marine haircut. He has aced three Naval Technical Training courses. The man knows his stuff. He can effectively troubleshoot any piece of photographic or computerized equipment on the RF-8G Photo Bird. For relaxation, he plays with his ham radio system. He and the Navy seem to be a perfect fit. Going on his eighth year, I'm sure Harry will be a twenty year lifer.

Our next ranking Petty Officer is Ray Hines, Photographer's Mate Second Class (PH2), age 24. Ray is a Colored Man from Tennessee, also with no college education but, as with Harry, he is an expert troubleshooter and repairman. Ray is highly dedicated to his work. Very slim, he stands about 5-foot-9 but can't weigh much over 140 pounds. Not exactly a Nat King Cole, Ray's face reveals a man who has seen too much bullshit in his young life. I'm sure that growing up Black in the South, he was expected to kowtow to Whitey in about every aspect of society. Many Southern Blacks have joined the military to escape the prejudice and discrimination of their hometowns. The Blacks, according to the rules and regs, are to receive fair and equal treatment in the Armed Forces. These rules have been in effect for many years although it has been alleged that in-country infantry has a disproportionate number of Colored Men in the front lines of combat. Not so with Navy service. The only time I see Ray really cut loose is when he invites his Southern brothers up to our compartment for poker. When together, the evening is filled with laughter and jive talk. It's like a foreign language. I can't understand a damned thing they're saying. It could be they like it that way. Part of me resents that exclusion but I have to remember where they've come from and what they've been through.

Photographer's Mate Third Class Richard Aden (PH3), who goes by Dick, is one of our two displaced intellectuals. Also 24 years old, he and I are the same rank but I'm a high school drop-out. Dick is only one semester from a Bachelor's Degree at the University of Wisconsin in Madison. I'm not sure how he ended up in Uncle Sam's Navy. I've never quizzed him about it but even with different educational experiences, I feel more of a kindred spirit with him than with the three others. Dick is introspective. He likes to read science fiction and heady books like Atlas Shrugged. Of medium height and build, his hair, when not completely shaved off, is a very dark brown, his eyebrows thick. He sports a wide, Arab-style mustache. Sometimes we jokingly refer to him as Mustache Pot. With three years under his belt, he's counting the days until he is released from what he calls "indentured servitude."

The other intellectual is Photographic Airman Ernest Levitt also 24. He is the most fascinating and frustrating man in our crew. With a very lackadaisical attitude toward personal cleanliness and hygiene, Big Ern, as we call him, stands 6-foot-4. His large frame supports 280 pounds of flabby muscle and fat. His gut bulges over his belt. He has a swayback that tends to exaggerate the size of his belly even more. Pepper hair grows wild atop his full, round head. Oily, smudged glasses cover his entire nose except for the red, bulbous tip and bubble nostrils. Boasting a Master's Degree in history, also from the University of Wisconsin, Ern is highly intelligent when it comes to academic subjects but woefully ignorant about simple, mechanical problems. For instance, you can name any event in human history and he can give you a five-minute synopsis including names and dates but he forgets which direction to turn a camera mounting plug. Clockwise, damnit! Righty tighty!

Ernest is an E-3, an Airman, with no desire to achieve the next highest rating. He postulates that in becoming a Petty Officer, he will be colluding with the military-industrial complex, a phrase coined by President Eisenhower just before he left office a few years ago. Actually, I don't understand why Big Ern even took the effort to join the Navy if he hates it so much. A great lover of books, Mr. Levitt submerges himself regularly, and once he's in his deep state of concentration, it's damned hard to bring him back to the real world. At times, Ern can be a great guy. At other times, he gnaws at our patience by his catty little statements or his insistence on the implementation of some totally impractical idea, like saving scrap pieces of film so we can recycle them. During carrier qualification, Levitt had a few close calls. On the Flight Deck, he almost walked behind a jet exhaust. On another occasion, he was carrying a camera down a ladder and slipped. He and the camera fell. He bruised his ass and broke the five-thousand dollar camera. Awkward and clumsy, he still rams his head on the low overheads. He constantly drops film magazines because, in his words: "The damned ship rocks too much."

Almost replaced in Alameda, he was given a final option as to whether he wanted the cruise or not. He thought about it and decided to go mainly because he wants to take photos of Spanish Missions in the Philippines to add to his collection of Mexican and

Southwest American missions. The Air War? That's just incidental to Big Ern. Funny guy, Ern.

The youngster of the group is 20-year-old me, Gerald MacLennon, Photographer's Mate Third Class (PH3). Together, we are just one sometimes happy, always sarcastic little family. We work, bunk, laugh, cuss and squabble together. Our working space is also our living space. In one small compartment called Camera Repair or the Photo Shop, we have our sleeping racks, lockers, personal gear, cameras, magazines, dark room, film storage area and work bench.

One of the Photo Intelligencemen, Walt Lehmann (PT3), berths and lockers in our compartment as well. I like Walt. He and I are about the same age. He looks like a younger, thinner Robert Young, from the television show, Father Knows Best. He takes his work quite seriously but once our day's labor is done, he jokes around and fucks the dog just as much as the rest of us. Already, Walt and I have had several discussions about politics and religion. He is definitely opinionated but I don't mind, especially when a man's opinions are born of intelligence and sound reasoning. I think as days turn into months, Walt Lehmann and I will develop a close friendship. All of us are doing our best to get along because we are fully aware that we'll have to tolerate each other in very tight quarters for over seven months. We have undergone two weeks of Carrier Qualification testing off the coast of California. All men and equipment have performed superbly. Now, we look forward to continued excellence as we leave the United States bound for Vietnam. That sounded awfully friggin' gung-ho. Didn't it?

CHAPTER V
STEAMING ACROSS THE PACIFIC

16 June 1967 ... the first day.
Alameda Naval Station, San Francisco Bay, California.

After all the preparation, we finally deployed at 1000 this morning from Alameda. Loved ones living in the area lined the piers to wave their farewells. The day was overcast and damp. I stood on the Flight Deck as the U.S.S. Oriskany steamed out of the bay, watching San Francisco glide by for the last time until next February. I thought to myself that actually I wasn't saying goodbye to much at all. I am indeed happy to be leaving the United States and traveling back to the mystical world of the Orient.

Clouds blanketed the top half of the Golden Gate. As we passed under the famous bridge, a dozen people waved to us from above. Gaining speed, we entered the Pacific Ocean, encountering gale-force wind about five miles out. Flight Quarters were called. But we did not fly today. The rough sea mixed with heavy rain. Bad weather remained with us. We used this evening to organize our shop and paperwork. I wrote a letter to my family.

> *Dear Father, Mother, Sister, Brother,*
> *So many, many things have happened since I talked to you all last. I hardly know where to begin. While undergoing preparations for the cruise back at Miramar, Dick Aden and I shaved our heads on the night of June 11th, partly because we knew we'd be in an all-male environment for a long time, so why be concerned about our looks, and partly because the Officers at the Naval Air Station were always on our backs about our hair being too long. So we went to the opposite extreme. We also bought pairs of miniature, circular sunglasses. When I wear them I look like Mahatma Gandhi with shades. I had photos taken of my Hindu guise for remembrance of a once-in-a-lifetime experience. As we expected, two days after we became baldies, the brass gods put out a directive against head shaving.*

We flew up to Frisco from San Diego on June 15th but before going onboard the Oriskany, Dick and I linked up with one of his friends in Berkeley. Hitchhiking in that direction, we were picked up by a girl and her father and given a ride all the way to the campus. Walking ten blocks, we arrived at the man's house. His name is Marvin Lipinsky. He is professor of ceramics at the University of California at Berkeley. Dick first met him at University of Wisconsin. Marvin was the founder of the glass blowing department on campus. His house is half ceramics workshop. His work is beautiful.

The three of us went into San Francisco and dined at a Chinese restaurant. Walking through the streets of the city, we were a visual comedy. Marvin's hair hangs over his shoulders. Dick and I have not a strand upon our skulls. Marv was dressed in his hippie clothes, Dick and I in our silly sailor suits.

To top off our evening of liberty, we brought Marv to the ship as a visitor and astounded him with our iron tub. His hair astounded the old Chiefs and Officers.

~ Love you all. I'll write more later,
Gerry

17 June 1967 ... 2nd day onboard the U.S.S. Oriskany, somewhere in the eastern Pacific.

High wind, murky, rough sea and scattered showers remained with us this morning. Flight Quarters, with all hands prepared for turn up and launch, did not go as expected. We secured at 1400. No planes flew because storms were anticipated. However, at 1500, the sky began to clear and the sun came out. Flight Quarters were reconvened. We launched and recovered two of our Photo Birds in late afternoon.

This evening Dick Aden and I made more room in the shop by obtaining an area previously occupied by the Ship's Company Photo Lab. We reshuffled our cameras, film magazines and cases to give our area a much more livable quality.

19 June 1967 ... 4th day.

Today, we awoke to a new world at sea. The sky was crisp and clear, the ocean lazy smooth. Each was a brilliant blue. Winds still prevailed but hardly as strong or as cold. With the temperature around 70-degrees, we were quite comfortable wearing just Flight Deck jerseys and no jackets. The weather brought everyone in the Air Group out in the open. During our entire Carrier Qual period it had been miserably cold and windy, just like the previous two days.

Our pilots took two birds out this morning and snapped good air-to-air photos of one another. In the afternoon, we launched plane number 603. Ninety minutes later, it returned to the Oriskany for recovery and unloading of film. The time was 1500. Harry Hedge and Dick Aden were walking forward on the starboard side catapult track to the recovery area. I was already ahead of them, in position, waiting.

I didn't see the mishap but I noticed a frenzy of excitement where several Yellow Shirts, our flight deck traffic cops, were gathered on the forward cat. I rushed over to find Harry on his back, squirming like a worm. His eyes were rolling spasmodically, his tongue vibrating. He was gasping for air, bubbling at the mouth. Blood soaked his flight deck cloth helmet. It gave me a horrible feeling to see him in such a state when just moments before he had been normal. In quick order, I was helping carry him in a Stoke's Litter to the Number One Elevator. The elevator descended into the Hangar Deck and we rushed toward Sickbay. I kept looking at Harry's face. At first, he had been kicking and fighting the straps that bound him. And then, he was dormant, his eyes closed. I watched his complexion fearing it would turn pale. Yes, I was thinking the worst and praying it wouldn't happen. Aviation Boatswain's Mate First Class Craig Danko came up, grabbed the litter, and ordered me back to the Flight Deck. I reluctantly obliged. Danko is a dickhead.

A short time later in the Photo Shop, Dick gave his account of what had happened. Harry was walking forward on the cat track when the shuttle, the portion that is normally chained to a launching aircraft, was accidentally unleashed. It moved swiftly, about sixty miles per hour, down the track ramming and scattering chocks and pull bars in all directions. The shuttle caught Harry in the back of his foot flipping him up off the deck. Airborne for a couple of seconds, he plunged back down on to the back of his head.

Medical personnel reported an hour later that he had received a slight concussion with large laceration requiring stitches. Yet, within two hours after the incident, Harry was conscious and his likeable self again, a great relief to everyone concerned. Our photo crew visited him tonight in Sickbay and gave him holy hell for scaring the shit out of us. The doctor told us he'll be working again tomorrow.

At 1900 this evening, LCDR Sonniksen spoke to the Det about several things. The main subject, as you might guess, was Flight Deck safety. In addition, the Old Man gave us a slide presentation that briefed us on our assignments when we reach Yankee Station.

Tomorrow, our Photo Birds take pictures of Hawaii.

20 June 1967 ... 5th day. Pearl Harbor, Hawaii.

I woke up in the middle of the night, 0330 this morning, dressed and stood four long hours of Aircraft Integrity Watch – just walking around the same planes and aviation parts in Hangar Bay Two. During my watch, by the rays of dawn, we arrived at the forever-green, palm treed paradise of Oahu and Pearl Harbor. As we moored, my duty ended and I darted down four levels to visit Hedge in Sickbay. His bandages were being removed. Before I could shower and dress, Hedge was already signed out, dressed and off the ship. Dick Aden and I departed around 0930, catching a bus to downtown Honolulu. I wanted to see some of the outer reaches of the island and not just another big city so I proposed we rent a jeep. Two other men from the Det, Aviation Mechanics, teamed up with us. We pooled our dollars and rented a Datsun because the jeeps had already been snapped up. Stopping at the Army Fort DeRussey Exchange, Dick and I bought swimsuits and changed into them, tossing our ugly Navy whites into the trunk. It was eleven o'clock when we hit the open highway with Dick at the driver's wheel. Taking the tourist route, he drove past Diamond Head, Koko Head, stopped at Blowhole then proceeded about seventy-five miles up the eastern coast of Oahu. Around 1500, Turner, one of the boys in the back seat spoke up, "Hey, Dick! Mac! I forgot to tell ya. I have to be back to the ship by 1730."

I spun around glaring at him. "Five-thirty?"

"Yeah." He reaffirmed.

"Me, too!" said his buddy beside him. "We both have special duty."

Obviously just as pissed as I was, Dick looked at both of them in the rearview mirror, "Why the hell didn't you guys tell Mac and me when we started out?"

"Shit, we didn't know you was planning on going on safari," Turner snapped back.

I stomped the floorboard. "Damn it all to hell!"

Dick reluctantly slowed down, flipped a looey and headed the Datsun back toward Honolulu choosing a mountain route so we would, at least, see some new terrain on our way. At 1700, Dick and I bailed out at Waikiki Beach allowing our two buddy fuckers to turn in the rental and find their way back to the ship. We walked to the beachfront where we absorbed some Hawaiian sun and occasionally tested the water. We lifted our spirits and certain body parts by leering at the gorgeous Wahinis – the Hawaiian word for young girls. They wore skimpy, two-piece bikinis, leaving little to the imagination. As evening approached, the two of us changed back to our ice cream suits at the Waikiki beach house. Strolling through the waterfront business district, Dick and I found a restaurant with tropical decor where we ordered and socked away 16-ounce steaks and four Primo draught beers each; lucky for me, legal drinking age in Hawaii is twenty.

After the fourth brew, I became heavy-eyed and drowsy. "Dick, I'm sorry to tell you this but I have to go back too. Get some shut-eye. I've been up since three-thirty this morning, man."

"That's okay, Mac," Aden replied, flicking an ash from his cigarette to his empty steak platter. "My heart hasn't really been in it anyway."

"Why's that?"

He raised his voice, "Well, they give us a one-day glimpse of paradise then send us to hell."

"The Philippines?"

I knew what he actually meant.

Dick continued with his thought, "You heard of General William Sherman, right?"

"Who?"

"The Union General who ordered the torching of Atlanta during the Civil War."

"Oh, yeah, Gone with the Wind... that Sherman."

"He's the one who said, war is hell. And he had created enough hell on earth himself to know what he was talking about."

"Yeah," I agreed, "I'm sure Nam is hell especially for those poor bastard's fighting in-country in the South. And, it'll be hell for our pilots, too. They'll be looking into the face of death just about every day that we're on the line."

"Hey, man," Dick came back at me, "working that fuckin' Flight Deck ain't gonna be a piece of cake, either. A lot of Enlisted Men die up there, y'know. It's one of the most dangerous jobs in the fleet."

"I spose you're right."

Dick replied, "I know I'm right. The stats back me up. We could be like most of the guys and just fuck as many whores as possible while we're in-port; drink till we pass out in our own puke but that doesn't change the fact that we're gonna be in a world of shit when we get to Yankee Station."

"Well, thanks for the inspiring words," I replied sarcastically..

Aden's somber face transformed into a demonic grin, "You're welcome, asshole!"

We both laughed.

That was our day in Hawaii. A few observations: it's a beautiful island, but if you're expecting leis on your shoulder, hula girls in grass skirts, and all that other tourist shit, you have to stay at the expensive five-star hotels. Honolulu is basically just another American city. The only major difference being the prevailing mix of races: Filipino, Japanese, Chinese, Polynesian, Malaysian and, of course, us Whiteys. Daily life seems to be more casual than back in the States. With a mild breeze constantly blowing in off the ocean, the climate is very inviting, the humidity level quite tolerable. The term, Blue Hawaii, is appropriate. The sky and ocean are bright azure, volcanic mountains in the distance appear blue through the haze. Diverse exotic plants glow emerald green. I found myself attached to the place after just thirteen hours but, as Dick said, it was just a tease. Maybe someday, when I'm a civilian, I'll return and spend a few weeks. Tomorrow we steam southwest to Las Filipinas and Olongapo City.

21 June 1967 ... 6th day. Back on the Pacific Ocean.

An extremely lazy day. The Oriskany steamed out of Pearl Harbor at 0930 this morning. Great weather all day. Flight Quarters were not called. Instead, many men spent the day resting on the Flight Deck, some sunbathed, others played catch, wrote letters or just meditated. It was a welcome rest.

This evening, after dark, I walked all the way forward on the Flight Deck to the catapult guides. Called canoes, two of them project beyond the leading edge of the ship's bow like two metallic monoliths laying on their sides. It's an awesome feeling to sit there on the front end and gaze forward into the vast darkness of the moonlit ocean, hearing only the gentle rush of the water against the ship's bow. In that place, I was to alone; free to meditate and listen to the whispering of the stars. I stayed for over an hour. I needed a sacred, peaceful evening.

23 June 1967 ... 8th day.
Somewhere in the Pacific Ocean

Another day like yesterday, except we are now concerned with Red Bear conditions. Every cruise of every U.S. carrier to Vietnam has been approached by Russian aircraft. Our planes are on standby alert, ready to be airborne within fifteen minutes to escort the Russian Bears or Bison as they attempt to fly over our Task Force. Our radar can pick up such aircraft at one-thousand miles out. Our fighter jets and Photo Recon Squadron 63's Photo Birds can be on them within five-hundred miles. We, the Photo Mates, have loaded Ektachrome color transparency film in our oblique cameras for photographing the Reds when they appear on our radar screens.

Tonight, we cross the International Date Line and skip a day. June 24 will be lost completely. What a strange feeling. We will jump from 23 June to 25. Coming back, we'll pick up the lost day.

25 June 1967 ... 9th day; Ibid.

A lax day. No flight quarters were sounded but we're still in Condition Red Bear. Our tanker ship, the one that was to refuel us at sea, had a side-by-side collision with a carrier in the Tonkin Gulf, the result being, no refueling during our Hawaii to Subic voyage. The

Old Risky must maintain a certain percentage of jet fuel at all times, so flight operations have been trimmed back. The situation is cause for joy for the Airdales; remorse for the brass gods.

26 June 1967 ... 10th day.
The Pacific Ocean, halfway between Hawaii and The Philippines

Early this morning, the Deity sent us a few refreshing rain showers, washing down the planes and cleaning the exterior of the ship. Flight Quarters were sounded at 0930. It was my turn to preflight inspect our Red Bear standby aircraft. We flew three regular photo hops today and two instrument-testing hops after dark. No Russians.

CHAPTER VI
OLONGAPO CITY

Many a cherry boy has been sexually initiated in Olongapo City. I was one of them. Any Navy man or Marine who has taken a WestPac Cruise or who has been stationed at a Subic Bay facility has stories about Sin City that they don't tell their mothers, wives or girlfriends back in the States unless, of course, they are the few who abstain from the erotic temptations in this most notorious of liberty ports. Liquor and beer sales, illegal drugs, prostitution and sex shows are multi-million peso industries in Olongapo. The bars and hotels are named to attract Yanks: Copacabana, Lone Star, Las Vegas, Lucky Lady, Long Branch Saloon, L.A. Night Club, Stardust, Flamingo Club and my favorite, Pauline's. Configured much like tenderloin districts of American frontier cattle-drive towns, the two main streets of town begin near the base entrance at Shit River Bridge then continue for nearly three miles. The north fork attracts the Colored servicemen and the girls who can take them on, or in, I should say. The south and longest fork hosts everyone else – no forced segregation, that's just the way it's evolved. The streets are lined with bars, night clubs, cheap restaurants, souvenir shops, money changers, ramshackle hotels and skivvie houses where Americans take their bar girls for short-time fucks.

In 1965, at the age of eighteen, I requested and received assignment to work at FIC PAC FAC, the Fleet Intelligence Center, Pacific Facility, Cubi Point Naval Air Station, on the south side of Subic Bay. It was a whole new venue for me, my first time out of the U.S. of A.; my first time in a foreign country. By day, I fulfilled my duties as a Photo Lab Technician. By night, dark angels lured me to Olongapo. Back home, I can't legally drink alcohol until I'm twenty-one. Hell of a deal, huh? An 18-year-old can be inducted and have his ass shot in Vietnam but he can't legally drink a beer in his hometown. No age limits in Olongapo.

In my first six months of residence, I indulged in all the vices the city has to offer. I was still a virgin when I came to the Philippine Islands, still timid around women, afraid to go all the way. I suppose a large part of my abstinence was born of my religious training: the principle that I must save myself for my wife on our wedding night. It was that and my adoration of the virtuous woman – still looking for that dream girl. At Lincoln Northeast High School, I had been fascinated, as most boys are, by the girls who put out. Every guy in school knew who they were and just about everyone considered them sluts and just about every guy wanted a piece of them. I dated a couple of sluts and could have gone all the way with them but I chickened out, no doubt my Christian conscience at work.

Whores were a new concept for me. They don't have hookers in Nebraska... not that I am aware of. The way I saw it at first was: whores don't make love, they fuck. They don't give a shit who you are, where you're from or what you do for a living. They don't want to get to know you. They're not romantic. They don't play mind games. They ask for only one thing: money, in exchange for services rendered. If I do business with a whore, I'm not seducing her. I'm not forcing her to do anything she hasn't already done hundreds of times before. She has chosen her lifestyle. And, even though King Solomon in his Book of Proverbs says to avoid harlots, you've got to remember Old Sol had three-hundred concubines. So what is he saying? "I'm the King of Israel. I'm rich and I can have all the poontang I want; but you, peasant, you're poor, so don't be visiting any harlots. Sure I get fresh pussy every night but don't you be trying it."

At the barracks, I felt like the Lone Ranger. I think virtually every sailor had been laid at least once. Me, I didn't even know what a cunt looked like. The peer pressure was on. I put it off for several weeks but I finally had my first sexual encounter. My favorite Olongapo hangout was the newly-built Pauline's Night Club. It was, by far, the classiest joint on the strip: a large building with live bands and Las Vegas-style stage entertainment. The hostesses were all hot, young, gorgeous and for sale. As soon as I would walk in the door, three or four hostesses would come running up to me, each one begging me to sit with her and buy her a Lady's Drink. It was always a tough choice because they all were such cute, little things with their shiny black hair, mini-skirts all the way to heaven and those tight, thin tops that made their nipples show through. In their little girl voices, they'd plead: "Hey Joe! Come seet with me, please! Buy me Lady's Drink. I show you good time, Joe."

My buddies at FIC PAC FAC had indoctrinated me on procedure for bedding a hostess. The night I lost my cherry, I did it by the rules. Inside the entrance of Pauline's, I chose the cutest one. Her name was Tida. She was 18 years old, about five feet tall, with a very long, coal-black mane cascading to her waistline. She looked at me with those brown almond eyes, and confidently exclaimed: "You be happy you pick Tida."

Yes, I was. She took me to a vacant table where we sat and exchanged small talk while listening to the live band. The place was packed with sailors, marines, officers and hostesses. The Filipino male band played current American hits – mostly British Invasion music by the Beatles, Rolling Stones, Kinks, and the Animals. I bought her a Lady's Drink for four pesos. I drank a few rounds of San Miguel beer while replenishing her drinks. We danced a couple of times even though I hate dancing.

It took three San Magoo's for me to get up the courage to ask: "Tida, how much for a short time?"

She transformed into business mode: "Thirty pesos, Mock." Thirty pesos convert to only about nine American dollars.

"And how much, Tida, to buy you out of the bar?"

"Mamasan she no like me to leave bar." Tida was negotiating. "I make her good money. Me a good hostess. If I leave bar she lose money."

"Well, I'll compensate Mamasan well for her loss. How about twenty pesos?"

She signaled a waiter to come over to our table. "You pay him," she said to me, then rattled off several sentences in Tagalog to the waiter that I didn't understand.

She held out her hand to me, "You pay me now for short time."

My friends had warned me of this. Don't give them the money up front because they'll ditch you. "No, Tida, I'll pay you after short time."

She tried to look displeased for a few seconds then smiled, stood up and grabbed my hand, "Okay, Mock, we go make fuck. You come now."

We walked out of Pauline's to the congested street. Dodging colorfully-decorated Jeepneys filled with drunken sailors, we ran across the street. Jeepneys, by the way, are left-behind World War II U.S. Army jeeps converted into street taxis. About a block down, we passed through a dark entryway to a dimly lit lobby. An old white-haired Filipino man was standing behind a cluttered counter top with a cigarette hanging from his mouth.

Tida pointed at the old man. "You pay him for room. Fifteen pesos. One hour."

I obliged and we climbed a creaky staircase to the second floor. She chose a door and turned the knob. It wasn't locked. I made sure it was locked from the inside because I had heard stories about sailors being assaulted and their trousers robbed when they were completely helpless, butt naked in bed with their hooker.

Being the professional, Tida wasted no time. She kicked off her shoes, pulled off her top and dropped her mini-skirt and panties together. She was totally nude in about 20 seconds. I was utterly entranced. I just wanted to look at her naked body for a few minutes and enjoy the vision. She looked like the girl in my fantasy – the jungle girl under the waterfall. So beautiful! Bronze skin, dark brown nipples perched on firm little breasts, a little bell-shaped ass, a small V-shaped patch of black hair covering her twat. Unlike my fantasy, she didn't call my name softly. Tida was in business mode. She pulled down the covers on the bed, propped up two pillows and jumped on the mattress. She prepared herself by leaning back on the pillows and spreading her legs. She noticed a comic book on the night stand by the bed and grabbed it. From her tits down, she assumed the position of a bitch mongrel dog who wants her belly rubbed. My dream girl was spread eagle with Daffy Duck covering her face. I was still dressed and just standing by the bed with my mouth open, looking like some kind of idiot, I suppose. I don't know... I guess I thought there might be a just a little romance, a kiss or a hug, something like that. Nope, I was dead wrong about that.

Tida lowered Daffy and gave me a command, "You take off clothes now. Come on. Why you wait?"

As I slowly undressed, I tried gently to divert her attention, "Tida, Tida, er, Tida."

Irritated, she tossed the comic book to the floor. "What? What? What?"

"This is my first time, Tida."

"First time with me, yeah."

"No, this is my first time ever. I'm a cherry boy."

"No shit?"

"No shit."

Her attitude changed. For a couple of seconds, she came dangerously close to being affectionate. "No problem, cherry boy, you come up here on bed. I show you how."

Little Mister MacLennon had been ready for action ever since she undressed. I climbed on the bed and positioned myself in front of her furry patch but I was unsure what to do next. Suddenly, she grabbed my hard-on saying, "Give me titi, damnit, I put in buto." And, yes, she did. She arched her back as I slid inside of her. I pushed all the way in, pulled back, and pushed one more time and... It was all over in less than 15 seconds.

"Wow!" she exclaimed. "Me think you set short-time record. Next time you be better."

I was already wilted. She jumped out of bed, walked over to a sink on the wall, hopped on it straddling it with her legs still spread. She grunted and purged her cunt of my jizz. Grabbing a towel from the rack, she wiped herself, jumped down and pulled her clothes back on. I was still naked on the edge of the bed watching her efficiency. This 18-year-old girl had gone through this routine way too many times.

Tida walked up to me and held out her hand, "Okay, Joe, my money."

I was G.I. Joe again. With a heave and a sigh, I pulled my wallet from my crumpled blue jeans, pulled out a few bills and paid her fifty pesos.

"Ooo, fifty? You pay Tida fifty?"

"Yes, thank you for my first time, Tida."

She kissed me on the forehead. "Yup, you no more cherry boy now."

"No," I laughed. "No more cherry boy."

She unlocked the door and left. I never saw her again.

In the course of that first six months in the Philippine Islands, I only hired hookers three times. Tida was the first. I don't remember the names of the other two. I remember the second one was 35-years-old. We had an overnight together. She was very patient and taught me how to improve my obviously inadequate skills. The third came out of a skivvy house in Angeles City, near Clark Air Force Base. That one gave me gonorrhea and non-specific urethritis. My cock burned like hell for five days, green puss dripped out of it, staining my white boxers. I finally submitted to a shot of penicillin in my ass at Sickbay. A week later I was healed. Because of that nasty ordeal, I amended my wicked ways. My Christian conscience took over, I guess. I stopped the bar scene. I stopped picking up whores. If I did go out to the bars with friends, I'd entertain a hostess but I'd try to become acquainted with her. I'd ask about her family. I'd ask why she had chosen prostitution. Most of the hostesses are Roman Catholics; most carry a heavy load of guilt for selling their bodies. Large percentages have children from unwanted pregnancies. Most come from rural, agricultural regions and small villages. They write letters telling lies to their parents and relatives. They say they are working at legitimate jobs in the city making good money. The last part is no lie. They do make excellent money compared to most Filipino professionals. In fact, they earn enough to support their extended families back in the provinces. Most hope to work as whores for just a few years then get legitimate jobs in Manila. Many say they are saving their earnings to buy a small business for themselves. The sad part is: the longer these girls live in the sordid world of prostitution, the harder it is to leave. They become alcoholics and addicted to drugs. Some contract fatal diseases. Most grow old before their time and die in their forties or fifties. That's why I devoted the remaining twelve months of my leisure time in the Philippines to personal ambassadorship: learning as much of the language as I could; visiting the rural villages and getting to know the real people; and when I had opportunity, I'd try to talk Filipina hookers into returning home or finding better vocations. Ain't I just a friggen saint?

CHAPTER VII
RUSSIAN BEARS APPROACHING

27 June 1967 ... 11th day.
Somewhere in the western Pacific.

At 0630, bright and early, the 1MC came alive with the Boatswain's Pipe, "Red Bear Alert! Red Bear Alert! Russian aircraft approaching! All hands stand at the ready!"

As soon as the Commies were sighted on radar, CAG launched five Fighter jets to escort them as they entered our airspace. Hundreds of Black Shoes had scrambled up to the Flight Deck with little, snapshot cameras in their hands. I looked on, surrounded by the crowd of spectators, with my cheapo 35mm camera poised and ready for action – just like my titi. Activating the superstructure speakers at 0725, the Air Boss, in his best god voice, announced: "Photographers, please turn your attention to mid-port side bow."

There to the far left of the carrier, emerging from distant rain clouds were two long, thin silhouettes. Advancing quickly toward us, I was amazed by their swift, straight, smooth pattern of flight. At 0730, two Russian Bears, red stars on their wings and tails, flew by, escorted by our F-8 Crusader Fighter Jets. Similar in design to U.S. Air Force B-52 bombers, but larger, our escorts were dwarfed by the Soviet TU-29D aircraft. The Bears are powered by two turboprop engines on each wing; each engine having two propellers turning in opposite directions, clockwise and counterclockwise, so I'm told. The Bears flew by twice: the first time about a half-mile aft of the ship and the second time, about a half-mile forward. The air show lasted about twenty minutes. It was a rare moment of adventure. In the air, our fighter pilots exchanged gestures of greeting as Yanks snapped photos of Russians and vice-versa. Actually, it's a fucking irony: our pilots all chummy with the same people who are shipping surface-to-air missiles into Haiphong Harbor for the express purpose of blowing the shit out of airborne U.S. planes... and pilots.

In the kick ass department, Photo Recon Squadron 63 was caught with her panties down this morning. Just like Tida. Our sole photo aircraft in up-status, was launched at 0830. Too late. The great delay was because certain incompetent personnel of Hangar Deck Control didn't have our bird spotted last night as ordered.

Subsequently, Hangar Deck personnel were in a panic trying to reshuffle dozens of aircraft so 601 could be moved to the Number Three Elevator and brought up to the Flight Deck. LTJG Beam rushed and hopped into the cockpit. Following what must have been one of the quickest preflight inspections and turn-ups in recent naval aviation history, he launched, in afterburner mode, and attempted to catch up with the Russians. Even at close to top speed, he was unsuccessful; they had already exited our sector. This failure to obtain photos created a butt-kicking chain reaction from Captain Billy all the way down to the lowliest Hangar Bay grunt. It was not our squadron's fault. Blame has been placed where due.

Fortunately the pilots of the Fighter escorts shot some outstanding close-up photos with their handheld 35mm Leicas and Nikons. Our squadron's Photo Intelligence has been busy all day working with their film and transparencies. It seems unreasonable for it all to be classified as Secret when I see many similar pics on office walls but that's what has happened. And, because of the classification, I am unable to secure any duplicates from P.I. for my private collection. Fuckin' Navy!

In other matters, the Executive Officer (XO) of the ship gave word today that the ship's water supply is down to fifty per cent. No showers tonight. No laundry service until levels return to normal. Fresh water on the Oriskany is produced by giant desalination units that convert sea water into something almost potable.

Dick, Ernest and I held a cleaning field day on the shop tonight in preparation of tomorrow's inspection. After finishing, we were informed that inspection has been postponed due to lack of fresh water. Goddamned fuckin' Navy!

28 June 1967 ... 12th day. Ibid.

Since leaving Hawaii, Ernest has been keeping track of our coordinates. According to Big Ern we have been steaming due west and today are only 300 miles away from the islands of southern Japan.

As we were gathered at the workbench this morning, I shared an idea with Ray, Dick, Ern and Harry, "Hey, guys, I think we should call ourselves, Photographic Aerial Reconnaissance Technicians. I can put the abbreviation on our Flight Deck jerseys with a felt-tip."

"Why?" Ernest asked.

"Well, Ern," I replied, "The abbreviation will be Ph-A-R-T."

Dick nodded and laughed.

Ern stood there, lips moving as he thought about it; a light clicked on in his head, his eyes widened, and he exclaimed, "Oh, I get it! Phart! Fart! Yeah, that's funny."

"So it's agreed then?" I asked the four of them.

"Sure." Ray, Dick and Ern agreed.

I turned to Hedge looking him in the eye. "How 'bout you, Harry. Are you a Phart, too?"

Hedge didn't find the idea personally appealing.

The first of three launches catapulted off the deck at 1000. We are developing our work pattern. I have a feeling it will soon become routine, then eventually monotony. Three launches for Photo Recon Squadron 63; three recoveries. The Pharts break out replacement film magazines and record their numbers, load them into our backpacks, walk through the same passageways lifting our feet over hatchways trying to keep our balance as the ship rolls. We pull on our helmets and goggles and, emerging from the superstructure, run like hell to the forward section of the Flight Deck dodging jet intakes and exhausts, turning props and NC-3 Mule service vehicles. We meet our photo aircraft, after her recovery on the wires, unload the camera stations; then, dodging hazards, run back to the superstructure with exposed film canisters and descend below decks to the Flash Lab, leaving the film with the processors. Backtracking to the Flight Deck, the four of us reload the cameras with virgin film. I fill out a new photo data card – I've been placed in charge of all paperwork – and slip it into the cockpit. And voila! The plane is ready for another flight if all the cameras are behaving.

Today they weren't. As we prepared 604 for launch, I noticed there wasn't enough film in the station three KA45 camera. Rushing to reload it, I discovered the loading curtain broken. With only ten minutes remaining before scheduled launch, Ray Hines, Harry Hedge and I pulled the camera, unhooked the cables and wires and installed a new camera. It was hectic, nerve-wracking work but our fast action prevented the mission from being scrubbed.

This evening, we held field day on the shop in advance of yet another inspection tomorrow.

19 June 1967 ... 13th day. Ibid.

The ship came within 200 miles of the Japanese coast then turned south running parallel to the Ryukyu Islands, on our way to the Philippines. The screeching pipe of the Boatswain's mate came over the 1MC first thing this morning. What a rude awakening! "Zone inspection previously scheduled for today has been cancelled due to rearrangement of the flight schedule." Goddamned Navy!

Three of our planes were scheduled to fly today. Only one made it off the ship. Last minute difficulties postponed the other two prior to launch. To top it off, this was our hottest day so far. This afternoon's outside temp was 85 degrees, inside temp 95. Humidity was so thick our books and papers wilted, our clothing was soaked with sweat but we don't notice the B.O. because we all smell equally foul. Fresh water showers are prohibited. And almost nobody likes the saltwater showers.

Typhoon Anita is sweeping along the northern coast of Luzon, Philippines right now. It's expected to track northwest into Red China but judging by the condition of the ocean tonight, I'd swear the storm is headed north. The Oriskany is rocking fore and aft. She occasionally begins jerking and shaking as if my whole metallic world is about to turn upside down. The wind is extreme. If it persists, there will definitely be no flights tomorrow.

30 June 1967 ... 14th day.
Western Pacific, approximately 200 miles east of Formosa.

The eagle shit. Pay day! This morning, Ship's Company and CAG personnel reaped the fruit of our labor. I had to stand in line for an hour in the steamy forecastle passageway to receive my moolah in cash. Added to the twenty-five bucks I've saved, plus the twenty-five that Morgan owes me, I'll have a walloping one-hundred fifty to spend in the P.I. Drawing on my past experience, it has been my privilege to inform the inexperienced boys about what's waiting for them.

CHAPTER VIII
BACK IN THE PHILIPPINES

1 July 1967 ... 15th day.
The northern coast of Luzon, Philippines.

Harry jolted us awake at 0700 today. He's an early riser, usually going to bed at 2030 and getting up at 0530 to fill out time cards, checking the day's flight schedule and performing other small duties before rousing the rest of us. We, who don't carry as much responsibility as our beloved First-Class, hit the rack around midnight.

"Gotta pull the oblique cameras and the 45's in station one. Ray, how many KB-10A's we got out?" Harry was holding reveille his way, "Gotta lotta work to do. Planes are going out at 11."

"Good morning to you, too, Mister Hedge," I grumbled.

It wasn't so fucking hot today, more like the pleasant Philippine climate that I remember so well. As I climbed up to the Flight Deck, I asked a passing Officer where we were located. He told me we were passing through the Babuyan Channel. I walked back to the edge of the deck and spotted small atolls in the distance. As we proceeded, larger islands came into view and soon, the northernmost tip of Luzon. Seeing the P.I. again warmed my heart as if I'd met an old friend after a long period of separation. Rugged, jungle-covered mountains lined the coast. Smoke arose from small mountain villages where farmers were burning off stalks. Green-hued water splashed against the sandy shoreline. Standing there about a half mile from shore, I had the urge to jump off and swim to some private paradise but I know I can wait because I only have seven and a half months to go until I'm discharged from the service. Freedom, sweet freedom. I'll come back as a civilian, God willing.

Hedge interrupted my reverie. "Get off your ass, Mac! Help us prep 601!"

Sonniksen and Lieutenant Sam flew 601 and 603 off the ship at 1130. Even as I write, those two are probably at Naval Air Station Cubi Point, relaxing at the Officer's Club with drinks in hand.

2 July through 11 July 1967
Cubi Point Naval Air Station, Subic Bay, Philippines.

Written after the fact:

In the grey of a heavy downpour, our ship moored at Leyte Carrier Pier. When I lived here, I watched incoming carriers from atop the hill in Barracks 14. Now I am one of those disgusting fleet sailors that I used to hate.

The first day in port, I grabbed my dungarees, my laundry sack and caught a taxi up the hill. After laundering my smelly clothes, I headed over to third deck, Barracks 22, home to the FIC PAC FAC boys. Most of my old gang is gone, reassigned. Only a handful remains. During our nine days in-port, I spent several hours at the barracks relaxing and shooting the shit with them. My best friend, Pepé the houseboy, wasn't working at the barracks. I learned he had a death in his family and was up in the province of Pampanga for a couple of weeks.

Taking along friends from Det Gulf, I braved Olongapo City three times. I should have known better but, on the first incursion, I wore my dress white uniform. Heap big fuck-up. I had no idea a fleet sailor is so ill-treated: two pesos for a beer; hordes of beggars, thieves, pimps and little brown demons smearing my whites with black polish when I wouldn't hire them to shine my shoes. My group of Airdales exercised restraint but the Oriskany Black Shoes were mostly out of control, insulting locals with racist slurs, belittling the Filipino culture, fighting with other sailors and Marines, hollering, puking, dancing in the streets, passed out in the gutters. Dozens were brought back to the ship in the Shore Patrol Drunk Wagon.

Birds 601 and 603 were parked on the concrete apron next to the ship. On the two days it did not rain, our pilots took photo flights from the Cubi Point airstrip to scenic areas on Luzon. I latched on to a few of the photo prints to save in my personal collection. It's a beautiful country.

My Det buddies ran out of dough in four to five days. Me, too. Liberty began to lag. Lax time became dull. I think most of us are just more focused on what lies ahead in North Vietnam. It has certainly weighed heavily on my brain since we left Frisco Bay – even though I try to divert my thoughts.

CHAPTER IX
ENTERING THE WAR ZONE

11 July 1967 ... 25th day.
Heading west from the Philippines across the South China Sea.

After leaving Subic Bay at 1000, we ran into foul weather: strong wind gusts, white caps dotting the ocean. Driving rain danced on the Flight Deck surface and soaked the poor swabs who had duties to perform up there. Despite the inclement conditions, the ship's Air Wing began to fly aboard around 1600, and continued their arrivals until well after midnight. It's challenging enough for a pilot to hit the wire in sunny, perfect weather. Days like this are extremely dangerous for Flight Deck landings.

Our Photo Birds were already onboard. They were crane-lifted to the Hangar Deck back at Cubi. We worked on the photo systems all day. Components were going bad as fast as we installed them. I don't know if it was from static charges or what. Rolling out my newly-purchased banana leaf mat on the steel deck at midnight, I went spread eagle directly under the air vent and slept there all night.

12 July 1967 ... 26th day.
Somewhere in the South China Sea.

An aircraft was lost today. One of the A-4E Skyhawks in Attack Squadron VA-163 had a cold cat launch. There wasn't enough steam pressure in the catapult to get the plane airborne. Knowing he was going in the drink, the pilot ejected out of the cockpit and parachuted safely to the ocean surface. The A-4E exploded when its red hot engine made contact with the cool sea water. It sank to the bottom of the briny blue. Sorry, American taxpayers! Uninjured, the pilot was plucked from the sea by one of our Angel helicopters. This evening it's still blustery and raining, as we sail to Yankee Station – staging area for our air strikes over North Vietnam.

13 July 1967 ... 27th day. South China Sea.

No flights today except for the mail plane. No letters for me. A lazy day, we Photo Mates didn't get up till almost 1000. Then we did nothing but hang around the shop. In the afternoon, I broke out my watercolors and painted a few landscapes including a picture of our beloved Old Risky moored at Leyte Pier.

This afternoon, we had our second encounter with Russians. Maneuvering through the Tonkin Gulf, disguised as fishing boats, these sophisticated, little electronic marvels are here for one reason only: to monitor U.S. military communications, if they're lucky enough to break our codes. One of the two trawlers came within a quarter of a mile of the Oriskany. That was too damned close. Our destroyer escort hustled over, pulling up between the trawler and our carrier, she swung her guns around pointing them directly at the Ruskis. It had the desired effect, the little trawler turned tail. Joined by the other trawler, they quickly faded into the horizon.

Harry Hedge, Big Ern and I sat out on the canoes tonight watching the sun set, and talking about tomorrow. This evening, according to Captain Billy on the 1MC, we are about 200 miles northeast of the DMZ, the Demilitarized Zone of Vietnam, where North meets South.

14 July 1967 ... 28th day.
Yankee Station, Gulf of Tonkin, North Vietnam.

The USS Oriskany and her Carrier Air Group returned to action this morning in a joint operation with the Aircraft Carrier U.S.S. Constellation. Our position is approximately 40 miles off shore. Together, the air wings of both ships bombed strategic bridges, storage bunkers, railroad lines and cargo trucks just north of the DMZ. This region is where the NVA, the North Vietnamese Army, accumulates munitions and supplies before making their incursions into the South to link up with the Commie guerillas, the Viet Cong.

Flight quarters sounded at 0500. We gave Photo Birds 601 and 602 thorough pre-flight inspections. Pilots to make the first combat photo recon missions were our boss man, LCDR Sonniksen, and combat virgin, Lieutenant JG Beam. They launched, carried out their assignment, making good photo coverage and returned safely at 1045. After catching the wire and parking, each pilot descended from his cockpit with a big, shit-eating grin. I think the Old Man was happy to be back in combat. Beam was happy to pop his cherry without bleeding.

Another pilot wasn't so lucky, on this first day of action, the CAG had its first war zone aircraft loss. An F-8 Crusader from

Fighter Squadron 164, was riddled by anti-aircraft artillery fire over enemy territory. It limped back out to open waters and was within a mile of the ship when the engine flamed out. The pilot, LTJG Cunningham, ejected and parachuted into the Gulf. Immediately on top of him, our rescue chopper, Angel-2, lowered the rescue cable and plucked the waterlogged Officer to safety. Cunningham was roughed up and bleeding a little but otherwise okay.

Lieutenant JG Charles Rudd flew his first Vietnam sortie this afternoon. I had the privilege of visiting with his family during the Dependent's Day Cruise. Of course, they are all concerned about his safety. I get the impression he comes from a very close-knit family. Charley's Mom was doting on him. That's got to be very embarrassing for an officer, you know, especially in front of the Enlisted Men. But Charley grinned and bore the humiliation.

During our squadron party at Cubi beach in the P.I. he was instigating wrestling matches, volleyball games, and chug-a-lug contests. Passing him this morning in the passageway, I asked, "Will you be flying this afternoon, Mr. Rudd?"

He grinned, "Y-y-y-y-yes." He exaggerated his response.

I could tell Charley was apprehensive but he didn't feel the need to hide it from an inferior Enlisted Man. When he returned safely from the mission, he was smiling from ear to ear, as if to say "Look at me! I'm here! I made it!"

Climbing from the cockpit, he had kind words for the crew. I encountered him as he was heading down below decks to the locker room. He gave me a brisk slap on the back. Nice guy. Rudd.

Flight quarters secured at 1900. I power-checked 602. All systems are go for tomorrow. Flight quarters will sound before dawn at 0430.

15 July 1967 ... 29th day.
Yankee Station, Gulf of Tonkin, North Vietnam.

The following article appeared in today's Morning Musket, the ship newspaper:

ORISKANY BACK IN ACTION.

I think the world will soon know that the Oriskany is back on the line," said Oriskany's Commanding Officer, Captain Billy Holder, as aircraft from the "Mighty-O" slashed enemy lines of communications through central and southern North Vietnam.

Oriskany yesterday returned to Task Force 77 on Yankee Station after a nine-month absence. Once again she flies the flag of Rear Admiral Walter L. Curtis, Jr., Commander Carrier Division Nine.

The Commander of Carrier Air Wing 16, Commander Burton H. Shepherd, of Kansas City, said, "Our younger aviators got a chance to check out their systems and gain experience by following old hands as they flew over the target areas."

A pilot on his first combat mission was LTJG Michael Mullane, 24, of Fullerton, California, flying an Attack Squadron 164 (VA-164) Skyhawk jet. "For almost three years, since I started Navy indoctrination, I've been working for this moment and I finally made it. Today's mission was the payoff. Just like a kid going to the circus – really exciting." he recalled. His target, the Ngon Rao Rheo Highway bridge, was reportedly destroyed.

* * * * * * *

The rest of the article consisted of various interviews and descriptions of bombed targets: bridges, trucks, rail lines, and so on.

Today was the second day of combat strikes. Lieutenant Harry Sampson flew his first sortie of the cruise at 0700. His mission was chasing Commie PT boats and snapping their pictures. This afternoon, LCDR Sonniksen and LTJG Beam flew a routine mission over the mainland.

Death came to Carrier Air Group 16 today. A pilot from Attack Squadron 152 flying an A-1 Skyraider was shot up by ground fire. The old propeller-driven fighter-bomber attempted to hobble back to the ship, but only a few miles beyond the coastline, the pilot was forced to ditch the plane in the ocean. Before hitting the water, he blew the canopy and jumped. Rescue helicopters reported that he did not survive the fall. He was too low for his parachute to open. Tonight, Captain Billy announced this first pilot loss over the 1MC, "It is to my regret that I must inform you of the death of a shipmate..."

A change in attitude has come over aviation personnel since we left Subic. Yesterday's plane loss and today's death is a rude awakening to the fact that this is all serious business. For me personally, the Vietnam War has seemed distant and surreal up to this point. I've worked now with jet aircraft for about six months. The routine has become boring. I'm accustomed to watching pilots climb into the cockpit, take off and return undaunted. Now, the faces of these aviators have changed. They remain expressionless as they turn up the engines and check out controls prior to launch. I look at them but eyes do not meet. Flashes of home, their families and their projected futures must stir in their minds. And they wonder as I wonder, "Will this be the day?" It is hard to accept the fact that I may see them alive today and inside a body bag tonight, assuming their bodies are recovered.

We, the ship-bound, remain separated from most of the bombing and horror. It is hard to realize that beyond that horizon a few miles is a land of suffering and misery. How do the Airdales experience the war? By receiving word that a plane and pilot launched this morning will never return; by seeing holes blasted in the skin of the planes by shells and flak; by the smell of burnt gunpowder on returning aircraft. This is our war. We see no enemy.

One isolated incident of cruelty was brought to my attention today. These kind of stories pass from man-to-man. We're never quite sure if they're true or just more scuttlebutt. I'll write it down anyway: A pilot was returning from a bombing mission. He had one bomb remaining and was looking for a likely place to drop it because you can't land on the carrier with bombs attached. Too fuckin' dangerous! So, over Nam, on a countryside road he spotted an old man riding a bicycle. Flying in low, he approached the cyclist from the rear and released his ordnance. The explosion was dead center, blasting the North Vietnamese man into a million pieces. They say that when the pilot related the story to his detachment crew, everyone had a good laugh. When I heard the story, I was pissed off. It was a needless killing. The man on the bicycle could have been some elderly gentleman who, even though brought to suffer under Marxist rule, had given his all to support his family. He had kept their stomachs full enough to avoid starvation. He has kept his children and grandchildren clothed; and tried his best to comfort them when bombs began to shake the floors. No matter what this man may have been, good or evil, he was not a penny arcade target to destroy just for kicks. But like I said, the story could just be bullshit.

During the evening prayer at 2200, our dear Chaplain said a prayer for one dead American. The people he killed before dying were not mentioned. The hundreds of human beings dead tonight because of our bombs were not mentioned. In his eloquent words, the duty Chaplain usually mentions love of mankind, the state of our world today and, of course, our devotion to duty and the honor and pride we are bestowing on our loved ones back home.

He reminds us that God is on our side.

I might sound like one of those San Francisco Hippies but... Come on, Chap! How do we really know that?

16 July 1967 ... 30th day.
Yankee Station, Gulf of Tonkin, North Vietnam.

Today has been a bitch! The gang was out of bed at 0430 to preflight 602. She was scheduled for a 0500 launch but was moved back and launched at 0615. Lieutenant JG Rudd was piloting. He was on a special PT boat search and photograph mission. Overflying the coastal rivers, he ran off all his film and returned to the ship 45 minutes early thinking that surely he had found some targets. When the processed film revealed none, we prepped the plane and launched him again for a second mission in the same area. We were humpin'. Unload, reload, preflight, check out, prepare new film magazines, unload, reload but... it was more stress on Mister Rudd.

Our next flight launched at 1300 hours. Again, it was aircraft 602 this time flown by LT Sam. This is his second year on Yankee Station. At 1600, LTJG Beam flew 601 over the Haiphong-Hanoi area. Lieutenant Commander Sonniksen was slated to fly 602 at 1745, but part of the radio gyro equipment broke and his mission was scrubbed. Today, as I said, the ship's air wing concentrated on targets along the coast and near Haiphong. Two barges were sunk. One PT boat was sent to Davy Jone's Locker and another was seriously fucked up. Also destroyed were a few trucks, a span on a bridge, a section of railroad track and other piddly targets.

Our Carrier Air Group has averaged one plane loss per day now and true to pattern, we lost another aircraft and another pilot today. All missions had been running smoothly for the bulk of the day, bombing, killing and destroying with minimum resistance from the North Vietnamese. Then, early evening, on the last strike of the day the pilots encountered strong opposition. Surface-to-air missiles were fired at them. Anti-aircraft artillery burst near the planes. An F-8 Crusader from Fighter Squadron 111 was hit by flak in the exhaust nozzle and tail but the pilot managed to return to the ship and catch the wire safely. Amazing! Another pilot, Lieutenant Commander Butch Verich of Fighter Squadron 162, flying an F-8, was not so lucky. His plane was peppered with ground fire. It burnt out. He ejected over land and parachuted into a relatively isolated area. Darkness was approaching; rescue attempts were discouraged by the coming of night. SAR, Search and Rescue forces, will try to locate him at dawn tomorrow but the chances of Verich evading the North Vietnamese soldiers all night are slim. Very slim.

Big Ern participated in a working party tonight. He helped unload groceries from a supply ship that came up alongside, transferring goods via highline but Big Ern was unable to procure any cumshaw. Two of the guys across the passageway in VA-163 swiped six large cans of peaches. They gave us one. So we retire to our racks tonight with peaches in our bellies.

17 July 1967 ... 31st day. Ibid.

    I guess I was too pessimistic in assuming that LCDR Verich would be lost to the enemy. This morning the Search and Rescue team, comprised of planes from every squadron detachment and the Angel helicopters launched at 0430 to find the downed pilot. At 0900, the Captain announced over the 1MC that he had been found and rescued. Verich returned to the Oriskany aboard Angel-1 and was immediately taken to the medical department for a complete physical examination. He is in good condition and good spirits after spending the night in the forests of North Vietnam. I wish I knew the whole story. 'Sounds like fodder for a good movie.

    This evening I loaded about a dozen film magazines while playing "Sergeant Pepper's Lonely Hearts Club Band" on my tape deck and channeling the sound through a gigantic amp and speaker system owned by a guy next door in VA-163. And we sweat, all the time. Damn, it's hot! My skin pores get one hell of a workout here in Nam.

18 July 1967 ... 32nd day. Ibid.

    "Fire! Fire! Fire in port diesel generator!"

    We were jolted out of our racks at 0400 this morning by the Quartermaster yelling over the loudspeakers. As I laid there in a drowsy haze, he came back on the system a couple of minutes later with bells clanging: "General Quarters! General Quarters! All hands man your battle stations!"

    We all awoke, jumped out of bed and paced around, lit up cigarettes as if we should do something but we didn't know what. After I finished my smoke, I said, "The hell with it," and returned to slumber land. About an hour later, the son-of-bitch came back on the 1MC: "Secure from fire drill. Secure from General Quarters."

    I rolled over, pulling the covers completely over my head, "Okay, motherfucker, I'm secured."

    Our first flight didn't go out until 1200 so all of us Photo Mates slept in until 1030. I was up first, dressed, grabbed my gear and headed for the Flight Deck to preflight 602. On the way up the steel ladder a couple of Airdales from VA-163 told me that two pilots had been shot down during the morning air strikes. They were both flying A-4 Skyhawks from Attack Squadron 164. Surface-to-air missiles struck both planes, the pilots ejected and parachuted to the ground, as their planes smashed into rice paddies and exploded. Search and Rescue Forces comprised of both Navy and Air Force fixed wing aircraft and helos rushed to the area and successfully rescued both pilots, returning them to our ship. That's the current story. It could change.

This afternoon our planes flew two missions south of Hanoi. Not everything was routine however. During the 1610 launch the usual monotonous voice of the Air Officer on the superstructure island was replaced by a sweet, young feminine voice: "On the Flight Deck the time is 1 - 4, temperature 88 degrees, altimeter 27.9..."

Dear God, it was wonderful to hear an American female voice.

"Standby to start engines..."

My engine was up and running.

"Check gear in pockets..."

Yes, it's there and it's excited.

"Helmets buckled, goggles down, sleeves rolled down. External power up and ready."

For a quarter minute we all stopped and just gazed up at the island, trying to catch a glimpse of the girl behind the glass window.

She continued, "Check for loose gear about the deck. Check fire bottles and chains, check intakes and exhausts. Stand clear of propellers."

Pause.

"Start the props!"

Pause.

"Stand clear of intakes and exhausts!"

Pause.

"Start the jets!"

Having successfully completed the procedure, the whole Flight Deck crew began cheering and waving toward the island. She's still here tonight as I write this entry in the diary. I caught a glimpse of her at supper: a twenty-something blonde reporter in a mini-skirt under very tight security. There's an Officer escorting her at all times, of course. We all know that Officers are as pure as the driven snow.

You should hear the Old Salts. They're cursing and ranting, "A woman on a ship is a jinx!"

I think it's nice to have a Femalus Americana onboard. It makes this goddamned steel tub feel just a little more civilized.

19 July 1967 ... 32nd day. Ibid.

    Okay, I think we got the true story about yesterday's downed pilots. News here ain't like it is back home. Most of the time we only receive the info that the military censors want us to hear, and as I mentioned before, if it comes to us through the grapevine, all kinds of scuttlebutt gets mixed in.

    Today's version goes like this: our planes offered cover as rescue copters from the U.S.S. Hornet moved to pick up the first pilot. The North Vietnamese troops had the grounded aviators surrounded. I'm told that the NVA deliberately leaves downed pilots unmolested so they can fire on the Search-and-Rescue force. Sure enough, chopper pilots spotted the downed Americans and as they were closing in for rescue, the enemy opened fire. A SAM missile hit the lead chopper which exploded in flames killing all four crew members. Before any more aid could reach them, the pilots were captured. Not the happy ending of the first version I heard.

    The Triple-A's and SAM sites were loaded and ready for our planes today. An Attack Squadron 163 pilot lucked out. A missile struck the belly of his aircraft without exploding. He returned the plane dented and scorched but otherwise undamaged. Popping the canopy and climbing down to the Flight Deck, that was one happy son-of-a-bitch.

    Some other pilots were not so fortunate. An A-1 Spad ditched in the ocean after being shot up. Nobody knows the pilot's status. The Captain has said nothing to us. Same goes for an A-4 Skyhawk that ditched after running out of fuel.

    One of our top CAG Officers died today. Commander Hunter, the Executive Officer of Fighter Squadron 162 had received heavy flak over North Vietnam. Not wanting to ditch, he flew his crippled aircraft back out to the Gulf and attempted a landing on the first carrier available, the USS Bonne Homme Richard. As he approached the fantail, his fuel tanks ran dry, the plane dropped and rammed into the aft section of the Flight Deck, flipping and crashing upside-down onto the deck. The F-8 Crusader disintegrated with much of it falling off the edge into the sea. You can imagine what happened to Mister Hunter. For the sake of his family, need to describe it.

I was working on the Flight Deck when the helo arrived from the Bonnie Dick – as we call her. The black body bag was dropped onto the deck. Medical Corpsmen picked it up, placed it on a stretcher and took it to their department.

Damn, we've been on line for only six days. And in six days, we've lost seven planes and four pilots. The cruise is beginning to resemble a kamikaze mission. At this rate, we'll lose our entire air wing in three months. It's kind of sickening. Our squadron flew two uneventful missions today. The Photo Mates worked late – until 2200 – replacing damaged cameras and mounts, pre-flighting the systems, doing paper work.

The heat is something we've learned to accept now – the heat rash, too. Showers were turned off today because the ship's fresh water supply is down to 40% of capacity. We have the option of taking salt water showers but those fuckers are cold and you can't get all the salt dried off. So, afterward, you just feel like a sticky potato chip, worse than before you showered.

20 July 1967 ... 34th day. Ibid.

This morning I awoke at 0700 and was greeted with the news of a lost plane from Fighter Squadron 162. The F-8 Crusader had a cold cat launch. The pilot ejected from underwater and was recovered safely. Old VF-162 has really been having some tough breaks.

Later today, Lieutenant Kuhl from Attack Squadron-163 flying an A-4 Skyhawk was shot down over North Vietnam. He was recovered immediately.

This is getting redundant. Captain Billy informed us today over the 1MC that one of the two pilots downed two days ago, July 18, is still in radio contact with SAR forces. He is surrounded by North Vietnamese troops. Night missions are being flown tonight to bombard the enemy encirclement and to drop supplies to the pilot. Tomorrow morning the major rescue effort will be undertaken.

Today the water supply dropped to 30 percent and the XO of the ship is nervous. Showers are off, laundry was turned off and the scullery was secured. We're eating with plastic forks and knives off paper plates, and drinking from paper cups. Water supply was secured in several sections of the ship for an hour each sector. This was done to determine the source of a very large leak. We have been losing fresh water at a rate of 1200 gallons per hour. The source of the problem was found late afternoon today: the valves were screwed up. Fresh water produced by the evaporator distilleries had been integrated into the salt water lines and pumped over the side as fast as it was being produced. Goddamned stupid fuckin' Blackshoes! It'll probably take a couple of days for the water level to replenish so we can operate normally again.

Some guy in Communications heard today that President Johnson is adding sixteen targets including an airfield, a railroad yard, two bridges, and twelve barracks and supply areas, all within restricted circles around Hanoi and Haiphong, to the approved hit list for bombing. This doesn't sound like Defense Secretary McNamara's de-escalation that he promised. I don't understand why LBJ and McNamara are running this goddamned war. Don't they trust the Admirals and Generals to do it? Maybe someday it will make sense to me. Maybe it never will.

CHAPTER X
REMINISCING ON MY SISTER'S BIRTHDAY

21 July 1967 ... 35th day. Ibid.

It's my **sister's** 17th birthday today. I wonder what Jeris is doing to celebrate; I'm sure that she and her girl friends have something cooked up.

Photo Bird 603 made a sortie run today at noon over strategic locations. Lieutenant Sam brought her back with all film in the camera stations shot except for the KA-68 panoramic camera. It jammed on him. He was only slightly pissed. At 1530 LTJG Beam came swaggering out to 602 to prep for his flight. We Pharts were working like hell on two cameras, trying to get them operational by 1600 launch time. I was sitting in the cockpit of the plane supplying power while Harry, Ray and Dick sweat it out in the camera bays.

Mr. Beam looked up at me and shouted: "Do you think you own that seat, MacLennon?"

I paused a moment thinking of a good sarcastic response that would be appropriate for an Officer's sarcastic question. "Do you want to fly with your cameras working... sir?"

He laughed.

After pulling the LA-28 and 68 film magazines and replacing them, the system checked out okay. Beamer was launched on schedule and we returned to the shop to hang out and listen to our music while our intrepid Navy flyboy flew into the war zone. It was only a one hour mission. He brought her back, catching the wire at 1700. We were on deck ready to unload and reload as he taxied forward and cut engines. To our surprise, he signaled that he had shot nothing and we just stood there like idiots with our mouths open wondering why not. He climbed down from the cockpit, offering no explanation. He was calm but headed directly to Officer's Country. Later on, the Chief told us that as soon as Beamer had arrived in the target areas, a Russian surface-to-air missile exploded about thirty yards in front of him. A few seconds later another SAM detonated just off his starboard side. Falling back on evasion tactics, he commenced a steep dive gathering 7.5 G's of force in his descent. That's .5 more than the plane is designed to withstand. As he pulled out of the dive, yet another

SAM shot by his cockpit narrowly missing the plane and exploding 100 yards to port. That was all Beamer could handle for one mission. He turned around and returned to the safety of the Tonkin Gulf and our pig iron home. Mister Beam... there's a guy, a damned nice guy, who is very happy to be alive tonight. Although there were near misses, no planes from any of the squadrons were shot down today. I stood an Aircraft Integrity Watch on Hanger Bay Two this evening. This time I read a paperback while I walked back and forth. That helped the time pass a little faster.

I sit here now in our berthing compartment at the checkerboard table. The day's work is done and I can think of more pleasant things, such as my home in Nebraska. I always remember the date of my sister's birthday. I have trouble remembering everyone else's but for some reason, Jeris and July 21st are indelibly written on my mind. The kid and I had 14 years together of growing up. She was born when I was three-and-a-half years old. I don't remember the actual day of the week she was born nor of Mother Norma being pregnant with her. The first memory that sticks with me is the portrait session at the Carlson Photo Studios in Red Oak, Iowa. She was 6 months old and I was almost 4. I was wearing my reindeer sweater and she was in her little, fluffy dress and not at all happy with the situation. The strange man with his flashing machine terrified her but eventually Mom was able to comfort Jeris Elaine to the point that the photog captured some good poses with fairly good expressions.

Back then, my role as big brother was not well-defined. Hell, I'd never done it before. Even so, Mother often tried to impress me with my duties and responsibilities to this delicate, little girl, as Mom called her. Sometimes I was loving and kind to my sister; sometimes I was nasty and just plain mean. It depended on my mood and the circumstance. I have a photo of little Jeris, sitting in Mom's clothes basket. In the early Fifties, before we had automatic dryers, Mom hung the wash on the clotheslines in the backyard. Jeris loved to sit in the basket, watch, and sometimes play peek-a-boo. We lived in an apartment on Washington Street in Red Oak, Iowa, a pleasant older neighborhood with two-story houses. The neighbors were all friendly. That prompted little Gerald to take frequent tours to each door hitting up the housewives for cookies. Did I share my cookies with Jeris? Only if Mom made me.

Those were the years of innocence. Dad would leave us every morning, going to work at the Standard Oil service station. Mom would stay home, taking care of little Gerald and Jeris, washing, cleaning, ironing clothes, preparing lunches, baking, shopping, and preparing a nice supper for that magic hour when Daddy entered the front door to spend the evening with us. Life was pristine, overflowing with daily discoveries: the Hollyhocks by the alley, hummingbirds drawing nectar from the flowers, the autumn aroma of dry leaves burning in the street gutters, the Iowa Highway Patrol car that our neighbor parked by the curb, and the old people living next door who always gave us big hugs. Our awareness of the world was confined primarily to a two block radius of our house but we made frequent trips in Dad's Studebaker to visit friends, and to Mom and Dad's relatives all who lived in Red Oak. Grandpa and Grandma MacLennon lived in a little house down by the scrap yard. We only went there about once a month. Grandpa and Grandma Hilding, Mom's parents, still lived on their farm northeast of Red Oak. I have wonderful memories of the farm. Unfortunately, Jeris has none. She was there but she was too young to retain the memory of the majestic, white two-story house with stately Lodgepole Pine trees in the front yard. She doesn't remember Grandma Florence's fragrant Marigolds planted by the front porch, the flock of chickens that roamed freely in the barnyard, the hog pen with the malicious sow, the cattle and work horses and the best of all playgrounds: the hayloft in the barn.

Jeris' permanent memories didn't take hold until after Grandparents Hilding retired from farming and moved to the modest two-story house in town. That house on the hill is our fortress of family stability. I say stability because Dad became a nomadic worker after a time. He was always restless, looking for greener grass. We moved from Red Oak to Atlantic, Iowa; then to Grimes, Iowa; then Des Moines; then back to Red Oak. After six months in our home town, we packed again and moved thirty-five miles south to Shenandoah, Iowa; and ultimately to Nebraska in 1955.

Grandparents Hilding were our favorites and probably always will be because they always made us feel special when we visited. They demonstrated their love in dozens of ways. I talk of Grandpa Gus in the past tense now because he died last year. It was a terrible loss for all of us. Full name, Gustav Emanuel Hilding, he was a native-born Swede who sailed the ship to America with his family in 1903. Grandma Florence was one of five daughters born to Joseph and Nancy Cate, an Irish-American farm family who had also moved often throughout Kansas, Iowa and Minnesota. It was in Minnesota that Gus first met Flossie, as he called her. The romance commenced when he and a threshing crew came to harvest Joseph's crop. Following a long distance courtship by correspondence, he drove up to Minnesota and married her. The newlyweds rented and settled into their first farm outside Red Oak where their only child, Norma, our mother, was born a year later in 1925.

My Dad, Neal MacLennon, spent as little time with his folks as possible especially his father. The way I heard it was: Grandpa MacLennon never missed a chance to tell his son, my father, that he was not good enough, smart enough or motivated enough to be a success in life. In 1946, at the age of sixteen, Dad accidentally shot and killed his best friend, Charles, while they were using rats for target practice at the Red Oak trash dump. His father still torments him with the memory, as if he really needs reminding. Poor Dad is still depressed about it. Maybe that's why he drinks so much. It's no surprise that Neal MacLennon preferred the kind, helpful parenting style of Gustav Hilding over that of his own flesh and blood. Gus was not wealthy by any stretch but he was very frugal with his money and rich in wisdom. He was also elated to have a grandson, me, in his bloodline. Even though Jeris and I were not aware of it at the time, Gus and Florence did much to help our little struggling family.

Grandma's house always entices with delicious meals, home-made cookies, ice cream and chocolate cake. Sunday meals around the dining room table are a family tradition that dates back to the earliest days of Gerald and Jeris' life. The dining table offers comfort food, as some people call it: roast beef, corn, green beans or peas, mashed potatoes and gravy and whatever wonderful dessert Grandma has baked for us that particular day. She still lives there, alone now. She has good memories plus many friends and relatives who all enjoy her company. She hasn't done anything with Grandpa's territory. His portion of the basement and the garage remain as they were when he was alive. I wept bitter tears when he died; so sad that I wasn't by his bed at the moment of passing on. Instead, I was on duty at FIC PAC FAC when Mother's international phone call came to me from 13,000 miles away. After she told me the bad news and hung up, I just excused myself from work, walked outside to the second-level deck, looked up at the stars, and cried like a baby. I tried to talk to his spirit hoping that he heard me say "Goodbye" and that I loved him. I don't know where Jeris was when that moment occurred. She was sixteen; I'm sure she shed a cascade of tears.

As I mentioned, Dad had a penchant for uprooting the family and moving on a moment's notice despite the protests of his wife and children. Jeris and I would just get settled in one place, make new friends, meet the neighbors and, shit! we were off to another town, new people, new neighbors, new situations. I don't think Jeris was affected by the instability as much as I was because she was three years younger and hadn't started school yet. She was busy playing house, playing with her baby dolls. She had her little family that went with her wherever we moved. I would make fun of her sissy pastimes as big brothers are supposed to do.

Honestly, I don't remember much about our day to day life in those many venues. I do remember the stupid stuff like the day in Grimes, Iowa when Jeris pushed a bean up her nose and couldn't get it out. Mom was near hysteria as she mined my sister's nasal passages with a variety of instruments as the kid screamed bloody murder. It eventually came out with a little help from someone. I think it was Uncle Glen, Dad's brother. After the frenzy passed, we all had a good laugh over it and, of course, I teased her about it for weeks. It was also in Grimes where the large, evil men came to our house and took away our furniture while Mom pleaded with them to leave us and our furnishings alone. Apparently Dad owed someone some bucks and was in arrears. So, the bad men repossessed our furniture. Jeris' age of awareness is probably more focused on Lincoln. Dad landed a job at the huge Sears Department Store downtown. I remember the downtown in its grand old days when all the major retail stores were still located there and shopping malls hadn't been invented. Christmas was mystical and wonderful for Jeris and I. Gold's of Nebraska had the biggest and best toy department of any store and the best Santa, too. During the Yuletide season, he sat there proudly on his throne like a king. We would tug on his beard and it wouldn't budge. Maybe it was real. We still have a photo of Jeris sitting on his lap. Christmas 1955 was snowflakes falling on shoppers dashing, Salvation Army bells ringing on every corner, choirs singing songs of the Baby Jesus born.

Family members would visit us occasionally. The most memorable visitors to me were Uncle Bill MacLennon and Marlin Hilding. They were both young men in their early twenties. The former was Dad's little brother, the latter was Mom's cousin, both of whom had grown up in Red Oak. Uncle Bill came to see us in 1956 just as the Elvis craze was sweeping the nation. Parents of teenagers were up in arms about this new hip-swiveling, greased-back, singer who was belting out a new kind of music called Rock and Roll. "Demonic," some called it. And here came Uncle Bill to visit us, greased-back and looking just like Elvis. It was cool. Mom and Dad were cool because they were still young, too. Dad was 27. Mom was 31. Then Bill scored a date with the beautiful, blonde girl across the street, the one who lay out on her beach towel every day and had a deep bronze tan. That was even cooler because Dad and I both thought she was the bee's knees.

When Jeris and I were children, we were oblivious to the pressures adults must endure. We just took certain things for granted like: there would always be a meal there for us morning, noon and night; we'd always have a place to live; we'd always have new clothes when we needed them. If we got sick, Mom would take us to the doctor; if our tooth hurt she'd take us to the dentist. As kids, we didn't understand that people exchange their labor for money and that money is often limited, and credit unavailable, especially for lower income families. We didn't understand that Father left us every day not because he necessarily wanted to, but because he had to exchange his labor for money to provide us with all the aforementioned. We didn't understand why Mom and Dad had arguments about money. Sometimes, they were very loud arguments and all Jeris and I could do was lie in bed, listen and tremble. Dad sold household appliances at Sears, then at Wards, and then at J.C. Penney's, where he is now. He is a silver-tongued devil with a smile that can melt a customer's heart, breaking down their will power. He is good at sales; hell, not just good, he is the leader of the pack. As a result, he was offered the Department Manager position but Dad turned it down because he only has an eighth grade education. He felt inadequate for the task because I'm sure he still hears the voice of his father in his head telling him, "You'll never amount to anything, kid."

Grandpa Gus had encouraged Dad to get into sales but the words of Grandpa Noel MacLennon restrained him from advancing up the ladder – even without being there in person. A bad seed had been planted. Neal MacLennon has the melancholy strain that runs through his Scots-Irish family. At times he is riding high; at other times he is deeply depressed and anxious but he has always been determined to show his father that he can succeed. To that end, he bought a brand new house for us in the Lincoln suburb of Eastborough in 1958. It was a one-story, ranch-style with basement and car port, with a price tag of $12,000. Mom, Jeris and I were incredibly excited not only about having our own house but having the privilege of watching it being built just for us. What had been a cornfield was now the site for the MacLennon family mansion – not in the truest sense, but considering the roach havens we had endured over the years, it was indeed a mansion. Dad was especially proud. This was his grandest moment. He could, at last, flip off his Old Man. After moving on up to the East side suburbs, Jeris and I transferred to Meadow Lane School. Like everything in the neighborhood, it was also new – just a couple of years old. We had good teachers and very large classes because we were, and are, members of the post-World War II Baby Boom. Fifty kids per classroom was not unusual. The Eastborough and Meadow Lane area was overflowing with thousands of little Boomers. The Fifties were prosperous times. Fathers earned enough to support the entire family. Mothers raised their children. The community was vibrant and every man had his name proudly displayed on the mail box by the street.

The MacLennons of Eastborough lived a very normal, American, suburban lifestyle for seven years. Gerald was in Boy Scouts. Jeris was in Camp Fire Girls. We went to school, we played with our ever-expanding circle of neighborhood friends. We were good kids most of the time even though I started two brush fires on two different occasions while playing with matches in the farm fields to the east of us.

The year 1961 began with shocking news from Mother and Dad. They had to sit Jeris and I down for it. Mom was pregnant. The Terrible Twosome was going to have a little bundle of attention competition. We were not sure what to think? Mom was 36. That seemed extremely old to be having a baby but there certainly was no debating the issue. So, for the next nine months, we watched her inflate. As the September due date grew closer, our anticipation and excitement increased. Would it be a boy or a girl? I was hoping of course for a boy. I didn't want two sisters!

On the evening of September 27th, I thought something horrible had happened. I ran upstairs from my basement bedroom and saw Mother Norma in her undergarments running up and down the hallway with a bath towel tucked in her crotch. "O Lord, Neal, my water broke."

I had no idea what that meant. At first, I thought she was referring to some sort of plumbing problem in the bathroom.

Dad rushed to her, then looked at Jeris and me. "We have to go to the hospital. Will you kids be okay?"

"Yeah, sure, but what's happening?"

With tears in her eyes, Mom shrieked, "I'm having the baby!"

So, they took off to Saint Elizabeth Hospital for an extended labor. My new little brother, Jeff, was born the next afternoon, the 28th of September. He was all ugly, with a scrunched up red face. I said, "This cannot be my brother."

"Don't worry," the nurse said, "He'll look better in a day or two."

Jeris now had a real baby with whom she could play mother but neither of us had any idea of how much of a pain-in-the-ass a real baby is! Crying in the night and keeping us awake became commonplace. We weren't accustomed to a family member shitting his pants. He was totally high maintenance but of course the brunt of the work fell on Mom. He was untimely born but big brother and sister initiated him into the ways of the family quickly before we had to leave home and enter the adult world. He would know and understand that we loved him, yes, but Gerald and Jeris were still big brother and big sister.

Jeris was a sixth-grader at Meadow Lane when I went on to high school in the fall. I worried about her. She would be entering the evil world of junior high school where everything your parents have taught you about goodness and purity is challenged. It's the age of sexual awakening and experimentation with all sorts of unhealthy, illegal and immoral things. I hated for my kid sister to be in junior high without my protection but she had been giving me clues that she didn't really need it anymore. My memories of our adolescent years, even though they are nearer in time, are not as plentiful. I think we became more self-absorbed from 13 on, less involved with family and more interested in socializing with our select group of friends. Jeris had several cute girlfriends and I was always pleased when she brought them over to our house.

We still had family gatherings, trips to Grandma and Grandpa's house in Red Oak, vacations in Minnesota, Christmas, Easter and the other holidays. Dad had always liked his Old Milwaukee beer but he was drinking more and more. His after work stops at the Hob Nob or Duffy's Tavern stretched farther into the evening, well past supper time. This would cause fierce fights between Mom and Dad. Instead of changing his ways and coming home earlier, he'd stay later and get totally shit-faced because he knew there was a fight waiting for him at home and he could handle it better drunk than sober. Things haven't changed.

I had been an honor roll student in seventh and eighth grade but I changed in ninth grade. The grades plummeted, my attitude went to hell. The only class I enjoyed was art because I was a natural. The kids loved the monster pictures I drew. Even so, I began playing hooky from school. Things were no better in high school.

In 1964, the pop music world was revolutionized by the British Invasion. The shaggy-haired foursome from Liverpool, The Beatles, captured the number one spot on the charts with I Wanna Hold Your Hand. That got the ball rolling for John, Paul, George and Ringo. And, the hits just kept on coming. Jeff had a favorite toy down in the basement, his hobby rocker horse. As Jeris and I played the Beatles' *She Loves You*, Jeff would rock with the beat and sing, "She lub you, yeah, yeah, yeah; she lub you, yeah, yeah, yeah." Along with every girl from 10-to-17, Jeris was caught up in the Beatles frenzy. I don't remember her favorite Beatle. Each had their own favorite; the one they wanted to marry.

Well, the Kid turned 17 today, the age I was when I joined Uncle Sam's Navy. We write to each other from time to time. I'm always interested in knowing about her Boyfriend of the Month but the details are usually limited. She has my car now, my boss '56 Chevy convertible and I know she's rodding it with her girlfriends – raising hell just like I did.

Anyway, it's late and I'm tired. We have standdown from air operations for the next four days which means we'll probably be cleaning, cleaning and cleaning for inspection of quarters and work areas.

Happy Birthday, Jeris. I love you, kiddo.

CHAPTER XI
ELUDING THE DOGS OF NORTH VIETNAM

Well, I guess this is the official story now. The following article from Star and Stripes tells about the ordeal of Lieutenant Commander Verich, the Oriskany pilot I wrote about on July 16 and 17.

DOWNED PILOT ELUDES N. VIETS' DOGS
By John Dittman, S&S Staff Correspondent

SAIGON – A U.S. Navy Pilot, shot down for the second time over North Vietnam, spent Monday night dodging Communist soldiers and scout dogs in the jungle 40 miles south of Hanoi before being plucked from a cliff by a Navy rescue helicopter.

As LT Cmdr. Demetrio A. Verich was being hauled up into the chopper, the door gunner cut into the North Vietnamese soldiers scrambling up the cliff toward the dangling pilot. "I hung on for dear life," Verich said.

Verich, now on his second Vietnam tour, was shot down the first time over North Vietnam last August 17. He managed to nurse his crippled plane to sea that time, where he bailed out and was back on his carrier within two hours. It took a little longer this time.

Verich took off from the carrier Oriskany at 3:30 p.m. Sunday for a strike against barge traffic on the Phu Bai River. The planes were met with heavy ground fire. Just before Verich started to roll in on target, an enemy anti-aircraft shell ripped into the tail of his plane, and Verich was forced to bail out. The Crusader jet crashed and exploded directly under Verich as he descended in his chute. "The wind was driving me right into the fireball so I pulled on my rear risers for all I was worth. I just managed to slip away."

LT Herb Hunter, Verich's wingman, circled the area for 30 minutes, getting an accurate fix on the downed pilot's position. Verich had come down on a steep rocky hill covered with thick jungle and trees. While the jet circled, he climbed several hundred yards up the slope, since North Vietnamese soldiers were already headed toward the wrecked plane. "I saw my wingman had fixed my position and would be back, but it was getting dark so I figured I wouldn't be rescued until morning," Verich said. "I thought the best thing would be to hide and then move after dark. I covered myself with branches and waited. The North Vietnamese were beating the bushes, some less than a hundred yards away."

Throughout the night, he could hear soldiers yelling, dogs barking and a strange sound like two pieces of bamboo being struck together rhythmically. "I decided to move at dawn," said Verich, "But just as the sun was coming up, a jet passed overhead so I stayed where I was and waited."

About 30 minutes later, another jet passed over and then propeller-driven Skyraiders swept in to cover the rescue. They were met with fire from the ground. Meanwhile, LT Neil Sparks and LTJG Robin Springer were maneuvering the Sea King rescue helicopter through the deep, bowl-like valleys trying to pinpoint the downed flyer. They couldn't see Verich through the trees, but, just as they passed over, he fired a flare. The door gunner spotted it and Sparks quickly turned the chopper around. The copter hovered over Verich and lowered its jungle penetrator. It came under attack from Communist ground positions, and one round hit just below Sparks, knocking out his radio and automatic pilot. Verich missed the line on the first drop, but the second time it came down about 10 feet from him and he was able to get to it. The line was being hauled in, by this time half a dozen Communist troops were climbing the cliff toward the dangling pilot. The other door gunner fired at the advancing soldiers with his machine gun as the 100 yard line between Verich and the chopper was reeled in. The helicopter had to hover until Verich was aboard because it was still 50

feet below the rim of the cliff. Verich was finally hauled into the chopper, which headed out to sea. It stopped at the destroyer Worden for fuel before heading for the Oriskany. Springer, later reported hearing that three MIG-21's had dived after them during the rescue but were chased off by Fighters from Verich's own group.
###

25 July 1967 ... 39th day. Ibid.

A foul weather warning came down from the bridge this morning. It has been issued for today and tomorrow.

For the last few days we've been in sight of a mountainous region on the North Vietnamese mainland near Hoang Du. Closest we have come to shore is 35 miles or thereabouts. Every day the ship receives unrep – underway replenishment. It is a never ending cycle. Utilizing high lines, Oriskany takes on fuel from tankers, ammunition from AE ships such as the U.S.S Pyro and the U.S.S. Virgo and subsistence supplies from refrigeration ships.

Sickness is on the increase and it's no wonder. The drinking water alone is enough to make us puke. It's mixed with JP-5 – highly refined kerosene. No official word has been released stating just how jet fuel gets into the fresh water. I've heard scuttlebutt that the storage vats below decks, when emptied of JP-5, are refilled with fresh water without first rinsing them. If true, I would think such negligence would be corrected by Captain Billy. He has to drink the water, too.

Then there's the food served at the galley. Most of the time it's barely edible but then there are times when it actually poisons some poor bastard. Yesterday, I was the bastard. I ate chow at noon and returned to the shop. About two hours later I developed stomach and intestinal cramps, headache and nausea. I barfed my lunch along with blood. Feeling like dog shit, I wove my way to Sickbay and was told to wait in line. Too damn weak and miserable to wait, I staggered back to the shop and heaved up more blood. Ray Hines insisted I go back down. He escorted me and got me directly into a treatment room. I explained my symptoms to a Medical Corpsman, he took notes, told me to sit on the bench and wait. So, I waited and waited, growing weaker.

I got pissed off after a half hour of waiting and returned to the shop again to lie down.

This time Dick Aden went down and told Mister Muffley the situation. The Lieutenant came to the shop and personally escorted me to Sickbay where I received immediate attention from a doctor. Brass has clout. Enlisted Men ain't got shit.

I was injected in the arm and sent to the ward room where I crawled into a bunk, fully dressed, and was nearly asleep when a little Corpsman jolted me back to consciousness: "Hey buddy, come here!"

He made me get up and sit beside his desk.

"What's your name? First, last, initial, service number, organization?"

He asked me that twice. For 15 minutes he deprived me of that bed. If I had the energy I would have decked him.

"Okay, I think I got it all. Get out of your clothes. Here put these greens on."

When I finally got back in bed, I had chills but was too weak to ask for a blanket. The closed-circuit television was playing some grade-B comedy. A group of patients was watching, laughing. For two long, long hours that goddamned television blared. Supposedly-sick Swabbies talked, laughed, yelled across the room to one another. It was a nightmare. Twice I jumped out of bed, ran to the head and knelt before the commode. The dickheads didn't even give me a bed pan. They gave me a capsule but I heaved it. I wasn't allowed water or food. My mouth and throat were dry as sandpaper. I couldn't sleep; couldn't get up.

The next morning, the 26th, I awoke feeling better, still weak but no longer nauseated. I drank a quart of water, ate breakfast and was examined by a doctor. A Corpsman gave me a painful shot in the ass. Taking in another hour of shut-eye, I was jolted back to reality by an ugly old man.

A face that had known too many years at sea and all the sins of the liberty ports spoke to me in a gravelly voice: "You can go now. But before you do, I want you to strip your bunk, get some new linen out of the pantry and remake your bed."

There ain't no frills for Enlisted grunts, even when we've been falling down sick. It's like I inconvenienced the Navy by getting sick even though it was probably their food that did it.

The old man wasn't through. "And after you make the bed, grab a broom, sweep down, swab the floor, lay some wax and buff the deck."

I was pissed but the motherfucker outranked me; so I complied and was released two hours later. They diagnosed my condition as viral flu but I still think it was food poisoning. Back in the shop, Ray, Harry, Dick and Ern were happy to see me up and kicking.

CHAPTER XII
MEETING MICHAEL GOLDBERG

This evening I ventured out to the front edge of the Flight Deck, and the canoe, to enjoy some solitary meditation. The sea was so placid it looked like a turquoise-colored mirror. As the sun descended to the horizon, it became a fiery orange ball peeking through the scattered jigsaw puzzle of clouds. It reflected in the water, sending an orange runner to the bow of our big, gray tub. I thought to myself: The eternal ocean has no concern for the affairs of man; it simply is, and always will be, long after our belligerent species has vanished from this emerald and aqua sphere.

It was all so peaceful, so contradictory to everything else happening around me. After an hour or so, the sky had completely cleared and the canopy of night unveiled millions of stars, far more than one could ever see living near a populated area. Scanning the heavens, I saw no gaps in the cosmos whatsoever. What a humbling experience: to know that God is so large and I am so small and insignificant in the grand scheme of things.

I was so entranced that I hadn't noticed I was no longer alone. I heard a faint rustle of clothing, turned and was startled by the presence of a dark figure behind me.

"Sorry. Did I scare you?" he asked.

"Yeah, sorta. Guess I wasn't paying attention."

As he came nearer, I realized that he was an Officer – a Lieutenant. That made me nervous. "You don't mind if I sit out here on the canoe, do you, sir?"

"Don't worry, sailor." His voice was kindly, "I'm not checking up on you. Matter of fact, I probably came out here for the same reason as you."

"Some peace and quiet, sir?"

"At ease, sailor," he replied. "Call me Michael... but only when it's just the two of us. Agreed?"

"Agreed, sir... er, Michael." It felt uncomfortable to break protocol.

Michael sat down on the deck beside me. In the moonless night, it was somewhat difficult to make out his features. His hair was black or very dark brown. His facial profile resembled that of a sculptured Greek bust. When he turned his head toward me, I could detect that he had dark, penetrating eyes – piercing but not menacing. I guessed he was probably about 25 years old.

He held out his hand, "Formal introduction... I'm Lieutenant Michael Goldberg."

We shook hands.

"I'm Gerald MacLennon, Photographer's Mate 3rd Class, but just about everyone calls me Mac."

"And so will I. Pleased to meet you, Mac."

"Same here... Michael." My conditioning makes it difficult to address an Officer by his first name, even with his permission. "Are you with the Air Wing, sir... er, Michael?".

"Yes, I'm a chopper pilot for HC-3, Helicopter Combat Support Squadron-3. We're home based in Oxnard Beach, California."

"The Angels?"

"Right, the Angels. What about you? Ship's Company?"

"No, Photo Recon Squadron 63."

"Sure, The Eyes of the Fleet." He hesitated a few seconds and then spoke again, "I think photographer would be a good rating. Are you an artist?"

I liked his perceptiveness. "Yes, that's why I chose photography. It was the only artistic rating I could find."

"That makes sense. If I were an Enlisted Man, I think I'd probably do the same thing. I'm somewhat of a Van Gogh myself."

"Really?"

"No. Not really. I dabble around, not what you'd call accomplished. I just do it for my own pleasure. Mostly nature and scenics."

"That's probably why we come out here, isn't it?" I observed.

"Pardon?"

"I mean, out here on the canoe at night. We're artists and we appreciate the beauty of nature."

"Definitely. I find peace in God's Creation."

He was very forthcoming with his mention of God; he didn't seem embarrassed in the least to acknowledge his belief. I was liking him even more. We were both silent for about half a minute, both looking up at the night sky.

Michael spoke, "Amazing, isn't it?"

"What's that?"

"The universe. The stars. The galaxies. Makes you feel very small, doesn't it?"

"Funny you should say that."

"Why's that?"

"Cause that's what I was just thinking when you walked over here, about how large God is and how very small and insignificant I am."

"I wouldn't say we're insignificant, Mac. Not in God's eyes."

He was taking the conversation into religion and theology and I was eager to go that direction but for some stupid reason, I changed the subject. "Did you say your last name is Goldberg?"

He nodded an affirmative.

"Like Justice Goldberg?"

"Well," Michael responded, "He's U.S. Ambassador to the U.N. now but yes, he did hold what they call the Jewish Seat on the Supreme Court before he resigned."

I hesitated for a minute. I didn't want to offend him but he read my mind.

"Yes, Mac, I'm Jewish."

"Really?" I was trying hard to find the right words. "I don't think I've ever talked to a Jewish person before."

"I seriously doubt that, Mac." His tone eased my discomfort. "Where are you from?"

"Nebraska."

"Maybe not but on the other hand, if there are Jews in Nebraska, they probably don't shout it from the rooftops. That's Bible Belt country."

"Bible Belt? Why should that be a problem?"

"You probably don't understand the not-so-subtle bigotry that Jews have to deal with, especially in places where we're a very small minority. Me? I just might be a target for bigotry in Nebraska because of my name."

"Goldberg? Why?"

"Well, like you said, you've had little or no contact with the Jews but anyone familiar with our people knows that the name, Goldberg is quite Yiddishkeit, it has 'Jewish' written all over it. Can't hide it."

"Okay," was my less than intelligent answer, then I attempted to change the subject.

"So, Michael," I asked, "Where are you from?"

"From the holy city."

I thought for a few seconds and asked, "Jerusalem?"

"No," He laughed. "Brooklyn. Brooklyn, New York."

I was puzzled. "Why do you call it that?"

"It's a local joke. There are more Jews in Brooklyn than all of Israel. That's why we say it."

He smiled. I smiled and laughed... but then, we fell back into silence for a couple of minutes, just enjoying the serenity of our oceanic outpost.

Michael was first to break the quiet, "Hey, Mac, did you hear about the Six Day War?"

"Ahh..." I hated to admit I didn't pay much attention to it. "Well, I guess I did hear something about it on the news but we were getting ready for this cruise and..."

He interrupted me. "That's okay, Mac. It probably didn't have much of an impact on you personally but for the Jewish people it was highly significant."

"Why?"

"Because we got our Temple back!" There was a surge of joy in the way Michael said it. Then, he turned to me and asked point blank, "You've heard of the Jerusalem Temple, right?"

I was confident with that question. "Yes, of course, it's in the Bible. I learned about it in Sunday School and Confirmation. It was the holiest site in Israel."

"And still is!" he was quick to add. "There's only a small portion of it left. That's the western wall of the foundation but, yes, it is still considered the holiest place on earth to my people and since 1948, the Jordanian Arabs have had control of it, the schmucks! They wouldn't let us go to our Wall to pray. They wouldn't allow us into eastern Jerusalem."

He was becoming agitated. "For nineteen long years, those Arabs have been desecrating our Jewish graveyards in the Kidron Valley. They used Jewish grave markers for paving their roads. They let our holy site fall into ruin. No respect! No respect at all for anything that was not Moslem but on June the fifth, we launched a preemptive war."

I broke in. "Israel started the war?"

"It was strike or be stricken, Mac. Nassar and his cronies in Egypt, Syria and Jordan were activating their armies making very real threats to invade Israel. When Nassar demanded the withdrawal of United Nations soldiers and closed the Straits of Tiran, Israel knew it had to act quickly. On June fifth, Israel's Air Force bombed Nassar's air fields and completely destroyed every Fighter jet on the ground. That very day, the Jordanian army began firing artillery shells into western Jerusalem and up in the north, Syrian soldiers mobilized to attack Israel from their perch up on the Golan Heights. Yes, the Israeli Defense Forces lashed out and struck hard on all three borders. In six days... six days, Mac, our little Jewish state captured the Sinai from Egypt, the Golan from Syria, the West Bank and East Jerusalem from the Jordanians. The IDF forced the Jordanian Army to retreat all the way back across the Jordan River where they belong!"

"Wow!" I was amazed. "All that in six days?"

"Yes, Six Days! Barukh Ha Shem!"

I changed the subject only momentarily. "What does that mean? That Ba roo ha shame?"

"Barukh Ha Shem. Bless the Name. Literally, bless the Holy Name of God."

"I see. Kinda like Hallelujah," I asked.

"Yeah, a lot like Hallelujah," he answered.

I wasn't sure how Michael would react but at that juncture I just had to ask him a question: "Michael?"

"Yes, Mac."

"Would you say then that the Six Day War was a good war."

"Yes, absolutely! It was good for Israel, the Jews and America!"

"Why America?"

"Because Israel is the only democracy in the Middle East and America's greatest ally in that region." He paused a minute to rehash my question, then spoke: "If you're talking political science, Mac... yes, I would say it was a just war. Justice was served. And if you're referring to religion, I must also say yes. It was good because evil was defeated. We Jews have a God-given right to our little sliver of the earth called Israel and any enemy who vows to push us out of our ancestral home and into the Mediterranean Sea is not a friend of civilization; nor of Ha Shem."

"Well, for the Arabs..." I began.

Michael jumped on it. "For the Arabs, it was a bad war, a terrible humiliation but they asked for it. You have to remember who was doing all the saber rattling and chest thumping! It wasn't Israel. Israel didn't pick the fight but they certainly finished it in rapid order."

"Yes, they did." I conceded to his argument but it wasn't really necessary. With Hitler exterminating six million Jews in Europe only two decades ago, I do believe that Jehovah God was moved to compassion and finally brought to an end nineteen centuries of Jewish exile. I read Exodus by Leon Uris last year. I was actually moved to tears when Ari Ben-Canaan's tough veneer crumbled following the death of Karen. Ari cried and I cried. Sitting there at Michael's side, I thought about how the Bible referred to the Jews as God's Chosen People.

Listen to me, I thought to myself, I don't sound like a Buddhist at all, do I? I thought I was taking up Buddhism. Make up your mind, MacLennon. What the hell are you?

"So, Mac?" the Lieutenant brought me back to the conversation. "Do you think the Six Day War was justifiable?"

"I pretty much agree with you, Michael." He looked up at the heavens again and said, "I bet I know your next question."

"You do? What is it?" I inquired.

"Do I think this war we're waging here in 'Nam is good... a just war?"

"You're right, Michael. It's been bothering me. Do you think it's right for us to be here?"

"Damned if I know." His response seemed out of character for someone who was so certain about the Six Day War. I was hoping he could offer me some wisdom regarding Vietnam. He continued, "When I was told I was being assigned to the Oriskany for a Vietnam cruise, I was ready to serve my country in a war zone. That's what I'm trained for. That's why I'm in the military, right?"

I didn't answer.

"Is this your first time on Yankee Station?" Michael asked.

"Yes," I replied. "and my last. I'm being released from active duty in February."

"I have two more years on my hitch."

"You're not making it a career?" I asked. "I thought all Officers were career bound."

"Not this Officer. Come 1969, I'll be back home in New York... probably in grad school. My father, from the time I was a little yeled, has drummed into my head that I will become a great surgeon."

"So, how did you end up here?" I was curious.

"Oh, it's a long story. I won't bore you with all the details. I turned eighteen and decided I'd had my fill of orthodoxy and kosher this, kosher that. And, I'd had enough of being goaded by my father so I chose my own way. I went to college all right but I did it on the U.S. Navy's meal ticket. It was a trade. They paid my way through college and, in return, I gave them a portion of my youth. I didn't want to take my father's money for tuition because, if I did that, I'd be indebted to him and I'd have to become what he wanted me to be. Aviation sounded appealing but I didn't want to be a weapon of war. I didn't want to fly a fighter or bomber so I set my sights on helicopter search and rescue. That way, I'd be helping people most of the time. I was lucky enough to land the schooling and training I needed and... heneni, here am I."

"Flying the Angels."

He grinned, "Yeah. The Angels of Mercy.".

I was determined to get an answer to the Vietnam question. "You and I both know, Michael, there are hundreds of thousands of North Vietnamese about fifty miles over there." I pointed to the west. "They'd prob'ly love to get their hands on us right now and tear us to shreds because of what this ship and others like it are doing to their people. Don't you think they have a right to hate us?"

"Of course!"

We sat silent for a couple of minutes, the only sound being the bow of the ship gently slicing through the gulf waters. I gazed at the stars for those minutes while he nodded his head in contemplation. He finally looked over at me and with a firm but gentle tone said: "Mac, I must believe that this is a just war. That's probably not the answer you were fishing for but let me explain. Communism in theory is probably the perfect form of government except for its promotion of atheism. It was formulated by a Jew. Did you know that?"

"No, I didn't." I replied and then asked, "Karl Marx was a Jew?"

"Yes, a wayward Jew but Jewish just the same. Marx is another one of those names that has European Judaism written all over it."

"You mean that Groucho, Harpo..."

"Jews. Yes."

"Anyway, the truth of the matter is that every country that has tried to adopt the Communist form of government has failed. Why? Because none has advanced beyond the first two steps which are: one, revolution, and two, dictatorship of the proletariat. And those dictatorships haven't actually been by the Proletariat, the working class. They've always had a ruling man or committee who supposedly spoke on behalf of the working class. You've got Ho Chi Minh in Vietnam; Mao Tse Tung in Red China; Lenin, Josef Stalin, the Politburo in the Soviet Union; Fidel Castro in Cuba... all iron-fisted dictatorships that show no restraint nor conscience in the systematic execution of thousands of their own people – in Stalin's case, millions – all in the name of Communism when it really isn't Communism at all. It's bondage. Slavery. It's evil, pure and simple.

"United States made a pact with SEATO, the Southeast Asian Treaty Organization in 1954 during the Eisenhower administration. It was for the express purpose of repelling the advancement of Communism. We, as a nation, have pledged to support freedom in this region of the world. That's what America stands for, you know? Freedom. And I believe it's our right... no, our obligation as the world's greatest democracy to help defend freedom wherever it's threatened, especially if the imperiled nation asks for our help. That's what South Vietnam did. And that's why we're here."

I interrupted, "But Ho Chi Minh is..."

"Please!" Michael raised his voice. "Please, I'm going to say this only once; so hear me out. I am an Officer in the United States Navy sworn to support and defend the Constitution of the United States of America against all enemies, foreign and domestic. When I was commissioned, I obligated myself to carry out the orders of my superiors including those of my Commander-in-Chief, the President of the United States. And, that's what I am doing. I do it without question. I do it because it is my duty. I believe it is honorable... and just... and acceptable in the eyes of my God." He paused. "I sincerely believe that."

I didn't speak. He made a good argument, the most rational one I've heard so far. And even though I've heard that the government of South Vietnam is more corrupt than Ho Chi Minh's dictatorship in the North, I didn't say any more. It's obvious that Michael is much more intelligent than I am and certainly better educated. So, it was good that I kept my mouth shut.

"Incidentally, MacLennon," Michael wasn't being my chum anymore. He had transformed back into officer Lieutenant Goldberg. "You took the same oath."

"What's that?"

"To support and defend the Constitution; to obey, without reservation, the orders of your superior officers and your Commander-in-Chief, Lyndon B. Johnson."

"Yes, sir." I was back to my military conditioning, and for good reason.

He stood up and stretched, "Well, I think that's enough for one night. I'll see you again sometime."

I wasn't sure how to respond; I chose humor. "Yes, I would like that. Maybe next time, we can take on the unsolved mysteries of the universe."

He laughed, turned and walked away. "See ya later."

CHAPTER XIII
BACK TO THE BOMBING

28 July 1967 ... 42nd day.
Tonkin Gulf, North Vietnam

    This morning the Captain made one of his rare talks over the 1MC. He revealed some new info: On July 25th, one of the pilots from Attack Squadron 163 was hit by the North Vietnamese ground defenses. His A-4 Skyhawk went down in flames. He didn't get out. Captain Billy also confirmed that one of our pilots was captured by the NVA from that plane that went down July 18.

    Last night, one of the A-3B Skywarriors, better known as Whales because of their immense size, launched at 2300 for a fly-off to the Philippines. It never arrived. Due to an unknown technical problem, the plane lost power and plummeted into the South China Sea. The crewmen radioed a distress call before bailing out of the ill-fated aircraft. So far, the pilot, LCDR Cabanaw, is the only man to be found and recovered. A freighter ship, on its way to Subic Bay, plucked him out of the drink. The two other crew members, PO 2 Hardy and Ensign Patterson, are still missing.

    Today, we saw sampans and junks for the first time, a whole floating armada of them. Initially, I heard some guy talking about them in the passageway. Not far behind him came two Airdales clutching their personal cameras. Staying on the 02 level of the ship, they dashed to the starboard side. I followed. From the open hatchway, I saw one large junk not more than 100 yards away. Still in my skivvies I dared not venture too far out to the exposed deck areas for fear of naval authority. So, I ran to the shop and told my fellow Pharts about the sailing vessels. Dick pulled on his work denims and grabbed his camera. I followed suit, ascending to the Flight Deck to zap off several photos. The junk that had been alongside the ship had drifted back to our wake and was almost out of camera range. Even so Dick and I took about ten exposures each. These unique Asian sea vessels are an awesome sight, just as the ancient Oriental murals depict them. These were about the size of a tugboat with golden-brown, ribbed sails rising like a dragon's wing from the ocean surface. Apparently the Old Risky steamed into a commercial sea lane that, I presume, extends from Haiphong to the Chinese ports and Hong Kong.

We sighted land again this morning and were told that it was the mountainous region of Hainan, the Red China island on the eastern side of the Gulf of Tonkin. Yesterday, we were 35 miles from Haiphong, the largest North Vietnamese sea port city.

Life out here is strange. It has come to the point where daily bombing and recon missions are like a regular job. We work, do our necessary tasks and finish about 1600 every day. Following supper, each of us settles down to his own bit of comfort. Harry may write letters or play with his electronic projects. Dick and Ernest will most often read books or magazines, if they're not dozing. Ray usually wanders off to the Ship's Photo Lab or to some place where he can enjoy the fellowship of soul brothers. No matter what we do, we attempt to forget the work, the ship, the Navy, and where we are. It is good that this tub is so big and complex. It gives me a feeling that there is much to discover if I care to explore. Just that thought can eliminate some of the isolation and claustrophobic feelings.

I had a patriotic moment on the Flight Deck late this afternoon. Below God's sapphire canopy dotted with neatly arranged puffs of white, I saw the Aircraft Carrier, U.S.S. Constellation about three miles to our portside; the Bon Homme Richard about the same distance to starboard. Each carrier had two destroyers following – six total. Mine sweepers and a few support ships were also within the collective formation. Junks appeared and disappeared on the horizon. In the air, dispatched from the bird farms, jet fighters and bombers created white etchings in the canopy. The entire sky dome was bustling with America's finest. It reminded me of a grand finale to an Armed Forces Air and Sea Show. Black Shoes and Airdale personnel gathered on the Flight Deck to witness the awesome sight – a good morale booster. Just look at all those men out there, all fellow countrymen, all working, living and some dying for the United States of America.

29 July 1967 ... 43rd day. Gulf of Tonkin.

Our forty-third day at sea started out just like the others. No one, but God, could have foretold that by the end of this day one-hundred thirty-two Americans at sea would be dead, with just as many wounded in what they're already calling the worst Naval disaster since World War II.

Early on, we saw small Vietnamese boats originating out of coastal villages. They were using our sector of the Gulf of Tonkin for fishing. Dumb shits. It was another one of those heavy, damp summer mornings when the humidity was so thick our Flight Deck jerseys were soaked in sweat.

At 1045, Big Ern, Ray Hines, Harry Hedge and I were on deck giving Photo Bird 602 a pre-flight inspection. After cleaning the camera-bay windows on the RF-8G Crusader, we stood by for the arrival of LTJG David Beam, today's target for the Vietnamese Surface-to-Air Missiles... the SAM's. At 1100, Beam was in the cockpit, grinning and listening for orders from the Air Boss on the loud speakers tower.

Before we received word to start engines, I heard a booming noise in the distance somewhere across the blue. I thought nothing of it at first. Probably just a destroyer firing off a practice round. Five seconds later... two, three, four, the percussions popped off like fireworks. I ran portside and saw a column of black smoke rising on the horizon. I couldn't see what was exploding. It was too far away. Maybe, I thought, a plane had blown-up in the ocean. No, there was too much smoke. The base of the smoke column was black and billowing and, as I watched, an orange fireball shot up, followed by another thunderous explosion.

Shock was my first reaction but it didn't last long. As a trained U.S. Navy Photographer, camera was my second. I knew then it was a carrier fire – a major disaster.

"I think you're right," I could hear Ray saying behind me as I jumped into the catwalk and ran down to the Photo Shop. Returning to the catwalk with my 35 millimeter, I snapped off several pics of the black column which, by then, was extending into the clouds. The Oriskany turned to port in the direction of the burning ship. I ran to the starboard Number Three Elevator to view the inferno as we approached it. By this time, all plans for today's aircraft launch had been scuttled. All hands on the Flight Deck were lining the starboard and forward areas of the ship. Apprehension was running through the crew. I heard rumors.

"The Bonnie Dick?"

"Yeah!"

"No, It can't be!"

"The Connie?"

"No, she left for Subic last night."

A Plane Director, in his yellow shirt, ran over and joined his friends on the elevator, "It's the Forrestal! I just heard it on the two-way. It's the Forrestal."

I didn't know the Forrestal was operating out here with us. She is the first of what are called the super carriers. All ships in our group: the destroyers, cruisers and minesweepers steamed toward the wounded Forrestal. Re-spotting of aircraft began immediately. The props and jets were moved forward on our Flight Deck. Our three helicopters were fueled and loaded with stretchers, medical supplies, fog foam, fire hoses and medical personnel. The 1MC address system screeched on with the Ship's Duty Officer barking out orders, "Man all lifeboat and rescue stations! Man all lifeboat and rescue stations!"

The Flight Deck Boatswain ran around shouting orders to the Blue Shirts, "Get all the stretchers you can find. Hurry!"

He spun and bellowed at a group of sightseeing slackers, "Hey, assholes! Go down and help those guys below get that fog foam up here."

A scurry of colored shirts covered the Flight Deck, men running and shouting in all directions. Even though it looked like chaos, there was underlying organization to it all.

The helos were launched.

I climbed a small platform protruding from the starboard side of the superstructure. Big Ern was there among the spectators. I asked to use his color-film camera because I had a better vantage point, and he complied. I watched as we closed in. Smoke kept billowing. A black layer clouded the sky blocking the noonday sun. The loudspeaker on the Oriskany's island turned on us, "All unnecessary personnel clear the Flight Deck! Only required personnel are to remain on deck!"

Hundreds of men would not budge. The Flight Deck Officer came around shouting threats at idle Officers and Enlisted Men. Slowly, the congestion began to clear.

"No cameras will be allowed on the Flight Deck!" Again, the loudspeaker blurted, "No cameras! I repeat. No cameras except for authorized Ship's Company Photo Mates."

Flight Deck officials began chasing photo amateurs off the deck. I wore my VFP-63 PHOTO jersey, so I hoped the bouncers would mistake me for Ship's Company and leave me alone. They did, for a while. As we neared the Forrestal, I snapped off one shot after another. Not until we got within a half mile could I actually see the scorched carrier behind the smoke. Two destroyers were steaming about one-hundred yards to each side aft of the Forrestal. Several helicopters swarmed around the ship like giant dragonflies; a couple of them were flying crisscross patterns behind the ship searching for men overboard. At the same time, helos touching down amidships off-loaded emergency supplies and then took on casualties, swiftly transporting them over here to us.

Our ship maintained a distance of about a half mile as we sailed parallel to the Forrestal. Peering through Big Ern's telephoto lens, I could see the tremendous damage. The rear half of the crippled carrier was totally blackened. Holes were ripped in the side. The aft sector of the Flight Deck appeared to be collapsed. And smoke – white, black and grey – gushed from the fantail. An aircraft fell off the port side of the ship. Portions of the catwalk were torn away draping down into the sea. After an hour passed, smoke diminished, becoming mostly steam; still a thin column of coal-black smoke persisted from the fantail.

I shot all twenty exposures on Ernest's camera and handed it down to him, asking him to change film. The Flight Deck Chief marched up to Ernest and stared directly into his eyes. "Get that goddamn camera below deck, Airdale!"

Ernest stumbled around, searching for words, "Ah, I'm a photo ... ah, VFP-63 photo ..."

"Get it out of here," the Chief repeated, "before I confiscate it and throw your fat ass in the brig." Ernest complied instantly, galloping back to our Photo Shop on the 02 Level.

Not wanting to leave, I descended from my perch and found Chuck Vesten, one of the ship's Photo Mates. He was toting a 16mm movie camera, camera gadget bag full of film and a tripod. I asked to carry the bag and tripod so I would look like a member of Ship's Company and be allowed to remain on the flat top. It worked.

Helo traffic was highly congested. Our three choppers, as well as others from the carrier Bon Homme Richard and AF's in the area, were landing and unloading four or five casualties at a time, taking on emergency gear and heading back to the Forrestal. Several would land simultaneously. It was a fast cycle. As soon as one took off, another landed. Fuel crews hot pumped them when their tanks ran low.

After toting the tripod and bag for another hour, I returned to the shop and smoked a cig with Dick Aden.

"Mac, you got A-positive blood, doncha?"

"Yeah. Least that's what my dog tag says."

"I think they called for blood donors for A-positive."

"You sure?"

"Well, first they asked for O-positive and then they said something else. I think they said A-positive."

"Where do they want donors? Sickbay?"

"Affirmative."

"I'm going down."

Four decks below, I entered Sickbay and walked down the passageway toward the lab. Casualties were strewn everywhere. I saw a young man lying in a stretcher on a table, covered with a sheet. A volunteer was standing by him holding a bottle of plasma; the tube led from the bottle to a needle that a Corpsman was inserting in the injured man's arm. On the Sickbay deck were three more men in Stokes Litters, plasma bottles strapped onto ship's overhead pipes and valves. One man's face was bright red, blistered and glossy from the salve that had been applied to it. Another poor SOB. lay belly-down nude with just a small sheet partially covering his pelvic region. Fragments of metal protruded from blood-clotted holes in his thighs and butt.

Through the doorway of the treatment room, I could see the naked, twisting body of a Forrestal Airdale. Corpsmen were attempting to calm him and treat his wounds but he was reliving his experience, crying out, "Please, please! Gotta get out! Jump! Jump! Watch out!"

Entering the lab, I asked a Corpsman if he needed A-positive blood. The answer was no. I could have left but I wanted to stay and help. The opportunity came. Passing by, a doctor ordered a med assistant to clean up a pool of vomit in the ward passageway. Grabbing a mop and bucket of water, I told him I would take care of it. He was more than willing to allow me the dubious privilege.

From that point on, I kept busy. Doctors and corpsmen from the Oriskany and other ships, and a throng of assorted workers ran helter-skelter administering treatment, transporting patients, performing hundreds of emergency measures. I helped carry the patients to the recovery ward, lifting them on to their beds. Sickbay has a capacity for about thirty patients. Today, all beds were occupied; other injured lay in litters on the deck. Virtually every patient was receiving plasma or blood. God, there was so much to do – so many men in need of immediate attention.

One young Black Man was bandaged in salve-soaked gauze from his feet to his neck. His face was horribly burned. Blisters had formed and burst leaving pink scars. Below the surface we all look alike. Body fluid oozing from his burns had seeped through the bandages, soaking the sheets and mattress. Another man had shrapnel wounds over his entire body. A chest tube ran from a vacuum bottle to a hole in his chest; a laceration on his skull had required over a dozen stitches. Many had bomb shrapnel wounds. I assisted a doctor as he was tightening a tourniquet. I helped another by swabbing out the holes in a patient's leg. After I had proved my worthiness, the Medicals began sending me after splints, bandages, surgical tubes and other necessities.

The injured were asking for help. I'd get help. Many asked for water. I would support their heads and hold the cups for them. Many just needed comforting and encouragement. All had been toe-tagged, so I tried to learn their names.

Petracelli was an East Coast city boy with heavy accent. Both of his hands had received third degree burns. His face was blistered. He lay still with his eyes closed until I approached him and said, "How ya doin'?"

Turning his head slowly, he looked at me and said, "I never thought I'd make it, man."

"What happened?" I asked.

"I was there, right in the fuckin' middle of it. The fire. Bombs goin' off. Missiles. It all happened so goddamned fast."

He paused for a moment and just stared at me, replaying the disaster in his head. Then with a burst of emotion, he said, "We didn't have time to run from the fire. I saw guys boining. My hands, they got boined. I looked at 'em and, God, they're black. I run over to the catwalk. I jumped down on the catwalk, y'know, and then over the side. I hit the water and just kept going down. I thought I'd never stop. Then, when I starts to come up, I thought I'd never get to the top. So I reach the top and this wave slaps me in the face and... I don't really know."

He paused again, shuffled his body to a more comfortable position and forced another smile. "When that chopper came, that was the greatest moment of my life. It looked so fuckin' great, and they dropped that line to me. They call 'em Angels, y'know. That's just what that thing was – an angel, man – a fuckin' beautiful angel. An' they pulled me in, and here I am." Petracelli was glad to be alive.

A sailor named Meyer had a chunk of shrapnel lodged in his left knee. A long-drawn, sandy-haired man about my age, he said to me, "I was real lucky. Those other guys, some of them are real bad off. I ain't so bad compared to them."

He had been working on the Flight Deck of the Forrestal when the chain of explosions occurred. "Yeah, they were parked in a line, y'know, along the back. A line of A-4 Skyhawks. It was one of them. It started spilling fuel and it ran under the other planes. Then the fire started. We got the fog nozzles out and were waiting for the foam to pump up but the damn stuff didn't come. Then it all went off. The whole fuckin' mess exploded. That's when I caught this thing in my knee." He paused to take a drink of water, then lamented, "So many killed! One of the CO's of this squadron was in his plane. He didn't make it out. Another pilot tried to get out. He tripped and fell on his head, and then the fire got him. I was laying there yelling for help. I was lucky. As soon as the helicopter landed, the Corpsman comes over. He grabs me and puts me in and then it takes off."

I spoke with another Airman. I couldn't find his name. No tag. Both of his hands were bandaged. He had been wearing his Flight Deck helmet and goggles. From the goggle line to the base of his neck, he was blistered and swollen. Unable to use his hands, I fed him a sandwich the galley had sent up.

"Four days," he uttered after downing the last bite, "four days we been out here, and this! And, we hadn't even started the Alpha Strikes yet! No, wait! Our first one was yesterday, and this was going to be our second. It's unbelievable."

He stopped, thought for a minute, then looked at me and pondered, "I wonder what it's all for, if it's worth all this shit. This whole fuckin' war seems so senseless. I'm not like one of these guys back in California, a protester and stuff, but the way they're fighting this thing seems all fucked up. They're jis gonna keep sending more and more guys to get killed, and the whole fuckin' thing will end up like Korea. If they'd just plant an atomic bomb," he stopped as if he was disclosing secret information; then continued in a muted tone, "If they'd take a small A-bomb and tell them that in 48 hours, we're going to drop it on Hanoi, that would give the gooks time to 'vacuate, and those that don't, to hell with 'em. Then, we wipe out the heart of Hanoi."

He could tell by looking at my stone face that I didn't agree with his strategy, so he changed the subject.

"You're a Photo, huh?"

"Yeah, in Photo Recon Squadron 63, VFP-63, flying the RF-8G aerial photo birds."

"Yeah, like VFP-62 on the East Coast. I was on a ship with them. Hey! When I got off the chopper today some guy took a picture of me. D'ya think you could get one for me?"

"I don't know. Those guys were from the Ship's Photo Lab."

"If you can, I'd 'preciate it."

I thought for a couple seconds, then told him, "Maybe they'll come out with it on the front page of the country's newspapers or something."

"Jesus, I hope not. My poor mother would die of a heart attack."

Several of the wounded mentioned their mothers, wives or sweethearts back home. Many swore they'd never go on a Flight Deck again. Some told me they just wanted to get the fuck out of the military.

* * * * * * *

Late this evening, Captain Billy Holder addressed the crew of the Oriskany on the 1MC. Harry, Dick, Ernest, Walt and I were all in the shop as the skipper spoke. I'll try to write his message as I recall it.

"Attention all hands! This is your Captain speaking. I come to you tonight with an overwhelming feeling of sadness regarding the events of this day, July 29, 1967, but at the same time I have a tremendous feeling of pride in the men of the U.S.S. Forrestal and of our own crew who turned-to in this time of crisis and displayed courage and tenacity in the midst of disaster. I'll try to bring you up to date on what happened today on the Forrestal. Our latest count shows one-hundred thirty-two Officers and Enlisted Men dead with some unaccounted for. From what I've been told, the fire started just before eleven-hundred hours this morning as the planes set on the Flight Deck turning up for the day's first launch. Something happened, we're not sure, to a Skyhawk manned by Lieutenant Commander John McCain. Most likely some kind of ordnance impact to his plane. McCain's fuel tank ruptured, dumping about two-hundred gallons of JP-5 on the Flight Deck. Two 1,000 pound bombs that had been attached to the wings of his A-4 dislodged and fell to the deck. The fuel ignited and spread under other planes. Officer McCain was able to crawl out on to the nose of his aircraft and swing down from the fuel probe and escape being burned to death but other pilots and men weren't so lucky.

"The bombs setting in the fire cooked off and exploded killing several men instantly. Apparently that explosion set in motion a chain reaction around the perimeter of the Flight Deck where other aircraft armed with bombs and rockets were spotted and prepped for launch. Many men were blown off the Flight Deck into the ocean by the force of the blasts. Our helos and those of the Forrestal plucked floating bodies and survivors from the water. One bomb blast created a crater in the Flight Deck that ran down two levels. Burning fuel poured into the hole and tonight as I speak to you, men are still trapped down there and firefighters are still working to extinguish the flames so they can rescue them. The Forrestal still has power and right now is steaming for Subic Bay. Most of her crew will be heading home. Some of the Forrestal pilots have already asked for reassignment to other carriers and I salute those Officers who still want to stay in action after what they've gone through today.

"Again I want to say how proud I am of those in the Oriskany's Air Wing, the helo pilots and crews, our medical personnel and all who helped the men of our sister carrier in this unforgettable time of tragedy and valor. Now, I'll turn the microphone over to the Ship's Chaplain."

There was a brief pause, and then fumbling of the microphone. None of us in the room said a word as we sat there, heads down, waiting for the 1MC to come alive again.

"Jesus said: 'Greater love hath no man than that he give up his life for another.'" After quoting the New Testament, the Chaplain called the crew to prayer: "Heavenly Father, we come to you tonight with saddened hearts. At least one-hundred thirty-two of your children have sacrificed their lives this day, many of them as they tried to save the lives of their fellow shipmates. We pray that you grant their souls eternal rest in your loving arms and so, too, do we pray for their families, wives and girlfriends back home who will be grieving their untimely deaths. Grant them the comfort of your Holy Spirit, Lord. For it is in your holy name we pray, Amen."

After his Amen, the squawk box began playing a scratchy recording of the Navy Hymn. I love the Navy Hymn.

> Eternal Father, strong to save,
> Whose arm doth bind the restless wave,
> Who bidst the mighty ocean deep
> Its own appointed limits keep,
> O hear us as we cry to Thee
> For those in peril on the sea....

As much as I fought it, tears began to well in my eyes and overflow down my cheeks. It's hard to believe that only six weeks ago we sailed out of San Francisco Bay and now this. Damn, things can change quickly.

30 July 1967 ... 44th day. Gulf of Tonkin, Vietnam.

Last night, all night long, helicopters continued flying. All but six of the Forrestal fire victims were transported from the Mighty Zero back to their home ship. The Captain spoke to the crew again over the 1MC and thanked everyone for their help.

Today, it was back to war as usual. We flew two hops. It was routine except for a KA68 camera in 602 that kept failing on us. Ray and Harry worked well past midnight trying to repair the motherfucker. No luck. So they placed 602 in down status and will continue dicking with the camera tomorrow.

The following is an account of the Forrestal mishap, written in Oriskany's Morning Musket:

FIRE EXPLOSIONS WRACK FORRESTAL

Aboard the U.S.S. Forrestal (CVA-59) in the Gulf of Tonkin, July 29 – "I was looking at one of the sampans on the port side when I heard an explosion. I looked, and smoke was billowing. I grabbed my unit one (first aid kit) and ran back there. I ran into a Chief with badly burned hands and helped him to the aid station. By then, people were streaming in."

That's the way hospital Corpsman second class Paul Streetman, of Gulfport, Mississippi, first saw the fire which occurred in this ship's first tour of combat duty in Vietnam.

Streetman, one of eight Corpsman assigned to the Forrestal, now has spent more than 11 hours on the mangled Flight Deck, treating the injured, and helping to carry the dead to a hastily constructed morgue in Hangar Bay one.

There is still no official count of dead and injured. Through the day, divisions and squadrons have gone through the laborious task of accounting for their men. The many men still unaccounted for may have jumped or been forced over the side of the ship to escape the blistering flames or as a result of bomb blasts. Many have been recovered by ships in the area.

Oriskany, which suffered a similar tragic fire last year, was one of the first to come to Forrestal's aid. She and the Bon Homme Richard both have flown doctors and corpsmen along with medical supplies to the stricken ship to augment her beleaguered medical staff. The more seriously wounded are to be transferred to the hospital ship U.S.S. Repose later this evening.

There have been many tales of valor born here that will be told by sailors for years.

Lieutenant JG Robert Cates, Forrestal's explosive ordnance demolition Officer, lowered himself down a rope into a smoldering compartment to defuse a live 500-pound bomb that could have exploded at any moment.

In the Hangar Bays, a Chief Petty Officer, his clothes plastered to him, ran from the burning Hangar Bay three and called for five volunteers. He got thirty. ABH3 Alonzo Turner is the Tractor Petty Officer. "I was on the fan tail with my tractor drivers. We were starting our tractors for a launch. All the aircraft were started except one. When the fire started burning, we jumped down in the catwalk and got a hose and started to fight the fire. Then the bomb went off and we were knocked down."

At the height of the fire, CAPT John K. Beling, Forrestal's Commanding Officer, went to Hangar Bay two. He watched quietly for a while, patted his men on the back and told them they were doing a good job and went back to the bridge. There was nothing more he could do. His men were doing all that could be done.

Filipino stewards, some who appear as though they weigh no more than 100 pounds, rolled 250 and 500-pound bombs to the deck edges and pushed them over.

"The courage that I have seen today and the way in which Navy men have acted to help other Navy men make it really all the worse," said LTJG Emory Brown. "You realize you have lost a lot of good friends," he added.

Aboard the U.S.S. Oriskany (CVA-34), morning air operations had been completed and a calm air pervaded Oriskany's navigation bridge. Suddenly a lookout reported an explosion on the Forrestal, followed by a fire.

Within seconds CAPT B.D. Holder had the Mighty 'O' closing on the blazing ship, whose cylindrical pile of smoke could be seen on the horizon some 20 miles away.

Captain Holder alerted various departments to prepare to give all possible assistance to the Forrestal – and it became plain that even more than the Mighty 'O' could provide might be needed.

Accompanying destroyers, the U.S.S. George K. MacKenzie (DD 836) and the U.S.S. Moore (DD747) were also ordered to the scene. The Mackenzie, in particular, got a chance to see the devastation at close quarters. The destroyer, in an effort to provide a cooling spray on gasoline tanks, bombs, and a magazine bulkhead, maintained station from three to five feet from the Forrestal's Number Three Elevator for an hour and a quarter.

Oriskany's helicopters, along with those of the Bon Homme Richard (CVA 31) and the Air Force's "Jolly Green Giants," also rushed to the scene with damage control material and medical supplies and returned with casualties from the Forrestal. Many were crewmen who had been blown into the water when explosions rocked the giant carrier's Flight Deck.

Conferring with CAPT Holder on the bridge was Oriskany Engineering Officer, CDR William G. Sandberg, who ordered the OBA's fog foam, flashlights and other gear which the Forrestal requested, or might need, to the Flight Deck.

Repair parties aboard Oriskany were manned on their stations and DCA LCDR Bennie J. Smith coordinated the transfer of needed materials to the elevators and Flight Deck.

On the Flight Deck, crews worked feverishly in removing victims from helicopters and reloading the choppers with firefighting gear and medical supplies.

As casualties were transported to Oriskany's Sickbay, the ship's doctors and corpsmen provided the necessary medical assistance. Their efforts were augmented by the addition of two flight surgeons and four corpsmen from the U.S.S. Intrepid (CVS 11). Other medical aid was provided directly by the U.S.S. Annapolis and the Bon Homme Richard to the Forrestal.

Oriskany Doctors Adeeb, Fahrenbruch and Edwards, along with 15 corpsmen and Dr. Gary Cooley of the Dental Department were among the first to provide on-the-scene medical assistance aboard the Forrestal.

By this time, Oriskany lifeboats had been dispatched to follow in Forrestal's wake in an effort to pick up survivors; nets were also rigged alongside for the same reason.

Among the helos making the shuttle between Oriskany and Forrestal was one piloted by LT Dave Clement, who, with co-pilot ENS "Butch" Eiland, was the first helo on the scene. Their helo was acting as a plane guard when the first plane exploded, sending the pilot into the water. Clement and Eiland picked him up. They watched as flames engulfed other planes on the deck. "There were people, planes and parts of the ship everywhere," said Eiland.

Between taking casualties back to the Oriskany, the helos managed to transport some 400 OBA's, 2,000 canisters, nearly 900 five-gallon fog foam cans plus 500 flashlights and 2,000 batteries to the Forrestal. The list also included 30-45 CO_2 fire extinguishers, sealed beam and battle lanterns, as well as assorted lengths of fire hose.

Aboard both ships, there were praises for both victims and helpers. Oriskany Chaplain J.E. Six, who visited the Forrestal said: "The entire matter was well handled and operating like a machine. I was particularly impressed with the way injured men made way and waited as the more seriously hurt were brought in for treatment."

In Oriskany's Sickbay, praises were aired for assistance which "was provided by everyone we turned to." Anonymous seaman and airmen, who filled in when additional corpmen were needed in the lifeboats, never bothered to leave their names. Marines helped in moving people and by giving blood. The galley provided food and ice. The laundry came through with additional linens. Eight "guest" NROTC Midshipmen also lent a helping hand.

DCA LCDR Smith helped sum it up by saying: "The action displayed by all hands in gathering equipment, assembling it in a timely manner and getting it to the helos for transportation was orderly, organized and very commendable. It was a job well done by all hands." ###

I'm glad I made an extra effort to be helpful. I didn't leave my name. I'm not looking for praise. Sometimes God gives you an opportunity to do some good, and you jump on it because it's the right thing to do.

31 July 1967 ... 45th day. Gulf of Tonkin.

Alpha Strikes today! Major targets were hit. And, as always during Alphas, a life was snuffed in its prime. A North Vietnamese SAM exploded under the belly of a Fighter Squadron 111 Crusader jet piloted by LTJG Charley Zuhoski. He had little forewarning; no time to blow the canopy, tug the straps and activate the rockets on his ejection seat. He is presumed dead... killed in action. KIA.

Tropical Storm Fran, with winds of thirty knots, is 260 miles southeast of Hainan. I'm wishing it would come here and delay our flights awhile. I think I could tolerate a typhoon.

Captain Billy addressed the crew on the 1MC today. The two missing fly boys on the A3D Whale have not been found. The search has been suspended. They are presumed dead... missing in action. MIA. I guess there's a damned good reason why career Airdales say that A3D stands for All 3 Dead. The Captain also read the scoreboard to us of targets we've destroyed so far this line period: three flak sights, one SAM site, three POL sites, a few bridges, barges, patrol boats and ammo storage sites – mostly insignificant shit. Not worth all the lives that are being snuffed out – ours and theirs.

1 August 1967 ... 46th day. Ibid.

The sweetest sound on that 1MC is the graveled voice of the Boatswain yelling, "Mail Call!" Today I received a ten-page letter from Mom, complete with twenty snapshots of the family's recent vacation, plus printed sermons of good, old Norman Vincent Peale, Mister Power of Positive Thinking. You betcha. Norma loves Norman.

The second best thing that can happen is finding the ship's Ice Cream Shop open. Today it was. So, we had a bone-ass day: mail and ice cream.

On the darker side, Big Ern fucked up royally. While unloading a KA53 camera, he dropped a rotatable mount too low in the camera bay. He broke off a pressure-sensitive roller on the track. To repair it we had to completely pull the camera and mount, take off the motor arm, replace it, re-align it, then return it to the mount and the camera bay. Ray, Harry and I spent about six hours restoring it to up-status. Big Ern is on our shit list. Dick Aden has been assigned a working party tomorrow, unloading crated bombs. Sorry about that, sailor.

What a hot, humid, long, tedious, fuckin' miserable day. I want to write a letter but can't get enough time. Diary comes first; then letters.

3 August 1967 ... 48th day. Ibid.

Yesterday was easy. Today we busted ass as LT Sam flew from 0715 to 0825; LCDR Sonniksen flew from 1100 to 1245; LTJG Rudd, from 1400 to 1545. An additional flight was announced at 1500. LTJG Beam was to launch at 1700. We readied 602 for flight, the pilot was in the cockpit, the plane was turning up when warning lights indicated trouble with the tailhook assembly. The crew inspected it but couldn't remedy the situation so the flight was scrubbed. Beam was perturbed. He sat in the cockpit grumbling and sticking his tongue out at the maintenance crew. That Beamer. What a card.

I got a package from home in today's mail call. In it were two bottles of contact lens soaking solution, a Flair felt-tip pen with refills, a bag of candy and a short letter.

Dick received the photos we took at Miramar with our newly shaved heads. Outstanding! I'm getting duplicates.

The Captain spoke to us this evening about the major Alpha Strikes we pulled today on various strategic targets. The combined Task Force flew a record 197 missions. The hit targets ranged from the Hanoi-Haiphong sector all the way down to the DMZ.

But the best news today was liberty! We're scheduled to pull into Subic Bay, Philippines on August 10, a week from today. We'll be in-port for ten days. Tonight, I wrote to Pepé at Cubi Point telling him to expect me for his birthday.

6 August 1967 ... 51st day.
Gulf of Tonkin (but not for long)

The daylight hours were lax. The night was cooking. Flight quarters sounded at 1700. Night strikes began at sundown and continued until sunrise. A North Vietnamese cargo truck parking area was targeted and bombed. However, out of 150 trucks, only twenty-three were destroyed. A massive war supplies storage area was also hit with secondary explosions sighted. This indicates either stored ammunition or fuel. The pilots love it when they see secondaries. It's a ya-hoo moment.

Our Photo Birds stayed home because we don't take pictures after dark. Yes, we do have photo flares for night photography but such missions are impractical. Hell, they're down-right suicidal. The ECM gear, anti-surface-to-air missile radar confounders, must be pulled out of the bird in order to load the flare racks and ejectors. And, no pilot wants to fly without his ECM gear. In addition, AAA tracking stations can easily follow an aircraft's flight path by tracking the intervals of flash cartridge bursts. Only one-hundred photos can be taken on one mission because of the limited amount of cartridges. Ain't worth the risk. We're required to bring flares, racks and ejectors with us on these cruises but chances are, we'll never use them.

Our squadron has a new designation as of today. We're now Det 34. We lost the Golf. Not sure why. Today was the last of our missions for this line period. Hot damn!

8 August 1967 ... 53nd day.
Gulf of Tonkin to the South China Sea.

All the weary war birds are nesting now. They're tied down on the Flight and Hangar Decks. Maintenance and repairs continue for a few but none will be flying for two weeks. We leave Yankee Station tonight. Free mail closes out at midnight. The majority of the crew is kicking back, writing letters, discussing what they'll be doing at Subic and Olongapo.

During the wee hours of the night, I stayed up with Merkin Muffley and PT3 Paul Duncan discussing and designing a cover for the detachment's upcoming newsletter. Everywhere I go, my artistic talents are exploited but that's okay. It doesn't hurt to suck up to the Officers a little. You never know when you might need a favor in return. The newsletter will be sent to squadron headquarters at Miramar and to the other carrier detachments. It will be read at Vietnam high commands and by the big brass in D.C. The cover features Yosemite Sam, our Det mascot, riding Photo Bird 601, enclosed in a circle with printing on the edge: NEWSLETTER ... VFP-63. On a scroll below the circle were the words: DETACHMENT THIRTY-FOUR. It was a good cooperative effort. I finished at 0430, ate breakfast a half-hour later, then hit the rack. Old Man Sonniksen wanted to talk to his boys at 1100, so I crawled out, and stumbled down to P.I. where all the men had gathered. The head cheese chewed on us, cussed us, praised us and warned us again about the potential hazards of liberty in Olongapo. Tell me something I don't know.

The stats for this first line period are: fifteen planes lost, six pilots killed, one pilot captured, two air crew members missing and presumed dead. And that's just *our* Air Group! It doesn't seem worth it. The Admirals and Generals could end this fuckin' war fast by blowing the living shit out of Hanoi and Haiphong. Firebomb the entire cities just like the Allies did to Dresden, Germany. Why don't we fight to win or just get the hell out of Vietnam? You're just an E-4, MacLennon. You don't know shit. Shut up and stand your post.

CHAPTER XIV
DOWN TIME OFF THE LINE

9 August 1967 ... 54th day.
Subic Bay, Philippines.

The pay line for Third-Class Petty Officers was the longest I'd ever seen. It ran the length of the passageway from the forecastle to the Hangar Bay. It took an hour to get my roll of cash bennies. Bennies: them's the benefits of selling my body to Uncle Sam and LBJ.

Summer rain welcomed the U.S.S. Oriskany to the Philippines Islands. Only the mountains on the north side of Subic Bay were visible as we entered from the open sea. Grey sheets of mist blanketed Cubi Point Naval Air Station, Subic Naval Station and Olongapo City. The U.S.S. Forrestal, still bearing visible scars, is tied to Leyte Pier. A silent, sad behemoth now, she is here receiving enough repair to get her home to California. The fleet mooring area in Subic was filled to capacity with repair and auxiliary ships, so the O-Boat had to drop anchor in the bay and shuttle her crew ashore with liberty boats. Thunder rumbled across the bay as evening set in, bringing heavy rain. Bad weather was no detriment to hundreds of freshly-scrubbed sailors in their ice cream suits. With money in their pockets, and boners in their skivvies, they waited, some an hour or more, for their ride on the liberty launch. I stayed onboard because of the weather, enjoying the solitude and updating this diary. Sheets of rain played music on the ship's metallic skin. I had peace for a few hours among the unexploded bombs and rockets.

The drunken hoards began returning about 2330, wave after wave of them until about 0130 in the morning. Their dress whites were now brown with mud, beer, and puke. They sang, shouted, cussed and laughed. The animals got their just reward.

"Let's get loaded and fuck a whore." It's always the same theme song every night in the P.I. They just can't get enough San Miguel beer and Filipina pussy. Ha! Listen to me. Don't I sound self-righteous? It wasn't that long ago that I was doing the same thing.

August 10, 1967 ... 55th day.
In Port. Subic Bay, Philippines.

We remained anchored. Liberty commenced at 1300 for duty sections one and three. I'm in section four so I stayed onboard and performed my new in-port job: Compartment PO for the Det's sleeping area. Big fun. I have to ensure that the compartment cleaner, Big Ern, keeps the space ship-shape: deck clean, bunks made, cigarette butt kits sifted, trash barrels not overflowing. I pick up and sort laundry for the boys. Not much to it but I have a feeling it may become a pain in the ass when we're back on line.

In addition to that job, Hedge assigned me to the Drunk Watch. I'm supposed to stay up and escort my drunken Det mates from the launch landing to their racks if they are unable to do so under their own power and intellect. I won't do it. I will not play nurse maid to a blubbering idiot. Any man who intentionally gets that fucked up doesn't deserve any kindness. Sorry, Navy.

It's still raining, raining, raining. It rains so heavily that leaks are forming in the overhead of the 02 level directly below the Flight Deck. Many compartments and passageways have 2 to 3 inches of water in them. Our Photo Shop is water tight.

11 August 1967 ... 56th day.
In Port. Subic Bay, Philippines.

0730, the detachment mustered for roll call, as it does every day in-port, just to make sure all the drunks made it back last night. There are always a few of the hundreds who don't. Some are sleeping it off in a roach-infested hotel room or skivvy house; some are in the Olongapo jail; some don't know where the hell they are; and occasionally, one is found, face down, in the mud, with a butterfly knife stuck in his back.

The rain stopped for a few hours today. The sun tried to peek through. Great timing because today was my turn. Harry and I, dressed in white, took our liberty commencing at 1300. The Forrestal pulled out at 0700 this morning making room for our tub at Leyte Pier, so we walked the gangplank ashore. Even so, we waited for almost an hour for transportation along with a multitude of impatient Swabbies and Airdales. Apparently, there were no arrangements for rides. Typical Naval efficiency. Finally a base cattle car, a tractor-trailer rig with sliding side doors on the outside; vertical poles, overhead straps and wooden seats inside, arrived and shuttled us through the base.

The two of us went shopping at the B-6 Annex Foreign Exchange in Subic. Harry bought several wood carvings and other typical Filipino souvenirs for his wife. I had hoped to buy some movie equipment but it was sold out. I decided instead to buy a Nikon 35mm camera but that, too, was sold out. The damned fleet had taken all the good shit. We returned to the ship around 1500, changed to dungarees, and left again, in a taxi for Cubi Beach. Our detachment was having a beach party. A couple of First-Class Petty Officers and a handful of underlings were scattered in the seaside nipa huts. G.I. cans were filled with ice and beer, hamburgers sizzled on the grill. A couple men in denim played a spirited game of softball. A few were swimming. It was dull. The old lifers guzzled beer and, as always, talked shop. The rest of us pretended we were having fun. I stayed a half-hour, ate two burgers, drank two beers and then returned to the ship. I grabbed my dirty laundry and left again, catching a base taxi for the Cubi barracks of FIC PAC FAC.

I stayed the evening visiting old friends while doing my laundry. Every time I return to the facility I see more new faces and fewer of the old gang but my best friend, Jose Pepé Gonzales, remains year after year. I met him briefly at the barracks today and got a big hug. Overloaded with work, he didn't have time for conversation but told me with a broad smile. "Mock! Sorry I am so busy. You come, please, to my house, for birthday party tomorrow. Noon. Okay?"

12 August 1967 ... 57th day.
In Port. Subic Bay, Philippines.

Damn! I dozed off after muster this morning. Next thing I heard was the squawk box at 1300: "Liberty call! Liberty call! Liberty commences for sections two and three and expires aboard the ship at times specified in the plan of the day."

Omigod, Pepé's birthday! I yanked on my dungarees, put in my contacts and did my permission to go ashore. The rain had stopped; the sun came out just for my friend's celebration. At the Cubi barracks on the hill, I found Steve Szczecina fast asleep. I slapped him around and got him on his feet. We dressed, both of us, in our civvies, and taxied to the Shit River Bridge. From there, we switched to a jeepney directing the driver to Pepé's house. A bumpy, dusty ride through the back streets of O-po City brought us to a green and yellow, double-tiered apartment complex with front-yard patio. Multi-colored ceramic tiles adorned the building's foundation. Windows were no more than wooden slats artfully arranged and tacked in place. A Spanish-style wrought iron fence traversed the street side of the complex. And there on the patio sat ten to twelve festive Fic Pac Fuckers and twice-as-many Filipino well wishers.

Pepé and Hermie rushed out to us, "Hey Mock! Mabuhay!" We didn't bother with western formalities. We just ran into each other's arms and hugged Filipino-style.

"I think maybe you warnt coming, Mock."

"I wouldn't miss it, Pepé. You know how much I value our friendship."

"Yes, Mock, you have always been a good friend to me."

We had known each other for almost two years.

"I want you to meet my wife, Leenda, and my children," he continued. Linda is a petite and gracious woman. Standing less than 5 feet tall, she looked up into my eyes, smiled and said, in perfect English: "Welcome to our home, Mister MacLennon."

"Please," I begged, "call me Mac."

"Mock?"

"Yes, Linda. Mock." What's the use?

Pepé has two sons, Roberto, age 1, and Reyes, 2.

This was my first time at his house, my first time to meet his family. It gave me new respect for him, my 25-year-old friend, Jose Gonzales. I have always regarded him as an equal, a brother, even though he holds the lowly title of houseboy. Boy, hell!

Pepé is older than most of the men in the barracks but because he is a Filipino, and because he is not well educated, and because he cannot speak fluent English, and because he is only 5-foot, 3-inches tall, and because he humbles himself for his sailor clients, he is treated like a boy, a slave boy to spoiled brat Americans. He and his 18-year-old helper, Hermie, take care of the barracks and its occupants. They wash the sheets and make the beds in the morning. They do laundry, pressing and folding every item. They shine shoes. They pick up after us, they clean, dump the trash, scrub the floors and keep the bathrooms and showers sparkling.

That's their jobs, very coveted jobs because with pay and tips, Pepé earns an excellent income for a Filipino. And, because of American friends, like Gerald MacLennon, he takes home coveted commodities for his family and friends, like Salem cigarettes. Filipinos love American menthol cigarettes. Pepé has typical Filipino features: bronze-colored skin, coal-black hair, brown almond eyes, pug nose and round face. His most endearing quality is his smile. When he's happy, his whole face shines like the morning sun on a spring day.

Even though it was his birthday, Pepé had bought all the beer and food and sent out the invitations.

"It seems like we should be throwing the party for you, Pepé, not you for us."

"Dat's okay, Mock. You don't worry. Wanna beer?"

Linda brought me a plate of pancit and Shanghai lumpia, and a San Miguel beer. Hermie, who has just earned his brown belt in Karate, had to demonstrate his newly acquired abilities on me. It's amazing how strong a kick that wiry, little body can deliver.

Pepé and I discussed my life on the ship, Vietnam, the Philippines and the world. As soon as I finished one beer, there was another in my hand. "Mock, many Pilipinos are unhappy," he confided. "President Marcos, when he start, was a good man but now he is a man for sale. He is a puppet of the crooks. I think before five years, we will have revolution. Democracy is not working in the P.I. When we vote for a man, we are voting for who we want to make rich because all politicians just make big money for themselves and forget the little man who put him into office. It is always the same. They start out good, they end up crooks."

Communist domination is spreading in the central provinces. The cost of living and unemployment is on the rise. Poverty is nationwide. Crime is rampant. The whole country is uneasy. If revolution came, Pepé doesn't know for whom or what he would fight. But, in our San Miguel stupor, we agreed we would be comrades, standing and fighting for the P.I. side by side. Semper Fi. I love this country and its people. Sometimes I feel like I should have been born Filipino.

Into the evening, we talked, laughed and performed stupid solo dances. There was a never-ending trickle of friends and relatives coming and going: Pepé's sister, mother, mother-in-law, uncles and aunts, cousins, dozens of well-wishers. I had no idea he was so popular among his own people but I'm not surprised. Most of the Americans left early. They got their supper, had a beer and left for the bars. Good riddance. Go fuck your whores.

Around 9 PM, a balut man walked by. I flagged him down.

"Hey, Mock. I think you do not like balut."

"That's only when I'm sober, Pepé."

He challenged me, "You'll eat one now? I don't think so."

"Just watch me, buddy."

Americans do not eat baluts because we are squeamish. It's always a big joke to Filipinos. They watch most Yanks bite into the duck egg, then run for the commode. The all-Filipino crowd gathered round to watch and laugh as Mac ate his first balut. I tried not to look inside as I cracked and peeled away the dark brown shell. Following Pepé's instructions, I sucked out the soup inside and quickly chomped into the little roasted duck, trying not to think about what I was eating or what was making it crunch as I chewed. Actually it tasted very good. So, good I had another, washing it down with more beer. I was applauded for my courage.

As the party neared its end, Pepé's mood turned somber. He expressed to me disappointment that only about one-fourth of the invited Americans showed up. He confessed that he had blown his wad for the party, spending his last centavo on food and beer. Before I departed, I discreetly placed sixty pesos under an ashtray, enough to get him through until next payday. He didn't see me. After one last farewell to his family, Pepé and I caught a jeepney back to Rizal Avenue, the main street of Olongapo. He walked with me to the Subic gate just to insure his old friend didn't get harassed by the crooks and con artists. At the Cubi barracks, I transformed from civvie-donned base sailor back to fleet sailor then returned to the big, grey tub. I was snoring in my rack by 2300.

13 August1967 ... 58th day.
In Port. Subic Bay, Philippines.

The monsoon rain is back and I was stuck with the dirty duties again. Everyone else is on liberty. Harry and I remained in the shop. He puttered with electronics as I recorded music on a virgin seven-inch reel. Peter, Paul and Mary just released a new album named ALBUM 1700. My favorite song is "The Great Mandella" written by Peter Yarrow. Ironic, isn't it? I sit in our warship enjoying anti-war songs. Well, I'm not here because I love war. So, why not? I don't think Hedge appreciates it but, to his credit, he tolerates my weirdness. So far in-port, we've done nothing related to photo reconnaissance, performed no work on the photo gear. Our det received a gift today from our Photo Recon Squadron 63 detachment on the Bon Homme Richard: an airplane. Thanks, boys. The fucking thing should be junked or pushed overboard it's in such bad condition. It will be a long, long time before it's operational as 604. I was supposed to stand another Drunk Watch tonight. I still won't do it.

14 August 1967 ... 59th day.
In Port. Subic Bay, Philippines.

The bus tour to Pagsanjan Falls that Levitt, Chapin and I were taking has been cancelled. The Oriskany is pulling out Wednesday morning, two days from now. Damnit.

The alarm clock went off at 0630 this morning. None of us paid attention. Consequently, the Pharts, were all late to muster arriving at 0810. Chief O'Brian was pissed. He chewed out Harry and, for punishment, has now decided to split us up. Richard Aden, Big Ern, Lehmann and I are to move out of our racks in the Photo Shop and let the First and Second-Class Petty Officers move in. We the photo juniors must move to the detachment's berthing compartment way up in the forward section of the ship. O'Brian knew, with all our Officers gone, this would be an opportune time to pull such a stunt. Harry Hedge to the rescue. He searched out and found LTJG Beam who was still onboard, unbeknownst to the Chief, and convinced Beamer that a hold should be placed on such a decision until our Lieutenant Commander returns. Chief O'Brian was all bent out of shape when he discovered that Hedge had gone over his head but he couldn't do a damned thing about it. This is the kind of micky mouse bullshit that occurs in the States, in the peace-time Navy, not when we're in the war zone but some old lifers just can't resist.

We started to configure our new plane with cameras today but work was cancelled because the clouds opened up again dumping a deluge. So, Harry, Dick and I went on liberty at noon.

We were in a crazy mood. Maybe we're all getting water on the brain from the monsoon. As Harry stood by, giggling, Dick and I bought some play items at the Exchange: a toy iron, a lucky shaver with cream, five big coloring books and crayons. We also bought Play-Dough, and my favorite, a Hayley Mills cut-out doll. I loved her at 10; I still love her at 20. I also bought a recorded Tagalog language lesson plus some actual necessities. We returned to the O-Boat late afternoon and played with our toys for awhile. Then, Hines, Ernest and Dick went on liberty. I stayed. Too much mud. Late in the evening, after all had returned, we commiserated over the fate of our little photo family. Will we be split up? Will our happy home be torn asunder by the cantankerous Irish Chieftain?

15 August 1967 ... 60th day.
In Port. Subic Bay, Philippines.

Hedge asked O'Brian if he needed us for any jobs today. The Chief said no, so the photo boys sat around playing music on our Akai and Teac Tape Decks... and coloring. We're all enjoying the hell out of "Sergeant Pepper's Lonely Hearts Club Band." I think it's the Beatle's best yet; plus we're having competition to see who indeed is the Crayon Master. I usually win. That was our morning.

I met Pepé at the Cubi barracks early this evening. Dressed in civvies, I treated him to dinner at the Admiral Restaurant in Olongapo. We snarfed my favorites: chicken fried rice and Shanghai lumpia again, drank a San Magoo or two and conversed.

Pepé is deeply concerned about his own future, too. Understandably, he doesn't want to be a houseboy forever. He is currently supporting his wife, two boys, mother and brothers in the barrios. He was slated to join the U.S. Navy, serving four years as Steward, followed by his occupation of choice for the remainder of his career. It's a special program begun when the P.I. was a U.S. Territory, and one that continues today by mutual treaty. It offers Filipino men a golden opportunity they could never realize in their own economy. Pepé has been on the waiting list for two years. Then early this year his number came up. He hurried to the recruiting station at Sangley Point, Cavite City. He returned several times at his own expense. He spent money on mandatory legal papers. He passed the written examination and interview with flying colors but he was unable to produce a birth certificate because the courthouse where it was filed was destroyed by U.S. bombing raids during World War II.

The goddamned Navy recruiters would not accept this. They told Pepé he needs a court document certifying his natural citizenship; the cost, about 200 US dollars. The poor guy has already shelled out over a small fortune to get this far. The worst part is the callous attitude of the recruiters as they removed the name of Jose Gonzales from the priority list and placed his name at the bottom of the general waiting list, where it may not reach the top for another two to three years. Pepé says he was shocked, bitterly disappointed, and angry. He openly sobbed in front of me and then, in rage, unleashed a torrent of curses, insults and obscenities, all directed at the U.S. Navy and it's heartless rules and regulations regarding Filipinos. Pepé recounted the incident, "It was easy, Mock, for him to say to me, 'Sorry 'bout that.' So damn easy for him to say. But it is my life and all my dreams that he throw in the shit can." I wish I had the power, the clout to help Pepé. But I'm just a grunt, an E-4, three levels above Scum of the Earth.

After supper and our conversation, Pepé and I met Hermie at a piano bar next door. We drank several rounds of beer. I played the piano. Hermie acquired a guitar and together we sang some Spanish-flavored melodies.

Hermie's friend, Joe, and some new guy from FIC PAC FAC joined our table as we conspired to go off-limits to a strictly Filipino Club where a beer is 35-centavos instead of a peso; to where there are no obnoxious Americans in white uniforms. So, we piled out into the dirt street and hailed a Jeepney. Pepé directed the driver to the Jose Rizal Club, a modest, unassuming little building in a lesser lit part of town.

We entered, took a table and ordered our first round.

A gorgeous, little hostess sashayed by the table. I spoke to her in Tagalog: "Magandang gabi. Ang pangalan ko ay Mac. Anong pangalan mo?" – Good Evening. My name is Mac. What is your name?

"Maria." She gave me a cute, girlish smile.

Probably about 19, Maria's brown eyes sparkled. Her skin complexion was a beautiful unblemished bronze; mid-length black hair flowed slightly below her shoulders.

"Maria, ikina gagalak kong makilala kayo." – I'm very pleased to meet you.

She giggled, and swung her hips in mock gyration. Very cute... like Lauren Bacall in the final scene of the movie "To Have or Have Not."

"You buy me Lady's Drink, G.I.?"

Pepé told her, in a harsh tone, that I was not a G.I. but a very light-skinned Mestizo, mixed race, from the southern provinces. That's why I didn't speak Tagalog as my first language.

"Oo. Hindi ko Amerikan." – That's right. I'm not an American.

We had her going. Then I sang to her in perfect Tagalog, a Filipina favorite: "Dahil So Iyo" – Because of You. She was hooked. If only I had more time.

We took turns dancing with Maria and buying her the obligatory Lady's Drink at 3-pesos a shot. Not even alcoholic, Lady's Drinks are usually 7-Up. 'Can't even get 'em drunk and lower their resistance but what the hell. We sang, danced, laughed until 2300 when it was time for all good sailors to return to their security blankets. At the gate, I said farewell until November to my dear friends, Pepé and Hermie. I changed back into my silly sailor suit and returned to the Mighty Zero.

It's still raining. Oh well. Tomorrow, it's back to killing Commies for Mommy.

CHAPTER XV
THE TONKIN GULF YACHT CLUB

16 August 1967 ... 61st day. South China Sea.

The ship departed Subic this morning at 0800. Wouldn't you know it? The rain had stopped, the sun was shining. Flight quarters were called at 1000. Lieutenant JG Rudd launched in Aircraft 603 flying back over the Philippines to take snapshots of Subic Bay, Clark Air Base, village churches and whatever caught his eye.

Our Officers called a conference this morning with the Chief and the First Class Petty Officers. They decided that the junior Photo Mates are to be evicted. Harry Hedge, our dear sea daddy, fought for our rights but was overruled by the micky mouse specialists. Of course, Craig Danko, Aviation Boatswain's Mate First Class, was there with his lips glued tightly to the Chief's ass, as they usually are. Danko is a wiry devil, skinny with piercing brown eyes, a dark-haired crewcut and a very sharp tongue. The man is just plain mean. He comes up very short on the compassion and consideration scale. No doubt he's intelligent. He advanced to First Class in just a few years but according to him, "couldn't make Chief, cause every time I went up for it, there weren't no billets open. I passed every goddanged test but got quoted every time."

The men of the Photo Recon Squadron 63 berthing compartment are elated to get rid of Danko. Today, as soon as the decree was handed down, he took over my rack in the Photo Shop... the son-of-a-bitch. And, he wasn't alone. All the First Classes came with him, along with one senior Second Class. Walt Lehmann, Dick Aden, Big Ern and I were ousted from our home. We did not go obligingly. Harry Hedge and Ray Hines will remain in the shop along with new boarders, Mike Koppler ADJ1, Arlington AMS1, Watson AT2 and, of course, Danko.

Between and after aircraft launches, we, the evicted, packed and lugged our gear to low grade Enlisted puke quarters up in the forward bow of the ship. Flight quarters secured at 1700. All birds were in up-status requiring no work but we just hung around the Photo Shop anyway creating little jobs that required a lot of pounding and metal scraping.

Tonight, I watched *Dr. Strangelove, or How I Learned to Stop Worrying and Love the Bomb Again*. It was this evening's cinema selection on the ship's closed circuit television. The film is Director Stanley Kubrick's parody of the best-seller, *Fail Safe*. It was very entertaining in a sardonic sort of way and probably closer to what would actually happen if the U.S. and Russia lobbed atomic bombs at each other. It portrays the military as bumbling and run by madmen. I watched while I unpacked and arranged my new locker and then climbed into my bed. It's the top rack on a tier of three. Each sailor has about 18 inches of head clearance. Right above my head is the casing for the steam catapult.

17 August 1967 ... 62nd day. South China Sea.

Damn! Heat just radiates off that fuckin' thing! I slept in sweat last night.

We're still on our way to combat zone. We'll probably arrive in the Tonkin Gulf tonight around midnight. No combat missions today. Even so, three of our squadron planes went out for practice runs and all came back with mechanical problems of one sort or another.

This evening, I finished configuration of our new bird, 604. It's a piece of shit. Hydraulic fluid leaks everywhere. She was parked aft on the Hangar Deck, packed like a sardine with all the other planes in repair. Space is at a premium. At night we have to work under red light conditions – red is not as visible to a seaborne enemy. The heat was insidious. I pulled off my shirt and crawled down under the nose of 604, opened the number-one camera pod and wrestled for two hours with a camera that refused to be installed. The connectors were damaged, threads partially stripped. The boys on the Bon Homme Richard really fucked over that camera. I was cussing and kicking, with rivers of sweat running down my face and over my chest, mixing with dripping, red hydraulic fluid. 'Looked like I'd been wounded in action.

The 1MC crackled on at 2200 hours, "Standby for the evening prayer."

Exasperated, I yelled, "God! Help me!"

He didn't. I gave up on the project. Someone else can tackle it tomorrow, maybe Ray. I went up to the berthing compartment, took a cold shower and hopped into my hot bunk.

18 August 1967 ... 63rd day.
Yankee Station, North Vietnam

We are back in war zone again, primed and ready to raise hell one more time. *Burn down their huts while humping their sluts.* The bombs were loaded this morning: 500-pounders, 1000-pounders. The missiles and rockets were placed in their launchers. Strikes resumed over North Vietnam.

Our Photo Birds had much the same problems as yesterday. Six-O-Three was scheduled to fly at 0930. It went bad. Six-O-One was brought up for a quick swap. She returned from the mission in down-status. Six-O-Two flew at 1200. It came back down-status. All our birds are grounded for repairs; all tied down and chocked on the Hangar Bay, looking like big sad ducks with droopy wings.

I stayed up late drawing pornographic pictures of beautiful babes in compromising positions. God, I'm horny but I think my days of humping whores is over – too much social disease. And, there ain't no Pollyanna's in liberty ports. And, if there were, they wouldn't be dropping their panties for American sailors. That's for damned sure. A lot of social disease on that side of the court, too.

20 August 1967 ... the 65th day. Ibid.

A few of the plane captains next door have a little band organized. They have a lead, a rhythm and a bass guitar plus an assortment of reverbs, amps, speakers and microphones set up. Romanesco is the instigator of the band. He played in a group before joining the Navy. Now he has two others with him and a drum-less drummer whacking a metal can. They jam virtually every night outside of our shop. A large audience usually gathers, the noise blasts through the steel bulkheads until the early hours of the morning. But hell, since I don't live there anymore why should I protest? Our dear First-Class POs are about to go batty. They say the noise keeps them awake and they are tired all the next day. My heart pumps purple piss for them. Meanwhile, we of the banished continue our work in the shop long, late hours just to antagonize our unwelcome resident boarders.

As the schedule runs right now, we will be on Yankee Station this period until September 15. The next day we steam north for R&R in Sasebo, Japan. Hot damn!

21 August 1967 ... 66th day. Ibid.

I'll be a son-of-a-bitch! They did it! All combined Carrier Air Groups have received clearance to bomb the capital city! The order came directly from Washington, D.C. Today we sent aircraft on major strikes over Hanoi. A power plant was destroyed as well as several other targets. A few planes were shot down and pilots killed from the carriers Intrepid and Coral Sea. Two of our A-4 Skyhawks from Attack Squadron 163 were shot up. One came back with 83 holes in her fuselage, the other had 127. All of our CAG planes returned safely.

Our first Photo Bird launched at 0730. Lieutenant JG Beam flew the mission. He returned at 0915 having shot all film in all stations. The second hop wasn't until 1600 so we sat around, slept and screwed around in the shop while Night Check Danko cut Z's in the rack formerly known as Mac's bed. At 1600, Bird 602 piloted by Mister Rudd and 601 piloted by LT Sam were spotted and turned on the aft Flight Deck. Charlie Rudd made it off the cat all right and flew his mission as planned. Mr. Sam didn't go because at the last minute his fighter escort blew a gasket and was unable to fly. Frustrated and pissed, he taxied 601 over on to Elevator Number Three so that returning aircraft could be recovered on the wires. The plane director motioned for Sam to get out of the aircraft.

"Hell no!" Lieutenant Sampson yelled, "I'm not walking out there when those planes are coming in. Take the goddamned elevator down."

So the elevator was lowered to the Hangar Deck and Mr. Sam climbed out and then stomped his way down the deck. A few maintenance men working on 604 waved and shouted a few choice words of sarcastic consolation. Sam stopped, turned, flipped them the bird, smiled and proceeded to his locker room.

23 August 1967 ... 68th day. Ibid.

Routine is setting in already as we continue our flight regimen from 0730 to 1830; two to three hops a day. Asshole Danko walked into the shop today like King Shit and started planning with PO1 Mike Koppler where they were to put their additional lockers in the newly renamed First-Class Quarters. Ray protested. Dick protested. I felt like decking the S.O.B. right there on the spot. I think his mission is to make us hate him more and more. He strutted around the shop deciding what equipment of ours he would move out of the way to install his additional lockers. Harry quietly went to see the Chief and discuss matters. So far, no lockers.

Mail call. I got a letter from the folks concerning their move to a new house on September first and Dad's release from the hospital after a little run-in with asthma and bronchial disease. He had quit smoking but he's back at it now; chain smoking his unfiltered Pall-Mall's. Jeris also wrote a letter in reply to the one I mailed a couple of weeks ago. She is beginning to sound more mature, more interesting. Seventeen is a good age. Damnit, what a beautiful dream is home. Back in the world. What a wonderful time I'll have when I return to my folks' house and then my own. Day Dreams can alleviate the boredom and drudgery of this life at sea.

24 August 1967 ... 69th day. Ibid.

This morning an Admiral arrived onboard the Oriskany via helicopter. Captain Billy Holder and the ship's Executive Officer were on the Flight Deck to greet the brass god. Eight Seaman Apprentices were issued clean, crisp, brilliant green, blue, yellow and red Flight Deck uniforms. They scampered alongside the helo when it landed and formed a line. The chopper doors slid open and out stepped a tall, sandy-haired, wrinkled man with shiny brass stars glistening in the sun. The Side Boys, as they are called, snapped to attention and saluted in sync. The skipper rushed forth with outstretched hand, an enormous shit-eating grin on his face. We put on a good show for our Navy god. God smiled in return, shook hands, and responded to the flurry of salutes. Then in a syncopated motion, the throng of gooney grins gaited toward the superstructure where they would disappear and enter that mysterious land called Officer's Country. Becoming increasingly annoyed, I stood by the door through which they would all enter. A plane director ran up to me, shouting, "Hey, don't stand there! Hey! Get out of sight. The Captain and Admiral are coming."

Being a good compliant grunt I did as I was told.

What is it with these people? Why couldn't eight regular guys on the Flight Deck be elected to be Side Boys? Is it that the Admiral cannot bear the aroma of physical labor? Are our armpits offensive to his delicate nostrils? Is the grease and grime on our faces and clothing unsightly? Doesn't the Admiral want to see the actual working men of the Navy instead of those squeaky clean eunuchs disguised as Airdales? That's right, those Side Boys aren't even from the Air Wing. They're Ship's Company.

25 August 1967 ... 70th day. Ibid.

"Enemy lines of communication suffered heavily as attacking A4 Skyhawks, F8 Crusaders, and A1 Skyraider aircraft striking from the Mighty Zero hurled their ordnance at targets between Vinh and Thanh Hoa in the central regions of North Vietnam."

That was the lead-in of today's Morning Musket. Every day it's basically the same story telling of the glory of our bombing raids. The pilots are quoted. Bridges, dredges, trucks, AAA and SAM sites are blown up and the ship's journalists go nuts with the superlatives.

Meanwhile Chief O'Brian, the old gunner, posted a list of compartment regulations today. It was approved by LCDR Sonniksen. It's just more of the same old shit that can be found in any Navy barracks with a few ridiculous additions, such as, no laundry bags are to be hung on our racks, only towels. We must, of course, straighten out our bunks after getting up. That's reasonable. Reveille is to be held one-and-a-half hours before the first launch of the day or at 0600 whichever is earlier. Even if the first hop isn't until noon, we must get up at 0600. Horseshit! No matter where you are stationed in the Navy, it's always the same. Things can be good, everyone happy and content with morale riding high and work performed willingly. Then along comes some old lifer with twenty years' worth of stripes on his sleeve that likes to screw up everything. Gotta be more military, more in-line with regulations. He stops addressing the Enlisted Men to their faces, barking orders to the stripes on their sleeves instead. He enforces the segregation of working classes according to seniority and pay grade level. It ain't no democracy! The majority certainly does not rule. Petitions won't help. Balloting is something done back in the world by free civilians not by men of the U.S. Armed Forces. We Enlisted boys are merely slaves of the brass gods and their goons, the CPO's. O'Brian wants to get a medal for outstanding leadership for this cruise. Danko is bucking for Chief. The men are bitching. Fights are breaking out. Morale is in the pits; all because we ain't regulation enough for the leadership.

26 August 1967 ... 71st day. Ibid.

Idle day, a welcome relief, thanks be to the Omnipotent God of Creation who brings us rain and fog. Ho Chi Minh walked to the office today carrying an umbrella. No Air Pirates, as they call us, dropped bombs on North Vietnam today. Uncle Ho's army of civilian workers takes advantage of days like this to rebuild bridges and buildings, repair roads and runways.

All scheduled flights for the day were cancelled as the light rain of morning intensified in the afternoon. Taking advantage of the downtime, Lieutenant JG Kanker asked PH2 Hines to shoot a photo job for him; just general shots of the squadron personnel at work to submit to the ship's Cruise Book – our version of a high school yearbook. Hines was reluctant for some reason, so I volunteered, eager to prove I am a true photographer, an artist on film, more than just a Flight Deck film changer. Hines procured a Nikkorex 35mm camera for me with wide angle, normal and telephoto lenses plus a Honeywell Strobonar 660 flash unit. It's going to be a blast if I can find enough time to process and print them all.

In a non-typical display of humanness, Craig Danko and I had a very pleasant conversation this evening talking about photography, fishing and home. It's a pity he can't keep his good side turned on all the time but I guess I don't either. This life at sea without the civility of home, without women, without the creature comforts that we spoiled Americans are accustomed to, can turn a guy sour. On the other hand, I'm sure the Jarheads would rather be out here on a carrier than in-country thrashing through razor grass and sleeping in the mud.

27 August 1967 ... 72nd day. Ibid.

Another day like yesterday. More rain. No flights. Chief O'Brian got a wild hair up his ass today and decided it was time for me to paint our squadron mascot, Yosemite Sam, on the tail of aircraft 604 as I did on the other three birds back at Miramar prior to deployment. I don't know why he was so eager for me to do it. Old 604 will probably be down for repairs for at least the next month. Harry won't tell me how I was volunteered to do the job but I made it known that my artistic abilities are not part of my military occupational obligation. They are my personal talents that I offer as a gesture of good will and not just another mandatory duty. Not all of my ass belongs to the U.S. Navy. My art and my soul still belong to me and the one true God whomever He, She, It might be.

I moped around the compartment, listening to tapes, procrastinating. Harry kept bugging me. "When you gonna do the Sam's, Mac?"

"Oh, probably tomorrow."

"Tomorrow?," raising his voice. "I told the Chief you'd do it today."

"Oh, it was you, eh? Thanks, Harry. Fuddy Bucker!"

"My pleasure, Mac." He gave me a demonic grin.

After gathering my art materials – stencil, paint, brushes – I headed down to 604 in the Hangar Bay and tried to figure out how I could elevate myself ten feet to reach the area of the tail where I was supposed to paint Yosemite Sam. I ended up standing on the fuselage and reaching up to pencil on the stencil. Wiley stood on the UHT and supported my butt so I wouldn't fall backwards. Looking straight up and stretching to the max, I succeeded in penciling in both sides of the tail but said to hell with filling it in. Not today. The Chief said he'd try to get me some sort of moveable platform so I could finish. He forgot. I'm glad. When I painted the tails back at the Naval Air Station in California, I used a mechanical rising platform with angled steps but they have no such contraption on this tub. Sorry 'bout that.

Mr. Sonniksen turned up the engine on 601 today making sure it was ready for flight. I shot some photos for the Cruise Book.

28 August 1967 ... 73rd day. Gulf of Tonkin, Vietnam.

The sun crept up over the eastern horizon to an unblemished sky this morning. It's a lovely day out here for the Tonkin Gulf Yacht Club. That means we get to cream the North Vietnamese again. The fighters and bombers hit their targets. We sent out two birds to take pictures... first one at noon and the other at 1600.

On the noon hop, poised with my Nikkorex. I snapped off a few of old man Sonniksen as he turned up, performed the systems check, then taxied to the cats. Rushing to the 07 level of the superstructure, I grabbed shots of his launch. Camera in hand, I was on the Flight Deck when he returned from his mission. He botched the first approach to the wire and was waived off by the signalman. I captured the fly-through. On the second attempt, he caught the wire and I immortalized it on film. I finished off the

35mm and turned to my regular task of unloading and reloading the large film canisters on the Photo Bird.

This evening, in the Ship's Company Photo Lab, I processed and printed contact sheets of the two black-and-white rolls I shot two days ago. The lab boys were in my way doing their official work. I had to squeeze in between their priority jobs so it took me six hours to do a two-hour job. I slumped into bed at 0200 in the morning after editing my proofs and running them by Kanker.

"Ah, yes," he said, in his best Officer voice, "You've got mostly shots of individuals here. Now if we could get more group shots, MacLennon, that would be good."

Good night, Kanker Sore. Oh, and you're welcome. He didn't even thank me for what I've done so far. Par for the course.

29 August 1967 ... 74th day. Ibid.

At 0600, compliant to new regulations, PO Morgan held reveille on our berthing compartment. Four hours, only four hours of sleep! Shit. Several guys tried to get my tired ass out of the rack and finally succeeded. After smashing my knuckles into my locker and cursing the Navy, I felt much better. Morning dragged on as we preflighted 601 and sent it on its patriotic way at 0730. Following recovery and unloading of film, I sprawled on the Photo Shop floor under the vent and slept until time for the next launch.

This evening down in the Photo Lab, the boys and I watched a dumb movie on the ship's closed-circuit television entitled, *The Russians Are Coming! The Russians Are Coming!* How ironic because we're out here in the Tonkin Gulf with Russians. They're performing electronic surveillance on us from their so-called fishing trawlers and bringing in more missiles and anti-aircraft artillery on their supply ships to Haiphong Harbor. The Russian boats and ships are off limits to our strike aircraft as is the harbor, thanks to LBJ and his cronies who are afraid this little Police Action of ours might escalate into a full blown war with Russia and China if we do anything to piss them off. Meanwhile American pilots are being captured and killed, grunts in South Vietnam are dying by the thousands because we limit our aggression. Too bad Johnson is running this war. If JFK was still alive, we probably wouldn't even be here.

30 August 1967 ... 75th day. Ibid.

 This morning, Lieutenant Sam and Mister Beamer launched in 601 and 602 for a special trip to Cubi Point Naval Air Station and back for reasons unrevealed to we the *untermenschen*. Speaking of sub-humans, PO3 Goetz, the lad with chronic bad breath, has been painting our planes since we left Frisco. It's a never-ending job because of salt-water corrosion that can eat right through the skin of a fuselage and mess up important components required for safe flight. Someone – I can guess who – put pressure on him to have me finish that fucking Yosemite Sam today. So after some whining I collected my art materials and descended to the Hangar Bay again. Goetz checked out a rising platform from Ground Support Equipment. Well I'll be a son of a bitch, I guess they do have one on this ship! I applied the color to the penciled art. It took about an hour-and-a-half each side of the tail. I was relieved to get it over. Catching the wire at 1300, Sam and Charlie said their return flight from Naval Air Station Cubi Point was through pea soup all the way and they didn't even have time to drink a San Magoo. Aw shucks!

 Mail call brought a letter from Mom today telling me about the family's vacation in Green Lake, Minnesota. It's the same place they always go in Minnesota. You'd think with 10,000 lakes they could vary their choices. Just Mom and Dad took the trip this year. They left little brother Jeff with Uncle Glen and Aunt Marilyn in Des Moines. Jeris stayed in Nebraska with her buddy, Diane Livingston. Sis is working full time as a waitress at a restaurant that just opened. Mom says, "It's the longest time we've been away from our kids, since Neal and I left you, Gerald, with Mom and Dad Hilding and drove to the Chicago Railroad Fair back in 1950."

 It sounds like everyone's happy. The folks are honeymooning. Jeris is on her own, probably raising hell with the girls every night. Jeff is with his favorite relatives. And big brother is floating around on a ship in the Gulf of Tonkin perhaps not quite as happy but hey, I'm preserving the American way of life. Yeah, right.

 Nevertheless, it's nice to know Mom and Dad are trying to enjoy each other's company. They've had a rocky relationship to put it lightly. I'm sure at Green Lake, he has a Pall Mall in his mouth and an Old Milwaukee in his hand just about every waking minute.

I've been thinking about my behavior on this cruise. Lately, it's been awfully pessimistic. If MacLennon can't change his attitude, he's going to end up a miserable old curmudgeon. I've been too self-centered. A brighter approach would be good. Promote goodwill instead of finding fault and bitching and in so doing, pulling down the spirits of my comrades. My mouth has been running off. I've made comments that were better left unspoken. But I have time to make amends. We have many more days on this ocean. The heat and humidity gets to everyone; so, too, the monotony of the daily tasks. Physical and psychological pressure can cluster and turn a man into a pussy. Sure, the Navy isn't the life for me but some truly enjoy this existence, especially the Officers. Yes, I fully realize civilian life can be just as bad, but it can also be much better. I'm going for the better. Here in the service, I feel like a white Negro of the South who's fighting for his civil rights: the right to be a mister and not just a boy, the right of common courtesy, the right to petition when I consider an action unfair, the right to use the same toilet as an Officer, the right to free speech without fear of reprisal, to be a free-thinking liberal in a liberal-minded environment. I know this brand of discrimination will not vanish from the military, so it is necessary next February for me to vanish from the military.

I have dreams of what I will do back there in the World. I dream of a life of productive, hard labor in the wilderness of God's Country. I'll live in a small log cottage surrounded by the scent of pine and within earshot of a babbling mountain stream. I dream of cool summer nights when the boughs whisper in the breeze and of raging winter blizzards when winds howl in the canyons – my cottage is shrouded with ten foot drifts. Wrapped in wild animal furs, I'll sit in front of a crackling hearth as smoke spirits rise up the chimney. There will be a loaded rifle on the mantle, a husky-wolf lying at my side and a exotically beautiful, bronze-skinned woman sitting in the darkness calling me to bed; her delicate smile sufficient to arouse intense desire night after night throughout this darkest of seasons. Warmth and affection envelop me. It's a simple life where I can work the land, dig my hands into the soil and assimilate with the richness and fertility of the earth. Our sons and daughters will grow up in the wilderness, learning to love, preserve and protect God's Creation as divinely-appointed guardians – a role that all humans have been given but that few assume. Our family will give to and benefit from the land. We will scale snow-covered ranges and wade through the marshes. Bears, wolverines, cougars, the forest tall, wild grasses and flowers, the ruggedness of rustic existence will create true men out of my sons and strong, hard-working, compassionate women out of my daughters.

Where can I find such a world? Probably nowhere. A friend once told me that romantics usually believe they were born in the wrong place in time. So many dreams and inspirations come and go. Tomorrow's fantasy will probably be different from todays. Maybe this typical-American lad is merely destined to live a typical-American life just as every other typical-American. But damnit! I'd like to put a dent in this world somehow. And I have no idea where to start. I could be satisfied as a writer if the content was useful to the lives of others. I could attempt to write of what must done to bring peace, harmony and contentment to the citizens of this earth – as soon as I figure it out. As I sit here writing, war planes loaded with rockets and bombs are setting on the Flight Deck less than ten feet over my head, ready to inflict anguish on fellow human beings. What a mind fuck!

The future begins in less than six months. I must go to college first. I must see more of the world. I must know what is common to humankind in order to speak to the world of the world. That sounds just opposite the isolated life of an Alaskan homesteader, doesn't it? Just call me: Mr. Contradiction.

And... what does it require to reach lofty goals? Answer: enthusiasm, optimism, and indomitable spirit! Running straight on a true and noble path. And if I stumble and fall, I pick myself up and forge on. Even at twenty, I realize how short my life span is. There is so damned much to be accomplished and so few years to do it. That's why I'm so eager to get this military service out of the way. That's why I get frustrated. Time will not speed up for me. Back on terra firma, I used to walk out to God's world, isolating myself from other people. On my solitary journeys, I would pray and meditate on the Why's of Life. Indeed, why life? Why the constant turmoil of mankind? Why war? Why peace? Why evil? Why try to make sense of it all? What's the purpose?

CHAPTER XVI
SECOND CONVERSATION WITH MICHAEL

Lieutenant Michael Goldberg was sitting out on the canoe tonight when I went up there to meditate. We hadn't planned the rendezvous. It was just coincidence.

"Hey, Mac!" He seemed genuinely happy to see me. I was surprised. "How are you doing?"

"As good as can be expected," I replied.

"Pull up the Flight Deck and have a seat."

"Thanks."

I was curious. "How did you fare during the whole Forrestal crisis?"

He shuddered and fell silent. After an introspective pause, he looked directly at me and said, "It was the closest to hell that I ever want to get, Mac. Those poor guys, dead, burnt. Did you know that volunteers had to pick up pieces of human beings and stack them in a pile and hope they could put them back together later. I have no idea how many shuttles I made that day. I didn't sleep for two days. And, I still have trouble sleeping. I keep hearing their screams as I transported them. So many of them calling out to God, to their mothers, their wives. I really can't dwell on it. Not even now. So, whaddya say we change the subject."

I nodded in agreement. No need to tell him about my volunteer work in Sickbay. It didn't come close to what he witnessed.

"Mac, I was thinking about our last conversation and I want to apologize."

"For what?" I asked.

"It was one-sided... me, me, me. After I went back to my quarters, I realized I hadn't really learned much about you. So, why don't you tell me your life story."

I laughed. "Now, that would be too long, Michael, and too boring. I can still call you Michael, can't I?"

"Sure, same rules apply."

I proceeded to give him a brief history of my origins, how I came to join the Navy and mentioned again that I had once been a good Lutheran boy but now considered myself somewhat of a Buddhist. He didn't question my religious conversion, just seemed to accept it. His only remark was: "So, you're on a spiritual journey for the Truth, whatever that may be."

I was pleasantly surprised again. "Yes, that's exactly what's happening."

"Many people are, especially in today's young generation. Me? As I said at our last meeting, I cannot accept bearded old legends and traditions anymore."

We just kept on talking about all the things we have in common. An hour passed and it only seemed like five minutes.

Pulling out my pack of smokes, I offered Michael a Lucky Strike Filter. He took it and we both lit up. A puff. Another drag. I spoke. "You know, Michael, I think God put you and me together for a reason."

"You think so? Why?"

"Because I get so starved for these kinds of conversations. People just aren't interested..."

"Or, just maybe, they don't want to try on new ideas. Maybe it scares them." Michael looked over at me with a shit eating grin, "Now that was a damned arrogant thing for me to say. Wasn't it."

"Well, hell yes!" I agreed with him. "Stuck up, for sure."

We both laughed and then fell silent again for a minute or two. Both of us sat there together scanning the marvelous display of stars and planets above our heads. I was the first to say more: "Michael, as long as we're being intellectuals..."

"Great intellectuals!" He chuckled.

"Okay, regular Einsteins! So tell me, Mister Wizard, what's your answer to the classic question?"

"Which one?"

"Why does a good God allow..."

"Allow evil to exist?" He finished the sentence for me, then said, "Hell if I know."

"Not good enough."

"Maybe we have to have evil to know what good is. Ever thought of that?"

"Yes," I responded, pretending to be smug, "Yin and Yang."

"Oh, yes, Yin and Yang. They were the cats in Walt Disney's Lady and The Tramp, weren't they?" Michael was entertaining himself but I held my posture, resisting the urge.

"No, the cats were Si and Am." I said.

Michael didn't want to be serious. "Are you sure they weren't Ting and Ling?" he laughed aloud and then added, "Mac, Mac. It's all just opinion. Mankind has many religions but God is One. That's what I think. Mankind has many religions but God is One. Now... how you define One is up to you."

"Sure, go ahead," I smirked. "Hush my mouth and shoot me down."

"Can't do it," he reminded me. "Remember? I'm Search and Rescue."

Calling it a night, we both stood and stretched, breathing in the mild but humid air. Michael turned toward the ship's superstructure and slowly walked away. "Good Night, Mac! God bless!"

"Yes sir, Godspeed."

He shouted over his head, "And how fast would that be?"

PHOTOGRAPHER'S MATE 3RD CLASS GERALD EDWARD LOGAN ALIAS GERALD MACLENNON, US NAVY 1965-1970 - US NAVAL ACADEMY AWARD-WINNING PHOTOGRAPH IN COLOR VERSION - ONBOARD USS ORISKANY (CVA-34) - MEN OF VFP-63 IN THE PHOTO SHOP - JAPAN - PHILIPPINE ISLANDS - HONG KONG

CHAPTER XVII
FROM SILLY SACRED TO DEAD SERIOUS

31 August 1967 ... 76th day.
Tonkin Gulf – Yankee Station.

This morning, Chief O'Brian approached me on the Flight Deck as we were turning a plane preparing for the morning launch. "MacLennon," he said, putting his hand on my shoulder, "That Yosemite Sam on 604 looks real good. Fine job!"

Well, blow me down and call me Popeye. I was dumb-founded. He actually appreciates my extra duties.

We were in full-scale action today. The Oriskany Air Group flew highly significant Alpha Strikes near the Chinese border. On one mission, several A4 Skyhawks of Attack Squadron 163 crossed a mountain range, beginning their approach to the drop zone in the river valley beyond. The target was a large bridge linking supply routes from China to North Vietnam. A barrage of AAA flak and SAM missiles greeted the Skyhawk pilots. Two planes were hit, spiraling down in flames. Both pilots ejected and parachuted down into the middle of a Vietnamese village eliminating any possibility of rescue. Lieutenant Sampson lost his F-8 fighter escort but continued solo – no rockets, armed with just cameras. Another A4, this one from VA-164 was also hit by ground resistance. The pilot managed to fly his crippled aircraft back out to sea but only a few miles from the coastline it exploded reducing the plane to smoking fragments and killing the pilot instantly. I don't have his name yet; nor the two who are now POW's. Our squadron flew three photo recon missions today, encountering a shit storm of enemy resistance. Mister Sampson preceded and then trailed the attack birds on their Alpha Strike snapping photos for Bomb Damage Assessment. He put his ass on the line. Hell, all of our pilots do. He was fifteen minutes late returning to the ship. We were worried a SAM or AAA had taken him out but he finally appeared out of the clouds, landed safely and all was well. Smiles on deck.

2 September 1967 ... 78th day.

Flight quarters from 0600 to 1800; three photo bird hops at 0700, 1200 and 1600, this is the routine during heavy overcast.

Night strikes were cancelled because of looming thunderstorms. This morning I began reading *Sarkhan*, a novel by Lederer and Burdick, co-authors of *The Ugly American*. It focused on American civilians living among citizens of the Orient, learning their language and culture and thereby earning respect and admiration of the Asian nations. Such Americans are the true ambassadors of good will and the best advisors regarding the attitudes and needs of the Asians. But, do U.S. Ambassadors and Diplomats take their advice? Do they even consult these good people? Hell, no. *The Ugly American* emphasizes how insensitive and misguided American policies actually allow Communism to get a stronger foothold.

Sarkhan is the name of a fictitious Southeast Asian country but it could very well be Laos, Cambodia, Burma or Thailand. Hanoi-trained infiltrators trick Sarkhan's royal court into thinking their country is being invaded by Vietnamese guerrillas. The king requests and receives military aid, including troops, from the United States. The Communists use the American presence as a propaganda tool to convince the peasants that their country is being invaded by the Yanks thus adding momentum to the People's Liberation Movement. In the end, the king is deposed by his own people and a Hanoi-puppet dictator assumes control of Sarkhan. The American troops retreat and withdraw. Sounds familiar. Doesn't it?

The book was so well written, so intriguing, I couldn't tear myself away. I stayed up until 11 PM and finished it even though I had gone about 40 hours without sleep.

I received a letter today from Pepé. He wrote a very brief yet heartwarming message telling me of his concern about the Philippines, the coming elections and what the future may hold. He asked about the Cruise and what I've been up to.

I missed water hours damnit. I had to go to bed smelling like a goat.

CHAPTER XVIII
FIGHT TO WIN OR GET OUT

3 September 1967 ... 79th day. Ibid.

Same schedule today. Same good photo coverage. Thanh Hoa bridge, just north of the city by the same name, was hit again. Very challenging to the pilots, every Air Wing on line has tried to destroy it but the most damage has been merely dropping a few steel girders. The supports of the bridge are massive blocks of carved stone anchored deep within the river bottom. Our attack aircraft made direct hits on the bridge today with 2,000 pound bombs. The bridge is still standing.

It's strange but I find myself gradually becoming an ambivalent blend of hawk, as the media calls it, and pacifist dove. I still hold that the bombing campaign is killing thousands of innocent Vietnamese people in the north. And, that is sad. At the same time, I must stand in support of the young American men who are being wounded, maimed and killed by the NVA and the Viet Cong with weapons supplied from the north. That, too, is sad and damned frustrating. Lyndon Johnson's policy decision to hamstring our air power has prolonged the conflict.

A few weeks back, I read an article in a discarded May issue of Reader's Digest entitled: "Let's Fight to Win in Vietnam." After reading it, I thought to myself, "Wow, someone has the balls to tell it like it is." And ironically that someone is the female military editor for the Digest, Francis Vivian Drake.

In her article she asks how much longer will this undeclared war drag on and at the cost of how many lives? A question just about every intelligent American is asking these days. She points out that LBJ and McNamara seem hell bent on perpetuating a limited action offensive. Why?

Drake points out that since the Gulf of Tonkin Resolution over ten thousand American boys have died with over 50,000 wounded in order to prevent the Commie takeover of South Vietnam. She then asks what can be done to shorten this war, and answers with info gathered from Navy and Air Force pilots who routinely bomb the shit out of the North.

The consensus opinion is to eliminate the restrictions. Fight to win or get the hell out! Don't use our massive air power to just take out trucks, bridges and coolie caravans. Target the big shit. Hit them where it hurts: the steel mills and factories, major transportation systems, ammo plants, trains and supply ships. The article was written in May of this year and yes, we have begun to do just that but there still are strategic targets that remain off-limits. For one, our pilots are not allowed to bomb the actual supply line materiel coming into Vietnam from China because the Washington foreign policy advisors don't want to piss off the Chinese. Why not? They're supplying weapons that are killing our men. Some say it will bring the People's Republic of China into the war but better analysts state the chances of that happening are virtually nil. Their military is no match for ours.

Secretary of the Air Force, Harold Brown is quoted as saying, "Yes, air power could destroy North Vietnam but it is not in our national interest to do so."

Well, hell, it's not even in our national interest to be here. That's a stupid argument. My words. And since when do we fight nice wars? That's an oxymoron. That's why the article is entitled: "Let's Fight to Win in Vietnam."

Vivian Drake points out that the quickest, easiest way to cut off war supplies from China and our buddies, the Russians, is to block the narrow sea channel that leads into Haiphong Harbor from the Gulf of Tonkin. The channel is so shallow; it has to be constantly dredged. Pilots say that all we have to do is destroy their dredging barges or sink one large supply ship in the channel itself and ninety percent of North Vietnam's war materiel will be cut off.

The Japanese did it in World War II. That was their first target in what was then called Indo-China. They sunk a big freighter in the channel and didn't give a flying fuck what country it belonged to.

There are between fifty to seventy strategic targets in North Vietnam, according to Drake, that we could destroy, severely crippling Uncle Ho's assault on the South but LBJ will only allow our bombs to wipe out about ten to fifteen percent of them. Again, apparently not in our national interest. Finally, she estimates that it's costing China and Russia only about two billion dollars a year to use Vietnam as a testing ground for their latest weaponry, including the new generation of SAM missiles. Those assholes are just sitting back and taking notes while our taxpayers fork out about 20 times that amount to finance the war and offer up our sons on the sacrificial altar of the world's military-industrial temples, including our own in the United States.

Masters of War indeed. Bob Dylan is right. We are just pawns in the big chess game.

5 September 1967 ... 81st day Ibid.

Flight quarters weren't sounded until 1030 this morning. Photo Recon Squadron 63's first hop was at noon. It was wonderful to sleep in. I arose well rested and amiable for a change. Yeah, the idiotic 0600 reveille didn't last for long.

The sun was beaming bright from a clear sky yet my instinct sensed a change. Sitting along the catwalk awaiting the return of our flight, I remarked to Dick, "It's going to rain tomorrow."

"Bullshit!" was his reply. "What the fuck makes you think that?"

"Just something in my blood, I guess. Maybe my Iowa farm heritage."

"Farmer my ass."

"Can't you smell it in the air?"

"All I can smell is jet exhaust. You're crazy, Mac!"

The day played out well. The cameras all functioned properly. This evening at the Photo Lab, I watched the movie, *This Property is Condemned*, with the beautiful Natalie Wood. I think I'm in love. Move over, Hayley. How do we get our own private screenings? The ship's Photo Mates are in tight with the guys from Ship's Services. A little bit of the 'you scratch my back, I'll scratch yours' sort of thing. After the movie, I collected my slides of the Philippines that I received in the mail today. My sweet sister Jeris had them processed for me. Making use of the light table in Photo Intelligence, I spread the color transparencies and showed them to Muffley and Kanker Sore. They like them so well they called the Public Affairs Officer and requested that some be considered for inclusion in the ship's Cruise Book.

6 September 1967 ... 82nd day. Ibid.

I was right. Rain! I woke up this morning and walked out to greet grey clouds skimming the white capped ocean and wind-borne pellets of heavy rain. The gun tub was flooded. The 02 was dotted with puddles. The ship is rocking and a-rolling. No flight quarters.

At the shop, I brought out my tape machine and put on some tunes. Dick and I gave the shop a thorough cleaning; even waxed and buffed the deck. I hope this weather stays with us for a few days. Countdown to Sasebo, Japan: 15 days.

Rain has continued into the night. The wind is incredibly strong. I look out over the catwalks and nothing is visible. Blackness and the howling of the wind, the slapping of the waves against the hull of our ship, the occasional blast of the foghorn – just a little eerie, like an old World War II movie.

7 September 1967 ... 83rd day. Ibid.

It was just too good to last. After an early morning thundershower, the sky cleared and it was war time again. We sent out two hops, both in the afternoon. One of the checkers, the men who inspect the catapult-to-plane linkage, was injured today. As he was checking out the nose gear prior to launch, the aircraft rolled forward over his leg and pinned it between the catapult shuttle and the wheel. His leg was fractured in four places below the knee. The ship's surgeon operated and is optimistic.

8 September 1967 ... 84th day. Ibid.

The injured checker was flown out to the hospital at Subic Bay Naval Station last night. Speaking to us on the 1MC, Captain Billy Holder informed us today that doctors in Subic had to amputate the poor guy's leg below the knee in order to save his life. I reckon that's why they give us hazardous duty pay for working the Flight Deck.

Another Flight Deck accident occurred during turn-up for the second launch of the day. A red-shirted Ordnance Man was wheeling bombs across the deck on the dolly. A tow tractor driver was freewheeling down the Flight Deck and blind-sided the Red Shirt, knocking him down. The poor bastard rose to his feet again, took one step and collapsed unconscious. Medical Corpsmen carried him down to Sickbay. No word yet on how he's doing. Those damned tractor drivers think they own the whole fucking Flight Deck.

The Air Wing lost a plane in combat today over Nam. I think it was an F-8 Crusader from Fighter Squadron 111. It was hit by AAA or SAM flak and severely crippled. The pilot maneuvered the plane back out to the gulf, to within five miles of the Oriskany where he popped the canopy, pulled the straps on his ejection seat and rocketed high above his aircraft as the plane spiraled into the water. The pilot parachuted safely to the surface, separated himself from the seat and was picked up by Michael and his crew in Angel-3. As the chopper landed on our Flight Deck, corpsmen with their stretcher and little black bags emerged from the superstructure running toward the water-soaked pilot who, in the meantime, had merrily hopped out of the helo, was jogging in place, and waving his arms in a gesture that said to everyone watching, "Hey, look at me! I'm alive!"

The Air Boss, our god in the sky, got totally bent out of shape. "Put the pilot on the stretcher!" He yelled so loud into his microphone that his voice was distorted on the Flight Deck speakers. This old fart was pissed. "Again! Put the pilot on the stretcher!" I'd never heard him so mad. Did anyone pay attention to the voice of our little god? Hell, no. The happy pilot just pranced through the superstructure's hatch and went down to his ready room. The corpsmen looked at one another like: What do we do now? They shrugged their shoulders and returned to Sickbay.

Lately, the primary targets in North Vietnam have been hidden by overcast so the planes have been reverting to secondaries such as coastal installations, enemy PT boats, WBLC's, trucks, and so on. Missions have been relatively safe but I suspect when those primaries are targeted again, NVA ground forces will be well prepared for defensive action.

CHAPTER XIX
PEGGY LEE

A letter from Peggy Lee came in today's mail call. Damn, I wish she'd just forget about me. Six months before this cruise began, I took two weeks leave and flew back home. I had fun partying with my old high school gang. Then there was Peggy. Nineteen-year-old Peggy Lundgren was a new face in the neighborhood. The guys had renamed her in honor of Peggy Lee because she was buxom, sultry and did it – just like torch singer Peggy Lee. "Fever! In the morning. Fever all through the night... you give me fever."

She had moved into the neighborhood sometime after I left in '64. In those three years, I think she had a fling with just about every one of the guys. So it shouldn't be surprising that when I came home on leave, she took a special interest in me, too.

Unfortunately, the attraction wasn't mutual. For one thing, big boobs don't turn me on, she had a broad ass and she babbled too much but she did seem to have a good heart. And, because not too many girls find me desirable, I was open to starting some kind of relationship with her – nothing serious.

My time back home was limited. Even so, Peggy and I spent some hours together getting to know each other. That evolved into kissing and petting. Most of this happened at her parent's house where she still lived. Her dad was, and probably still is, a Methodist preacher – a very stern, no nonsense sort of man. He immediately made it clear that he did not want Peggy and I to leave the confines of his house. He'd let us sit in the living room while he and his wife retired to the basement to watch television. He seemed excessively over-protective of Peggy. The son-of-a-bitch probably spied on us too but I didn't care. It didn't stop me from making out with her. Sure didn't stop her either.

Time passed quickly. And then, one night I learned that Peggy Lundgren had some awful secrets. I had talked her into crawling out her bedroom window about 2 o'clock in the morning and meeting up with me. Together we rode out to the country in my '56 Chevy and parked near Steven's Creek, surrounded by cornfields. I had decided I was going all the way with her that night if she was game.

And... we were on our way. I had made it to first base and wanted to head for second. With my hand creeping up the inside of her thigh,

I had just reached inside her panties when she suddenly went berserk on me, bursting out in tears and sobbing hysterically.

Backing off, I yelled at her, "Damn, Peggy Lee! What the hell's wrong?"

"Don't call me that!" She screamed in my face.

"Okay. Okay. I'm sorry... Peggy. Can you tell me what I did wrong? I thought you were ready and willing."

She didn't answer but continued sobbing uncontrollably. I gave her time to pull herself together. It took about ten minutes. "I'm sorry," she finally said, wiping her eyes. "There's something I have to tell you."

"Well sure, Peggy." I responded in the most sympathetic voice I could muster. "I'm listening."

"I had a baby last year."

"Ah... Really?"

"Yes, really. And I had to give it up for adoption because my Mom and Dad didn't want to be shamed by their daughter."

I nodded, and urged her to go on.

"Dad was afraid of what his parishioners and higher-ups would think. He was afraid he might be asked to resign because he couldn't control the behavior of his own family. I'm a P.K. y'know – a preacher's kid. I'm supposed to be a shining example of Christian parenting. Bullshit! I'm not going to live in a glass house. I don't care what people think. Just the same, him and Mom decided to send their pregnant, little tramp to this stupid home for unwed mothers in Des Moines. Yeah, that's what they called me – a tramp! And... I stayed there in that damned place for seven long, boring months until the baby was born."

"Why didn't you tell me about this before?"

"I was trying to work up the nerve but..." Peggy was fighting back more tears. "I never got to see my baby. I don't even know if it's a boy or a girl. I'm so angry! And so pissed! And so..."

"Didn't you want to marry the baby's father?" I asked.

She went silent for about fifteen seconds and then looked straight into my eyes.

"The baby's father is dead."

Another jolt for me. "Dead?"

"Yes, he was killed in Vietnam. I think you know him. Jack Bradford?"

"Sure, I know, er, knew him. Not real close. We were in junior high and high school together, same grade. He was kind of a J.D. like me. You know... rebels."

"Jack and I were in love," the memory made her smile for a second. "The night before he was to leave for Vietnam, we were together – all night. My folks thought I was at a friend's house. Yes, we made love but I didn't know... I didn't know until about two months later that I was carrying his baby."

Another long pause.

"Then I found out from the newspaper that Jack had been killed in combat. And then my father got pissed when he found out about me and the baby and I just hated him... I hated the way he treated me. Some kind of Christian he is! Damned hypocrite!"

"And then your folks sent you away?"

"Yes. Send their little tramp 250 miles away." The flush of anger showed through her tear-covered cheeks. "So I hope you understand, Gerry. What we were just doing brought back all the memories and I thought about getting pregnant again, and of you going off to Vietnam. And I just couldn't..."

"That's okay." I pulled her to me and gave her a big hug. She dampened my shirt with more tears. "God, the poor girl," I thought to myself. "She has been through all this shit and here I am acting like some kind of horny animal out here in the dark, in the country. What a fuckin' moron!"

We just sat there and talked for a couple of hours. I guess the experience brought us closer together but, at the same time, also confirmed for me that I shouldn't be getting so serious with Peggy Lundgren. It wasn't right. I didn't love her. I was just taking advantage of her and that wasn't right. It brought me to my higher senses and made me grow up a little.

The night before I flew back to California, to my squadron, I told her that we should end the relationship but, darn her, Peggy Lee keeps sending love letters. I guess that I'll just have to ignore them. I know that's awfully cold-hearted. But what else can I do? I'm not going to marry her out of pity... and I'm sure that she'll eventually find the right guy, have more children, and will be reasonably happy. Right now, she just can't see that far ahead.

CHAPTER XX
THE MICKY MOUSE CLUB

9 September 1967... 85th day.
Yankee Station, Gulf of Tonkin, North Vietnam.

Lieutenant Commander Sonniksen flew the 1600 flight and as usual had a perfect landing on first attempt during recovery. Prior to that we had some action in view about three miles from the ship. Two Air Force pilots were returning from a mission over North Vietnam when a fuel malfunction forced them to eject from their F-4 Phantom. Oriskany's Angel-2 picked up both pilots and brought them aboard the ship. Our helo personnel snatched them from the sea before saltwater could even soak through to their socks. The pilots were part of the 8th Tactical Fighter Wing based in Ubon, Thailand. An Air Force Jolly Green helo came aboard tonight to pick them up and return them to base. That thing was friggen' big compared to our choppers.

On sortie today, pilots of Carrier Air Wing 16 destroyed the Dong Lo trans-shipment point 23 miles south of Hanoi. A boat repair facility was also wiped out. Yippee. I'm sure Uncle Ho will be surrendering any day now.

10 September 1967 ... 86th day. Ibid.

On the first launch at 0800 this morning, Attack Squadron 163 lost yet another A-4 Skyhawk. They are losing the most planes in the Air Group; only ten birds left, seven operational. One was shot up yesterday and will need extensive repair work. The A-4 this morning was the victim of a cold catapult. It plopped into the water; the pilot ejected and was rescued by Michael and his crew. LT. Dale Landroth was piloting the A-4 when it lost power. The entire ejection and rescue sequence took place about 50 yards off the starboard side of the ship in a span of about five minutes.

A-4s and F-8s from the Ole Risky hit a virgin target today: the Cam Pha port repair facilities. They not only popped its cherry, the place was almost entirely destroyed. The AAA site defending the facilities was obliterated by CDR Burt Shepherd, Carrier Air Wing 16 Commander. The Phuong Dinh bridge, six miles north of Thanh Hoa, was dropped by our bombs today. Last night, the Cam Pha mines were hit during night strikes. Containing the largest coal deposits in

Vietnam, our bombs collapsed and blocked off the entrances. I'm sure they're be reopened in a couple of days.

11 September 1967 ... 87th day. Ibid.

This evening the U.S.S. Cimarron, a tanker, was making her approach alongside the Oriskany to transfer fuel. The aft end of the tanker began to drift sideways. I was sitting in the shop when this weird sound came over the squawk box.

Dick Aden dropped his book. "What the hell was that?"

"The collision alarm I think."

We ran up to the Flight Deck as did dozens of others. The Cimarron came within two feet of crunching into the Oriskany's Number Three Elevator. There was excitement for a short time but no collision. Eventually shot lines were passed, fuel hoses suspended between ships and the underway replenishment proceeded without further incident.

On the squawk box tonight, CAPT Billy told us that the combined Air Wings of all the carriers on Yankee Station made heavy raids today on Haiphong and its suburbs in a major effort to isolate the largest port in North Vietnam from the rest of the country. Apparently, just about all road and rail traffic to and from the city has been cut off. One of the Photo Intelligencemen told me there was damage to foreign ships in the harbor but that's what they get for supplying Uncle Ho with the tools of war—the dumb shits. Even with today's extensive raids on Haiphong, the sea passage into the harbor still remains off-limits to our bombers... LBJ's orders. Even dumber but I'm just a grunt. What do I know?

At 2100, PH2 Jackson telephoned us from the Flash Photo Lab inviting us down for what he called educational 8-millimeter motion pictures. As I mentioned previously, the flash lab is a small compartment containing two of the large processors that develop our aerial reconnaissance film after we unload it from returned aircraft. Jackson works down there by his lonesome. So he has developed some diversions from his boring job. For about an hour Jackson, Lehmann, Duncan, and I watched men and women participating in more types of sexual activity than I ever knew existed. It was my first time to see porn flicks. I was mesmerized and damn! Did I ever have a major hard-on! A couple of times I almost lost my rocks right then and there – major pud pounding under the sheets tonight. Ironic, isn't it? Tonight, the North Vietnamese are licking their wounds and, thirty miles out in the Gulf, sailor boys are jacking off in their bunks. I think that captures the essence of this whole operation.

12 September 1967 ... 88th day. Ibid.

This evening at 1800, I mustered in Hangar Bay Two for my first major working party. The U.S.S. Mars was to pull up alongside and transfer groceries to us at 1845. My particular group, dubbed Traffic Control, consisted of Third-Class Petty Officers only. We were supposed to have some type of supervisory position but for an hour-and-a-half, until 1930, we did nothing but sit on our asses. At that time, I left to eat on the mess deck; wandered up to the Photo Shop afterwards, had a smoke, and went back down to the Hangar Deck at 2000. Damn, the whole deck, fore to aft, was filled with boxes, crates, and bags stacked around, in-between, and under parked aircraft. Hundreds of men were working pallets of groceries, sliding boxes down roller tracks to reefers below decks, passing stores hand to hand by human chain. Forklifts scampered in every direction carrying loaded pallets. Finally pitching in, I helped stack pallets for a while. A Chief told me to take a case of blueberries and apricots up to a forward reefer. Instead, I took them to our Photo Shop and stashed them away for my buddies.

On my way back down to the Hangar Bay, I ducked under the intake of an F-8 Crusader and rose up on the other side directly into the edge of a UHT horizontal stabilizer on another F-8. I grabbed my head, yelling, "Son-of-a-bitch!"

There was a big gash with blood flowing. I descended a ladder down to Sickbay. Wouldn't you know it? I thought to myself. Instant karma for stealing food supplies.

A Sickbay Medical Corpsman shaved off a patch of hair, applied antiseptic and sewed up my wound with five stitches. Asking no permission after treatment, I secured myself from work detail, ascended to the berthing compartment, showered and hit the rack. I figured I deserved it. Wonder if I can get a Purple Heart for being wounded in action?

CHAPTER XXI
THE DEVIL WITHIN

After seeing those porn movies two nights ago, I can't shake the images out of my mind. They just replay over and over. I get a hard-on every time I think of them. Yes, I screwed three whores in the Philippines but I've never made love to a Round Eye back in the States. I tried with Peggy Lee but only got to first base. And, because she stopped it, I'll never really know if I had what it takes to go all the way.

Am I a sicko? I know I have a dark side. I am an artist. I draw my own pornographic pictures. They're very realistic; well-drawn. I could probably sell them to an underground dealer and make a lot of money on them but I don't. They're just for me; for my own personal satisfaction. And the next day, I'll rip them up. I've been doing this for a couple of years now. It's like a drug addiction.

In junior high school, I drew monsters. It made me popular with the other boys. It was my social bridge to acceptance. If not for the monsters, I would have been just an ugly, pimply-faced nerd that nobody wanted to know. My art teacher, Mrs. Verna Mae Peterson, encouraged me. I made a painting with tempera of this large, muscular, werewolf-type creature. It was carrying the body of a dead woman. Her abdominal cavity had been torn open. Her intestines were hanging to the ground in a pool of blood. The guys thought it was really cool. The girls found it totally revolting. I took pleasure in both responses. Imagine my surprise, when I came to school the day after I had completed the painting and found it displayed on the wall outside the art room. It stayed up there for almost a month, the subject of much controversy.

Mr. Alexander, my shop teacher, called me out into the hall one day to have a confidential chat. Frowning and rubbing his chin, he made this observation: "Gerald, I don't know what your home life is like but I see some disturbing behavior in you that should be addressed. You have a wonderful talent in your art, son, but these pictures of monsters and blood and guts are, like I said, disturbing."

I remember my reaction. I smiled. I was pleased with the power I was wielding. My artistic talent not only caused emotional reactions in my fellow students; it was worrying the teachers.

"I think you need some counseling, son. Have you ever thought about that?" He continued to blather but I tuned out the rest. I had heard it before. People who knew me couldn't seem to figure out if I was gifted or hexed. They still can't. I like it like that.

That painting on the art room display board was my personal vengeance on those goddamned junior high bitches; those that giggled at me from their hallway huddles when I walked by them. In high school, my art teacher, George Rush, recognizing my advanced ability, allowed me to do my own independent projects. One of those was a pen-and-ink drawing of Nero's garden party. I had read how the evil Emperor killed Christians, soaked their bodies in oil, hung them upside-down in his courtyards and ignited them, using them as lighting for his all-night wine-guzzling orgies. I drew the scene in all its nauseating detail. Again, the boys said, "Cool!" And the girls said, "Gross!" I don't even pretend to understand it all. I was president of the Luther League, the youth group of our church. I was a good kid and a bad kid at the same time. I was looking for a very nice girl but also a very bad girl. Do all young men have these conflicts? And, what about whores? Well, in my mind, prostitutes are bad girls. Matter of fact, they are professional bad girls. As I said earlier in this diary, you don't make love to whores, you fuck them. There's a difference. They don't require love and courtship, all they want is my money. I go to the bedroom with them and do the deed with no affection. They take my money and leave. All my life I have been told that girls who have sex outside of marriage are bad girls... sluts. I've also been told by my dad, "Son, sex is the most beautiful expression of love in a marriage."

Although I can appreciate the difference, that being, sex is meant for marriage only; my psyche has some difficulty reconciling the two messages. Sexually active girls are bad but sexually active wives are good. I'm afraid that someday if and when I wed the Pollyanna I'm looking for and fulfill my husbandly duty with her, I'm going to feel like I'm turning a good girl into a bad girl. In other words, I change my wife into a slut. And here's the weirdest part: if my wife becomes a slut, the good boy in me will reject the bad girl I created in her. My angel and devil will be in a clinch hold.

Who are the good girls in my life? My sister comes to mind immediately. Who are the good women? My Swedish great-grandmother, Sofia, was a saint. My grandmothers, Florence and Mildred, are good women, and so too is my mother.

Is this some kind of Freudian thing? What about my porn drawings? Would I want the good girls and good women of my life to be treated like that? Absolutely not! So, I must be punishing the bad girls, right? And, in so doing, I get aroused. So, do I hate myself, too? Well, the good boy hates the bad boy but the bad boy is taking orders from his balls and they seem to be happy about it all. Maybe it's hormones out of control. Or maybe I just have a bad habit of analyzing the shit out of everything.

Or, maybe I am insane. Maybe Mr. Alexander was right.

CHAPTER XXII
FIRST PERIOD FINALS

13 September 1967 ... 89th day.
Gulf of Tonkin, North Vietnam.

Same unpredictable weather. All sunrise sorties for the entire carrier air wing were cancelled because of rain. Flight schedule was altered. Two missions were flown by Photo Bird 602 at 1200 and 1500. Today's COD flight transported four of our fucked-up cameras back to Cubi Point. From there, they'll be flown to Naval Air Station Atsugi, Japan for repairs.

This evening in the Ship's Photo Lab, we watched *Sylvia* starring George Maharis and Carol Baker. Damn, that Carol Baker is a sultry and gorgeous creature! What I would give to have a night in bed with someone like her! She is a bad girl of course.

September 14, 1967 ... 90th day. Ibid.

Dick, Ernest and I flocked together under the protective wing of our aircraft on the Flight Deck and yelled to the heavens, "Keep it coming!" And the god of precipitation replied with sheets of rain. But the voice of the demigod on the superstructure said, "Start the Jets!" That particular god is an idiot. So we sent Ronald out into the fog and rain. He returned an hour later having taken no photos because of overcast conditions over yonder in Commie Land.

We were on standby the rest of the day as the warlords prayed for the weather to improve but it didn't. The rain intensified and finally at 1700 flight quarters were secured. O beautiful, beautiful rain! It cools the air, causes the weary to slumber and, for a day at least, stops the Air War.

15 September 1967 ... 91st day. Ibid.

More rain, wind and choppy seas. No flight ops. More bullshit. I had to stand an Aircraft Integrity Watch today from noon to 1600 – four boring hours of walking around the Navy gray birds making sure no saboteur has thrown a monkey wrench into the jet turbine or punctured a hole in a fuel tank. Fat chance but you never know.

The Hangar Bay was jam-packed with A-4s and Spads inches apart from one another. Mechanics were swarming over the dormant war machines like little worker ants. It seems ridiculous that a guy should have to walk around maintaining aircraft security when dozens of squadron personnel are doing the same thing at the same time but who am I to question the wisdom of my great Naval leaders?

During the vigil I was baptized by the Gulf of Tonkin. The opening on port side Number Two Elevator was completely exposed to the elements. It was a great show. I could see violent whirlpools and curls of seawater rebounding from the swift hull of the ship. A dull grey sheet of precipitation hung in the sky as puffs of translucent vapor swirled in the wind below the grey. Peaks of salt water, capped with foam, rose up from the sea – peaks and valleys undulating and then slamming together in an explosion of mist. Gales howled through the nets, rigging, antennas and external structures of the Old Risky. It was a magnificent demonstration of God's dominion over the elements. Our escort destroyers, the Eton and the MacKenzie were tossing and rolling like children's bath toys. Their bows would rise from the water, pause and then plummet down into and under the surface of the water creating a white tempest over the length of the ship. Attempting to lessen the turbulence they eventually fell in line behind the Oriskany and rode in our wake. Even our massive carrier rolled and jerked about.

As I stood in awe, the ship rolled to port and a gigantic wave crashed into the hull, rolled back, hit the supports for the elevator and shot a geyser of water directly into the Hangar Bay and directly on top of me. I was soaked head to toe. The mechanics who saw it happen thought it was fucking hilarious. I had two more hours of watch duty so I finished my beat, looking like a drowned rat with hecklers everywhere that I wandered. I must admit it was somewhat amusing.

This evening, showered and sporting a dry uniform, I hung out in the Photo Intelligence area drawing ideas for the cover of the next VFP-63 Det 34 Cruise Report. Slugging down coffee and smoking Lucky Strike Filter's, I eventually tired of the cover art and began detailed drawings of naked women. In P.I. I don't have to look far for inspiration. Their bulkheads are covered with Playmate centerfolds.

September 16, 1967 ... the 92nd day. South China Sea.

The sun has returned. The Photo boys and I awoke, dressed and made our migration down to the squadron Photo Shop, now known as Danko's Penthouse, and prepared for the day's labor. Lieutenant Muffley decided that we needed to pull the KA53 monster cameras out of stations three in 602 and 603 and replace them with KA45s for air-to-air photographs on tomorrow's flights. They wanted wider angle lenses for taking vanity shots of one another as they departed the carrier and flew north to Japan for R&R. Apparently, we steamed out of Tonkin Gulf overnight and are now on the first stretch of our voyage to Japan. This line period on Yankee Station is officially complete, no more combat missions. We lucked out this month because many hops were rained out. I'm sure the brass and the cowboys who love bombing the living shit out of the Vietnamese didn't see it as luck. Tough titty. Only five planes were downed during this period with one pilot killed. Two aviators were captured by the North Vietnamese.

By late morning, we encountered heavy cumulus clouds. Once again we had rain and gales of almost typhoon strength. Ray and Dick were installing KA45s when the storm hit us. Sheets of rain dumped on the Flight Deck and my fellow PhART's were forced to abandon their tasks. Throughout the day, an occasional volunteer would go topside trying to complete the installation but each one returned soaked to the bone, having accomplished nothing.

17 September 1967 ... 93rd day. South China Sea, I think.

The old man, LCDR Ronald G. Sonniksen is flying out tomorrow for a little golfing vacation in Atsugi, Japan while the ship docks in Sasebo. He ordered us to remove the two big cameras in 601, cover the bay windows with cardboard and padding and in the empty compartment load his luggage and golf clubs. R.H.I.P. Rank has its privileges.

18 September 1967 ... 94th day.
Between Taiwan and Okinawa in the East China Sea.

No flights today. Tomorrow we arrive in Japan but of course, this being Uncle Sam's Navy, the Officers could not let the day go by without some sort of micky mouse bullshit. The boss couldn't decide if he wanted to use 601 or 602 for his Golf Cart Special. Therefore to be sure he is pleased with either decision, Dick and I were ordered to pull the big cameras out of 602 as well, taping down cardboard and padding in those bays. In addition we loaded some color film in the forward nose bay so Ron can take pretty pictures of Mt. Fuji.

At 1300, the entire gang of Photo Recon Squadron 63 Detachment 34 shed our denims for our dress blue uniforms. We mustered on the Flight Deck for our official Cruise Book group portrait. A memorial service was held at 1400 on the Flight Deck for LCDR Perry, the only pilot killed during this line period. None of our detachment was required to attend. So we didn't.

19 September 1967 ... 95th day.
Somewhere south of Japan.

The eagle shit for all personnel this morning, so I wove my way through the corridors and hatches up to the forecastle of the ship where I stood in line for nearly three hours waiting for my thirty seconds with the disbursing clerk. U.S. Servicemen visiting Japan use Military Payment Certificates – more commonly known as Funny Money. Each bill has the face of a Hollywood glamour girl, such as Jane Mansfield, instead of an ugly president. I collected $339 worth of Funny Money adding it to the money saved from our port period in Subic. Total is $618.

At noon, Mr. Sonniksen was catapulted off the ship. He decided on 601. The rest of us were busy. Hebb covered the launch. Dick and I held field day on the Photo Shop straightening up the old farts' shit house. Last night while I was working in the ship's Photo Lab, the poker boys were busted. Five of them, Watson, Koppler, Arlington, Nicholas, and good old Hines were in the squadron shop playing cards and betting. Gambling is strictly forbidden onboard ship. Someone ratted on them. The Chief Master-at-Arms walked in and placed them all on report but the Det is a tight group. Because all the violators were Senior Enlisted Petty Officers, they will, no doubt, receive nothing more than a slap on the hands – if that.

CHAPTER XXIII
THE LAND OF THE RISING SUN

19 September 1967 ... 96th day. Sasebo, Japan.

Entering port was a great occasion even though I had duty today with no liberty in the evening. Islands, islands everywhere. The day was hazy bright, the water calm. Craggy rocks protruded through the seawater surface. It's called Ninety-Nine Islands. As the Oriskany meandered through the obstacle course following the well-marked channel into Sasebo Harbor, sailors lined the catwalks and Hangar Bay openings surveying the shoreline for glimpses of those wonderful creatures that they hadn't seen for weeks: women.

The city of Sasebo is sprawled out at the base of a mountain. The fog-blanketed valleys and lush green peaks reminded me of Subic Bay. The layout of the lower quadrant reminded me of Pearl Harbor. An immense shipyard hugs the waterfront with docked vessels flying colors from many countries. The O-Boat tied up across the bay from the city proper at a U.S. Army Fuel Pier positioned directly below a foliage-covered miniature mountain rising perhaps 800 feet from base to summit. The air is cooler here, invigorating. Hines and two of his soul brothers put on their liberty whites and their sunglasses and headed down the gangplank for a night of wine, women and song. Me, I turned in at 1830 and fell fast asleep. I had been awake for 36 hours.

20 to 30 September 1967. In Port, Sasebo, Japan.

Danko went to the military hospital in Sasebo for a hernia operation. He may be there a awhile. Rumor has it that he may even receive new orders and be reassigned. No Danko for the rest of the cruise? Damn, that would tear my heart out.

On the second day in-port, I finally made it off the big iron tub for my first encounter with Japan. I had expected something similar to the Philippines and Olongapo City but was pleasantly surprised. First impression was the cleanliness of the city, the homes, the people – everything and everyone is neat, orderly and clean. I hopped in a taxi by the pier and was amazed. The exterior of the car was polished: no dents, scratches or chipped paint. The interior had not a scrap of paper or spot of dirt. It was clean. It smelled cleaner than any Filipino taxi or jeepney, even any American taxi. Traffic in Japan runs on the left side of the street, like England. Driver's seats are on the right side. It's weird. Riding to downtown Sasebo, we passed through the ship yards: ships in dry dock, ship hulls, tankers, freighters, gigantic hammerhead cranes, trestle cranes, huge brick buildings housing the furnaces and forges of the steel molders. Japanese people in the yards wear the same work uniform, male and female alike sharing the same tasks. Equality of the sexes. And, considering what a potentially grimy job shipyard work can be, all the laborers were still well-groomed.

The business district downtown is remarkably clean. No trash blowing through the streets. No garbage in the gutters. I didn't even see a cigarette butt on the sidewalks. In Japanese culture, I suspect, people are taught from infancy that cleanliness is a serious matter. I have never ever seen an American city or town that could compare to Sasebo.

There is nothing old or backward about this nation. Comparatively speaking, Japan is more advanced than the U.S. as far as modern conveniences are concerned, at least in the areas I visited. The department stores, the motion picture theaters, bus stations, restaurants all reflect a beauty of design in architecture that is both attractive and highly functional. They make the most of limited space and do it with style.

In most locations, the benjo – water closet, restroom, head – is a common area for both male and female. Apparently this has been an accepted practice in Japanese culture for centuries. Men and women bathe together at public baths. They have a healthy attitude toward bath and toilet matters and nudity. We could learn a lesson from them. In Japan, you don't see billboards with half-naked women advertising products. Japanese movie ads do not highlight erotic scenes with provocative language. There are only about three skin mag titles sold on the newsstands. Lack of interest? I doubt that. After all, how long have Geishas been around?

It seems the Japanese have not been corrupted with western attitudes. I surmise they see life for what it is and live it realistically. Sex is a part of life. They look upon it as just that: a part of life. It's not blown out of proportion, distorted, twisted, and made into something dirty as it is in America. By the way, I bought all three skin mags titles for my sea chest.

The people of this country are quiet, extremely courteous, and very warm-hearted. They don't speak unless they have something to say. Traditional courtesies and respect are still expected: bowing to one who is senior to you in social order or age; women avoid eye contact with men until they know them well. Highest honor is accorded the elderly because of their presumed wisdom. I must learn more about the religion of Japan. I must admit it is a little confusing. There seems to be an indigenous form of Buddhism practiced but there is also a folk religion with even more ancient roots called Shinto – in Japanese, Shinshu. On the altars of the temples and shrines I visited, three figures predominate. I don't know who they represent. This seems to be a much different than the Theravada Buddhism I studied in California. The temples and shrines are built in the ancient architectural style, that is, corners of the roofs curved up and the torii gate at the entrance to the holy place with ends curved upward. I am told this prevents demons from entering within. Majorities of the housing in the outlying residential areas are also built in the old traditional manner with rice paper or frosted glass panels, low furniture, tatami mats on the floor, curved corners on the roofs.

Very few people here speak English which goes to prove how self-sufficient this country is, how little they rely on American assistance unlike the Philippines where at least half of the population of Luzon speaks English in order to be educated with their printed-in-the-USA textbooks. In Japan, bar girls, Navy Exchange employees, and some taxi drivers speak our language. Otherwise, you're out of luck, G.I. Joe!

With compulsory public education for all children, the Japanese are very literate and academically advanced. They are also very fitness oriented. Participation in some sport is mandatory for every student. I didn't notice the type of rebellious youth we see in America. They all tend to conform to the accepted standards. They're clean-cut, healthy, and all wear uniforms to school to prevent the sort of class bias we have in the states because of the type and expense of clothing students wear to school. The boys wear blue trousers, white shirts, blue jackets and a blue cap. The older ones also wear ties. Girls wear blue plaid skirts and white blouses, white socks and blue slip-ons. I've found the kids to be well-behaved and respectful to elders when I encounter them on the streets or on buses. There are no giggling, shouting or heckling groups of trouble makers. None own cars. Their objective is education and landing a good career. Social activities take a back seat to academics. Schools in Japan run a different schedule than those in America. They divide the school day into two shifts: morning and afternoon. They attend school six days a week. There is no summer vacation as we Americans know it but rather three semesters in the year, each three months long, each followed by a one-month vacation. Inspired, I would say. Japanese students seem to be very aware of world events and cultures beyond their own. After school, record shops are crowded with little blue-cloaked bodies listening to and buying the latest 45 rpm singles by the Beatles, the Rolling Stones, Jefferson Airplane, Donovan... the British Invasion has also invaded Japan. They even dig the psychedelic tunes. Maybe in their own little worlds at home, they dress in mod clothes and miniskirts but in public they please their elders.

The farmers' and fishermen's market is one of the old-style businesses that still thrive even in the big cities. In a street lined with small booths, each operated by one family, one can buy all the living necessities from fabrics to fish, flowers to herbs, ceramics to home-grown vegetables. Food from the sea is available in the fish markets featuring, in addition to fish, such delicacies as squid, octopus, shark, eel, and seaweed. Many men and women solicit their fruit, flowers and veggies from portable carts. Looking around, it seemed to me that most of the farm folk bringing their products to town are elderly. Perhaps it's a fading tradition soon to be overtaken entirely by the supermarkets.

The atmosphere of Sasebo was so very enjoyable that I found the small nightclub strip, with its sailor bars, to be grossly out of place. I probably spent a total of three hours in the bars during my ten day vacation. I didn't even try to engage the services of a prostitute of which there are very few. And the few that do solicit generally prefer Japanese clientele not American.

With visions of females in heat, a thousand squids made a beeline everyday straight for the drinking and fucking district while in-port on liberty. They'd drink until midnight and stagger back to the ship vomiting in the clean streets, vomiting in the clean taxis, vomiting in their racks where they spun out and crashed into an inebriated coma. These guys visit a foreign country and don't even care to experience the cultural differences of that new land? Many of them will have nothing to relate to their children and grandchildren of their time overseas, except: "Well, I went to Olongapoo, drank San Magoo and got laid by a whore. Then I went to Japan, drank Asahi beer, and got ripped off by a whore." Hell, they won't be able to tell what they actually did to their kids, grandkids, girlfriends or wives, so they'll just maintain their collective code of silence about their escapades as military youth. Sharing it with their buddies every so often down at the VFW. Sea stories.

With a wad of Funny Money bulging in my front pocket, I taxied over to the Navy Exchange on my first day in Sasebo and bought the camera of my dreams: The Nikon F with Photomic TN finder. I also lucked out and bought the first telephoto zoom lens made by Nikkor. It's an 85mm-250mm zoom, about 15-inches long, weighing about 3-to-4 pounds. And even though it contains 16 elements, it still has wide open aperature speed of F4.5. Additionally, I bought an electronic flash, shutter cable release, a variety of filters, lens shade, and twenty-five rolls of film and mailers for each roll. Total expenditure: $525. During our Rest and Recreation period in Sasebo, I shot up 13 of those 25 rolls.

I did a lot of shopping around the city – mostly, window shopping. I did get the Karate Gi for Hermie the House Boy that he requested. It was 1500 Yen. I bought a pair of walkie-talkies for my little 6-year-old brother Jeff for 3800 Yen, a little over $10 American. Jeffrey's birthday was September 28. The gift will be a little late getting to him but I'm sure he'll enjoy it whenever he gets it.

Most of my transactions with the Japanese people were somewhat comical. The language barrier is a problem. Case in point: On the third day, Dick Aden and I approached a taxi driver in downtown Sasebo.

I asked him, "Where can I get a good sukiyaki dinner?"
He looked at me bewildered. He didn't know English.
So I merely said, "Soo-key-yah-kee! Soo-key-yah-kee!"

Dick said to me, "I don't think they pronounce it the same as us. They say it more like ski-YAHK-ee."

When Dick said this, the driver's eyes lit up and he said, "Ski-YAHK-ee? Okay! You get in. I take."

The driver took us out of the city and we started climbing the zig-zag roads that led up the face of Mt. Yumihari which I had discovered by then was the name of the beautiful green mountain overlooking Sasebo. We diverted off the main road into a forested area. If this had happened in the Philippines, I'd be afraid that we were being delivered to a base camp of Hukbalahop, the Communist guerillas but, I felt safe in Japan. No Huks.

Set back in and among the trees was a wonderful traditional-style house. We thanked and paid the driver. Opening a wooden gate and meandering down a stone path we were met at the entrance by three smiling women wearing kimonos.

They bowed and greeted us, "Komban wa," which means Good Evening.

We returned the greeting.

The youngest of the women, probably around 25 years old, could speak a little English. "My name ees Akiko. Prease remove shoe, prease."

We pulled off our Navy-issue black shoes and put on comfortable house slippers they provided for guests.

"Forrow me, prease." Akiko was not a raging beauty but not ugly either. She had a full-moon face with lovely brown almond eyes, short black hair with bangs. Not my Asian fantasy girl by any means but she was woman and I hadn't been treated nicely by a female for a while. I loved the way she attempted to speak our language. And, she was so short, so petite. So cute. Erotic thoughts passed through my mind briefly, then dissolved. Akiko was not a bar girl. An elegant, burgundy kimono covered most of her body. She wore little, if any, makeup; no jewelry. She was the kind of girl I could marry, not just fuck. I appreciated her modesty and gentle manner. Those traits, in turn, brought out the civilized gentleman in me — even though I was wearing a silly, sailor suit.

Dick and I were taken to our own room. It was just what I had been looking for: the real Japan. The name of the inn was Hakuun Banriso which translates as: a place in the clouds. The architecture was exposed beam. There were dark wooden panel walls on three sides with a scroll painting hanging on one panel. An exotic potted plant set on a teakwood platform. Tatami mats covered the floor. Centered on the floor of the approximately 20-by-20 foot room was the low square table where we would be served dinner. Four cushions were in place for seating. The south side of the room had traditional rice paper sliding panels walls, that when pulled back, led us out onto a deck overlooking the entire city of Sasebo, the bay area, and islands beyond. It was evening by now and the city sparkled like illuminated diamonds on black felt. The last hint of daylight created a deep reddish glow on the water. A cool but comfortable breeze filled our room; fragrant incense was burning. A feeling of total serenity embraced me. We had been on that damned ship for so long – that never quiet ship. It hums, clanks and groans constantly like living in the belly of a gigantic beast. But Hakuun Banriso was so quiet, all I could hear was a faint ringing in my ears, the sound of my own blood flowing through me.

Akiko invited us to take our place, cross-legged, at the table. Dick and I sat on our cushions not speaking a word as we were served hot sake. Pronounced SAH-kee, it is Japanese rice wine that tastes terrible cold but is quite good warm. An elderly mamasan entered, setting a bottle of propane gas just inside the doorway. She came back and set a burner plate on the mat and placed a metal bowl on top of it. Akiko entered with a tray of sliced beef, onions, rice noodles, a variety of vegetables and other mysterious ingredients for our sukiyaki. Both of the women kneeled on the tatami and began cooking the meal. With what few words and phrases she had learned, Akiko conversed. We offered her a cigarette and she smoked with us. When the meal was cooked, three bowls were placed before each of us: one with steamed rice, one with a beaten raw egg, and the third with the sukiyaki. We were given hashi chopsticks and shown how to use them. The sukiyaki is to be picked up, dipped in the egg and then down the hatch. I mastered the hashi quickly. Good food. Good company. Peaceful atmosphere. I felt like I had died and gone to heaven.

Following sukiyaki, we were served green tea in a steaming pot. Both Dick and I had small tea cups; Akiko struggled to continue the conversation as she poured. She stayed as we sipped. After five minutes, we became so amused by our inability to communicate, the three of us were reduced to laughter. The other two older women came in with more hot sake. The five of us enjoyed laughter, sake and smokes. Only too soon was it time to call a taxi and return below to that goddamned hunk of pig iron floating in the bay.

    I enjoyed that evening so much that I returned two more times: once with PT3 Chapin and once with PT3 Walt Lehmann. On those occasions, we had overnight passes, and not only ate at Hakuun Banriso but slept there, too. As soon as we arrived for the overnighters, we stripped off our government garb, placing robes on our bods. Prior to the meal, we took a 120-degree hotsy bath. Returning to our room, supper was served. When slumber time arrived, the table was removed from the center of the room and the ladies brought out bed rolls from hideaway closets. The mattress with sheet and quilt was laid directly on top of the tatami. And, we drifted off to a peaceful utopia. Believe it or not, the bath, dinner and overnight lodging only cost 15,000 Yen each. That's about 20-bucks American.

                  *   *   *   *   *   *   *

    The central park of Sasebo is built on steep hills on the north side of the city. Ancient stone-laid paths wind through the dense trees and shrubbery. Little Shinto shrines and Torii are built in secluded areas for those who wish to come meditate in solitaire. With new camera and telephoto lens in hand, I stepped lightly. Down the slope, perhaps two-hundred feet below my vantage point, a middle-aged Japanese woman in simple kimono knelt on the earth, facing a small wooden shrine. Beams of filtered sunlight cast kaleidoscopic patterns around her. I raised my camera and captured the tranquil moment.

    Some of the boys in other squadrons decided to take a daytrip over to the resurrected city of Nagasaki, about 100 miles northwest of here. They asked if I wanted to come along. I thought about it for a day. I pondered the irony of that tranquil moment in the Central Park compared to the horror and anguish America unleashed on Nagasaki and Hiroshima 22 years ago. Yeah, the two atomic bombs brought a halt to Japanese aggression in eastern Asia and the Pacific islands but at what cost? Around 200,000 civilians – men, women and children – were killed instantly; more died later because of radiation sickness. Yes, I've heard the justification. Wiping out those non-strategic Japanese cities saved the lives of perhaps a hundred thousand American troops because the U.S. didn't have to make an invasion of the mainland in order to win the war. Okay. I did some quick math and realized just about every Japanese citizen over the age of thirty has some recollection of World War II. As I explore Sasebo, I am continually encountering people who remember that I was once the enemy. Enemies then. Friends now? Who knows what thoughts, what sorrows, what grudges they may carry. Do some still hate us? Or, do they hate what Tojo did to their country? Strange the turn of events in merely two decades: back then, Japan was our enemy; China, an ally of sorts. Today, China is our enemy; Japan, an ally. Back then, Germany was our enemy; Russia, an ally of sorts. Today, Russia is our enemy; Germany, an ally of sorts. The enemy of my enemy is my friend. What a friggen' mess we humans make. No, I didn't need to visit Nagasaki. Even though I was born in 1947, I have relived the disaster hundreds of times on television ever since T.V. entered our homes in the early fifties.

Despite our history, the people of Nippon, their name for Japan, have been good to me. I thought I was in love with the Philippines but Japan has absolutely captured my heart. We had ten magnificent, sunny days. The nights were so cool I needed a blanket. No place has ever made me feel like going AWOL as much as Sasebo.

While in-port, our squadron duties were kept to a minimum. Most of the time, the Photo Mates just moped around until we heard those magic words, "Liberty Call!" I did have one four-hour Aircraft Integrity Watch, again, on Hangar Bay Three where I witnessed hoards of drunks staggering back aboard ship from 2200 to midnight.

Many were cursing the Japanese: "Fuckin' whore, she took my money and disappeared."

"Goddamn gooks kicked me out of the bar. 'Called the fuckin' Shore Patrol on me."

"Slant-eyed bastards! Couldn't find even one bitch who'd fuck, no matter how much money I gave her. Little prick tease!"

"We shoulda dropped the A-bomb on the whole goddamned country!"

Sometimes I am so ashamed to be an American serviceman especially when I get lumped in with any criticism of these shit-faced, bigoted assholes.

During duty nights in-port, I was usually down in the ship's Photo Lab printing Cruise Book pictures or personal stuff to send home. We mustered every morning at 0745 wearing our white Dixie Cup hats instead of the usual denim caps because we must look like regulation fleet sailors in-port.

CHAPTER XXIV
BACK TO THE CARNAGE

1 October 1967 ... 107th day.
Leaving Japan and steaming south back to Vietnam.

The U.S.S. Oriskany (CVA-34) has been ordered to depart Sasebo immediately and proceed full steam back to the Gulf of Tonkin. Not sure why. Peons are not privileged to that information. Last night, I raised my final glass of Akadama plum wine to Japan saying, "Sayonnara for now."

This morning at 0800. the ship pulled in its lines, maneuvered the channel and set forth to open sea. We go in peace. I'm well rested and mentally revived. The men have had their fun each in his own way. Just about all of us are out of money. I didn't think I would ever hear myself saying this but it's good to be back at sea doing my recon photo thing again. There's a rumor afloat that the Air Wing will be doing a lot of night flying this line period. I like that. It means less photo missions and more late morning sleep-ins.

Flight Quarters were sounded at 1130 today but Photo Recon Squadron 63 didn't fly so we just screwed around, dozed and, from the catwalk, watched the frothing ocean slap the sides of the ship.

*   *   *   *   *   *   *

Lieutenant Commander John McCain came onboard yesterday before we pulled out of Sasebo. He apparently asked for reassignment to the Old Risky and Attack Squadron 163, the Saints. It was his A-4 Skyhawk that may have been hit by a rocket on the Forrestal; his ruptured fuel tank that saturated the flight deck aft. He narrowly escaped with his life. I would think he would be happy as hell to go back to the States but I hear that both his father and grandfather were Navy Admirals so I reckon he has something to prove.

2 October 1967 ... 108th day.
In the western Pacific, heading south.

We had payday this morning. In addition to my regular salary, I received my hazardous duty pay for working the Flight Deck. Combined, it came out as $210. I could have used that a couple of days ago to buy my Nikon wide angle lens, bellows extension, slide copy attachment and other accessories. What the hell, I can get them in Subic; if not in Subic, then Hong Kong; if not there, than in Yokosuka on our way home.

Today's flight schedule was royally fucked up. It had us, Photo Recon Squadron 63, down for six flights. We only have three birds now. We gave 601 to our squadron detachment on the Constellation and only one of the three birds we have is in up-status. We were scheduled for six but we only flew once and secured. I detest these days when the big boys don't have their shit together.

Speaking of the big boy, Captain Billy finally spoke to us today. He didn't have much to say: "Congratulations men for your outstanding conduct while in Sasebo."

Apparently, we left no one behind in jail or the Sasebo morgue. He also told us indirectly why we left three days early. Something big is about to happen in North Vietnam. All available air power is gathering for a major strike somewhere. So, the Old Risky was called out to participate in the fun and games. Hey, maybe LBJ finally decided to seal off Haiphong Harbor.

3 October 1967 ... 109th day.
In the western Pacific, south of Taiwan.

While we were frolicking in Sasebo, pilots from the carrier U.S.S. Coral Sea destroyed the last intact bridge that carries the only major road and rail line out of Haiphong. Four bridges in Haiphong have been destroyed since September 11. I also learned that this upcoming operation is going to target two or three Russian MIG bases, petroleum storage areas and a major power plant. Additionally, we'll try to destroy as many bridges as possible along the Vietnam-China border to stop the influx of war materiel from Chairman Mao.

Regarding R&R, I've been informed by LT Merkin Muffley that the Big Zero is traveling to Yokosuka next month after this line period instead of Subic Bay as scheduled. During the period that was scheduled, another carrier will be parked at Leyte Pier with a CVS anchored in the bay. Plus, the Philippine elections on November 14 and 15 will close the gates to Olongapo because those hot-blooded Filipinos become homicidal during elections. It's a shaky democracy they have, replete with mucho corruption.

Because we've had to pull out of liberty port early the last two times, the brass thought we deserve something better. So word has it. We'll be in Yokosuka – pronounced yah-KOOS-kah – in November. It's on the outer rim of Tokyo bay. I'll experience Tokyo, one of the world's largest cities, for the first time. Captain Billy Holder has to officially confirm before we can get too excited but I'm sure his heart is in the right place.

Mister Sonniksen, flew back aboard today. He returned in Photo Bird 601, the one we thought we'd never see again. According to the grapevine, he got the runaround during his vacation. No sooner had he arrived in Atsugi and he was ordered to fly to Cubi Point, Philippines. The brass gods were arguing amongst themselves as to where 601 should go. Some of the other detachments are hurting for aircraft more than us. From Cubi, Sonniksen flew out to the Coral Sea for four days where he did nada. He returned to Cubi.

Damned determined to have himself some sort of R&R, he caught the shuttle bus up to Angeles City, Pampanga, the town outside the gates of Clark Air Force Base. I don't know if he played golf but there are plenty of other diversions..

The Oriskany had a minor collision today with the U.S.S. Hopewell, a destroyer we were refueling. The two ships were steaming side-by-side with hoses strung between. The destroyer lost rudder for some reason and her tail end began drifting toward the O-Boat. Collision alarms sounded, the starboard antennas were brought up to vertical and the Number Three Elevator was folded. The Hopewell scraped against our starboard side aft. Fuel lines that had been transferring black oil snapped in half and sprayed like a garden hose gone wild. The tails of the aircraft hanging over the flight deck were blackened. The starboard hull of our ship that had just been painted in Sasebo was spray-painted black. Fortunately only minor damage was sustained by either ship. No personnel were injured. The Number Three Elevator was whacked and will be inoperable for the remainder of this line period, only two operational. What a pain in the ass for the Hangar Bay boys!

Six flights had been scheduled for today but thank you, Grandfather Spirit, we only flew one mission. Photo Birds 603 and 604 were preparing for launch when the collision occurred. All flights for the rest of the day were cancelled.

4 October 1967 ... 110th day. South China Sea.

The ocean has been nasty since we left Japan. Large swells cause the ship to pitch heavily at times; the sky overcast but no rain. I hear monsoon season has fully set in now for Southeast Asia. Maybe it will just rain steadily for the next month. We should be arriving on line this evening or early tomorrow to support and defend the Constitution of the United States of America.

We're losing 601 after all. Early this morning the Photo Mates rigged her up for departure. Each camera bay has to have mounts in it but with no camera. Universal mounts as well as rotatable had to be safety wired into bays 3 and 4 snugly so they don't bust loose when the plane hits the wire upon landing. I don't know who's getting that piece of shit, probably the Coral Sea or the Connie. Have fun, boys!

5 October 1967 ... 111th day.
Gulf of Tonkin, North Vietnam.

Back Yankee Station and the sky is sunny and clear; the water calm. Alpha Strikes were carried out today on the Thanh Hoa's POL sites. One pilot said after his bombs hit, the petroleum ignited causing "the largest goddamned secondary I ever seen." The Thanh Hoa railroad-highway bridge was crippled by our ordnance but not destroyed. A coastal defense site sustained heavy damage. Photo Recon Squadron 63 flew two missions today. LTJG Charlie Rudd piloted the morning hop. LT Sampson took the afternoon flight snapping photos. All camera systems were A-OK.

On this, the 111th day, Fighter Squadron 111 had a pilot and aircraft downed during strikes. Captain Billy hasn't spoken about it yet. Information I received is still vague, not certain if the pilot had engine failure or was hit. Nevertheless he ejected over enemy territory ditching the plane and parachuting into a heavily-foliaged mountain area. Search and Rescue aircraft went in to find him but had no luck. They'll probably head out at sunrise tomorrow.

6 October 1967 ... 112th day. Ibid.

There's no better alarm clock than an A-4 on your roof turning up its engines full blast at 5 o'clock in the morning. God, I couldn't hear myself think. My rack was vibrating; my brain rattling against my skull. I've noticed we're making a hell of a lot more launches every day. Around noon today, every available fighter and bomber was gone, somewhere over North Vietnam.

Early evening, I heard a disturbing report. Someone in the radio shack picked up Hanoi Hannah on the receiver. She was saying that one of yesterday's bombs hit a school house killing 33 children and wounding 28. Dear God, I hope it's a false report. Mistakes do happen in war. Many innocents are hit by off-target bombs. It makes my heart ache but it's the reality of this so-called police action. Six-year-olds are dying because of the political feuds of the adult world – six-year-olds, like my little brother Jeff. Shit! War sucks!

Tonight it was time for Harry Hedge to make out quarterly evaluations on all of his Photo Mates. I wrote my own evaluation and gave it to him but he said I cut myself down too much. He proceeded to write, as is his responsibility, the report in his own words. I was pleased. He had a lot of nice things to say about me even though I've been a pain in the ass to him.

7 October 1967 ... 118th day. Ibid.

As with yesterday, photo launches were scheduled for 0800, 1200 and 1600. Again, the first hop was cancelled due to lack of escort from the Fighter Squadrons. The two hops at noon and 1600 were piloted by Mister Rudd and the boss. They had a special mission to Da Nang Air Base in South Vietnam to photograph the runway. Not sure why. Maybe the allied forces have experienced mortar rounds from the NVA or VC, and the runway's fucked up. Prior to taking off, Charlie Rudd was in his usual happy mood. He walked up to his plane. Birdsong, the plane captain, was still in the cockpit checking out systems. So Charlie stood in front of the aircraft in the plane captain's usual location and pretended he was giving Birdsong the checkout signals. He ended up with his right hand clenched in a fist, fitting inside his left hand and then quickly pulled it out. That means: get your head out of your ass and think.

When our aircraft returned, we unloaded film and carried it down to the flash lab, as usual, for processing. The final product was of uncommonly good quality. Maybe Jackson dropped his dick long enough to change the chemistry in the processors. The Air Wing hit various targets of strategic importance today. I'm still wondering when the big operation is supposed to start. Maybe this is it and I'm just a mushroom.

Buck Gordon is a detachment AK Storekeeper. He works in concert with Ship's Company. Somehow he pulled some strings to get a free ride in an E1-B aircraft, a Willie Fudd. It's a radar detection aircraft used to forewarn pilots of enemy installations and SAM tracking sites. Buck said the Fudd flew along the coastline of North Vietnam, "I could see the explosions from the strike force's bombs. Those motherfuckers kick ass."

Buck was allowed to listen in on the radio banter. He heard one of the A-4 aviators from VA-164 holler out when his bird was grazed by a SAM. Although badly damaged, the pilot, LT Hodges, tried to fly back over the Gulf instead of ejecting over land. Over the radio, Buck could hear other pilots pleading with Hodges to eject before his plane exploded but he didn't heed their advice. About a mile from the coast, the A-4 went up in a fireball along with the Lieutenant.

"It was sad," Buck commented later. "But those guys just don't wanna parachute down into gook territory cause they know 'bout the horrible shit that happens if they're caught by the NVA."

The Big Cheese of Photo Recon Squadron 63 is over here, visiting from Naval Air Station Miramar. Commander Hegret choppered onboard today from the Coral Sea. He's sky hopping from carrier to carrier, visiting all of our detachments. Hegret, of course, received the royal brown-nose treatment from all of our Officers. As of yet, only a small number of us enlisted pukes have seen him. The ship's fresh water supply dropped down to 50 per cent today. All showers are secured until further notice. What moron is pumping fresh water overboard this time? I'll bet CDR Hegret has plenty of fresh, hot water up in Officers' Country. R.H.I.P.

8 October 1967 ... 114th day. Ibid.

Lehmann in P.I. told me that a couple of days ago the combined Air Wings flew 34 strikes on bridges up along the Chinese Border. They also hit a power plant southeast of Hanoi and various other targets. And yesterday, for the first time in the war, our Navy Pilots bombed and destroyed several Soviet-built helicopters on the ground. It's good to see we're being more aggressive and not so damned afraid of what Russia and China are going to say and do about our actions.

Commander Hegret walked in to our Photo Shop today. We anticipated that he would eventually get around to seeing us so we made a big banner that read: "Welcome Commander Hegret. We love you." He was speechless. Even though we were being sarcastic, I think he actually liked it because he mentioned it several times and had nothing but praise for the sign and us. Of course, then again, maybe he was just toying with us too.

We had two routine photo hops today. Commander Hegret was scheduled to take the 1600 hop but for some reason unknown to us, Rudd flew the mission instead. Cold feet? Surely not.

Elsewhere, it was another day of tragedy. Mister Zissu is MIA. An Early Warning Aircraft – a Willie Fudd – went down in a mountainous jungle region between Da Nang and Chu Lai in South Vietnam. The reason for the crash has not been determined. Apparently all indications were that the plane was having a routine flight and then radio contact was lost and the Willie disappeared from radar screens. Lieutenant Junior Grade Zissu was piloting the aircraft. Most of us Photo Mates, both Ship's Company and squadron, knew him well. He was a photo bug himself; loved to hang out in the lab in his free time. He'd develop film, print, and sit around shooting the shit with the Enlisted Men. He wasn't your typical Officer, more like my friend Michael. Just a couple of days ago, he put up a list in the Photo Lab offering rides in the Fudd for any of the Photo Mates who wanted to go. I considered signing up but, for some reason, didn't. If I had, I'd be an MIA today and Mom would be receiving the "We regret to inform you..." letter from the Pentagon. On the flight with him were LTJG Wolfe of Airborne Early Warning Squadron 11 and Seaman Journalist Raul Guerra who had gone along just for the hell of it. A search is underway but no encouraging words so far. Up until now, most of the deaths haven't affected me personally but this one got to me and I had to shed a few tears for some good men lost – all the while thinking I could have been, or maybe I should have been in Guerra's seat.

I received two letters today: one from home. Everything sounds hunky-dory back there in Nebraska. My family has moved into a new house and they love it. Father is becoming more interested in home life now. Mother is socially active again. Jeris and Jeff are busy with school and extra-curricular activities. Life goes on in the U.S.A. The other letter was from a long-lost friend: Good Lutheran lad, Nathan Hausmeier. He's been to Bible College and is now at some small school in Iowa. It was a pleasant, how-de-doo letter and deserves a reply even though we have parted company not only by physical distance but theologically as well.

Even with the letters from home, I could not overcome the sick feeling in my stomach from the Willie Fudd going down. It's true, you never know when your number's up. First, that shit and then I was volunteered to participate in an ammo working party tonight; my first one and I hear they're a bitch.

9 October 1967 ... 115th day. Ibid.

At 1930, last night, Parachute Rigger 3rd Class, John Nicholas, and I mustered in with Chief Carr in Hangar Bay One as the squadron's assigned slaves for the ammo party. About three-hundred grunts from various divisions were present to help Division 6, the ordnance crew, as the U.S.S. Pyro pulled up alongside the Oriskany, shot over unrep lines and transferred tons of bombs, rockets and cannon shells. Forklifts and shuttles worked at maximum speed carrying crates of ordnance from the starboard sponson into the Hangar Bay. Nick, Spanky the chubby Ordnanceman and I worked as a team. We began with 500-pound bombs. The 500s are stacked on pallets three layers high with three bombs on each layer. We had to cut the bands on the crates, throw the wooden pallets overboard, and bodily lift the big mothers on to an ordnance dolly – or skids, as they're called. It's a steel contraption with two wheels; concave depressions on top with nylon straps for secure transportation and a long rear handle for guidance. The skids can hold two five hundred pounders at a time – half a ton. After each loading, the three of us wheeled them down to bomb elevators where other crews took them down below decks to the ammo magazines and stacked them. Loading a quarter-ton bomb is a gut-splitting chore. With the bomb in horizontal position, one man grabs hold of the thin nose as two men, using a heavy nylon strap, lift the fat base end and, on the count of three, heave it from the crate over to the skid. Our team worked with several other teams on the 500s for about an hour. At that point, the Chief gave us a break and reassigned us to

250-pound bombs. We had twelve pallet crates of those to unload totaling 144 altogether. With the lighter load, we were able to become a little more systematic and efficient. Nick, Spanky, and I worked on these sons-of-bitches until 3:30 in the morning taking a one-hour break at midnight for chow and rest and, of course, griping about our sore bodies and talking about what we're going to do when we get back to The World.

Nick and I had lost our youthful vitality somewhere around 2300 and worked in agony for the remainder of the so-called party. Both of our backs went bad on us. After 0100, we could hardly bend over but we kept hacking it. By the time, we secured, my eyes were fogged, my brain in neutral, my spine warped and my body one big ache.

Two words from Chief Carr never sounded so good: "You're secured!"

I double-timed to the berthing compartment wanting so much to go directly to the rack but I was a salty, sweaty, smelly mess covered with rust, mud and crud so I grabbed my towel and douche bag, climbed up one level to the Flight Deck and walked aft to the salt water showers. Cold salt water felt good after eight hours of torture. Never thought I'd say that. After showering and putting on fresh clothes, I stopped at Photo Intelligence for ten minutes to talk with Chapin, who was on night shift. We chatted. I had a couple smokes. He pulled out the first aid kit and applied Merthiolate to the dozens of scratches and cuts on my hands and arms. Returning to the berthing compartment, I discovered a pile of clean laundry on my bunk that had come back the previous day. I did not want to do it but I did. I folded and put away clothing and towels in my locker, finishing at 0430. Done with my earthly chores, I dragged my brutalized body into bed and was instantly asleep.

"Reveille! Reveille!" the ship's Master-at-Arms yelled over the 1MC. "All hands up and about the decks. The smoking lamp is lit in all berthing compartments."

I opened my eyes and yelled as loud as I could: "Fuck!"

It was 0730. I had three hours of sleep and had to start a new day – no special favors for ammo party members. I tried to roll out of the rack but my body wouldn't respond. "I am so freakin' sore I can't get up. Can somebody help me?"

Aviation Machinist's Mate Johnson came over, laughing, "What time did you secure last night, MacLennon?"

"Three-thirty this morning."

"No, shit?" He was still smiling, finding some kind of sadistic joy in my misery.

"But I didn't get to sleep until 4:30. And, wipe that shit-eating grin off your face, will ya?"

"A little sore, eh?"

"You could say that."

"First ammo work party?"

"And last, I hope."

"It'll make you a better man."

"I think it made me a eunuch. I'm not sure I have any nuts left."

"Just stretch for a while. You'll feel better."

And to prove there's no rest for the wicked, I had to muster in with the rest of the squadron at 0800 hours in Ready Room Three. It was the first time most of us Enlisted Men had been in Officers' Country. The Ready Room is where the pilots get their daily briefings before flying their sorties. Commander Hegret had a little heart-to-heart chat with all of us – Officers and Enlisted combined. He told us, of course, how well we were doing and he told us about the squadron back home at Miramar. Our east coast counterpart, Photo Recon Squadron 62, is being decommissioned. All of their aircraft and personnel are moving to Miramar so when we return to the world, our squadron will be twice as big as when we left. The brass are moving us down to the big hangars. Unmarried PO2's and PO1's are now being given BAQ status and allowed to live in their own apartments ashore with a Navy stipend. Very nice for the lifers but I'll be a civilian a month after we return. The meeting mercifully lasted only a half hour. I high-tailed it to the squadron Photo Shop, grabbed one of the old men's racks and slept until 1300. Harry and the boys left me alone; they knew I was exhausted. Bless their hearts. While I was cutting Zs, the old man himself, Commander Hegret flew the noon hop out over North Vietnam and shot up every last inch of film on 604. In PI's words, "He got outstanding photo coverage." I don't know if they're just kissing his ass but I guess he has plenty of experience. That's why he's head honcho over the squadron.

During leisure time this evening I took the three boxes of slides that arrived in today's mail, down to P.I. to view pics of Sasebo on the light tables. That makes me feel good. While I was down there LTJG Charlie Rudd struck up a conversation with me as he was enjoying a Brahms symphony on his tape deck. We talked about Japan, classical music, Buddhism and many other subjects of interest we have in common. It's too damn bad we have to be segregated by military protocol: Officer and Enlisted Man, night and day. The big brass would tell us we should not be fraternizing.

10 October 1967 ... 116th day. Ibid.

As anticipated, night flights were scheduled to begin today – noon to midnight. That made the boys of Photo Recon Squadron 63 happy because we can sleep in until 1000 and secure from missions at sunset. We had two hops lined up but as it turned out, no birds in the Air Wing flew because the weather turned shitty over all of North Vietnam thanks to monsoon rain. The Enlisteds are happy. Our pilots are happy because they don't have to worry about dying or being captured today. The North Vietnamese are happy because no bombs will drop on them today. Hell, let's all pack it in and go home while everyone is happy!

This evening in the P.I. area, Det Airman Bobby Guthrie – kind of goofy little shit – had his hand down his pants scratching his package. He latched on to something down there and pulled it out.

"Oh, no!" I could hear him mutter as he examined a little black speck in the palm of his hand.

"What is it, Bobby?"

"If it's what I think it is..." He took the speck over to PT3 Duncan who, in turn, positioned it under the 30X magnification lens on the light table. "Yip!" shouted Duncan. "It's a goddamned crab."

The others in the room began laughing. "Did ya have a good time in Sasebo, Guthrie?"

"Hey Bobby, did she give you something to remember her by?" They were cracking up.

Obviously pissed, he fired back, "No, I did not have a good time like you're thinkin' I did! I didn't even get laid so how the hell did I get this thing?"

Ensign Kanker Sore offered an explanation, "Probably off a toilet seat, Guthrie."

"You mean – oh my God – I got the crabs from another sailor?"

"Couldn't even get 'em honestly." The boys were close to rolling on the floor.

"Shit!" Bobby tried to be serious but the humor of the situation began to curl the corners of his mouth and soon he was laughing along with the rest of us. He called us all over and let us all look at the crab louse through the microscope. "Look at this ugly, little fucker!"

It was translucent and hairy with six-legs. By golly, it did look like a crab. Guthrie left immediately and ran up to the showers, stripped and examined himself. It turns out his whole pubic region is infested with crabs. He'll have to report to Sickbay tomorrow to be de-loused. If Bobby has them, there are probably others who are picking them up, too. Heck, it could turn into a plague of biblical proportions.

11 October 1967 ... 117th day. Ibid.

A little past noon today, the Oriskany passed under a puffy, little nimbus cloud not more than two miles wide but very dark. There, in the midst of an otherwise bright and sunny sky, this little, energetic cloud was releasing a steady column of heavy rain. It fell on us, drenching the Flight Deck and the parked planes topside. We were on stand-down waiting for word from the tower as to when the day's flights would commence. In the interim, CAPT Billy got a wild hair up his ass. He wanted to navigate the ship under the little cloud as the deck crew held field day. On the double, the boys went down to their berthing compartments and changed into swim trunks and shower shoes, grabbed the long-bristled push brooms and 5-gallon cans of Terco from their work shops, regrouping on the Flight Deck. Not to be outdone, the Squadron Chiefs got caught up in the excitement and ordered us underlings to the parked planes with buckets of soapy water and rags. Captain Billy took the ship under the cloud again and drenched us with rain water. As we exited the precipitation column, all hands began brushing, soaping and scrubbing our little hearts out.

The O-Boat made a wide turn and re-entered the rain column for a rinse. And so it went, over and over. I'll bet we passed under that cloud a dozen times.

Some of the grunts were grumbling, as always, but most were taking it in stride, having a good time, enjoying the novelty of it all. The rain was cool and refreshing. I didn't mind getting sopping wet. After all was cleaned, we sailed steadily in the drying sunlight. Our Photo Birds looked better, much better. Ready for action. Happy birds.

The only action our squadron saw today was one hop at 1500. Mister Beam flew a 75 minute mission and despite mostly cloudy conditions over Nam, clicked off some good photo coverage. He accomplished that by flying below the cloud cover at about 3,000 feet. Very dangerous. Night ops began for the other squadrons at 1500 and lasted nine hours. Hello, North Vietnam, here's some 500-pounders in your backyard. Sorry if we disturbed your dinner plans.

The exam results for rate advancement came in today from California. Lord, the nightmare has come true. Danko the prick made Chief Petty Officer but hold the phone, this may be a blessing in disguise. Our detachment doesn't need two Chiefs so when Danko is released from the Naval Hospital in Japan maybe he will be reassigned to some other squadron. I can only hope.

12 October 1967 ... 118th day. Ibid.
"Mac! Mac!" A voice was invading my dream. "Wake up!"

It wouldn't go away. I eased open my lids and there towering over my bunk was a Fu Manchu mustache with food particles stuck in it. Not the first thing one wants to see in the morning. It was Big Ern.

"What time is it?" I muttered.

"Ahhh, about zero six hundred."

"Zero six hundred? Are you fuckin' crazy? Go back to bed and leave me alone!" I tried to roll over but he caught my arm.

"There was a death on the Flight Deck last night."

Eyes wide open, he had my attention. "Who was it? How did it happen?"

"I don't know for sure but everyone's talking about it."

Curiosity overrode the urge to sleep in. I thanked Levitt for the news, hopped out of my bunk, showered and headed down to the mess hall for breakfast. After listening to several accounts of the incident at the mess table, I think I compiled a fairly complete and accurate account: Night flight ops were still in full swing. A launch was being prepared. All aircraft, props and jets, were turning up. An Ordnance man from Attack Squadron 152, the A-1 Skyraiders, was standing about ten feet in front of one of his Spads. The prop was spinning as the old plane awaited its turn for takeoff. In front of the Ordnanceman an F-8 Crusader pulled out of park position and with a blast of its jet engine spun around toward the catapults. The exhaust blast caught the Ordnanceman by surprise. As he staggered and turned to avoid the searing heat, he was pushed by its force directly into the spinning propeller. Without going into the gory details, I'll just say that he was chopped up; dying instantly. One of my friends working on the fuels crew told me he was standing behind the Skyraider, and was sprayed with human fragments and blood. Placed in a body bag, the dead man was taken down to the refrigerator room below decks and placed between the cheese and the butter. An ignoble end. Two of the men from the Ship's Photo Lab had to go down and document the incident by photographing what remained of the poor guy's body.

Trudging up the port side metal ladders after breakfast, I entered our shop to find Harry, Ray and Danko stretched out on the bunks laughing.

"Where've you been, Mac?"

"Just got back from chow," I replied

Smiling, Harry asked, "Did those breakfast steaks taste a little funny this morning?"

"Huh?"

"Yeah," Danko chimed in, "Did they taste a little like... Airdale?" They all broke out in belly laughs.

"Coulda been worse," Ray added. "It coulda been... squid." Again like a bunch of deranged hyenas they were reveling in their little macabre comedy. I didn't see the humor.

Angrily, I shot back at them, "You all work up there! You know the hazards! That poor son-of-a-bitch could just as well been one of us." That remark sobered them up a little.

I continued, "I don't get it. How can you make jokes about it?"

In his usual condescending manner, Danko said, "Hey now, Mr. Third Class Pussy Officer doesn't like our conversation, men. Ain't that too fuckin' bad for Mister PH3 MacLennon?"

"Yes!" I fired back at him. "It's too fuckin' bad for me but worse for three assholes who have no compassion!" There was an awkward silence.

I spoke again but timidly. These three all outranked me. I was treading dangerous water and making them mad. "Look guys, if you can't handle death then I think you should just be quiet about it."

At that point, Harry stood up, pointed at some small parts on the counter and ordered me topside to replace a camera bay door fastener on 601. Nothing more was said about the dead airman for the rest of the day.

Today Photo Bird 602 flew both of the scheduled hops at noon and again at 1600. The Air Wing's strike force today hit the Haiphong shipyard. The A-4 and F-8 pilots reported heavy damage to the ship repair facility, several dry docks, and surrounding support structures.

One pilot said, "The bombs were packed so tightly together that the resulting smoke looked like one huge column billowing up 6,000 feet."

The early afternoon raid left a heavy black pall of smoke hanging over the target zone. Despite heavy AAA flak all planes ran a successful mission and all returned to the ship safely. This was one of the big ones we anticipated this line period.

A POL site was also destroyed north of Thanh Hoa.

More death. I heard today that search planes have sighted aircraft wreckage on a rugged mountainside between Chu Lai and Da Nang. It was positively identified as the E1-B Willie Fudd that carried Ensign Zissu, and the two other men. Helicopters haven't been able to get in there yet. The search pilots say there are no signs of life – relatively little hope of finding anything more than three burnt, decomposing bodies. God bless their souls. God bless Journalist Guerra. His fate could have been mine. Sometimes I think the Creator gets a kick out of playing craps with his children.

13 October 1967 ... 119th day. Ibid.

It's Friday the 13th. I slept in until 1030. Showers are completely shut down today. Our water level is down to 40 per cent, just enough for basic necessities. A clean body is not one of those necessities.

Our first launch was at 1230. Lieutenant JG Beam climbed into the cockpit of 603. Huffer and power were hooked up, the engine turned up. While Harry, Ray and Dick were busy checking out the KA68 in bay 4, Beam signaled to me that camera bay one, under the nose of the plane, was not working properly. I told Harry and whamo! It plunked his magic twanger. He turned on the panic button. While Harry ran around in circles waving a screwdriver spastically in the air, Ray Hines and I calmly opened the station pod and turned the film to release a jam caused by dampness. By that time Harry had zeroed in on us and was pushing his way into the pod as sweat broke out on his forehead. We informed him that we had the situation under control and he slowly backed off. In spite of Nervous Nelly, Ray managed to get the camera in place and back together. He and I buttoned up the pod. Beam checked out the cockpit camera control and everything was cool. Harry wiped his brow. And, after all that, the hop was cancelled anyway because the fuckin' tail hook wouldn't drop. Beamer was pissed off at his mechanical support team.

Later in the afternoon 603, piloted by our flying Admin Officer, Charlie Rudd, was launched with all systems up. Sometime during his flight, gremlins crept into the innards of the aircraft. Charlie was rolling in over his target, he pulled the camera trigger and nothing happened. Spittin' fire mad, he made a fast turn around and full-throttled back to the ship. On the way, his radio went dead. He made two attempts to land missing the wire both times. He finally caught it on the third go round. Man, I thought Beam was pissed but Rudd was ready to rip someone's head off. I'm sure the Chief caught holy hell and passed it on to Hedge. We investigated the problem and found the camera bays overheated, the entire circuit breaker panel was blown, the shutter in the KA53 had ripped out and when Hines opened the door to camera bay two the window broke.

Rudd, according to Walt, stomped into P.I., slammed his knee board down on the table and stomped out the door issuing a few obscenities as he exited. I guess Charlie was expecting someone to pat him on the head and say, "That's all right, Charlie! We'll make those dirty, little Enlisted Men pay for the nasty thing they did to your airplane." Pilots seem to think they are the only ones risking their lives every day. They get all the glory and we get our butts chewed out for every little thing that goes wrong.

CBS television reporters and cameramen arrived today aboard the COD from Cubi Point. They stayed about 15 minutes on the Old Risky. A helo came over from the Constellation, picked them up and whisked them away. I reckon our old tub just isn't big enough or modern enough for news coverage.

In contrast to all the hassles today, the weather was beautiful. Between air ops silence prevailed – no wind. Sunlight, diffused through the heavy haze, created a fluorescent sky. The sea was smooth as glass, the air autumn cool.

This evening, we played a dirty trick on Big Ern. Because he is now pulling night duty in the chow hall, he sleeps during the day in the shop. Ern was sawing logs with a note attached to the rail of his bunk reading: "Please wake me up at 5:15."

I crept over as he was sleeping and turned his wristwatch one hour ahead to six o'clock instead of the actual time of five. I tore off the note and shit-canned it. Then Harry yelled out, "Hey, Levitt! What time did you want to get up? Ern!"

Groggy and foggy, Ern pulled his watch up to his half-opened eyes. "Six o'clock? My gosh! Why didn't you guys get me up at 5:15 like I said in my..."

He was looking around frantically. "My note! Where is it?"

"Note? Did you see any note, Mac?"

"No, I didn't see a note. Did you, Hines?"

"Nope."

Ern stumbled to his feet and rushed out the door whacking his head on the way. "Ow! Damnit all!"

The poor guy was sure that he had been late for chow hall muster. He came back into the shop a couple of hours later during one of his breaks and looked around at us, all 6-foot-4 of him looming like a pudgy panda. "I oughta throw all of you over the side!"

He wasn't as angry as he tried to be. He held a straight face but after a few seconds we all broke out laughing. Ernie's an okay guy. I mean, after all, last night he cumshawed two cases of apple juice from storage and brought it up to the shop. We discreetly hid it behind the film and camera gear.

14 October 1967 ... 120th day. Ibid.

There was an All Hands Squadron Meeting this morning in Ready Room Three. Lieutenant JG Kanker presented a slide show of North Vietnamese strikes. The photos were taken by A-4 pilots with their personal 35mm cameras. It gave me a weird feeling to see North Vietnam in living color. Our photos are all on black-and-white film. It's a beautiful place with lush, blue-green mountains and valleys, azure rivers, and real people trying to live normal lives in their cities and villages despite political turmoil and the threat of death on a daily basis.

A picture of an airfield reminded me of Miramar Naval Air Station and the way it looked from the air when we took off headed to Alameda. I can better visualize now what is happening down there to those people on the ground as they see our bombers coming in and blowing the place to smithereens. It's like ole Mac putzing around in the hanger as usual and KA-BOOM! I'm dead.

With that image still in my mind, the presentation ended and Kanker Sore sat down. That was the cue for head honcho, LCDR Sonniksen to stand up. He sauntered over to the desk up front, moved a telephone and parked his butt on the corner. He wiggle around a little, decided he didn't like that perch, got up and walked over to a chair and planted his foot in the middle of the seat, hunching over. After that splendid John Wayne portrayal, he lit up a cigarette, cleared his throat and spoke: "First of all, I want to congratulate you men for your outstanding attitude and performance during Commander Hegrat's visit. Unfortunately there's some other issues I have to bring up."

It was inevitable. First the Attaboy then lower the boom.

"Some of you guys seem to be in a mid-cruise slump. I think you've become a little overconfident in your work but yesterday we had two fucked up planes."

The room became deadly silent as we all sank a little deeper into the leather aviator chairs.

"Pilots look into the face of death on every mission. We never know when we take off from that catapult if we'll ever see this ship again or our homeland or our families. It takes a hell of a lot of courage to fly into a war zone. And the last thing we need as we're getting our asses shot at by triple-A and SAM's is a malfunctioning aircraft. That's where you boys come in."

Boys. Of course, they're the men and we're the boys.

"I expect 110 per cent out of all of you. You've got to do your jobs and do them right. Pilot's lives are depending on you and you've gotta be alert at all times. We all know what happened up there on the Flight Deck the other night. If that Red Shirt had been more alert, he'd still be writing letters to his sweetheart back in the states. You must be aware of everything!"

Wait a minute. Were we responsible for killing that poor Airdale? I was eager to hear what was coming next.

He stood up straight. I could tell he was preparing for his conclusion.

"Many men have given their lives in Vietnam. We know the dangers but we continue to fly our missions every day because we love our country. Now, you all know our purpose over here. You know why we were sent here; why we're fighting this war."

Just when I thought he was about to offer some logical explanation for this crazy war, he turned the subject back to us. "Knowing the sacrifices, the lives given, I believe you should give your all, do your work eagerly and cooperatively with no bitching."

He took a deep breath and this time bellowed it out, "No bitching!"

He could have saved a lot of time and verbiage by just saying, "You guys screwed up, don't let it happen again, and stop bitchin' and moanin'. We're not on a Caribbean cruise."

I guess Sonniksen, being the Officer and the gentleman that he is, never heard the old Navy adage: "It's a sailor's right to bitch."

We were dismissed and ushered out of the Ready Room back to our humble servants' quarters. No plush leather chairs for the boys.

* * * * * * *

Flight quarters began late afternoon and ran through the night. Photo Birds 602 and 603 flew at 1600. We were worried about 603 wondering if she'd blow her circuit breakers again or if the camera bays would overheat. We really hadn't found anything out of the ordinary and were still mystified as to why they went bad on yesterday's sortie. Before the launch, we checked and double-checked all systems and cameras for discrepancies but found none. So we crossed our fingers as we watched Sampson and Sonniksen take off for the Ma River and that damned Thanh Hoa bridge that refuses to die. Both planes worked like a charm. All the cameras operated flawlessly, both pilots especially LT Sam got outstanding pre-and-post strike coverage. SAM'S and AAA flak was heavy. Coming home, our fly boys both caught the wire on their first attempts. And hey! we Enlisted Men did it all without any bitching. Do you suppose Sonniksen will call a meeting tomorrow to tell us how well we did? No. We were just doing our job the way it's supposed to be done. This evening, after finally obtaining a photo job order from the Ship's Company Photo Mates, I processed the roll of Ektachrome shot in Sasebo that I had overrated at ASA 250. I was in the final wash at 0030 when suddenly the lab was invaded by a mob of sleepy-eyed photo mates, most wearing only their trousers.

"There's a fire! A big fire! Starboard side!"

They were panic stricken so naturally I became a bit edgy myself. I left the film in the wash and ran out the door, across the Hangar Bay and up to our Photo Shop on the port side. It was not a good time for a fire. Night crews were uncrating bombs and ammunition throughout the Hangar Bay.

Reaching Airdale country, some of my fellows informed me that the so-called big fire was merely a parachute flare that had dropped off a plane as it was being catapulted. The magnesium flare ignited and burnt with great intensity on the forward starboard side of the Flight Deck. It looked bad but there was no damage; no injuries. You can't blame Ship's Company for panicking considering last year's conflagration. The flare was extinguished and firequarters were secured at 0100. I did manage to dry my slide film despite all the hoopla and hit the rack at 0200.

October 16, 1967 ... 122nd Day

    I am James Dean.
    I'm mad at the world
    because I know
    how it could be,
    and should be,
    if only ...

> There is a fiery heap of metal
> beside a desert highway,
> my funeral pyre
> but there are things I must do
> before I keep that appointment.

My two resident college boys say my poetry is juvenile and unrefined. They can kiss my rosy red ass. I enjoy writing. While the others amuse themselves playing poker, watching the ship's closed-circuit television or screwing around with their stereo equipment, I write. It takes me to a different world and helps me put this one in perspective. A little bit.

> I delay my demise because
> the hope of beauty
> keeps me alive,
> beauty and innocence.
> Somewhere, out there.
> She exists.
>
> Virgin, pure-hearted,
> undefiled by this ugly, polluted world,
> she is that one special girl
> who can rescue me,
> who can transform my world
> from depression to ecstasy,
> from death to eternity.
>
> I fell in love with Hayley Mills
> when she portrayed Pollyanna.
> Then one night while camping
> with Cub Scout buddies
> they popped my bubble
> by telling me perverted tales of sex.
>
> It took a long time to overcome that shock,
> to find innocence again.
> But I did.
>
> I discovered her
> deep in the emerald jungle.

I see her there,
alone, bathing in a stream
next to a waterfall.
I watch her from the reeds.
She sings.

Her skin is a deep, natural bronze
and her hair as black
as midnight of the newest moon.
Petite, muscular,
the curvature of her naked form
bends with the boughs
of the breeze.
And through the mist,
She dances.

Eighteen years old perhaps,
difficult to tell.
She holds a leaf and with it
traces down her shapely limbs.
Her flesh is dotted
with shimmering drops that
refract the midday sun.
She dreams.

And as her almond dark eyes
follow a descending jungle hawk,
her hands form two cups under
sweet little breasts.
Reddish-brown ridges encircle
firm, erect nipples.
She desires.

Touching the tips,
her lips open softly.
Expectation flows as
she whispers a word,
seductively,
a name,
my name ...

"Hey, Mac, what the fuck you writing now?"

It was James Son-of-a-Bitch Carson from the Aviation Mechanics Shop.

"Nothing, asshole."

He was persistent.

"No, come on." He approached my desk. "What is it?"

"You wouldn't understand."

His horse-like face contorted into a goofy grin, "Try me."

"Okay, but you'll laugh."

"No, I won't."

"Yes, you will."

"Come on!"

"Okay." I took a deep breath and began reading, "I am James Dean ..."

"James Dean? Ha! In your dreams, motherfucker."

Pissed off, I slammed my writing pad down on the desk. "See, what did I tell you?"

"Hey, feller, don't get upset. I just came over to catch some cool air from your vent."

I looked over at my lounging associate. Dick Aden was lost in his latest science fiction novel ignoring both of us.

"Hey, Aden!"

Dick peered over the top of the pages, perturbed, "Yeah, Mac?"

"Don't guys like Carson bug the hell out of you?"

"Whaddya mean?"

"Like when he comes into the shop with nothing in mind except to stand under our vent."

"Well, I guess that's ..."

"I mean, y'know, I don't give a shit if he wants to cool off but he seems to think he has to strike up a conversation or attach his lips to our butts just to get some free air."

"Hey, Mac!" Carson jumped in. "Fuck you! Okay! Just fuck you!"

"Sorry, sweetheart," I scowled. "You're not my type."

He flipped me off, turned around and stomped out of our shop.

I returned to my writing pad and wrote below my poem: Gerald MacLennon, rebel without a justifiable cause.

October 17, 1967 ... 123th day.
Yankee Station, Gulf of Tonkin.

CBS Television was aboard yesterday and today. I reckon they decided Oriskany was worth some footage after all. Maybe they will do some sort of news special to be broadcast back in the States about all of us sailors and pilots over here in the Gulf of Tonkin. Our mummies and daddies will see it and be impressed but most average Americans will switch the channel selector to their favorite Western. Vietnam or Gunsmoke? Hmmm. Gunsmoke.

Race car driver, Roger Ward, came aboard today via helo. Decked out in light blue slacks, light blue stretch t-shirt, blue sneakers and carrying a Firestone suitcase, he sure looked spiffy. I didn't know who he was or what he did until I asked one of the Ordnance Men. The Red Shirt looked at me like I was an idiot.

"That there is Roger Ward! Indy 500 Winner! Everybody's heard of him!"

I reckon I've been missing out on the more profound aspects of life. Stupid me. Ward gave a motion picture presentation of his Indianapolis 500 competitions and then chatted with the troops. I hear it was a treat for many of the guys. I chose to go up to the shop and listen to my Bob Dylan tapes.

17 October 1967 ... 124th day. Ibid.

The first launches weren't until noon today so all of us photos slept in the shop until 1030. Chief O'Brian disapproved. The old boy had reiterated his rules and regs: everybody should be up at 0600 regardless. Not long ago he told us: "If you sleep in, do it in your workshop, not in the berthing compartment."

This morning, he told Richard Aden, "If you're going to sleep in, do it in the berthing compartment, not your workshop." Then as he turned to leave, he had a second thought in his obviously corroded brain, "And... I don't want you sleeping in late in the berthing compartment."

So there you have it: Navy logic at its finest. The lunatics are running the asylum.

I've developed yet another attitude of indifference to all the Navy chicken shit. I have absorbed so much of it for the past three years that, at this stage, I'm like a sponge that is totally bloated and can't suck in any more. On 15 February 1968, less than four months now, I'm wringing it all out.

A big double went out today: 602 and 603 at 1200 piloted by LCDR "John Wayne" Sonniksen and LTJG David Beam. They accomplished their missions over Nam and returned with gripes. David's exposure meter conked out. Ronald's KA-68 didn't fire. Beam just blew it off as he usually does. Sonniksen, on the other hand, was compelled to melodrama. After the landing, Hedge waved for a signal from Ronald but the boss just flipped Harry the finger. He does that often. The Photo Mates are supposed to get a signal from the pilot as soon as he lands letting us know which cameras were shot so we can turn-to and get our job done. All the pilots are good about this except the old man. He just farts around, opens his canopy slowly, cuts his engines, and is half way out of plane before he gives us the signal. I think Sonniksen and the Chief both hate photo reconnaissance planes and the Photo Mates. The Lieutenant Commander would rather be a bomber pilot. And, I think the old Chief longs for the days when he was a battleship gunner back in the big one, World War II.

Death came to another Blue Shirt today down in the Hangar Deck. The poor motherfucker was working in the aircraft tire shop inflating a tire to the required 500 pounds pressure when the rim separated and it all blew up in front of him. His face was pushed to the side of his head; his chest and abdomen split open. He was lying in a large pool of blood when the corpsmen arrived, transferred him to a litter and carried him down to Sickbay. He lived for about ten minutes and was pronounced dead by one of the ship's surgeons. Bill Miller, one of the plane captains on 604, watched as they carried him over the UHT of our Photo Bird. Bill had to clean up blood afterwards. This evening the Chaplain prayed for his soul over the 1MC. And, Danko had his cute ass remarks: "Roast Airdale for dinner tomorrow!" I guess Danko was just born to be an insensitive prick.

An Enlisted died today. And an Officer died today. One of the pilots from Attack Squadron 164 was killed when his A-4 was hit by hostile fire over Nam. No further details at this time. We loaded film tonight until bedtime. The sea is rough with heavy rolls expected throughout the night and into tomorrow. The air temp was unusually cool today, high of 76. There's been a rumor running through the ranks tonight that a typhoon may be heading for us.

19 October 1967 ... 125th day.
Leaving Gulf of Tonkin heading south.

"Typhoon confirmed," read the 0800 report. "Carla is on a west-southwesterly course and expected to continue. This poses a threat to Yankee Station. Winds in excess of 30 knots not expected prior to 1200, 19 October on station. Heavy seas will be encountered if the ship moves south to evade the storm. Secure all gear and aircraft for heavy rolls. Typhoon Diana is 1200 miles east of the Philippines increasing in intensity, following same course as Carla."

The Old Risky headed full steam out of the Gulf today to evade the Pacific Ocean's version of a hurricane. Destination: coastal region of South Vietnam. Yes, we did encounter the heavy rolls promised. Back and forth, back and forth all day long, it felt like the ship was nearly lying on its side sometimes. There were a few sea sickness cases in the Air Wing but most of the Airdales have become salty enough now not to puke in heavy weather. One thing unavoidable however is when a guy is walking the passageway and suddenly the damned ship rolls and slams you into the bulkhead. That smarts!

I had not been scheduled for an Aircraft Integrity Watch tonight but in typhoon conditions the watches are double teamed, not sure why. I suppose if one poor bastard gets blown over the side, he'll have someone there to wave goodbye to him. So, I was volunteered to pull the 2000 to 2400 Flight Deck Two Watch. Four of us Airdales, three from VFP-63 and one from VAW-111, were assigned Flight Decks Two and Three – the rear two-thirds of the Flight Deck. No aircraft were parked forward. Lord, it was one hell of a four-hour stand; cold, dark, rainy with unceasing gales. The wind across the bow must have been a steady 40 miles per hour with gusts to 60 or higher. And, stupid me, out there wearing just a t-shirt, Flight Deck jersey and dungaree jacket, the bitter wind cut right through and chilled me to the bone. Around 2200, from the darkness overhead, torrential sheets of rain unloaded on us. About that time we said, "Fuck aircraft integrity," and all huddled together behind the ship's superstructure opposite the wind. There we were, like four drenched ducks, ten o'clock at night, staring out over the starboard side at an expanse of black fury. A full moon was hidden behind the overcast but every so often would break through and cast a diffused glow on the ocean's raging surface – incredible white caps, mountainous swells.

Thank the powers that be. We were relieved of our watch at 15 before midnight. Back in the dryness of sleeping quarters, I lost the wet clothing immediately and took the hottest shower tolerable – yes, we have fresh water again – then crawled into my rack and curled up fetal position under my warm, wool, Navy blanket. Carla rocked me to sleep. The last thing I remember thinking, as I drifted off, was: "If this is the edge of the typhoon, it must be hellacious in the Gulf of Tonkin."

23 October 1967 ... 129th day (four days later).
Yankee Station, Gulf of Tonkin, North Vietnam.

We waited out the storm four days from a safe distance, and returned to the line yesterday. We have had technical malfunctions every day this line period. It's like all of our birds are infested with gremlins. Damned frustrating; weighing heavily on us. As a result, we become edgy and nasty to one another. That's part of life at sea, according to the old salts. Hell, a man can't live with his own wife this much without becoming tired of seeing her face. Sea Daddy, Harry Hedge; sea veteran, Ray Hines; mustache pot, Richard Aden; Big Ern; and MacLennon... we're together 15 hours a day, seven days a week. We are developing pet peeves. I have mine, probably too many, but they just seem to happen. Maybe we're having a mid-cruise slump; just going through the motions every day.

Attack Squadron 163 lost a plane and a pilot yesterday, October 22nd. The A-4 Skyhawk was hit directly and exploded before the pilot had a chance to eject. 'Don't know any more.

24 October 1967 ... 130th day. Gulf of Tonkin.

Late last night, General Quarters was called and Airdales went ape, running like Keystone Cops through passageways, tripping over knee knockers, ramming into each other. GQ isn't called on the line unless it's for real. An hour passed before we learned what the hell was going on. The Captain finally addressed the crew. Two UFOs had been heading our direction. They weren't responding to our radio IFF – Identify Friend or Foe. Nervous minutes ticked by in the communications shack but eventually the UFOs became IFOs. It turns out they were two crippled U.S. Air Force jets – Zoomies. Both had been struck by enemy flak – both had dead radios.

This morning, we had yet another scare. The 1MC crackled around 0930 with Master-at-Arms shouting, "All hands take cover! All hands take cover!"

That was it. No one knew what the fuck was happening. Some guys hit the deck. Others just put their hats on, most just sat in silent apprehension waiting for an atomic bomb to incinerate us, or whatever. Likewise, this scare turned out to be no big thing. The Big Zero was taking on fuel when the tanker's rudder failed, again, causing their ship to drift away from us. Fuel hoses connecting ships began to stretch and tighten. It was feared they would snap and whiplash. That was when the 1MC warning was given. An emergency break was made by chopping the ends of the hoses on both ships. Fuel splattered and ran over the starboard Oriskany sponson where the refuel crew was working. Praise the Deity, it didn't ignite.

Today was another of those major Alpha Strike days foretold by the Skipper. Here's how The Musket reported it, ex post facto:

Oriskany pilots flew into fierce enemy defenses in the first attack on the Phuc Yen airfield eleven miles north of Hanoi. Oriskany pilots and aircraft, together with other Navy and Air Force units, pounded the 9,000 foot airfield with 500 pound bombs. The attack climaxed one of Oriskany's busiest days on Yankee Station.

The Hai Duong railroad yard and station as well as the Haiphong railroad yard and warehouse area (west) were hit prior to the afternoon strike on Phuc Yen airfield where several Soviet MIG's were parked.

Led by Commander of Air Wing 16, CDR Burt Shepherd, Oriskany planes scored dozens of direct hits on the runway leaving it heavily cratered.

"This was the first time we've seen SAM's in quite a while." said one of the pilots, "There were plenty of them."

Lieutenant Commander Dean Cramer was strike leader on the Haiphong attack, flying an A-4 Skyhawk. He reported seeing a SAM fly directly under his plane on a flat trajectory. "I couldn't see where it hit," he commented, "but it was headed for the center of Haiphong."

Commander Lighter, Executive Office of VA-163, said, "This was the most flak I ever saw over Haiphong. I couldn't find a place in the sky where there was no flak, so I just drove right through it. There was no place else to go."

An A-4 Skyhawk, piloted by LTJG Taber of VA-163, suffered hits by flak. He managed to maneuver his aircraft out over water before he was forced to eject. A rescue helicopter was immediately on the scene to snatch him from the water and return him safely to the ship. [End of Report]

Meanwhile, Mister Sonniksen and our three other pilots obtained very significant targeting photos over North Vietnam, obtaining complete advanced coverage of Haiphong and Phuc Yen airfield for the big strikes today. We knew we did a damned good job and... it didn't go unnoticed. A message came through from Rear Admiral Weinel, Commander of Task Group 77.0:

"The success of our attacks on the Haiphong RR Yard (w) is due in large part to the direct result of the photo reconnaissance conducted by Oriskany Photo Det. Please convey my appreciation to the Officers and men of your Photo Det for an outstanding performance and my wishes that 'The Eyes of the Fleet' continue to guide the Navy Sunday Punch."

A similar message arrived from Admiral Michaelis, Commander of the Seventh Fleet. It's nice to be noticed and appreciated.

Yokosuka in two weeks! We'll be wearing dress blue uniforms for a change because central Japan is close to the same latitude as Nebraska. It's autumn at home and in Tokyo.

25 October 1967 ... 131st day. Ibid.

No Photo Recon flights today. It was, however, another hectic day for strike aircraft. Phuc Yen was hit once again. All fighter and bomber aircraft were utilized in the strike effort. Maybe the brass think VFP-63 deserves a day of rest after doing such a fine job over Hanoi, Phuc Yen and Haiphong.

26 October 1967 ... 132nd day. Ibid.

Out of the frying pan into the fire. Phuc Yen airfield – because of the cooperative efforts of all the carriers on Yankee Station and U.S. Air Force bases in Thailand and South Vietnam – has been put out of commission for a long time. Today the united air strike groups hit Hanoi... finally. The Captain gave one of his now rare briefs over the ship's 1MC concerning what's been happening on strikes for the past few days. He talked about Phuc Yen but didn't say much more than the ship's newspaper has already related. He did boost our squadron morale by reading the message from Admiral Weinel that commended the Photo Det for our outstanding work. This was the first time Captain Billy has ever mentioned Photo Recon Squadron 63 over the squawk box. Every Airdale, Black Shoe and Snipe on the Oriskany heard it.

It amazes me how much U.S. military spokesmen in Washington, D.C. try to bullshit the American public. In a United Press International (UPI) release printed in this morning's Stars and Stripes the following was written:

> "There were no U.S. planes reported lost in Wednesday's raid although pilots said they had to fly through a fierce defense around the airfield. Radio Hanoi reported, however, that two of the attacking American planes were downed over Phuc Yen." [End of blurb]

Hanoi Hannah was correct.

An almost fatal mishap on the Flight Deck a few days ago was just brought to my attention today. It seems one of the F-8 Crusaders was pulling out of spot on its way to the catapults when one of the Blue Shirts walked in front of the jet intake and was swept off his feet; sucked into the plane head first. An alert man on one of the plane crews saw the Blue Shirt being pulled into the bowels of the aircraft and quickly ran over, grabbed the man's feet and pulled him out. The Plane Handler was saved from a grisly death in the grinding blades of the jet turbine. His Flight Deck helmet was pulled off his head by the suction and it severely damaged the engine. Better an engine damaged than another Airdale killed.

Today is the first anniversary of the tragic fire that killed 44 men on the Oriskany. Memorial services were going to be held on the Flight Deck in memory of those who died but the call to arms was considered more important. Services were cancelled and Alpha Strikes were launched. We kill citizens of Hanoi in remembrance of those Americans killed last year on this day. Irony. Later this evening, a 15-minute break was made in the flight schedule. The memorial services were quickly staged at 1715. I attended even though last year at this time, I was working at the Fleet Intelligence Center, Pacific Facility at Cubi Point. The original plan this morning was for the men to wear ceremonial white uniforms but that was changed this evening to work blues. I stood at the rear of the formation amidships and couldn't see a fuckin' thing that was going on up front. The ship's Chaplain stepped up to the P.A. microphone and gave the eulogy commenting on the fact that many heroes of the disaster were still serving onboard, recalling how "heroes were the rule not the exception" during the fire and "such men undoubtedly saved the lives of many shipmates, as well as the ship, through their unselfish acts." Following a brief account of the fire in the bomb storage area, the Chaplain delivered a prayer to the Great Father asking him to hear our pleas of mercy, love and all that. He prayed for "the souls of our dead shipmates now in heaven." Following his meditations, some of the ship's Jarheads smartly dressed in their peacock uniforms marched around, stopped and fired a 21-gun salute. The bugler in the Admiral's band played Taps. And it was over. All non-essential personnel, especially Marines, cleared the Flight Deck and the last strike group of the day landed, completing a successful day of destruction in North Vietnam.

Yesterday, Oriskany strike aircraft slashed through a heavy concentration of surface-to-air (SAM) missiles and flak ringing the city of Hanoi to unleash their bombs on the Hanoi thermal power plant, the main power facility located at the city's center. This was the second strike against the major target, untouched until two months ago, when Oriskany A4 and F8 jets struck the power plant on August 21 for the first time. Enemy defenses were said to be intense but pilots agreed they were heavier this time.

The power plant was severely damaged. The roof caved in. Flashes of electrical arcing could be seen by pilots. Smoke blanketed the area after the full package of bombs had hit their target.

Between 20-to-25 SAM's were seen. Three planes from Oriskany's Air Wing were struck. Only one of the damaged aircraft made it back to the ship. Lieutenant JG Rice of Fighter Squadron 162, was forced to eject when his Crusader was hit by one of the Russian-built Surface-to-Air Missiles.

Lieutenant Commander John McCain of Attack Squadron 163 was forced to eject when his A-4 Skyhawk was disabled by NVA anti-aircraft artillery. Pilots who circled back report that McCain parachuted into Hanoi's Truc Bach Lake and was apparently rescued by Vietnamese civilians. Soldiers, most likely, seized him as he was brought ashore and whisked him away.

Both Rice and McCain parachuted into the heart of the capital city. No rescue attempts were made. If the two are still alive, the Hanoi Hilton – the name captured pilots have given to the Hanoi POW prison – will have two new guests checking in tonight. McCain must have a hex on him. First he barely escaped being fried to death in the Forrestal Disaster, now the poor bastard is a POW for God knows how long.

Also today, an A-4 flown by LTJG Nelson of VA-164 was damaged by AAA flak but was able to fly back to the ship and land safely.

One of the pilots from our neighboring carrier, the Constellation, was involved in an aerial dogfight with a Russian-built MIG-21 aircraft over Nam. After a 15 minute battle, the Connie's pilot delivered a fatal air-to-air missile strike to the MIG and sent her down in smoke. So far this cruise, Oriskany's Air Wing has recorded no MIG kills... but I'm sure our fighter pilots would welcome the opportunity.

27 October 1967 ... 133rd day.

Today is my third anniversary of joining the U.S. Navy. Yes, three years ago in Denver, Colorado, I held up my right hand, took the oath, and signed myself into military service. Along with the anniversary comes a small pay raise. Ironically, it's also Navy Day. I didn't know that when I signed up. So, in honor of my third anniversary, a special noon meal was served in the chow hall: steaks grilled to order; a huge cake was cut and served. The cake was a 6-by-4 foot map of the United States with a Navy Flag on the top of it, all made with scrumptious frosting. It was a terrific work of culinary art by our ship's cooks.

So, three years in the Navy and what do I have to show for it? I've traveled. Where else could I live in Pensacola, Florida; San Diego, California; Miramar, California; Subic Bay, Philippines; and onboard an Aircraft Carrier at sea all within three years, working for the same employer? I've been to Mexico, the Southern U.S., the West Coast, The Philippines, Japan and will visit the British Crown Colony of Hong Kong before 1967 is over. I've experienced the three major types of duty in the Navy: shore station in the United States, shore station in a foreign country, and sea duty. I've been through photography school, graduating at the head of my class. I have worked at both ends of photographic reconnaissance: the mental labor at FIC PAC FAC at Cubi Point, P.I. and now out here, the physical labor working with the cameras. A lot of water under the bridge in three short years.

29 October 1967 ... 135th day. Ibid.

The only photo recon mission of the day went out at 1100 flown by none other than our fearless leader, Commander Sonniksen. This was undoubtedly the most screwed up launch we have had to date. The Old Man hopped into 602 and turned up the engine. He found a discrepancy in his ejection seat and the fighter aircraft assigned to be his escort went bad during turn up. So Sonniksen cut the engine and climbed out. Nicholas, Parachute Rigger 3rd Class, immediately corrected the ejection seat problem. When Ron arrived below decks to his locker room, he was informed that another plane had been designated escort and that 602 was up and ready. So he sauntered back up to the Flight Deck and went through the whole start up procedure again. He gave the signal to apply compressed air into the turbine. The turbine wouldn't turn. The engine was frozen. Six-O-Two went down hard this time. Was Ronald pissed? Is the Pope Catholic? The next strategy was to bring Photo Bird 604 up from the Hangar Bay. After cutting power on 602, Ron dismounted and walked over to the Number Two Elevator and waited for 604. Evidently she was parked all the way aft in Hangar Bay Three. It took over fifteen minutes to extract the bird and push it on to the elevator. In the meantime, Sonniksen lost his patience and stomped back down to his locker room abandoning any hope of flying today. Chief O'Brian had to go fetch the boss one more time. Dodging jet exhausts of aircraft lined up behind the cats, Ron ran back across the Flight Deck to 604. He preflighted the aircraft, climbed in the cockpit and repeated start-up procedure. Everything checked out. His spirits were rising. He just wanted to get off the damned ship and into the wild blue yonder.

But luck continued to elude. Incidents on the Flight Deck delayed his launch for a half hour. An F-8 Crusader from Fighter Squadron 111 was pulling out of spot taxiing up to the cats when its wing crunched into another F-8 parked along the way. This created a major gang fight of angry Chiefs and Officers. Then a Crusader from Fighter Squadron 162, was on the cat all hooked up for launch when smoke began pouring out of the exhaust vents. "Fire on 2-0-0, starboard cat!" the air boss yelled. In seconds, a hoard of crash crew personnel was climbing over the plane poking CO2 extinguishers into the smoldering engine. The Purple-K chemical extinguisher truck pulled up alongside the bird and began pouring its chemicals into the plane. Men in asbestos suits appeared on the scene. The fire was declared extinguished about a half hour later. The damaged aircraft was towed off the catapult. Then and only then was Sonniksen cleared for take off.

I must admit the Old Man did a relatively good job of keeping his cool throughout the whole ordeal. Sometimes I catch myself being proud of him. If we have any differences, it's all in the family. He powered up, taxied to the cat, punched his afterburner – that's like laying rubber with my '56 Chevy – and was jolted off the ship. Fortunately, he flew a good mission and all cameras worked. The plane came back in up condition. No problems.

The flying day was over at 1300. The rest of the day I slummed around meaning to write some letters but didn't have the ambition. Miley, our illustrious Yeoman, walked into the shop this evening delivering the Plan of the Day as he does every day.

"Well, only another day to live," he blurted.

"What the fuck you talkin' about, Miley?"

"We're supposed to sink tomorrow. Didn't you hear?"

"No, Miley!" I replied sarcastically. "I didn't get the news. Tell me about it." I knew what was coming.

"That woman that predicted Kennedy's death and all that other stuff said we're gonna sink. She said she could see a 34 under water."

"Oh for Chrissake!"

"Better say your goodbyes now," Miley advised.

I couldn't restrain myself, "Why in the hell does everyone pick on Jean Dixon? Goddamnit! She did not predict any such thing. Where'd you hear this bullshit?"

"Oh, some guy down in IMA said..."

"There! You see! Some guy made it up. More fuckin' scuttlebutt!"

I get upset because I have a soft spot for prophets and prophetesses, seers, clairvoyants and the like. I've read Edgar Cayce and Jean Dixon. She has a wonderful gift of prophecy and I hate to see such a gift trivialized and abused by ignorant people with phony predictions.

30 October 1967 ... 136th day. Ibid.

The sea was uncommonly smooth today. The ship must have been close to shore because the water was green; assorted little marine plants were floating on the surface. During preflight inspections at 0730, god came on his loudspeaker announcing: "The ship is maneuvering to avoid small boats."

I rushed over to the side and saw about six junks and sampans. Around each were about a dozen small fishing boats. The Oriskany came within a hundred feet or so of one of the fishing boats. Sitting in the small boat was a Vietnamese man and woman wearing their Coolie hats. They had nets and lines hanging over the side into the water. They stared at the huge ship as it moved swiftly by them – their mouths gaping in astonishment. I wonder what they thought of us? Dozens of sailors lined the side of the ship in mutual interest. I took a few photos. These poor fishers are supposed to be our enemies but I couldn't help but feel the deepest compassion for them and somewhat ashamed of our presence in their fishing waters. I'm just not a good player in this war game.

We flew two missions over their homeland today, another 0830 and 1130 schedule. Both went well. No gripes. Strike groups from the ship today hit the Vong Bi thermal power plant complex, 20 miles north of Haiphong. Bombs and missiles from Oriskany fighters and bombers completely obliterated the entire complex. Photographic bomb damage assessment was flown by our birds piloted by Sampson and Rudd. BDA photos revealed that not only was the power plant area hit but a stray bomb exploded in a nearby village. The photos showed approximately thirty thatched roof houses on fire. Undoubtedly many innocent civilians died. But they're our enemies, too. Right? Son-of-a-bitch, I hate war.

31 October1967 ... 137th day. Ibid.

My Swedish great-grandmother, Sofia Lovisa Hilding, would have been 95 years old today. She passed away three years ago. I miss her. I'll always remember her telling me, "Yerry – she couldn't pronounce the J-sound – Yerry, I want you to preach the Gospel of Yesus."

I wonder what she would think about me being here in Vietnam? Am I doing the work of Yesus, Grandma?

Back in the states it's Halloween and millions of little American beggars will be going door to door asking for candy but nobody here really gives a shit. If you think about it, it's an absurd holiday: kids dressing up in frightening costumes for fun. Over here the most frightening thing for kids is the sound of air raid sirens warning them that another round of bombing is about to begin.

October will be remembered as the all sea month; the only month of this cruise where we spent the entire 31 days at sea. In two days, the Mighty Zero sets sail for the port of Yokosuka, Japan. We should arrive there on 7 November. It will be a nice R&R: cool weather, possibly snow, and dress blue uniforms.

Our morning schedule was hectic. We had a launch at 0830, another launch at 1000, a recovery at 1015, a launch at 1130, a recovery at 1145, and a recovery at 1300. Around 1100 the processing machines broke down in the flash lab and progress was stymied for the rest of the afternoon. The PT's didn't get their film until late. This evening at 2000, the Photo Recon Squadron 63 night crew was turning aircraft 602 on the Flight Deck checking out the engine. I was sitting in the Photo Shop writing this diary. Suddenly the squawk box crackled and a Boatswain yelled: "Fire! Fire! Fire aft of aircraft 602 on the Flight Deck, port side!"

Six-O-Two was directly over my head. I walked out the door and was nearly trampled by the crazed crowd running up toward the catwalk just to rubber neck. You fuckin' idiots! I thought to myself. If that fuel tank blows you'll all be dead. Sure, I was curious, too, but I wasn't going to run directly into a fireball. Instead, I hustled through the 02 passageways over to the starboard side then went up to the Flight Deck and watched from a safe distance. There was the usual mass confusion of spectators, crash crew, Blue Shirts, Yellow Shirts, Officers and Chiefs. After the fire was extinguished and the crowd dispersed, I walked over to join the men of my detachment. They were all there. The story I got from them was that 602 had the engine turning. They were trying to kick in the afterburner but with no luck. Some mechanic stupidly pumped up extra fuel for afterburner ignition. Again it failed. The excess fuel began to pour out of the tail and the heat of the engine ignited the JP5 inside the engine chamber and on the Flight Deck. Ship's firefighters quickly extinguished the fire but the engine is ruined and will have to be replaced. Sorry taxpayers! That means we currently have only one flightworthy aircraft. The wrath of Chief O'Brian most assuredly will befall some poor jet mechanic; the whole maintenance crew will be paying the price. Those poor bastards work their asses off as it is. They don't need more chewing.

1 November 1967 ... 138th day. Ibid.

Another time in another world I remember November. In those days, I climbed the Colorado mountains. I stood on high peaks and surveyed the autumn landscape. Leaves of red, orange, golden brown and yellow blanketed the earth below. Hints of the coming winter storms whitened the ground at night. In the mornings, the leaves and trees sparkled in the rising sun with crystal frost.

My little sister and I climbed Bear Mountain. We scaled the boulders like young, frisky mountain goats. The wind made streamers of her hair. She got a run in her hosiery. Silly girl, you don't climb a mountain wearing panty hose.

2 November 1967 ... 139th day. Leaving the Gulf of Tonkin.

This afternoon at 1500, Detachment 34 had an all hands gathering in Hangar Bay Three for presentation of promotion certificates to four of our mechs. Commander Air Group 16,

Commander Burt Shepherd, was there to present the certificates and shake hands.

In this, the last morning of strikes for this line period, Oriskany's Air Wing hit only petty targets: trucks, barges, boats. Damn, a pilot was killed on this final sortie. Lieutenant JG Knapp of Attack Squadron 164 was diving in on a SAM site in his A-4 unleashing his rockets when his aircraft was struck by ground artillery. His plane burst into flame and smashed into the ground. Mister Knapp was killed instantly. It was untimely misfortune because the O-Boat secured Yankee Station operations at noon, did a 1-80, and steamed out of the Gulf. By this evening we were in the South China Sea heading on a northerly course toward Japan. The ocean is becoming rough. Heavy rolls and stormy seas are expected throughout our four day transit. Typhoon Diana is still active in the Okinawa-Ryukyu Island area. There is a possibility that we may run into her or her into us.

This month has been a costly one. According to my calculations, the Air Wing has lost ten aircraft. Eight pilots have died. Five Enlisted Men were killed. Three pilots were captured by the North Vietnamese. In our first line period, we lost 15 planes and recorded 8 deaths. So far for this lovely Vietnam Cruise: 30 aircraft lost, 21 men killed, 6 now residing at the Hanoi Hilton but everything is relative. If you think about those soldiers pulling combat duty in the jungles and rice paddies of South Vietnam, 21 men dead is the toll from a small skirmish with the VC. Our only true combatants out here on Yankee Station are the pilots and they don't have to meet the enemy face-to-face unless they're forced to eject and parachute to the ground. It must be a shock to go from their privileged lives here on the ship to a dank, dark prison cell.

Speaking of cushy comforts, tonight around twenty of us crammed into the Ship's Photo Lab to watch feature film, Judith, starring Sophia Loren. What a sultry piece of work she is. My groin twitches just watching her smile.

3 November 1967 ... 140th day.
Somewhere in the South China Sea, near Taiwan.

The showers have been off for several days now and boy, do I stink! Of course, so does every other body. The squawk box fired off at 0700: "All today's commissary working party muster on station!"

I had been invited to the party three days ago. Because I stayed up late until 3 AM writing, I wasn't too ambitious or cheerful. I dressed and mustered with the PO in Charge on Hangar Bay three. We were not sent to work immediately so I crawled on top of an F-8 engine and slept through all the noise for about an hour.

"Hey, Airdale!" someone shouted me awake. "Get your lazy ass over here and get to work!"

He made me carry two slide rollers down to the Number One Elevator pit. I took care of that and secured. I walked up to the Det Photo Shop, said, "Good Morning" to my fellow Photo Mates, then fell fast sleep in our overstuffed chair for three hours.

In the afternoon, Paul Duncan and I went up to the Flight Deck with our 35mm cameras to take pics of the angry sea. We were sailing north today, somewhere near Taiwan. Bad weather remains with us. This was the first time that I had ever seen water coming over the bow. It takes some damned big waves to reach over a forty foot bow. Paul and I stood on the Number Two Elevator photographing the gigantic waves as they crashed into the ship. The wind was so strong we had to lean into it at a 70-degree angle to avoid being toppled. Lieutenant JG Kanker, Mister Beam and LT Sampson joined us with their cameras and we snapped photos of each other.

On the aft end of the Flight Deck, I used my new telephoto lens to capture the drama of our destroyer escorts fighting the sea. They were being slapped right and left by the swells. They attempted to ease their ride by steaming in the Oriskany's wake but it didn't work. Their bows would rise above the surface of the water and then crash down into frothy sea, inundating the front half of the small vessels, creating an explosion of salt spray. I took about thirty photos of our tin cans. I think I might have some outstanding coverage.

The ocean was worse tonight. All hands were told to stay off all weather decks and catwalks. The waves slammed against the hull of the ship with a distinct thud. Geysers of sea water poured into the sponsons and guntubs. The forecastle was flooded. Many of the boys were seasick. I even saw a salty, old Boatswain's Mate in the head puking his guts out.

CHAPTER XXV
TOKYO CALLING

*5 November 1967 ... 142nd day.
In the West Pacific, off the eastern coast of Japan.*

The ocean was beginning to calm this morning. Flight quarters were called and the pilots manned aircraft for fly-off operations. Photo Birds 602 and 603, piloted by LCDR Sonniksen and LTJG Beam respectively flew off to Naval Air Station, Atsugi, Japan. Six-O-Two will be there for the next month for a total sand-down and paint job as 601 was this month. Six-O-Three will just have a little touch up work.

The crew received their payroll checks this morning. I waited in line for two hours to pick up my $326 in cash, liberty money for Yokosuka and Tokyo.

*6 November 1967 ... 143rd day.
In Port - Yokosuka (pronounced ya-KOOS-ka), Japan.*

By noon, the Old Risky was well into Tokyo Bay. Anchor was dropped a few miles outside the Naval Station where all aboard waited impatiently for a cruiser, U.S.S. Providence, to vacate our berthing space and find one of her own. Earlier, as we had neared Japan, the temperature gradually dropped. Upon arrival, it was downright cold with a penetrating breeze and dimly lit sky enveloped in the mist of an autumn morning. I stood alone on the forward Flight Deck wearing two jerseys and a dungaree jacket yet still shivering. Several Japanese fishing boats floated by the Old Risky, slowly, cautiously, as if not to be molested by the gigantic iron monster. The Japanese fishermen waved to me. I returned the greeting. In a detachment meeting at 1100, Sonniksen briefed us on Yokosuka and Tokyo liberty policies then congratulated us on our outstanding achievements this period. At 1515 this afternoon the 1MC announced: "Ship is moored! Shift colors!" As soon as the crossovers were hoisted and dropped into place from ship to pier, liberty call was sounded for Sections 1 and 3. Unfortunately I'm in 2 so I stayed aboard watching eager young sailors offloading like a herd of wild buffalo and stampeding toward the nearest fire water holes. The boys looked smart in their dress blues.

The Oriskany is moored in a cove; slipped into a pocket where granite hill and woods form a semi-circle around the aft end. It's good to be in a climate similar to that of back home. The trees are flaunting their fall hues. I wasn't allowed to enjoy the scenery for long because, as always, there's work for the duty section. Six-O-Four, our only Photo Bird remaining onboard, needed to be washed. The duty section farted around for a couple of hours as Koppler ADJ1 tried in vain to obtain water hoses and wash gear. That project ended up being scuttled.

Craig Danko returned to the ship this afternoon following a month's absence. He was gay and chipper, happy to see all of us again. Well, most of us. He scampered around after returning to the Photo Shop, putting his clothes away, reclaiming his bunk. The asshole had to tell us about all his adventures in Sasebo and Yokosuka; about all the love-starved women that he had satisfied. He is so full of shit. He was off the ship, out on liberty about an hour after his return.

Tonight, I hung out in P.I. until midnight then walked up to our berthing compartment just in time for the return of the drunken, cursing, fighting, staggering and stumbling young non-rated Boatswain's Mates in the neighboring compartment. Some were carried in unconscious. Their deck was spotted with pools of pale pink vomit, the stench horrible. One sailor lay passed out; his uniform torn and soaked with beer; his head positioned face down in a puddle of regurgitated beer and food particles. He had waited 35 long days for this glorious moment.

7 November 1967 ... 144th day. In Port – Yokosuka.

This morning all Det hands turned to and washed 604 Flight Deck aft. At 1300, I put my foot on Nipponese soil – liberty call in dress blues. With me were Richard Aden, Robert Chapin and Bart Gordon, one of the Ship's Company P.I.'s. We headed directly to the A-33 Foreign Merchandise Building where I bought a 55mm Micro Nikkor Auto lens, a slide copy attachment and other photo accessories. From there we headed into downtown Yokosuka clutching bags of civilian clothes purchased at the Navy Exchange. We rented storage at the Hide Away Locker Club for 1000 Yen. Conversion rate is Y360 to one U.S. dollar. After changing out of my silly sailor suit into civvies black Levi's, sport shirt, and black jacket, I felt human again and commenced Operation Hedonism. Knowing not what the evening would cost me in pride and pocketbook, I decided to give the night spots a whirl. All four of us walked to the bar and night club row with its neon lights, narrow streets and streetwalkers – the din of a hundred juke boxes all played different American tunes. This district is known to veterans as Thieves Alley. Signs were prominently displayed outside of each club with amusing messages such as: Welcum U.S. Hero, Come in and shoot the shit; Beautiful Girls, Lousy Service; Had Any Lately? Find Some in Here; Beautiful Girls-Good Booze-Cheap Price and the one that made me burst out laughing: Intercourse if you like.

We entered one of the dimly lit night spots and took a table. I was soon to discover that Japanese bar girls are the same as their counterparts in every port of call. After two minutes, we all had beers in front of us. After four minutes, we all had gals sitting on our laps. Lord, they were trashy looking: heavy messy eye makeup; gaudy cheap western-style dresses; their hair, probably washed in laundry detergent, was supposed to look like the work of a fine hairdresser but was definitely do-it-yourself.

The hooker next to me introduced herself, "Hi, my name is Miko. What's yours?"

"Mac."

"Mock?"

"Mock-san to you."

"What sheep you on?"

"Oriskany."

"So, Oriskany. Why you wear civvie clothes? Maybe Officer, yes?"

"No."

"Chief?"

"No. I rented the clothes."

"A so desu."

The chit-chat warm-up aside, she got down to the big question: "You buy me one ladies' drink, prease?"

"No."

"Prease? I only ask for one."

"How much is it?"

"500 Yen."

"500 Yen? Damn, that's a buck, fifty!"

"Only one time."

Melting from her cute, little child-like voice, I gave in: "Okay, Miko, just one time."

I stayed there longer than I should have because that only one time became two times, then three, then four. She was drinking iced tea, of course, staying stone sober while I was downing beer after beer getting drunker by the minute. That's when she came up with this line: "I think tonight we go to my house, have few drinks, then we make love to each other, just two of us with bodies close. We make beautiful love, Mock."

For some reason that pissed me off. Angrily, I shot back at her: "Do you know what love really is, Miko? What's in this for you? It's just business. I'm not an idiot. Do you think all American sailors are sex crazy? That we do nothing but drink and fuck, drink and fuck?"

She looked confused. She lowered her head and said to me in a sweet, shy voice: "But you been out to sea long time. No booze. No girls. All sailors get horny. Want girl when come to Yokosuka."

But I was in rare form. "All sailors not alike, Miko." I got up from the table and began to leave. I paused and turned around and addressed my little Japanese bar girl one last time, "I hope you find a better job and a nice man someday so you can know what true love is."

This always seems to happen if I get too drunk. I start preaching like some kind of holier-than-thou, self-righteous jerk.

I left the bar alone, leaving behind Chapin, Aden and Gordon who were still clutching their bitches and blowing their money. I went into another bar, sat down alone, and ordered hot sake. Why the hell did I do that to the poor girl? I was thinking to myself. I am an idiot... just a lost, drunken fool in a world of money-hungry devils. Why did I come down here anyway? Some men get rowdy and violent when drunk. I get depressed and weird and preachy. Around midnight, I returned to the locker club changing back into uniform. Rushing, running, stumbling, I just barely made it back through the main gate before it closed at 0100. Back on ship, I slumped into bed and was fast asleep.

10 November 1967 ... 147th day. In Port, Yokosuka, Japan.

The past three days haven't been much to write about. The Tokyo Bay area, with all its cities and mobs of people, doesn't have the charm of Sasebo. Yes, it's new territory but life is different up here, more like the big cities of California. People dress western-style. It's a faster pace; everyone seems to be in a hurry to get from place to place. Traveling about 60-to-90 miles per hour, the high-speed electric trains are an interesting phenomenon, something we sure don't have in the Midwestern U.S. And some of the modern innovations are quaint, such as glass panel doors that slide open automatically when a person approaches them. I think it's because of some little electronic eye that detects movement and triggers the open switch.

I've traveled around with a couple of the P.I. guys. We've snapped photos from the moving trains and taken shots of each other at the stations – again, nothing too interesting. Tokyo is a massive metropolis. Sidewalks are choked with short Japanese businessmen dressed in their dark suits, white shirts and ties rushing feverishly to their designated appointments while checking their watches every other minute to make sure they're not losing the rat race. The Ginza business district of Tokyo is crammed full of corporate headquarter buildings, each displaying their company name in bright neon Japanese characters and English. I was impressed by the SONY name display. Yes, if you seek it out, you can still find comforting traces of the old Japan but they seem almost out of place amidst the towers of glass and steel, the busy streets jam-packed with little compact cars violating traffic rules. We stopped at various eating places, from street corner food vendors to high-priced, fancy restaurants. I still enjoy the traditional food. And, actually being in the place where Nikon produces their cameras and photo equipment has given me the opportunity to complete my entire photo system at a price far less than I would have paid in the States. I'm thankful for that.

The problem here is: the urban Japanese seem to be as materialistic as their American counterparts. Tomorrow I think I'll search for some spiritual peace by visiting the ancient holy town of Kamakura.

CHAPTER XXVI
THE GREAT BUDDHA

11 November 1967 ... 148th day. In Port – Yokosuka.

    Japan is predominantly Buddhist. Westerners make fun of Buddhism. They just don't understand or try to understand. Another one of Christianity's downfalls is its attitude of spiritual arrogance – the idea that only Christians have knowledge of the absolute Truth. Personally, I think it's much more spiritually uplifting to know that my choices in life will bring about my salvation as compared to "You must believe that Jesus Christ died for your sins or you will spend eternity burning in the flames of hell."

    *   *   *   *   *   *   *

    Today, Walt Lehmann, my friend from Photo Intelligence and I went on a spiritual pilgrimage of sorts. Kitakamakura is a beautiful little village amidst tall, majestic pine trees. As everyday has been so far, it was cold and overcast but the weather didn't dampen our enthusiasm. In fact, it made us more attentive, alert and energetic. At Kitakamakura, we entered beneath an ancient Torii gate into the grounds of the Zen Buddhist priests. They live there in small houses. Several large temples and shrines dot the conifer-covered park. We had no guide or information in English so we knew not exactly what we were looking for. Walt and I walked down the narrow highway from Kitakamakura toward Kamakura, stopping along the way to eat at small refreshment stands and to gaze at monuments and small roadside shrines. Catching a taxi after we realized it was a damned long walk, we went to the Hashiman Shrine and Temple, a magnificent place. Entering under the very large Torii on to the grounds, we crossed an old arch bridge and walked through the gardens of golden autumn trees, stone paths, willows and lotus ponds. I stopped and purchased a Buddha medallion at a small tourist stand. I now proudly wear it around my neck. We paused at a tall wooden shrine with the traditional curved-edge corners on the roof. Climbing a hundred steps at a 45-degree angle, Walt and I visited the magnificent red temple at the top. Two stone lions guarded the temple doors. Tourists are not allowed to enter the main temple because priests still worship and pray there. In the outer corridors of the temple was a small museum containing religious relics. All the descriptions were in Japanese. It probably would have been very interesting if I could have understood it. I shot three rolls of film.

On our way to Daibutsu, The Great Buddha, Walt and I stopped into a Chinese eating house. Removing our shoes, we were escorted to our private room by a pretty, young Japanese girl in a kimono. We ate our meal in solitude and silence, the way it should be done. Seated cross-legged on floor cushions, Walt enjoyed Peking Chicken. I had General Tso and sake.

Looking upon the Great Buddha of Kamakura for the first time will, no doubt, be one of my most memorable experiences from this Vietnam Cruise. I've seen Daibutsu in a hundred photos. Every book about Japan includes a picture of him. And, because I've read and studied Buddhism so much, this moment in time was almost sacred. I must have taken over fifty photos with my Nikon. I stood at the base of this 45-foot bronze statue and engraved it into my mind. Sitting cross-legged in the traditional lotus position, the Enlightened One, with eyes cast down in meditation, exudes the spirit of absolute tranquility. Laying on his lap, palm up, his two hands meet. Thumbs and index fingers form an elliptical hole. The tourist pamphlet explains that such a configuration is typical of all Amida Nyorai statues in Japan. Whoever or whatever that is. Just the same, I felt so temporal knowing that the Daibutsu statue has been here for 800 years. It preceded me, and will be here long after I'm food for worms.

Walt, being the staunch Roman Catholic that he is, had nothing but criticism for the Daibutsu and Buddhism in general. He referred to the people praying and lighting incense at the base of the statue as idol worshipers and heathens.

"That's kind of a harsh judgment. Don't you think?" I asked him.

"Well, look at 'em. They're praying to this statue!"

I didn't respond but thought to myself: You know, Walt, when I was growing up in the Lutheran church, a lot of people called Catholics idol worshipers because you guys kneel down in front of statues of Jesus and Mary and the Saints. You light candles and incense and appear to be praying to them.

At that point, I stepped up to the decorative burning thing. It reminded me of a pot-bellied stove. Anyway, I lit my own stick of incense and stood there in silence to show my respect. I was not worshiping the statue – just using it for focus.

In my opinion, it's the same for most Buddhists; they just use the statues to focus on the person who was the Buddha, the Enlightened One, and his teachings. The Theravada school of Buddhist thought doesn't believe that Prince Siddhartha Gautama was God in the flesh as Christians do with Jesus. He was their flesh-and-blood spiritual leader. From what I've read, the Buddha made a final request to his disciples as he lay on his death bed. He asked that his followers never deify him. Yet, contrary to his request, some schools of Buddhism have done just that. I reckon it's just human nature to want a visible god. That's the reason for the Commandment received by Moses that prohibited the use of graven images. End of religious commentary.

Catching the 1700 train at the Kamakura station, Walt and I watched the sunset as the electric train sped us to Tokyo. Following an unsuccessful attempt to see the Imperial Palace grounds, we traveled downtown to the Ginza for a Kobe steak dinner at a small restaurant. We also found a high-class night club patronized primarily by Japanese business men. For 1000 Yen each – less than three bucks – we had a couple of mixed drinks, watched an entertaining floor show with live band. The night club is called The Showboat and is modeled after a Mississippi River stern-wheeler. The waiters wear little sailor uniforms. They look ridiculous but they're friendly and extremely courteous.

At 11:00 p.m., Walt and I walked back to the train station in a cold rain and caught the late rush train to Yokosuka and our ship, the end of a very pleasant day.

12 November 1967 ... 149th day. In Port – Yokosuka.

Duty calls for the young Mac-san. No liberty today. There was no work for the duty section so I just slummed and slept most of the day. I was to stand the 2000 to 2400 Aircraft Integrity Watch on Flight Deck One this evening, however only two men were needed on the Flight Deck. The other two watches were E-3 Airmen. I'm a 3rd Class PO, an E-4. So guess who got to opt out?

I watched some of the Nipponese TV programs on the ship's closed-circuit television this evening. It wasn't much different than back home; too many commercials and not enough programs. I started to watch an American movie, Colorado Territory, starring Joel McCrea but couldn't hack it. Who wants to hear the manly Joel McCrea speaking Japanese in a squeaky little voice?

13 November 1967 ... 150th day. In Port – Yokosuka.

The weather today was perfect: clear sky, cool autumn temperature. After walking Early Liberty Chits through the chain of command, Big Ern and I put on our dress blues and were off the ship by 0900. At first, he was reluctant but I talked Ernest into renting civilian clothes at the locker club. Levitt has taken time to gather maps and information on areas around Tokyo Bay and is well versed on what railroad lines and highways to take to see interesting out-of-the-way places. Again we rode the train twenty minutes to Kamakura. I introduced the Great Buddha to Big Ern. Today I used black and white film. We also took in several temples that I didn't know were there. I was awestruck by the grandeur of Buddhist architecture and craftsmanship. There was the Hase Kannon, a 30-foot wooden statue of a standing Buddha covered with gold leaf. We visited many small shrines and the temple and pagoda at Enoshima.

In Ofuna we climbed a large hill topped by a 50-foot high, white marble statue of Maya, the mother of Buddha. She looks very much like Christendom's depictions of Mary, the mother of Jesus. From that exhilarating perch, we watched the sunset and then took time exposure photos of Maya after dark.

Deciding to call our day of cultural expeditions to an end, Ern and I returned on the train to Yokosuka and walked over to Club Alliance, the Enlisted Men's watering hole to down a few mixed drinks. At the locker club, we changed back to Navy blues and returned to the Big Zero at 2200.

14 November 1967 ... 151st day. In Port – Yokosuka.

Our last day in Japan! Lord, I hate leaving this beautiful, cool autumn and returning to hot, damp Yankee Station. Last month one of our sister carriers, the U.S.S. Intrepid, was here in Yokosuka. Four sailors, three 19-year-olds and a 20-year-old, deserted. They went AWOL in Tokyo during an anti-Vietnam War street protest. They never returned to the ship. Desertion in war time is punishable by death or a very severe prison sentence. I don't know what they were thinking. Apparently they're still being sheltered by the Japanese Peace in Vietnam Committee, a left wing socialist organization. The four Americans have issued public statements to the news media denouncing U.S. involvement in Vietnam. The Intrepid will be home in the U.S. by Christmas. Who knows where these four fucking idiots will be? Probably Peking or Moscow.

I practiced using my soroban today. I picked it up at Thieves' Alley a few days ago. It's a computing device with rows of beads that most of the merchants here use to calculate sales. It's much the same as a Greek abacus, an amazing little device. I'll learn how to use it and then teach it to my little brother Jeff when I get home. He can take it to show and tell at school and amaze his teacher.

Final reflections of this final day: The urban young people here are much different than those of Sasebo. They're Americanized. Many boys and girls have grown their hair like San Francisco hippies. Tokyo authorities have had problems with these kids and their mass demonstrations. Society's elders are worried that their children are abandoning the old, traditional ways, and picking up bad habits and behaviors that they see on American television programs. Hot dog and hamburger joints have not invaded yet. The Japanese still prefer their native foods but who knows how long that will last?

As modern and materialistic as the New Nippon may be, I still see a reverence for long-lived traditions and for the abiding faiths of the country: Shintoism and Buddhism. Having said that, I look back to Imperial Japan and World War II and wonder how practicing Buddhists could have committed the sort of atrocities that Japanese soldiers carried out on the people they conquered. And, how could true Buddhists accept the concept of a divine Emperor? From what I understand, a faithful Buddhist would rather die than snuff out another human soul. It's one of the genuine religions of peace and non-violence. Maybe someone can explain the paradox to me some day. Then again, maybe most Japanese are just Jack Buddhists. My friend, Roger, at FIC PAC FAC called himself a Jack Mormon. It meant he was a member of the LDS church but didn't really practice the faith or believe all of their doctrines.

CHAPTER XXVII
TYPHOON GILDA

15 November 1967 ... 152nd day. Back to the Briny Blue.

Ninety-two days and a wake-up, and I will be bussing out that gate at NAS Miramar, saying "Good riddance."

This morning the Det mustered at 0745 in Hangar Bay 3 as it does every day in-port. At exactly 0800 the 1MC announced our departure: "Ship is underway! Shift colors!" The Oriskany steamed out of Tokyo Bay churning the calm inland waters. Today was much like the day when we entered port: grey overcast, a penetrating cold wind with drizzle. Only one day was clear and sunny during our Yokosuka stay: November 13th, the day Ern and I visited Kamakura. I'm not complaining. I've enjoyed the cold.

The open sea was choppy. White-capped waves dotted the dark blue depth of the Pacific. As we proceeded, the cloud cover broke and Old Sol showed his face again but didn't warm us. The farther out we got, the more the wind increased – blizzard winds sans snow. Our big iron tub pitched, rolled, jerked and shuddered.

Lieutenant Commander Sonniksen and LTJG Beam flew 601 and 603 onboard at 1400. They had just left Naval Air Station Atsugi. Both Photo Birds looked primo. They have been completely repainted and revamped during our R&R period. The Big Cheese of the Det encountered some problems in 601. After hitting the deck and detaching the cable, he advanced the throttle to taxi forward but got no response from the engine. It remained in idle. The jolt of the landing must have finished off an impending discrepancy. If the throttle had gone bad during his flight, we'd probably be mourning loss of plane or pilot right now, maybe both. It was a close call. Sonniksen can't blame this fuck-up on our Det mechanics. The Aircraft Maintenance Division (AMD) at Atsugi made the error while overhauling the aircraft. My complaint is that most of my Yosemite Sam illustrations on the tails were sanded off and painted over. I'll hold off as long as possible but I know I'll have to repaint the little motherfuckers. Ron likes Sam.

Today's mail call brought a surprise package addressed to our fearless leader. It was a large mailing tube from Personality Posters, Inc. addressed to: "Ronny Sonniksen." Inside it were two 30-by-40 inch posters: one of Mao Tse Tung and one of Black

Panther Stokely Carmichael. Sonniksen was in Photo Intelligence when he opened the tube. Walt Lehmann and Duncan were watching as smoke began to billow from the boss' ears, his face turning bright red. Before storming out the door, he threw the posters toward Walt and yelled, "Tear them up!"

Big Ern is now avoiding LCDR Sonniksen for some strange reason. I've got to hand it to Levitt. He's a trip.

16 November 1967 ... 153st day.
Somewhere in the western Pacific Ocean.

Yet another typhoon is in the area south of Japan and northeast of the Philippines. This one is called Gilda and is worse than Emma which, I'm told, wreaked havoc on Manila and Subic Bay and made seas rough out here last month. Winds near the center of Gilda are 125 miles per hour. Today, even though we're several hundred miles away from her, the Oriskany is encountering heavy seas. We are at Typhoon Readiness Condition 3. If the ship heads back to Yankee Station by the usual course, chances are, we'll run directly into Gilda. Captain Billy and his navigators have decided to take an alternative route around the east side of Luzon, then steam through the San Bernardino Strait to the South China Sea.

No flight ops today. No photo work. No one is allowed on the catwalks or weather decks. So, we're stuck inside like ants in a beer can on Colorado River rapids. That damned fast-stopping elevator sensation is twice as bad in my forward berthing compartment. Once I am in the rack tonight all nestled in my cradle, I looked forward to being gently rocked to sleep.

In the photo shop, using a little measuring device that we created out of string, a wrench and angle radius, we measured the rolls. They were 15 to 20-degrees throughout the day. One larger 25 degree roll slammed our pea coat locker flat on to the deck and thrust rolls of canned 5-inch film off of the shelves.

Those poor bastards on our destroyer escorts get rolls as strong as 45 degrees. I've heard that everyone just goes to bed except for the man at the wheel.

Danko lost his familiar name today. From now on he will be addressed as Chief Danko. He packed and relocated to CPO Quarters. Good riddance.

November 18, 1967 ... 155th day.
Somewhere in the Philippine Islands.

The air temp is rising. We must be close to Luzon because several F-8s and A-4s flew on from Naval Air Station Cubi Point this afternoon. We had no launches. All of our Photo Birds are up and ready for action.

The inevitable happened already. Chief O'Brian commanded me to repaint the Yosemite Sam's on the tails of our aircraft. Reluctantly, I grabbed up the paints and worked throughout the day. I had to do 603 from scratch. The painters hadn't totally fucked up 604 so that was a retouch job. I was unable to do 601 because it was parked by the elevator and covered with salt spray. I'm brokenhearted about that.

CHAPTER XXVIII
FROM TEMPEST TO MADNESS

19 November 1967 ... 156th day.
Back on Yankee Station, Tonkin Gulf.

We're back in the war zone following our four day transit from Yokosuka. The sea is smooth, the sun is shining and the Grim Reaper is back onboard. A fatal mishap occurred on the Flight Deck today. One of Fighter Squadron 111's Crusaders, piloted by LT. Ed Van Orden, was linked to the catapult ready for launch. He turned up. The cat built pressure and was released. Halfway down the cat track the coupling of the shuttle to the belly of the plane broke off. The F-8 skidded off track and although the pilot was bearing down on his brakes, he continued forward diagonally across the deck on to the port side canoe. He panicked, apparently believing that the plane was going over the bow into the drink. The Lieutenant punched out his ejection seat. The canopy blew off and the explosive charge under his seat ignited, rocketing him about thirty feet into the air. Still strapped in his seat, the pilot descended and crashed face down in the portside catwalk. Had the seat descended only ten feet to the left or ten feet forward he would have entered the water and possibly survived unless of course he was sucked into the ship's screws and chopped to pieces.

The Flight Deck crew worked feverishly to unstrap him from his seat and corpsmen rushed him to Sickbay on the litter but he died on the operating table. Ironically his aircraft did not go over the bow. The nose gear collapsed and it came to a halt on the edge of the cat guide. Had Van Orden stayed in the cockpit he would have lived but he was faced with a split-second decision and sadly made the wrong one. Investigators said the cause of the catapult linkage break was too much steam pressure. It jerked the plane forward breaking the chain halfway down the track. Catapult force is adjusted according to the weight of each individual aircraft. I'm told that it's possible to mistakenly set steam pressure too high but no one is saying that's what happened. Four F-8s had been launched prior to the ill-fated Fighter Squadron 111 aircraft. All are in down status now awaiting that inspection of their catapult coupling bars.

As a Navy photographer, I had to take photos of the ejection seat in the catwalk. I feel like a vulture hovering over the scene of death but I wasn't alone. Dozens of Ship's Company and Air Wing personnel were snapping photos. I guess we all have a little vulture in us.

We thought there may be another tragedy in the making later in the afternoon. A damaged A-4 Skyhawk was unable to drop its tail hook for landing so the Flight Deck crew quickly set up the nylon-web barricade to catch the speeding plane. No death or injury this time. Pilot and plane were safely brought to a halt.

Tomorrow, we begin bombing North Vietnam again. While reading a stateside news magazine a couple of nights ago, I found an enlightening article concerning Phuc Yen airfield, the big one our Air Group hit on October 24 and 25. The story claimed that the Russian MIG base was back in operation less than a week after our heavy bombing. Such a rapid repair job is typical of the North Vietnamese. Apparently Defense Secretary McNamara had argued that such puny results are not worth the risks taken by our pilots but that heavy pressure from Congress and the military high commands force decisions to bomb targets like Phuc Yen just the same.

What the hell? Did McNamara get cold-cocked by reason and common sense while we were on R&R? He's right by golly. That particular set of Alpha Strikes cost our Air Wing alone four aircraft, two pilots captured by the NVA and one was killed-in-action. Maybe we should put some of those senators and top brass in a Willie Fudd and fly them over Phuc Yen. I reckon they'd say, "Phuc no!"

20 November 1967 ... 157th day.
Gulf of Tonkin, North Vietnam.

The first strikes of this our last complete line period were flown today. Three photo hops were scheduled but gremlins struck. Dave Beam in 601 and Harry Sampson in 603 were turning up on the Flight Deck in preparation of a double sortie but before they could begin their taxi to the cats, 603 overheated and popped several circuit breakers. Mr. Sam's flight was immediately cancelled. Then 601 developed photo problems. The KA68 and KA53 cameras weren't relaying info to the cockpit panel indicators. Harry Hedge was in his emergency state of frenzy jumping around like a crazed dervish with visions of his promotion to Chief going down the drain. Obviously displeased, Mr. Beam, surveyed the Photo Mates from his cockpit as we looked for the source of the problem. Ray Hines, our best troubleshooter, found it. One of the cannon plugs on the junction box was in the wrong socket. He corrected it and all systems were go. No one is pointing fingers but I think I'm the one who made the fuck-up. Oops.

Maybe the Flight Deck problems were an omen. Beam's mission over Nam was harrowing. Two surface-to-air missiles were launched at 601 and his F-8 fighter escort. Upon his safe return to the ship, Beam let us listen to his flight recorder during the missile scare. We could hear the eerie sound of the SAM warning system in the cockpit. Then we heard Beam's escort pilot shouting, "Pull up! Pull up!" Beam had taken the evasion tactic of going into a steep dive but he was going so fast he built up 7 Gs, seven times the normal pressure of gravity, placing both aircraft and pilot in danger of collapse. One of the SAM's exploded to the rear of 601. The second SAM grazed the belly of the escort at which time the pilot could be heard loud and clear on the tape yelling, "God Damn!" The two planes cheated death today and following the SAM incident went on to fly an excellent photo recon mission.

First day and the pilots were back into the thick of it. Lieutenant JG Earl of Attack Squadron 163 was diving on one of his targets in his Skyhawk when small arms shells penetrated the nose of his aircraft. One of the shells passed through his left foot and lodged in his right leg just below the knee breaking his tibia. Bleeding profusely and growing weak, Lieutenant Earl turned his bird back to the ship escorted by his strike leader who talked to him all the way trying to keep him conscious. Because he was physically incapable of operating the foot pedals and because Captain Billy Holder wanted to make sure the crippled pilot and aircraft were trapped on the first landing attempt, the nylon-web barricade was once again rigged on the Flight Deck.

Hitting the barricade and brought to a safe stop, LT Earl, I'm sure, was saying, "Thank you, Jesus." His aircraft was engulfed by dozens of Flight Deck personnel, by fire trucks, fog foam hoses, a platform forklift, and medical staff with litter and equipment. The platform forklift was raised to the cockpit with stretcher and two corpsmen. They eased the pilot out, his face grimacing in pain. He was lowered and rushed below decks to surgery. The 1MC announced that Type A+ blood was needed from the crew. I went down to donate but there were already dozens of A-pluses waiting in line, so I figured they had enough and returned to the Photo Shop.

Good news tonight from Captain Billy in his evening report. Lieutenant JG Earl is listed in fair condition and his leg was saved.

21 November 1967 ... 158th day. Ibid.

Clouds today over the pock-marked face of North Vietnam. Three photos hops were scheduled but only one flew: that one was by our swashbuckling, poster ripper, Ron Sonniksen in 601. During his mission, the camera bay ventilation system overheated as it has before and blew circuit breakers. The cameras stopped operating. He returned to the ship. The Photo Mates was braced for another royal ass chewing but Sonniksen wasn't pissed. Neither was Chief O'Brian. What's wrong with them? Our afternoon hops were cancelled due to lack of fighter escorts. There is a critical shortage of F-8 Crusaders in Fighter Squadrons 162 and 111, the latter having four planes down awaiting x-ray inspection of the catapult coupling bar.

CHAPTER XXIX
LESSER MEN DIE; PRESIDENTS DON'T

22 November 1967 ... 159th day. Ibid.

As long as I live, I'll never forget November 22nd. My beloved President was assassinated by that fuckin' little Commie in Dallas four years ago today. November 22, 1963, I was in the high school hallway, near the cafeteria when the loudspeaker came alive. It was Mr. Taylor, the principal: "Attention all students and faculty! We have just received word that President Kennedy has been hospitalized in Dallas, Texas, after he was apparently hit by gunfire. We don't have details yet but again, let me repeat, President John F. Kennedy is in a Dallas, Texas hospital possibly injured by gunfire. I'll have more later."

I was frozen in place. The world had just stopped. No one was moving. They just stood in place with mouths gaping, unable to grasp the shocking news. A few minutes passed. Hallway traffic resumed but at half speed. Many of the girls were sobbing. Boys were making stupid jokes. Teachers huddled and talked amongst themselves.

It seemed foolish to continue classes as if life was normal but we didn't know what else to do. The next period was American History with Mr. Mueller. It was a pud course because if we didn't like the lesson of the day all we had to do was ask Old Man Mueller about his World War II experience and he'd spend the rest of the period lost in the past. But on November 22, 1963 we didn't talk about war. Sullen and long-faced, he attempted a few reflective words but they came out of him as half-hearted garble. So we just sat there uncharacteristically quiet, looking at the pages of our books, and waiting. Some cried. Some prayed.

Surely, I thought, it was only a wound. Someone might shoot the President but they can't kill a President. He has the best doctors and surgeons in the country. Lesser men die. Presidents don't.

The school public address system crackled on. Our attention was immediately riveted to the cloth-covered box above the blackboard. "We have just received word that President Kennedy has been the victim of an assassin's bullet. I'm sorry to announce that President John F. Kennedy is dead. Again, our President... is dead."

Tears flowed freely. And it wasn't just the girls. No one was too hip, too bad, too cool to hide his grief. Even Mr. Mueller, tough old war veteran, was reduced to tears.

A few hours later, we all became aware that the entire nation was in mourning with us and virtually everyone had responded the same way when they heard the terrible news. The United States of America wept together for its fallen leader, the charismatic, young senator from Massachusetts who had charmed his way into the nation's hearts. He and his glamorous wife, Jackie, and two children, Caroline and John-John, had epitomized the vibrancy of this new era. They weren't old fogies like Eisenhower, Truman, and Roosevelt. They were like us: young and alive, free spirited and filled with ideals for a better tomorrow. We had laughed at Jack Kennedy's wit. Vaughn Meader's comedy parody album, The First Family had topped the album charts for almost a year.

But on November 22, 1963, Camelot ended. There was no Thanksgiving that year. All three television networks cancelled regular programming. During that holiday break and for days to follow, I gazed at the black-and-white screen in our living room, witnessing the aftermath of Kennedy's assassination. Misty-eyed news veterans Walter Cronkite, Chet Huntley and David Brinkley talked me through my grief.

Yes, there was the initial shock of the November 22nd afternoon but then there was the aftershock at home as I saw the suspected assassin, Lee Harvey Oswald, shot and killed on live television. At bedtime, I lay there alone sobbing, angry at God, wanting to ask somebody, anybody, Why?

I wrote a letter to the White House asking for a photo of the fallen President. Next morning, I returned to the television. I camped there for the return to Washington, the public viewing, the procession, little John-John's salute, the funeral, the burial, the lighting of the eternal flame.

* * * * * * *

We had three photo hops scheduled today but no escorts were available. So our pilots enjoyed a safe and secure day off. Already the Ship's Company is making preparations for our return to the states. In the Plan of the Day, we were asked to convey to our correspondents not to send any 2nd, 3rd, or 4th class mail after the first of December because it will be retained in Alameda until our return.

This afternoon Chief O'Brian came into the Photo Shop, where we were lounging and sleeping, and told us he needed the total weight and cubic feet of all Navy and personal gear that we'll be sending on the trucks from Alameda to Miramar. After the Chief left, Aden had a little tantrum. Keeping my short-timers cool, I turned to and started dragging out all of our cameras, cases, ejectors and other paraphernalia. Borrowing a hanging scale from maintenance, I worked for six hours weighing and calculating.

23 November 1967 ... 160th day. Ibid.

It's Thanksgiving Day. I didn't even think about it until I went down to the mess for lunch. Hot damn, decorations were hanging from the overhead. The tables had autumn-theme centerpieces, so very appropriate here in the sub-tropics. And God bless the cooks, we had the finest meal so far this cruise, all traditional: turkey, stuffing, sweet potatoes, cranberry sauce, pumpkin and minced-meat pie. Delicious. After the feast, I went up to our Photo Shop where Harry, portly Ernest, sarcastic Aden and soul-brother Ray were either napping or talking shit. I sat down with my notebooks and wrote several pages of trivia. I spent the evening in P.I. talking trivia with P.T.'s and Officers. All in all it was a very trivial Thanksgiving Day.

Today's front page of the Pacific Edition Stars and Stripes had a feature story about the U.S.S. Intrepid's four deserters. They're in Moscow! There was a photo of the dumb shits all spiffy in their cheap suits, white shirts and ties. One was being patted on the back by a grinning, little Russian bureaucrat. The traitors have made hundreds of anti-American statements and will, no doubt, denounce their American citizenship, too. I reckon they're staying for life because, as I mentioned before, a U.S. military man committing treason during a time of war still gets his sorry ass shot dead by a firing squad.

What is this ideology called Communism? Just about every American has an opinion, usually negative, but relatively few know the basic concepts of Communist theory. I have studied about it in my spare time. I tried reading Karl Marx' Das Kapital but gave up.

It's written in economists' language and I guess I'm just too stupid to comprehend.

From each according to his ability to each according to his need. I did learn enough to know that a true communistic form of government would be mankind's crowning achievement but it will never be realized because of the common weaknesses in human nature. As Lieutenant Michael Goldberg pointed out, every so-called Communist government so far, following The People's Revolution has become bogged down in the developmental stage called The Dictatorship of the Proletariat. And in most cases, that has degenerated into just plain, oppressive dictatorship by a single ruler or group of rulers. Case in point: Ho Chi Minh, claims that his country is Communist but in reality, it's a dictatorship under the iron hand of Uncle Ho. Still I sometimes ask myself if a unified Vietnam under the banner of Communism could be any worse than the vice and corruption rampant in the South Vietnamese government. Could it be any worse than the continual fighting, death, bombing, broken lives, broken homes and general heartache of war? Seditious thoughts, I know. Seditious and damned confusing. That's why I keep them to myself. Lord knows I don't want to sound like any of those American traitors in Moscow.

24 November 1967 ... 161st day. Ibid.

Two birds went out this morning on weather reconnaissance flights. Again no fighter escorts available so 601 and 603 escorted one another. It's overcast and raining in North Vietnam. Same here. We had heavy rain last night. Our pilots have been restless. That's why they arranged the double weather flight, not because it was necessary but because they wanted to log some flight time. They shot no photos which, of course, made us happy. The Carrier Air Group strikes as of late have been nothing remarkable. They're bombing water-borne logistics craft, trucks, barges, bridges and the like. No Alpha Strikes so far this line period. The rest of the day was devoted to personal interests. Maintenance had a few gripes to work on but our cameras are in good shape. I began a letter home, sending some photographs and wrapping a miniature Buddha for my kid brother, Jeff.

Harry W. Hedge III, my 24-year-old Sea Daddy has changed lately. Since Big Ern returned from the mess decks, Harry treats him as if he's not needed anymore and largely ignores him. Harry has decided to do something that he said at the beginning of this cruise he would never do and that's become a member of The First Class Lounge, the old men's sea story center. Harry re-enlists on 15 December for a six-year hitch. O' well, that's his choice; his life. The U.S. Navy needs men like him. Otherwise it wouldn't be the best damned sea-going fleet in the entire world. Aye! The devil, they say, still rides the waves in the soul of a seafaring man.

26 November 1967 ... 163rd day. Ibid.

Today began as an official Stand Down Day. No shit. Buy me ladies' drink. Today's flight schedule showed no ops whatsoever and then, all of a sudden, we were pre-flighting 603 for a photo mission. Ours is not to wonder why; ours is just to do and fly. The brass decided they wanted five combat and one photo sortie before securing flight quarters at noon. An Air Wing Awards Ceremony was planned early afternoon. Then the ceremony was cancelled. This made us happy because none of us likes changing into our ice cream suits. Then the gods announced that we were going to commence Alpha Strikes. We waited an hour for final confirmation before we got too agitated. Then they announced that Alpha Strikes were cancelled. There you go! SNAFU: Situation Normal, All Fucked Up.

Chief Danko strutted into our shop around 1500 today and relayed to me a message from Chief O'Brian: "Since you have nothing to do, this would be a good time to finish that Yosemite Sam on 601. Okay?"

Fuck Yosemite fuckin' Sam! I'm getting so goddamned sick of painting Yosemite Sam cartoons on airplanes. I cussed and pouted but ended up doing it. Of course.

27 November 1967 ... 164th day. Ibid.

"No, We do not use anti-personnel bombs on the North Vietnamese." Back to his normal self, Secretary McNamara has been trying to bullshit the American public again.

Hell, we used them today. Our official rationale for using them is to terminate personnel operating the AAA's and SAM sites but who knows who else might be in the area? And, sure, once in a while Cluster Bomb Units – CBU's – go astray and wipe out civilians going about their daily lives but collateral damage is to be expected in any war. Doncha know?

These CBU's are cleverly-devised killers. The bomb is a large pod that splits apart upon impact releasing dozens of softball-shaped, metal grenades. These scatter and then explode penetrating any person or object close to them with large pellets. Ordnancemen claim this bomb wipes out all life in an area the size of a football field. The North Vietnamese media claims that dozens of women and children have been killed or mutilated by them. But can you trust the North Vietnamese media? Then again, can you trust McNamara?

Alpha Strikes were flown today; major targets were hit by the Big Zero's Air Wing. Kien An was one of them. I don't know the extent of the damage. Frankly, it's all redundant. We destroy; they rebuild; we destroy again; they rebuild again; et cetera ad nauseum.

I stayed up late, perfecting and finishing my song tonight. It's dedicated to my friend, Lieutenant JG Zissu, and others who have died on this cruise. It goes like this:

FADE ACROSS THE BLUE SEA

Mere man cannot heal the thing that has died
In the boy who was wed to a blood-stained bride.
A house in the meadow, a child and a wife,
Set sail with the dreams that once were his life.

The sun withholds its beckoning glow
Dead flowers are crushed under blankets of snow.
They say that he lives but he only exists
For, no man can capture the dream that he missed.

A damp, blade of grass fade across the blue sea
Buried in winter and no longer free.

In silence, he breathed the hot, boiling flame,
He stood in the blast of a murdering plane.
A propeller spun and ground to the bone,
His blood sprayed the wing that will carry him home.

A jagged, high peak grabbed the life of a friend

Death and red steel, flesh burnt in the wind.
Charred and forgotten, a young dream no more,
A spark is smothered in ash and the gore.

A damp, blade of grass fade across the blue sea
Buried in winter and no longer free.

In calm surface sea off of enemy shore
A thousand explosions in deafening roar
Scar minds and faces, hardened and grey,
Ending all hope of meadow bright days.
In the mud and the oil of a field somewhere
Mangled metal and eyes that only can stare
Look up to nothing, nothing but red,

Red of the fire, the blood and the dead.

A damp blade of grass fade across the blue sea
Buried in winter and no longer free.

28 November 1967 ... 165th day. Ibid.

Life amidst the bombs! The designated ammo storage areas are overflowing so the ordnance people just park the bombs on their carts anywhere they can find space. Standing in line at the ship's post office, we have to straddle bombs. Sitting in the chow hall eating our breakfast, we watch as the Red Shirts wheel bombs and rockets by our tables. During ammo unrep – underway replenishment – the Hangar Bay surface is coated like an overpopulated ant colony with bombs of all sizes, varieties, and killing capacities — bombs for North Vietnam, courtesy of the citizens of the United States of America.

We flew two flights today: one at 0800 and the other at noon. Each returned with nothing because of the cloud cover over target zones but "Never Say Die" Muffley arranged another flight at 1500 in one last desperate attempt to take some pictures. Charlie Rudd flew the hop and shot all of his film. This ruined our no-hitter but made Navy Intelligence officer Merkin Muffley one very giddy and gratified Ivy-Leaguer.

In the strikes today, Air Wing 16 pilots slammed through intense flak in a major strike against the western Haiphong railroad yard and a nearby railroad highway bridge. The key railroad yard, one and a half miles southwest of Haiphong proper, is the second largest rail facility in the area. It is located on the main line leading to Hanoi. Take that, you bastards! I'll bet that puts you out of commission for at least two weeks.

29 November 1967 ... 166th day, Ibid.

Lieutenant Junior Grade David Beam, as previously mentioned, is the 24-year-old pilot in our detachment. He's mischievous and loves practical jokes. His light-hearted attitude and fraternization with Enlisted Men is frowned upon by Regular-Navy Officers but Beam could give a damn. In Sasebo, Olongapo, and Yokosuka, he went bar hopping with the crew just like he was one of the boys. He often visits our Photo Shop under the pretext of official business when actually all he wants to do is shoot the breeze and match wits. He enjoys being contrary. He hates putting on his dress uniform to eat supper in the Officer's ward room.

"The State Room!" Laughing at the irony, he makes fun of the name of the Officer's berthing compartment: "The State Room my ass!"

I think Beamer doesn't want to be a career Officer and refuses to act like one. It's always nice to have him visit because laughter follows him in the door.

Beam did one hop this morning but the weather closed in on us this afternoon and all Air Wing flights were cancelled for the rest of the day. I was uneasy today. I'm smoking too much – up to two packs a day. Every time I pull out another cigarette, I undergo a mental trial-and-punishment period but usually light up anyway. I've become friends with tar and nicotine mostly out of boredom. It fills the gaps on those days when there's not much to do. On the other hand, I want to live a long, healthy life but I certainly will not if I continue to be a slave of the American tobacco companies.

I was hoping to have some peaceful time in the Photo Shop today to catch up with this diary but then two of the plane captains from VA-163 came over and asked Harry if they could use our work bench to set up their tape recorders. He gave them permission. Almost all of us have reel-to-reel tape recorders: either Akai's, Teac's, or Sony's. The reel tapes will hold up to four or five complete albums of music depending on whether you use seven and a half inches per second or three and three quarters inches per second running speed. A lot of guys make custom reels of just their favorite songs but we all borrow from one another. I think just one person bought the reel tape of "Sergeant Pepper's Lonely Hearts Club Band" and within a few weeks everyone had dubbed it to their own personal tape by patching from one tape unit to the other. So much for my solitude. Within two hours of the first appearance, we had more plane captains, and one of Harry's amateur radio friends. The counter was set up with three tape decks, tuner-amps, two sets of large speakers and a ham receiver.

I heard some scuttlebutt in one of the passageways. A radioman was saying McNamara has resigned. Surely Not!

I wasn't in the mood for a music and ham radio party so I just left the shop and roamed through the ship passageways and cul-de-sacs for a couple of hours looking for that next turn where I would step through a mirror and find myself in a vast, green valley with blooming flowers and cottonwood trees rustling in the summer breeze; a small stream, perhaps, with brown trout, frogs and tadpoles; jack rabbits bounding through the Buffalo Grass and no other human within sight. Damn! All I could find were steel bulkheads, steel decks, steel overheads, ventilation pipes, steam pipes, water pipes, valves, bundles of power cables, hatches, bulletin boards and hundreds of faces. I see new faces every day because this ship is a city. Still uneasy this evening, I paced and smoked.

30 November 1967 ... 167 day. Ibid.

We're socked in by heavy weather: overcast, heavy rain and high winds – same over North Vietnam. How the hell are we going to win this war if we can't drop our 500-pound bombs on boats, trucks, tool sheds, grass huts, schoolhouses and old men riding bicycles?

It's interesting how the attitudes of people have changed during the course of this cruise. Chief O'Brian has turned over many of his duties to newly-anointed Chief Danko. I see him smiling a lot more because of that. O'Brian retires in March after serving his country for 26 years. Enlisting in 1941 at the age of seventeen, he'll start drawing his pension at forty-three. Chief O'Brian is a veteran of World War II, the Korean War and now Vietnam. Even though it's hard to respect some of his orders, you've got to respect his service record. He was a warrior when I was still a tadpole swimming around in my Daddy's scrotum. And, O'Brian was in the big one, World War II, back when U.S. Ships were enemy targets and thousands of sailors died at sea.

Lieutenant Commander Sonniksen has changed. Maybe he had a religious experience. Instead of being the grumbling grouch we've come to know and avoid. he now smiles when he meets us in the passageways, even says, "Howdy." When returning from his photo missions he doesn't fuck with our heads anymore but promptly tells us what cameras he shot and how much footage.

1 December 1967 ... 168th day. Ibid.

Only seventeen more days for this line period. I learned yesterday we'll be anchoring in Hong Kong for Christmas. Cool.

A few strike aircraft went out today but the Photo Birds remained grounded due to the shitty weather. The monsoon season comes to Southeast Asia this time of year and continues through January. Chances are, our flights will be very limited for the remainder of the cruise. For a lot of the guys, this cool, damp weather wets down their spirits but not me. It's such a welcome change from the first months out here when temps were in the 90s approaching 100 and the humidity was stifling. Now, I sleep under a blanket every night.

A book arrived in today's mail call that I ordered two and a half months ago. It's called "Mansions of the Soul: The Cosmic

Conception." From the Ancient Mystical Order of Rosae Crusis in San Jose, California, it explains the doctrine of reincarnation from their perspective. I read a few pages up until 1900 when duty called: another four hour Flight Deck Aircraft Integrity Watch. Again, I walked the cold, lonely post on the silent deck making sure no saboteurs messed with the parked fighters and bombers. It rained intermittently. The Petty Officer of the Watch – we call him the POW – equipped me with a Mae West life preserver just in case I fell over the side into the drink. The preserver, made of rubberized canvas, is shaped like a vest. At the bottom in the front are two cords that are linked to compressed CO_2 cartridges. If a man goes overboard, he pulls the cords when he hits the water and the preserver inflates. The front side, when inflated, looks like two mammoth breasts hence the reference to buxom film star Mae West.

Taking an unauthorized break from the watch, I moseyed down to Photo Intelligence to warm myself up with a cup of coffee. Lieutenant Muffley was there with the PT's doing nothing in particular. When he saw me come in, he walked up to me with a shit eating grin on his face, and grabbed my Mae West cords.

I smiled back, "You wouldn't do that, would you?"

He did. I inflated instantly. The boys all had a good laugh at my expense.

Embarrassed but amused, I walked back up to the POW in the ship's superstructure. His eyes bugged when he saw me.

"Why the hell did you do that, MacLennon?" He barked.

"Ah, I didn't do it," I replied.

"You better have a good excuse or I'm writing you up!"

"One of our pilots came up to me while I was on watch and thought it would be funny to pull my cords. He's kind of a practical joker."

"An Officer, huh?"

"Yeah, Lieutenant JG Muffley."

As much as the POW tried to retain a serious face, a few seconds of silence passed and he broke out laughing. "Well, I guess we'll have to get you another one, won't we."

"Thanks for understanding."

Re-equipped for falling overboard, I returned to the Flight Deck. The rest of the four hour watch passed without consequence or embarrassment.

2 December 1967 ... 169th day. Ibid.

Today our illustrious Harry Hedge III reenlisted in the U.S. Navy for another six years. In a brief ceremony on the bridge, Captain Billy Holder did the honors. Hedge is officially on his way to becoming a lifer. For the rest of the day, Ray, Dick, Big Ern and I were flipping him shit but it was all in fun. Three flights were scheduled for Photo Squadron 63 today but they didn't happen. All the other squadrons flew but not us.

3 December 1967 ... 170th day. Ibid.

The days are racing by. Our Plan of the Day briefed us on rules and regulations while we're in the British Crown Colony of Hong Kong.

The ship's fresh water supply is up to 98 per cent. So far this line period we've had plenty of water, no special shower hours. Whatever was causing us to lose water must have been discovered and fixed. It probably required one plumber extracting his cranium from his colon. The Eagle shit today. I elected to keep my pay on the books until we pull into port. With the addition of Hazardous Duty Pay, for working the Flight Deck, I'm earning $112 a week. Damn good money when you consider it's all gravy. My meals and lodging are free.

Sorry to say, we broke our silence today by launching two Photo Birds at 0900. Lieutenant Sam and my bud, Charlie Rudd, flew together in what was supposed to be a weather recon mission. They changed their plans and flew over target area Hon Gai taking publicity photos of other aircraft in action plus a few photos of each other. Even though the photos serve no strategic purpose, they often end up on in the pages of Stars and Stripes and other publications, and quite possibly, future books about the Vietnam War. The weather turned to crap while the fly boys were out taking snapshots. When it came time for landing and recovery, the ship was enshrouded in a cold drizzle. I wore a duty jacket under my green jersey and still shivered. A wind of 30-to-35 knots didn't help matters. I pitied the pilots having to land under such unfavorable conditions. Days like this really test their metal. Fortunately they all touched down and caught the wire safely. Confident that they hadn't shot very much film in weather like this, we weren't prepared for complete unloading and reloading. When they told us they had used all of their cameras, we had to quickly race below, grab our loaded canisters, dash back up to the forward deck and change them out. It's hell trying to load film in the rain. The emulsion gets sticky. Excessive moisture is our biggest gremlin. Unbeknown to him, all of Charlie Rudd's cameras failed during the flight mission because damp film had jammed up the cameras. When he returned, Charlie was about as pissed off as I've ever seen him: cursing, hurling insults, kicking things around and slamming the side of the Photo Bird with his fist. 'Guess I can't blame him. He put his ass on the line and has nothing to show for it.

4 December 1967 ... 171st day. Ibid.

Stand Down today. No flights. I was surprised because the weather was beautiful: sunny, blue sky and gentle breeze but P.I. said North Vietnam is in the throes of monsoon conditions. So, we just farted around.

Ernest Levitt is growing a Fu Manchu mustache but the Navy gods don't like it. When he was mess cooking, Ern was ordered to stay clean shaven but now that he's back with us, he's bucking the system again. It's just in his nature to be contrary. Kimball, the Ship's Photo Lab Warrant Officer, told Levitt yesterday that he is not allowed in the Photo Lab with that "fuckin' Mongolian mustache."

Ernest said, "Fine! I just won't go to the Photo Lab anymore."

Tonight when I told him that the movie of the night was James Michener's Hawaii, Big Ern made the personal sacrifice of shaving it all off. And, subsequently was granted permission to enter the lab. The movie was threaded in the projector and ready to go when Captain Billy called down from Mount Olympus and said he wanted to see Hawaii in his State Room. There's no disputing the skipper so the photo boys obliged, scrounging up another flick: Two for the Road, starring Albert Finney and Audrey Hepburn.

Big Ern began to rage like a rogue elephant. Stomping and fuming, he blasphemed the skipper: "Fuckin' Captain! Why does he have to screw up everything? Motherfuckin' Captain!"

That didn't settle well with Mr. Kimball. My big, chubby buddy was expelled once again from the Photo Lab – this time, according to the Warrant Officer, it's for the duration.

5 December 1967 ... 172nd day. Ibid.

Back to work big time! We sent out and recovered four photo missions today. The sky cleared over North Vietnam and all the carrier groups lambasted the little nation with wide spread bombing raids.

On the third photo hop of the day, Mister Sonniksen's escort, an F-8 from Fighter Squadron 111, developed an internal malfunction over hostile territory. Their photo reconnaissance mission concluded, the two of them turned their Crusaders toward home but the escort caught fire while still over Nam. With the boss alongside keeping close watch on the intensity of the flame, he advised the fighter pilot to stay with his bird until they were over the Gulf. It worked out okay. Just as the escort's situation was becoming critical they cleared the coast. The nervous pilot blew his canopy and pulled his ejection rings. Nothing. He pulled again. Nothing happened.

"Son-of-a-bitch! Who the hell cleared this plane for flight? Nothing's working!"

"Yank it again! Hard!" Sonniksen yelled at the pilot over his radio. "Hard!"

He did... and again... and again...and finally, it worked. The underside ignited and rocketed the whole seat out of the Crusader. Upon reaching apex, its parachute deployed, allowing the pilot to safely float down into the drink. He was plucked from the water by crew members on a nearby Navy destroyer. From there the Oriskany's Angels cable lifted and transported him back to the Old Risky. As he made foot contact with our flight deck – relieved and happy to be alive – he walked up to his plane captain and declared: "The bottom of the ocean is best place I can think of, to park that goddamned piece of shit!" And he laughed.

Hedge had hernia surgery today. He was his usual sassy self when I visited him in the medical ward tonight. All propped up in one of the most comfortable beds on the ship, he was more than eager to show me his stitches despite my protests to the contrary. He also said that he doesn't intend to come back to work for the rest of this line period. We'll see.

6 December 1967 ... 173rd day. Ibid.

Clear sky was short lived. Monsoon rain is pounding our Flight Deck today. Even so, CAG ordered bombing sorties and one photo hop. They must be getting desperate to meet their quota of dead Vietnamese before we head to Hong Kong to celebrate the birth of the Prince of Peace. Nevertheless, our photo mission was a bust. All clouds. Nothing to photograph.

Two dames came aboard today on the Cod flight. One was an old Wave Lieutenant. The other was an ugly public relations lady with black, horn-rimmed glasses. This evening the Oriskany's Executive Officer, Captain Nordberg, escorted the two women around the ship. Bad luck, you know — having women onboard ship. The smiley little threesome walked into the chow hall as I was eating supper. The P.R. lady started mingling and talking with some of the guys as they stuffed their mouths with food: "Ohhh hello, boys! Are we having supper? Is it tasty? And how are you boys doing tonight?"

Believe me, this didn't settle well with the troops. If the XO hadn't been with her, a few guys probably would have had some choice words for her. We're out here in this iron bucket doing our duty for Uncle Sam and here comes this self-styled mother figure patronizing us and calling us boys. She may mean well but we don't need the hassle.

Speaking of mothers, I received a letter from home today acknowledging my previous letter about being a Buddhist. Mom thinks I'm just going through a stage and will eventually return to my senses and to the open arms of the Lutheran Church. Fat chance. Even if I returned to Jesus, I wouldn't return to the organization that claims to represent him.

Down in the med ward tonight, Harry was all smiles. He got his shipping-over bonus today of two-thousand dollars. That's a hell of a wad but is it worth signing over six years of your life to the micky mouse club? I think not but that's his choice. It's his life. I did some errands for Sea Daddy: procured some money orders, mailed some letters and left him to his closed-circuit TV show at 2100.

The goddamn ship's laundry has lost three pairs of my dungaree trousers in the last month. I can't see buying new britches since I'm out of the Navy in 71 days and a wake-up. Walt Lehmann was kind enough to give me three pairs of his boot camp dungarees.

CHAPTER XXX
MUSIC TO SOOTH THE SAVAGE

7 December 1967 ... 174th day.
Gulf of Tonkin, North Vietnam.

Twenty-six years ago this morning, Japanese bombers attacked Pearl Harbor, Hawaii. Most of us weren't even born then but the old timers, the Chief O'Brian's among us, will never forget where they were when the news came to them. It's kinda like my generation and the assassination of John F. Kennedy. We'll never forget.

And who should we get for Pearl Harbor Day but Connie Francis! Yes, the pop star of the 1950's arrived today on the noon Cod flight. A mob of sailor's, obviously more informed about her arrival than I was, gathered around her to exchange greetings and snap photos. She came to Vietnam to entertain the troops on land and at sea. Her performance was at 2030 this evening on Hangar Bay One. Richard Aden and I were probably more excited about it than anyone else in the Det. We loaded our personal 35mm cameras with high speed, low light film but first, Mister James Norville Muffley got a wild hair up his ass that we, the squadron Photo Mates, should go down into the bowels of the ship and pick up a large, new shipment of 500 foot-by-5 inch Plus-X black-and-white and Ektachrome color film; and once we had it toted back to the Photo Shop, change out all the cameras for tomorrow's flights so the pilots can shoot color pictures of one another in flight – more P.R. bullshit. We had to locate our Photo Birds in the red-lighted darkness of Hangar Bay 3 and fumble around with the cameras as show time neared. Fortunately, we got it wrapped up by 2000; quickly cleaned up and headed to down to Bay One.

Normally crowded with aircraft and ugly Aviation Boatswain's Mates shouting orders to peasant plane pushers, the Hangar Bay had been cleared with a central, elevated stage set up. Ship's signal flags were draped from the overhead, a large, backdrop covered the Elevator Number One pit and an orange banner read: "Oriskany Welcomes Connie Francis!"

I'd estimate that at least half of the Ship's Company and Carrier Air Group were packed into that relatively small space, more than 1,000 men, I'm sure. Men were perched on pipes, huffers, drop tanks, forklifts, ventilation pipes, and ledges along the bulkheads. I stood on a deck hatch ledge that elevated me about a foot. A musical trio played electric piano, guitar and drums. Dick Lord, some sick comedian, got up before the mike and recited a series of what were supposed to be humorous stories. He didn't get many laughs. Thank God, that didn't last long.

"Attention on Deck!" was shouted over the ship's 1MC. A path cleared from the Officer's Country hatch and down to the stage strolled Captain Billy and Connie Francis. A collective, thunderous cheer broke out from the assembled Black Shoes, Airdales and Officers. Connie didn't look like the gal I'd remembered in the movie, *Follow The Boys*. Her hair was deep black and swept up into a cone style with a fall in the back about two feet long. She wore a one-piece leopard skin miniskirt. She had flesh-color tights and black, spiked high heel shoes. Her eyes were thick with make-up, I'd estimate she's about 5-foot-2. She's buxom and stout but to a thousand guys who have been starved for months to see a young, female Round Eye, she looked gorgeous. This particular woman on the ship was definitely not a jinx. As soon as Miss Francis climbed the stage steps and sat down on the rotating bar stool, a raucous cheer went up from the guys in front of her. Apparently, she had spread her legs as she was taking her seat. Cheap thrill. She turned on the mike and scolded the horny bastards: "Now, boys! Behave yourselves."

That prompted another cheer and laughter. Funny, but having Connie Francis call us boys didn't seem so bad; not the same as when the hags in the mess called us boys. The music began and she sang like a nightingale. What a beautiful voice! I was immediately transported back to my childhood with the familiar old hits: "Ivory Tower," "Lipstick On Your Collar," "My Happiness" and a dozen others. She did a wonderful rendition of "God Bless America." There were tears in many eyes. Connie tried to get up and dance a little as she sang but the poor girl doesn't have her sea legs. In fact, she appeared to be getting pale from sea sickness but she held out. Between songs, she'd ad lib and talk to individuals in the crowd. This made the moment even better. At the conclusion of the show, Captain Billy came up on stage and presented Miss Francis with a surprise birthday cake. As it turns out, Connie was born on Pearl Harbor Day. Reversing roles, one thousand grateful men sang "Happy Birthday" to Connie Francis. She was overwhelmed, grinning and crying at the same time. The performance was two hours but, as far as the crew was concerned, it could have lasted all night. She was asked to sing four encores and graciously complied. As she finally said "Good night and good bye" to us, she told us that her little entertainment combo was heading back to mainland South Vietnam tomorrow. Whispering closely into the microphone, she got another round of cheers when she declared: "I don't want to go. I want to stay here with you."

When the men quieted down, she added: "There aren't any bugs and snakes out here." Laughs.

8 December 1967 ... 175th day. Ibid.

Operation Rolling Thunder is losing its thunder because of monsoon season. No flights today. We're preparing to go home and the North Vietnamese are busy repairing and rebuilding everything American bombs have destroyed. Six more days on the line and we steam into Subic Bay for about a week, then cross over to Hong Kong. This may turn out to be the first line period with no pilot deaths.

Before Connie Francis departed today she visited Sickbay to cheer up the ailing sailors. There are no war casualties down there just people like Hedge with sundry medical problems. Miss Francis and her band took the Cod flight out at noon.

Later in the day, I visited Harry and asked him if he met her.

"Yeah, she came over and talked to me for awhile."

"What did she say to you?" I asked.

"Not much, just a 'Hope you get better soon'" – you know, shit like that."

"What did you think of her?"

"She had about 40 pounds of makeup on her face; cute nose; black hair with white roots but she was wearing real tight, black Levis. Had a real nice ass on her. Not bad topside either."

CHAPTER XXXI
ROLLING THUNDER

9 December 1967 ... 176th day. Ibid.

After getting up at 0630, dressing and eating breakfast in the mess hall, I sauntered to the Photo Shop and tried to do a little reading and writing but the Chicken Shit Patrol caught me being idle. I was ordered to the Hangar Bay to help the squadron maintenance men sand, tape and paint 601. I pretended I was working for about an hour. Hell, they have 19 people already designated to do this work and we were just getting in each other's way.

By mid-morning, I was in P.I., shooting the shit with the boys and working on Christmas cards that I'm designing myself. Afternoon slipped into night. Walt Lehmann and I decided at about midnight to record Christmas tapes for our families back home. We screwed around trying to come up with something clever but eventually trashed the project. Up on the flight deck there was heavy rain all night long. This old tub is leaking like a dilapidated house. Lehmann and Chapin were kept busy through the wee hours emptying their buckets of collected rain water. Many of the ship's passageways on the 02 level are flooded again with a couple of inches of water. Outside the visibility is nil – just one big, overwhelming mass of grey.

I stayed up until 0300 reading *My Secret Life*, the erotic diary of an English nobleman who must have fucked hundreds of women. He recorded all the graphic details in his diary. It's been a popular book onboard ship. I've seen dozens of horny sailors reading it, prepping themselves for the whores of Olongapo. My sex life is boring. 'Think I'll break up with my right hand and start going steady with my left."

10 December 1967 ... 177th day.

A strange dream last night. I was back in the Nebraska Sandhills, a beautiful part of the country of which most Americans are unaware. For as far as I could see in all directions were the magnificent sand dunes, the remnants of an ancient sea bed, now covered with lush, green grass. It's open range country with hundreds of thousands of cattle grazing in the place where buffalo used to roam. I was living in a small house atop one of the dunes overlooking a placid valley dotted by small lakes fed by underground spring water. On the far end of the valley was a ranch with several corrals.

As I stood outside my house, a very dirty, unkempt Shetland pony approached me. It was saddled and bridled but had no rider. I mounted it and rode it down to the ranch thinking it must have been one of their stock. I was right. A young girl, about 16-years-old with braided, blonde hair, came out to meet me. She said that the Shetland must have been abandoned by his rider. She explained that her elderly father owns several Shetlands and rents them to visitors for children's rides asking a $20 deposit up front. That seemed weird because we were hundreds of miles away from any population center.

"Well, since I returned the pony," I queried, "Shouldn't I get the $20 deposit for a reward? One of your clients obviously abandoned the little guy."

Instead of agreeing with me, she gave me some promotional pamphlets and brochures. I protested, saying: "Look, I could have kept the pony and sold it for 200-dollars. Is $20 too much to ask?"

"No, you didn't know it was ours but you brought it back to us anyway. Your loss."

"Your ponies are filthy dirty and they stink," I changed the subject. "Do you mind if I at least wash the filth off my hands in your horse tank?"

She reluctantly consented.

As I washed, I scolded the girl, who was standing about ten feet away holding the bridle straps of the pony: "You know, girl, it's a bloody shame that humanity must be so cruel to these poor, little animals. They don't deserve this kind of treatment."

She took the pony and just turned away, saying nothing in response.

I'm not a biblical Joseph so I'm not sure how to interpret the dream but it probably had something to do with Vietnam... or maybe it's just a longing for home.

12 December 1967 ... 179th day. Ibid.

The rain subsided enough this afternoon to allow several attack bombers to venture out in search of available targets. Hot Dog Sonniksen took the opportunity to fly a weather recon mission. He launched without a fighter escort because it had been predetermined he wouldn't enter hostile territory but Hollywood Ron decided, on his own volition, to go take color pictures of North Vietnam. It's hard to tell what was in his mind. Was he trying to earn more metals for service above and beyond the call of duty? Or, does he just have a death wish?

Crappy weather conditions moved back in while the jet jockeys were playing over Nam. Rain began to fall in sheets across the Flight Deck. We, the flight service personnel, had to stand in the downpour awaiting the recoveries. Soaked to the bone, my teeth were chattering. The A-4 Skyhawks came in first and taxied forward. I intentionally positioned myself in the exhaust path of the A-4s just to warm up. Because of the low ceiling, landing conditions were hazardous. A couple of aircraft missed the wire and had to rocket off the angle deck, circle around and try again. Lieutenant Commander Sonniksen caught the wire on his first attempt. I hate to admit it but the guy is one hell of a pilot.

This evening in the Photo Lab, we finally got to see Hawaii starring Julie Andrews and Max Von Sydow. Good flick. Too bad Big Ern screwed himself and was unable to attend.

13 December 1967 ... 180th day. Ibid.

Despite shitty conditions, the strike groups took another swipe at North Vietnam today. Our Photo Birds stayed home. On the Flight Deck this afternoon, a young plane captain, his mind obviously preoccupied with other matters, walked directly in front of an F-8 intake as the bird was turning up. He was instantly sucked off his feet and pulled down into the jet turbine tunnel. Fortunately, someone saw it happen and frantically signaled for the pilot to cut his engine. Once silenced, two squadron crew members crawled into the intake to rescue the dumb shit or what was left of him. They found his body wrapped around the generator hump directly in front of the turbine blades. He had miraculously avoided being chopped to pieces like steak in a meat grinder. The corpsmen rushed the unconscious airman to the medical ward. Doctors performed surgery on him late into the evening. He suffered multiple internal injuries. His rib cage was crushed on one side; his lung punctured. His spleen was damaged beyond repair and had to be removed. Captain Billy told us on the 1MC tonight that the misfortunate Airdale was still alive but in critical condition. And of course the skipper couldn't pass up the opportunity to give the Flight Deck crew a little lecture about the hazards of walking in front of intakes, exhausts, and propellers. Yeah, sure, we're all fuckin' idiots, Billy, and you da smart one.

This evening, LTJG Beam recruited me to do the artwork for the upcoming detachment newsletter. Following approval of my rough layout, I proceeded on the real thing working with pen and ink on 18-by-24 inch white poster board. The cover picture is of the three Magi en route to Bethlehem guided by the Star however one of the Magi is Yosemite Sam. I didn't get too far into the project because Lieutenant Muffley decided that the KA45 cameras in our birds should be replaced with KA53's. Ray, Dick and I took care of it and hit the sack.

14 December 1967 ... 181st day. Ibid

Weather improved today, good enough to launch the attack aircraft. The Air Wing recorded a first for the cruise: two of our fighter jets from Fighter Squadron 111 were aerially assaulted by four Russian-built MIG-2 aircraft. A long, harrowing dogfight ensued. One of our fighters finally struck and downed an enemy jet using heat-seeking air-to-air missiles. That one kill scared off the rest of the MIG's. Our Crusaders returned to the ship safe and unscathed. This will be one for Stars and Stripes.

This evening in P.I., I sat down intent on finishing my Yosemite Sam newsletter cover. I had just started when our Yeoman, Jerome Miley, called me up on the telephone: "Hey, MacLennon! Why didn't you muster for the working party? They're gonna write you up as U.A. if you don't get down here."

I was pissed. "What the fuck are you talking about? No one told me about any goddamn working party. Anyhow, I just had one eleven days ago."

"Well, I don't know about that. All I know is that if you don't get down here, your ass is grass, buddy."

* * * * * * *

I later found out that 2nd Class Arlington put me on an extra working party for making some racist comments during the last corrosion control working party. As a black man, he was understandably upset; he angrily ordered me to shut my trap. I apologized to him but got punished anyway. That's okay. I deserve it.

It's hard to shake off a lifetime of racist indoctrination. I learned it from my old man and he from his dad. It probably goes back many generations – probably all the way to Ireland and Scotland. I know the world is changing and the descendants of Africans in America, especially in former slave states, are beginning to exercise their new civil rights agenda. Dr. Martin Luther King has become a strong spokesman for them. The rational Lutheran part of me knows that black folk shouldn't be treated in the disgusting ways I witnessed in Pensacola, Florida. Everything was segregated there: Men, Women and Colored restrooms; Colored sections of restaurants and buses; many businesses had signs hanging on their front doors: No Coloreds. Some even said, No Coloreds or dogs. In my heart and soul, I know that such discrimination is not acceptable in "the land of the free and the home of the brave."

As Bob Dylan wrote and sang, "The times they are a-changing." And, Gerald MacLennon needs to change with them. I seriously doubt if my old man ever will.

I mentioned earlier in this diary that I had read about the disproportionate number of Blacks who are placed in the front lines of their combat platoons down in South Vietnam. I don't know if that's true or just scuttlebutt. Suffice it all to say this: When men lie wounded on the battlefield, the color of their skin doesn't matter, for they all bleed red.

*   *   *   *   *   *   *

It was a commissary working party. We were taking on tons of food. I worked from 1800 to 2200 pushing food around on bomb skids. Then until 0200 in the morning, a bunch of us were stuck six decks below in the reefers passing down stores by human chain from the Hangar Deck. There were crates and boxes filled with carrots, potatoes, lettuce, cabbage, tangerines, apples, oranges, onions, butter, milk, spinach, corn, green beans, ad infinitum. We secured from work detail at 3 o'clock in the morning.

15 December 1967 ... 182nd day. Ibid.

Hines shook me awake at 1000 this morning informing me that I had already missed one launch and recovery and the second one was coming in at 1030. I took care of it and retired to the Photo Shop where I found a corner to curl up and sleep all afternoon. No one bugged me. Awake and alert at 1800, I headed down to Photo Intelligence to work on my newsletter project. Determined to finish it, I worked until midnight. It's a damn fine piece of artwork, if I say so myself.

Around 2300, Mister Sonniksen walked in and looked over my shoulder: "That's a beauty!" he said, "There's no other words for it but that's a beauty!"

The Old Man was impressed. That makes me feel good. All in all, it was an unusually special evening. I enjoyed the company of intelligent people while I created. We drank fresh-brewed coffee and listened to our taped music.

16 December 1967 ... 183rd day. Ibid.

It's the last day of this line period and I guess Captain Billy wanted to put on a good show before we retire to R & R. The sun shone brightly over North Vietnam; the Tonkin Gulf had just a smattering of light fluffy clouds, a perfect day for Alpha Strikes. Our air wing bombed Haiphong today. The Photo Birds went out for bomb damage assessment. The processed photos confirmed that the missions had been highly successful.

Four photo hops launched and recovered today. We were strapping it from 1100 to 1730. Once secured from flight ops, the Photo Mates were busy into the night loading film, installing cameras, testing the systems for operational readiness. Big Ern was having a tough time of it. He banged his head on the overhead at least four times. He dropped a 35-pound camera on his fingers. He stumbled and hurt his toes on the arresting cable. The poor guy is a natural klutz.

Harry was passing scuttlebutt that our line period was being extended for 15 days. He had me depressed until I heard Captain Billy on the 1MC tonight announcing that we depart for Subic Bay tomorrow.

"Hedge, damnit," I yelled at him. "You had me going all day. And all along you knew it wasn't true, didn't you!"

He gave me a wry look. Then a cynical laugh gurgled up from his gut.

Around 2200, I placed the finishing touches on my newsletter cover art. It goes to the ship's print shop tomorrow.

17 December 1967 ... 184th day. Departing the Gulf of Tonkin, heading into the South China Sea.

Our Photo Birds launched at 0830 this morning heading to Cubi Point Naval Air Station, on the south shores of Subic Bay. Lieutenant Commander Sonniksen piloted 601, Lieutenant Sam took 603 and Mister Rudd, 604. Incidentally, there's a rumor afloat that Sampson has been recommended for the Distinguished Flying Cross for his action at Thanh Hoa Bridge on 14 October. I don't know if it's true but if he has earned the DFC, so have our other three other pilots. At least, that's the way I see it. The rain returned this afternoon but who gives a flying fuck? We're on our way to my old home, the Philippine Islands.

Forty five days remain for this WestPac cruise of the U.S.S. Oriskany (CVA-34). This line period one pilot died and that was from catapult malfunction. The plane captain sucked into the intake remains in critical condition. One aircraft from Fighter Squadron 111 was lost. The cruise tally is now: 22 men killed, 31 aircraft lost, 6 pilots captured by the North Vietnamese, now captive in the Hanoi prisoner of war camp.

CHAPTER XXXII
PHILIPPINE BEAUTY & DEBAUCHERY

18 December 1967 ... 185th day.
Arrival at Subic Bay, Republic of the Philippines.

The Oriskany was already entering Subic Bay when I awoke at 0700. Damn, the Philippines look good! It's ironic how miserable the weather was on the line and here it's sunny, warm and dry. Someone said the temp was around 85 degrees.

The carrier, U.S.S. Kitty Hawk – or the Shitty Kitty, as the sailors call her – just arrived in Subic from California. She's here to relieve the carrier, U.S.S. Constellation which was tied up at Leyte Pier in Cubi Point. Our ship had to drop anchor in the middle of the bay. The bottom must be mush because it took four attempts to set anchor. The skipper finally got her stabilized at 1500. Liberty boats arrived from the Naval Station pulling up to the side-mounted ship pier. All the fine sailors dressed in their dress whites and young Officers in their dress tans boarded the launches one after the other while visions of beer, bar girls and poontang danced in their heads.

I didn't go to Olongapo today. I had duty; not that there was much of any duty to perform. It basically means you stay on the ship and occupy space, and if an Officer or Chief approaches, look busy. As usual, I found myself farting around in Photo Intelligence admiring my detachment newsletter cover that came back from the print shop this morning. I collated and stapled the cover to the confidential guts of the newsletter as I listened to anti-war songs on Lehmann's tape deck. Sonniksen would probably confiscate the whole tape if he was to walk in and hear it but he's probably sitting in the Officer's Club right now at Cubi Point downing whiskey and water. I don't know if that's actually his poison of choice but John Wayne drinks whiskey and water so I venture to guess, so does swaggering Hollywood Ron.

Bob Dylan's Greatest Hits album came out this year and we've been playing the hell out of that but I also like some of his less publicized work. I was listening to the lyrics of "Masters of War" this morning. It's about us. Actually, it's more about the military-industrial complex – not the grunts.

The Kitty Hawk had an onboard fire this afternoon. Half of the 02 level was blackened with smoke when a stack of aircraft tires ignited into flames. Strange. Tires are not easily ignited. The ship's fire crew worked for nine hours to bring the fire under control. She was scheduled to pull out tomorrow morning for the Tonkin Gulf. It looks like the crew will have more port time than they expected. I'll bet that breaks their little hearts.

Down in the ship's Photo Lab this evening I printed 8-by-10 photos from several of my black and white negs. I have a cool one of Mac at the Great Buddha of Kamakura and a few of Dick and I shaving each other's heads back in June prior to the cruise. Damned rebels!

19 December 1967 ... 186th day.
In Port – U.S. Naval Station Subic Bay, Republic of the Philippines.

We're still anchored out here in green, murky Subic Bay. Liberty for Mac Day! Richard Aden and I pulled on our ice cream suits and hopped in the bobbing liberty launch at 1000. Misted with salt spray, we took the ten minute ride through the choppy water to the Subic Naval Station pier. A grey bus transported us to the Subic Navy Exchange. I had $450 in my pocket to blow and I think I chose well. For my sweet, little sister, Jeris, I bought a service-for-eight stoneware table setting. For Mom, I purchased a beautiful set of Noritake silverware. For the old man, who likes to take snapshots, a Petri 35mm camera with simple automatic controls. It was a top-of-the-line stereo system for Mac-san: a Sony tape deck, a Sansui AM/FM tuner and amplifier, reverberation unit and a boss set of Sansui speakers. A Navy Exchange van hauled us and our loot back to fleet landing. It took some doing but we finally got it all back onboard ship and safely stowed in the cage of our Photo Shop.

Our uniforms were soiled and I had ripped out the seat of my pants when I lifted my sister's stoneware into the launch so we changed into clean uniforms and headed back to terra firma for a night in sin city. As soon as we entered Olongapo, we became just two more targets in white for all the pickpockets, beggars, pimps and street walkers. One Filipina kid tried to divert my attention while his little buddy reached for the wallet in my chest pocket. I slapped his arm away just in time; he ran away holding his sore limb. Little creeps! We ate a Mexican dinner at another of my favorite restaurants, Papagayo's, and of course were overcharged because we were dressed as fleet sailors. The base sailors, who wear civvies when they go to town, get much more reasonable rates. Being an ex-base sailor, I argued with everyone who tried to overcharge us from the restaurateur to the bar hostesses to the Jeepney drivers. In the end, I would just give them what they were really worth and walk off with them raging at me, "Cheap motherfucker!" or some other equally endearing curse.

We ended up spending the rest of the night at one of my old favorite haunts. As with every large nightclub on the Magsaysay Strip, a neon sign nearly as large as a theater marquee spelled out the name of the club in glowing red, orange, blue and green: The Victoria Club. Aden and I passed through the double-door entrance into a cavernous room made acrid with the stench of spilt beer and cigarette smoke. Moving silhouettes of hundreds of sailors, marines and hookers were backlit by colored spotlights on the walls. Up on the stage a rock and roll band of six young Filipinos was in the process of murdering Rolling Stones' lyrics. The lead vocalist was doing his damnedest to imitate Mick Jagger. But, of course, he did it with a Filipino accent: "I can geet no sateesfaction. I can geet no sateesfaction but I try and I try and I try and I try..."

He was trying in more ways than one. The singing and playing were atrocious but, mercifully, they were overpowered by the din of the drunken crowd and giggling whores. Dick and I bought two bottles of San Miguel beer at the bar, one peso each, searched for and found a table for four. The usual parade of tiny hostesses in their skin-tight dresses came over to our table asking to sit with us. Dick chose the third candidate, cute but not the kind I'd pick.

She introduced herself. "Hi, my name ees Christina. You buy me Lady's Drink?"

"Sure," Aden replied, motioning her to sit. She signaled the bartender for the 4-Peso glass of 7-Up.

"Do you wanna dance?" Aden asked her.

"Okay, Joe."

"The name is not Joe. It's Dick."

"Your name Deeck? I like deeck."

"I'll bet you do." He stood up. "C'mon, Christina, let's go dance."

They left and wove their way through the mob to the purple linoleum dance floor.

I was left to make my choice without any prompting from Mr. Aden. I had decided that because this was probably one of my last nights in a Filipino night club where the girls come to me instead of back in America where I have to make a fool out of myself asking Round Eyes if they will have a dance with me and then get rejected.

Yup, I had decided that I was going to hold out for one very special beauty. I must have turned away a half dozen little scags and was beginning to think that the night would end up a wash out when I saw her sitting alone at the bar. Oh my God! She was beautiful. She looked just like my fantasy girl, the one bathing under the waterfall in the jungle.

She wasn't playing the hostess game. Perched on her swivel seat, wearing a sleeveless, high-necked white dress, she appeared to be lost in thought, her mind somewhere far away from this den of animals. The hair was perfect: pitch black, straight, flowing halfway down her back. Her deeply, bronzed skin told me she was probably not a city girl but newly arrived from a distant farming province. Unlike the whores, she wore very little facial makeup. She didn't need to. She was a natural beauty.

Brushing off another approaching hostess, I got up and brazenly walked over to the bar, to my dream girl.

"Magandang Gabi sa inyo." I said Good evening to her in Tagalog.

Surprised, she looked into my eyes and I felt my knees grow weak — such lovely, brown, almond eyes, so expressive, so penetrating, so soft.

"You speak Tagalog?" she asked.

"Oo, kaunti." Yes, I did speak a little Tagalog.

I introduced myself and asked her name, "Ang pangalan ko ay Mac. Anang pangalan mo?"

"Angie."

I told her in her language that I was very pleased to meet her and invited her over to my table to sit and talk.

"Sorry, Mock. Boss man, he only let me sit with sailor if you buy Angie ladies' drink."

"Of course, I'll buy you a ladies' drink. I'll buy you five ladies' drinks." I raised my voice. "I'll buy you ten if you will do me the pleasure of sitting at my table!"

She laughed. My heart melted a little more when I saw her endearing smile. It was an authentic smile, not a bar girl's Cheshire grin. It was the look of sad innocence trying to be happy. I offered my arm. She took it and I escorted her back to the table. Dick and Christina were still dancing. Angie just looked out of place here. I wanted to steal her away, stow her on the ship and take her home with me.

I was too bold. "Angie, you are one of the most beautiful girls I have ever seen."

She lowered her head and smiled again.

"Would you like to go to America?"

"Ev'ry girl want to go America," she replied. "But it jeest a dream."

"I could write to you when I get home and maybe..."

"No. All sailors say that. Then they go home to American girl friend and forget Angie."

"I wouldn't forget..."

She held up her hand and stopped me in mid-sentence. A tear came to her eye. "I belong to Filipino man. Cannot leave. Must stay here and work." She shook her head. "Cannot leave."

Then it hit me. She was probably a victim of the sex slave trafficking. If she made any attempt to leave, she'd be either severely beaten or killed. And, there was nothing I could do about it. I felt so damned helpless and sad. Leaning toward her, I stroked her hair, looking straight into her eyes. "Angie?"

Then, out of the blue, she floored me with a hustle: "You want to go short time with Angie?"

My fantasy snapped; shredded with one sentence. So beautiful, so young, so innocent she was... so violated by God only knows how many men. I was enraged. "No, Angie!" I yelled in her face, "I do not want to go short time with you. I love you."

Tossing her head back and laughing, her shiny black hair rippling like ocean waves, she parroted me: "I love you! Okay! Mock love me. All sailor love me. All fucking sailor boy love Angie because Angie pretty."

She jumped to her feet knocking over her chair. "Bullshit! Nobody love Angie. Go home and fuck your long-nose girlfriend, Cherry Boy!"

She turned to walk away, then remembering that I knew some Tagalog, looked back at me and screamed: "Walang hiyah ka!" I don't think it has an English equivalent but it's about the worst insult in the native tongue.

So much for my romantic naiveté.

"No girl yet?" Good timing. As soon as Angie walked off, Dick returned to the table without his whore.

"No," I lied to him. "They're all VD-infested sluts. Speaking of which... where's Christina?"

"The little puta tried to lift my wallet while we were dancing."

"No shit?"

"Yeah, no shit. I dragged her over to Mamasan and turned her in. Mamasan kicked her ass out the door. You missed all the excitement."

"Guess I did."

Dick could tell I was not really amused by his exploits and that I probably wasn't going to be any fun for the rest of the night. Hell, I hadn't even touched my beer.

"Hey, MacLennon. Let's just get the hell out of here and call it a night. Whaddya say?"

"Good idea."

Goodbye, fantasy girl. You don't really exist, do you? Sometimes it just seems like all innocence has been corrupted. Who is the devil? Who is the angel? Who is good? Who is evil? To a North Vietnamese, I'm evil. To the Johnson Administration, I'm good. To Bob Dylan, I'm evil. To John Wayne, I'm good.

20 December 1967 ... 187th day. Ibid.

This morning at breakfast, Richard "Deeck" Aden and I both agreed that we wanted to travel out into the Bataan Peninsula, meet and photograph the real people of the Philippines. About an hour later, we submitted request chits for early liberty this Friday the 22nd to do just that. The Oriskany remains anchored in the bay. Our Photo Birds are parked on the apron at Cubi Point Naval Air Station. Chief O'Brian decided mid-morning that he wanted to take a small contingent of Photo Recon Squadron 63 personnel over there to power check our planes. I was chosen along with ten others. We took the boat and bus ride arriving about an hour later only to find that the Kitty Hawk crew had first dibs on all the ground support equipment. We could do nothing. Old Man O'Brian just flopped his arms, shrugged his shoulders and said, "The hell with it! Everybody might as well secure."

That gave me opportunity to shuttle up the hill to the Cubi NX Cafeteria and grab some lunch. With a belly full of burgers and fries, I hoofed over to the FIC PAC FAC barracks and reunited with my good Filipino friends, Jose Gonzales and Herminio Sanchez. After warm hugs and handshakes, we sat in their work room and shot the breeze for over an hour. I'm already regretting my final departure from the Philippines because Pepé has been such a close friend over the past two-and-a-half years. I'll probably never see him again. Knowing that, we made a pact to get together this Friday night, the 22nd, to make our last night together one we'll never forget.

21 December 1967 ... 188th day. Ibid.

This morning, Dick and I were pleased to learn that our early liberty chits for Friday have been approved. At the same time, we were ordered to submit special requests to attend a Photo Recon Squadron 63 party tonight in Olongapo. Lieutenant JG Kenny Kanker made the reservations and promises us plenty of food, beer and a special surprise. It doesn't take much imagination to figure out what that's going to be.

Harry got a wild hair up his ass this morning, ordering Aden and I to ride the launch and take a taxi over to our planes and, once there, reconfigure the camera systems. Ours was not to wonder why... so we strapped on our tool pouches and headed out. We located 601 on the apron next to the Kitty Hawk and removed about 200 pounds worth of cameras and mounting brackets. Harry wanted us to place them in 602, which was parked in Hangar B on the opposite end of the airfield. We flagged down a pickup and bummed a ride sitting in the truck bed clutching our cameras to keep them stable and secure. Dropped at the hangar, we thanked our driver and began the search for 602. It took us an hour. We finally found her about a quarter mile away. Someone gave us bum information but on the bright side, hey, our muscles got one hell of a workout. Another SNAFU.

After installing the cameras, I backed off and took a look at our little RF-8G Crusader jet comparing it to a beautiful RA-5C Vigilante parked next to it. I love Vigilantes; they're large, sleek and stylish and when they're landing, the engines screech like an Irish banshee. The Shitty Kitty CAG flies them. It was good to work again on solid concrete, like we do back at Miramar: plenty of elbow room, fresh air and best of all, we stripped naked from the waist up soaking in that penetrating tropical sun.

The squadron party was at D'Cave. Never heard of it. After showering and donning our dress whites, we headed for Olongapo, again walking down the strip fighting off the hordes of low-life rabble. D'Cave is a small bar. The owner had apparently smeared plaster on the ceilings and walls and painted it grey. Such creativity. The only resemblance to a cave was the darkness. He probably kept it dark so we couldn't see the cockroaches scampering across the floor. There was just barely enough chairs for our detachment. Five square-top tables had been pulled together to make one large surface so we could all sit together. A young pig skewered on a spit had been roasted over a blazing fire pit. Because we arrived late most of the pork had been eaten. Dick got the last of the meat. I drank a couple of whiskies with soda to loosen up, then, on a dare, ate the pig's tongue and brains. I figured if I can eat a balut, what the hell.

Kanker's special surprise was a Filipina slut named Linda. She waited until the boys were adequately drunk before making her grand entry through a beaded curtain. About 5-feet tall, she wore spiked heels, a leather miniskirt, and tight, red half-top that exposed her flat midriff. Her black hair piled into a beehive looked ridiculous. She wore heavy makeup with false eyelashes and flashed gold fillings in her teeth when she smiled.

"Hi boys, my name ees Leenda and I come to make you happy."

Someone shouted, "I'm always happy when I cum!" Everyone laughed.

"You think maybe you geet some pussy tonight, huh Joe?" She sassed back.

One of the mechanics yelled, "I know I'm geeting some pussy tonight, baby," mocking her accent. "But it sure ain't gonna be yours!"

"We see bout that, sailor." More laughter.

Linda climbed a chair, stepping over to the table top and then kicking empty beer bottles to the floor to make room for her performance. "I theenk maybe you like to see some titties, huh?"

"Yeah!" they roared with approval.

My God, the owner had the David Rose recording of The Stripper. He put on the record from somewhere behind the beaded curtain and the cheap, little ceiling speakers crackled with the music. Linda launched into her routine, trotting up and down the table as drunk Airdales grabbed at her ankles. Then she pulled her top up over her head and threw it in the face of the mechanic who had insulted her. Laughs.

Next she bent down in front of Kenny Kanker and whispered in his ear. He smiled. She spun around and he unsnapped her black lace bra. Everyone cheered.

Standing up, the bra fell to her feet revealing two cute little breasts – high-chested and firm with dark brown nipples. More cheers.

She danced and spun, knocking off more bottles and spilling cocktails.

"Hey boys, you want to see Leenda's pussy?"

This girl was going all the way. The strippers can't do that in the night clubs – local ordnance – but it must be okay for private parties. And yes... of course, the squadron wanted to see Linda's pussy! She slowly unbuttoned and unzipped her skirt and walked over to Sea Daddy, who was drooling like an asylum escapee. She looked him in the eyes and said, "Pull eet off, big boy."

Good ol' Harry, always happy to oblige a woman who needs a little help. The skirt came off and all that remained was a very skimpy set of pink lace panties. Damn, this girl was skanky but she had the Det whipped into testosterone frenzy. She smiled and looked around at the Airdales and Officers. Then, she winked. "Okay, I theenk I go now! Show over!"

"No!" everyone shouted back, including me. And we all started pounding the table, randomly at first and then in unison. Linda held up her hand to stop the pounding. Her eyebrow arched, "So, you want more?"

"Yes!" we cried.

"Okee dokee," she replied.

She slipped both thumbs under the waistband and slowly, so agonizingly slow, she pushed the panties down revealing first her shapely little ass. Whistles and hoots. And then, in one fast motion, she pushed them all the way down and stepped out of them revealing her sweet, little shaved pussy. Chapin couldn't restrain himself. He jumped up on the table and lunged at her.

"No!" she yelled at him, "Bad boy!" He stopped.

She bent over, picked up her panties, walked up to Chapin and stuffed them in his mouth. We all just split a gut laughing. He looked so gooney standing there, drunk as hell, weaving, with a pair of panties hanging out of his mouth.

"Now, you geet down off table!" Linda scolded him. And he complied.

She continued to dance and writhe thrusting her cunt toward the men. Then she squatted down in front of Chief O'Brian. Even in the low light, I could see his face turning bright red with embarrassment. He had a cigar in his mouth. She removed it, reached between her spread thighs and inserted it up her vagina, just far enough to make the lit cigar stay in place. I didn't think we could get any more raucous but that just about brought down the plaster ceiling. She danced, bowlegged, up and down the table with the cigar hanging out like a big, brown turd. I couldn't believe what I was seeing. Then she reached down, pulled it out and stuck it in Koppler's mouth. He loved it. He took a big puff and passed it to the next guy; and on and on it went down one side of the table and up the other to all the Enlisted personnel until it got back to Chief O'Brian who refused to take a drag. "You guys can all get syphilis of the mouth but I sure as hell ain't."

We all laughed. He was probably the only clear thinking man in the bunch.

"Thank you, boys!" Linda picked up her clothing from the table top and yanked her panties out of Chapin's mouth.

"You like taste of Leenda's pussy?" she asked him.

"Ah, yeah," he muttered.

"Too bad. That all you get." And with that comment, she climbed down from the table as we all applauded. She turned and took a bow, then disappeared behind the beaded curtain from whence she had come.

That was the climax, excuse the pun, of the party. After Linda's arousing performance, we all got up. Sonniksen called for a special round of applause for Lieutenant Kanker thanking him for putting together such a stimulating party. Yes, he did a good thing. It's crazy shit like this that helps to build morale.

The night was young and the Victoria Club was just a block away. I knew I shouldn't but I just wanted to sneak inside to get a glimpse of Angie. After Linda, I was so horny, I thought I might just apologize and take her up on her short-time offer. But I saw her sitting at a table near the bar. Angie and another incredibly beautiful girl were entertaining two Navy Lieutenants. Smart girl. She goes for the brass. That's probably what she was waiting for last night when I invaded her territory.

"Ah, hell, MacLennon," I told myself. "Just get over it."

I headed back to the ship, hit the rack and made love to old lady five fingers. She's always faithful and I know she's clean.

22 December 1967 ... 189th day. Ibid.

Early liberty! Richard and I were dressed and off the ship by 0830 with camera cases in tote. In addition to camera gear, we had stowed civilian clothes in our bags. Upon reaching terra firma, we taxied up to the Cubi barracks and changed out of our uniforms.

By 1000, we were at the Victory Liner bus depot in Olongapo. A throng of Filipinos were in the terminal also awaiting the first bus departure. The Victory Liner, I'm told, has been in business since the end of World War II, hence the name. And by the look of the busses, I think they're the same ones that have been operating since 1946. They're old; the cab and engine compartment are metal but the passenger box is made of wood. Below a thick coating of dirt is a faded coat of red paint. The passenger windows are merely sheets of sliding plywood that are always open except when it's raining. It's probably a good thing because in addition to the human passengers, we also ride with crates of chickens and geese. Today, an old man even brought a pig with him.

We took off finally after the driver had crammed as many people and animals on to the bus as possible. I was fortunate to get a window seat. The old bus chugged down Magsaysay Street heading north to the MacArthur Highway. Not much of a highway, it's cratered with pot holes and the driver managed to find every one of them. Each bump shook and rattled the entire passenger area. Filipino mechanics have yet to discover that modern innovation called the shock absorber.

For a few minutes, I pondered last night, shaming myself for getting so caught up in the ugliness of the drunken party and the stripper. Today, I chose to make amends with my soul by interacting with the real Filipinos, not the dregs of sin city. I had taken this trip dozens of times when I lived at Cubi. Climbing the zig-zag road up the jungle-covered coastal mountain, the beauty of nature was personally revitalizing for both Dick and myself. He was all smiles. On the other side, we came into flat lands covered with a light brown quilt of rice paddies. The crop was ripe and farm families – men, women and children – were working the harvest. Along the road, elevated on stilts to protect them during the flooding season, stood the peasant nipa huts: simple, wooden houses with thatched roofs and ladder staircase entries. Here and there, we'd see carabao resting in the shade of exotic trees or wallowing in small ponds. Some were pulling sledges piled high with bundles of cut rice. Magnificent beasts they are, large, dark brown, muscular with ominous horns in the shape of a inverted crescent moon. They are so gentle that 3 or 4 kids can climb on one carabao and ride him around just for fun.

This was the scenario until we reached the city of San Fernando, Pampanga. We were taking a risk because we were 35 miles outside of our authorized limits. Both of us would have stood Captain's Mast if Shore Patrol or military police had caught us but we hadn't seen any gringos since we left Olongapo so we felt quite safe from the strong arm of Uncle Sam's rules and regs.

Because Spain occupied the Philippines for 400 years, most of the central Luzon towns look very Mexican. The Catholic Mission Church of San Fernando was built in the same architectural style I have seen in the American Southwest. It was beautiful. Leaving the bus, Dick and I walked around town recording on film the Spanish cathedral, the smiling faces, the simple houses of humble people, the storefronts, the colorful Jeepneys and the calesas – horse-drawn passenger carts that have for centuries offered the cheapest form of transportation, other than walking and cycling of course. We bought lunch from a street vendor then sat on the edge of a wooden walkway eating and planning our next destination.

We wanted photos of the rural people so we caught the next Victory Liner heading back toward Olongapo planning to stop somewhere along the way. There's no problem disembarking at any point along the highway because a bus comes along just about every hour.

We traveled about 20 miles re-entering the Province of Bataan. We talked about this area. We were probably on the same road as that taken by the Japanese when they force-marched thousands of starving Filipino and American prisoners during World War II. In the Bataan Death March, thousands of good men died or were killed on the spot when they couldn't keep up or slumped to the ground from heat exhaustion and hunger.

The old Filipinos still remember the brutality of the Japanese occupation forces. When I was stationed here in the P.I., one of the older maintenance workers on the base told me about the day the Jap soldiers came into his village in 1944. They decapitated the village leaders with their Samurai swords, raped the young women, they sliced open the bellies of pregnant women, infants were hurled in the air and impaled on rifle bayonets. Throughout the massacre, the Japanese soldiers laughed and cheered each other on. The old man said to me, "I still hate Hapon."

What is it about sustained combat and male peer pressure that turns civilized men into monsters? I'd like to think that Americans are immune to such depravity but I've heard too many stories coming out of South Vietnam that are not unlike that which the old man witnessed 23 years ago. The U.S. commanders designate a peasant village a Viet Cong stronghold and that seems to give American soldiers license to storm in, murder, rape and burn the thatched-roof homes to the ground. The Viet Cong do it. The G.I.'s do it. And the poor peasants – who just want to be left alone to live their slow-paced agrarian lifestyles – become the victims of politicians and generals whom they've never seen and will never know. They've done nothing to deserve it. There have been many persecutions: the North Vietnamese Army, the South Vietnamese Army, Viet Cong Marxist guerillas and before that: the French Army, fighting to retain their colony which at the time was called Indochina.

Most of the older generation of Filipinos will never forgive the Japanese for their atrocities. And conversely, most of them still love Americans because we're remembered here as liberators. That's why when Dick and I left the bus and entered a small fishing village we were warmly welcomed by men, women and dozens of children. The kids were jumping up and down, announcing our arrival: "Americanos! Americanos!"

Competing with one another, the village elders were inviting us into their houses for food and drink. We thanked them profusely but declined, telling them we would like to take some photographs. They gave us their blessings and said: "Our home ees your home."

A little boy probably about 10 years old introduced himself to us: "Hello, Joe. My name ees Pedro. I speak good English. You follow Pedro and I show you good pictures."

He captured our hearts instantly. "Hi Pedro." I said. "Ikina gagalak kong makilala kayo." I told him in Tagalog that I was very pleased to meet him.

"You speak Tagalog?" he asked.

"Ka-un-ti," I replied. "But please, let's speak English."

He smiled. "Okay, Joe."

We told Pedro we wanted to go out to the fields. He took us out to a barren area where a very old man, wearing a coolie hat was struggling behind a primitive, single-blade plow pulled by a carabao ten times his size. We talked to the gentleman through our young interpreter. He was cordial but I could see the strain of hard labor in his face. Sunbaked, wrinkled, he told about how the monsoon rains were so heavy, they had caused the nearby river dikes to break. His meager portion of land was flooded with silt and sand. The rice paddies were destroyed. He was now trying to plow the hardened earth so he could plant melons in the hope of producing some sort of cash crop.

It was sad. I had Pedro tell him, "We were sorry for his bad luck and that we wished we could help in some way."

We offered him some money but he refused it. He was a proud man. So, I offered him a pack of Salem cigarettes, the Filipino people's favorite brand, and he gladly accepted. He opened the pack, took a smoke for himself and offered one to each of us, Pedro excluded. We lit up, smoked and chatted for another ten minutes then bid him a warm-hearted goodbye.

Jesus must have been talking about people such as this man when he said, "Blessed are the meek." We took photos of him and then walked a quarter-mile to a rice paddy brimming with ripened grain. Nearby in an open area, workers were separating the rice from the chaff by leading their carabao over the harvest that had been strewn on the ground. I was thinking, This is probably the way it's been done for over 2,000 years. More photos.

On the way back to the village, we passed some kids playing with a carabao. I asked Pedro if I could ride the animal.

"Yeah, sure, Joe." He motioned, "Come on!"

The carabao was difficult to mount and once I was on it, even more difficult to remain in place. Apparently, it didn't like gringos because the surly critter began whirling around and trying to nip my leg. He threw me off and I rolled out of the way just before he stepped on me. The kids were all laughing at me. Big joke. Yankee falls on his ass.

Brushing off the dust, I jumped to my feet and asked Dick, "Did you get a picture before I fell off?"

"Yes, I did."

"Good."

The sun was getting low in the western sky, so our little threesome walked back to the village where we took a few more pictures of the fishermen with their banka river boats made from hollowed out logs. I captured on film a charming, little girl, probably about 7 years of age, squatting by the river bank washing clothes on the rocks.

Walking back up to the MacArthur Highway, Pedro waited with us for the next Victory Liner. We gave him ten pesos for being our guide (about $2.50 American) and his eyes bugged.

"Ten Pesos!" He exclaimed. "Thank you, Joe. Thank you. Thank you."

I could tell he'd probably never seen ten pesos in his life, let alone possessing them all for himself. Knowing the nature of the people, I'm sure he took the money home later and gave it to his father for the benefit of the entire family.

The bus came along. Pedro ran out into the highway to flag it down with his arms.

"Paalam," we said as we boarded.

"Paalam. Goodbye, Joe! Goodbye!"

Forty-five minutes later, we were walking the sidewalk in Olongapo being harassed by flocks of disrespectful little beggars again. What a contrast.

* * * * * * *

Dick returned to base and the ship taking my camera and exposed film with him for safety's sake. Because I was meeting Pepé at 7:30 pm, I stayed in town and treated myself to chicken fried rice and Shanghai lumpia at the Shamrock restaurant.

I won't attempt to repeat the extensive conversation Pepé and I had over the course of five hours. He took me to a quiet, all-Filipino bar and grill in a more civilized sector of the city where we could relax and enjoy one of our last nights together. I truly hope that Mr. Gonzales someday realizes his dream of coming to America with his wife and kids. No one is more deserving. We rehashed fond memories of my FIC PAC FAC days. We talked about the future – uncertain as it is for both of us. At half-past midnight, he rode in a Jeepney with me to the front gate where we hugged.

I bid him farewell for now. "See you again in a couple of weeks, Pepé."

"Take it easy, Mac," he replied. "You be safe out there."

"Don't worry. I'll be back."

23 December 1967 ... 190th day.
Depart Subic Bay into the South China Sea.

We were well out to sea when I awoke at 1000 – back into the pitch and yaw of rough waters. It was merely a travel day. Tomorrow we reach Hong Kong for Christmas. This evening Chief O'Brian and Charlie Rudd gave the entire detachment a lecture on the resident dangers in the British Crown Colony and how to avoid them. They reminded us that Hong Kong is surrounded by our enemy, the People's Republic of China, and that many anti-American Communists inhabit the Kowloon district.

"So, be cautious and, above all, do not enter any Communist propaganda stores."

Later, after the meeting, Big Ern and I decided we'll just have to go to Kowloon and check out one of these Communist stores for ourselves. Yes, we do misbehave... but consider this: Is not one of the best tactics of war, the ability to get into the mind of your enemy, learning how he thinks?

CHAPTER XXXIII
CHRISTMAS IN HONG KONG

24 December 1967 ... 191st day - Christmas Eve.
In Port - British Crown Colony of Hong Kong.

   This morning I rolled out of the bunk, walked outside and voila! There before me was Hong Kong. It's strange living on this gigantic mobile home that takes me to Hawaii, Japan, Vietnam, the Philippines and now Hong Kong. The air was downright cold – a very penetrating Nebraska December cold. We are anchored in the middle of the bay between Victoria City on Hong Kong Island and the peninsula city of Kowloon on the mainland. Spiffed up in our custom-tailored dress blue uniforms, Big Ern and I were on the first liberty launch. It took us to the Navy pier in Victoria. From there we caught the Star Ferry, a two-tiered passenger boat built like a water-borne bus. We enjoyed the scenic ride, about a mile perhaps, over to Kowloon. A never ending flotilla of ferry boats transports people back and forth between the island and the mainland, predominant fleet being the Star Ferry Company.

   Looking very much like San Francisco, British-dominated Victoria is built on a gradual mountainous slope dotted with modern skyscrapers, upscale apartment dwellings, office buildings, high-class retail and dining establishments. Virtually all the exterior signs are in English. A thin blanket of fog lay over the city this morning. Victoria peak was hidden in clouds. By contrast, Kowloon is a uniquely Asian city: two and three story buildings in ill repair compressed into narrow streets. The pavement was flooded with Chinese pedestrians, bicyclists and motor scooter riders. The majority of the signs in Kowloon are written in Chinese characters.

   Upon disembarking, Big Ern and I distanced ourselves from the Navy Blue mob, hailing a taxi and climbing in. The klutz, of course, bumped his head as he squeezed into the little compact car. "Ouch! Damn it!"

   I laughed. Just like on the ship. The Navy and Asia are not configured for tall boys.

   Our spindly, little Chinese driver turned around and asked, "Where to you go, sailor?

   "We go to Communist bookstore," I replied.

   "Where it?"

"I don't know. You find for us. Okay?"

Not comprehending or just playing stupid, the driver asked, "What store?"

"A Communist store! You know, Mao Tse Tung. Chairman Mao books."

"Ah!" his eyes lit up. Apparently Mao did the trick.

It's always stupid to ask an Asian cabbie to locate anything for you. The place you're looking for may be only three blocks away but he'll take you on a five mile trip winding through remote neighborhoods and outlying industrial districts just to rack up the meter time and money. We took the chance. It didn't matter really because everything here is so damned cheap. After about a twenty-minute drive, he pulled up to a nondescript, tan, stucco building. I had no idea where the hell we were.

"This is it!" Big Ern smiled and pointed, "Look at the sign above the door. It's Chinese writing with a big red star!"

We asked the cabbie to wait for us while we shopped. He was pleased to keep the meter running. We stepped out into the crowd of Asian faces, no Caucasians to be seen in any direction. Six-foot four-inch Ernest towered above the sea of coal-black heads like a jolly Goliath with Fu Manchu mustache wearing a white Dixie Cup. I laughed again. It would have made a great picture but we had left our cameras back at the ship for fear they would be snatched from us by a street thief. Old men on the street glared. When we entered the Commie store they begin to point, chatter, and flail their arms like crazed chimps expressing their amazement. Not a common sight, I reckon.

Inside were tables and bookshelves filled to overflowing with books and Maoist miscellanea. Most of the books have tan covers except for a table of little red books. They're all purported to be written by Chairman Mao himself. Damn, the old boy must have spent fifty percent of his life writing! There were about twenty Chinese civilians in the store, also shoppers I assumed. They tried to be polite and not stare but the tension was so thick you could stab it with a chopstick. Ern and I just acted like it was no big deal.

"Hey, Ern! Here's Mao's book about protracted warfare! Do you think I should get it?"

"Yeah, that's a good one," he replied. "That's the tactic Mao is coaching Uncle Ho to use in Nam, y'know. Just dragging it out until the folks back home in the states get so sick and tired of it, they tell their senators to throw in the towel."

Nodding my understanding, I tucked the tan book under my arm and moseyed on to the table of red books. "What are these, Ern? D'ya know?"

"That's the Quotations of Chairman Mao. It's the bible of the Red Guard Movement."

Looking at a poster on the wall depicting Chinese students in olive drab proletariat uniforms, I noticed that the red book hoisted over their heads was one and the same.

"Damn, Sam! I gotta get that for sure." I picked up two of the English versions. Ern grabbed a couple.

"Hey, Mac!" Ern had discovered something. "Look! Lapel Pins!"

He was all excited. "Look at this one, Mao in the middle of a red star with gold border; and this one, Mao and one of his quotations. And look! There's some plain red stars."

"Yeah!" I shared in his enthusiasm. "And lookie here, up on the wall. Will ya? "

I walked across the room to a sales display. Still babbling I pointed out the Red Guard calendar for 1968. "And look over there! North Vietnam postage stamps! They have illustrations of our planes being shot down. And, goddamn! They have North Vietnamese propaganda magazines! This is great stuff to use in my post-cruise slide show. My audience will be able to see both sides of the war."

Ern wasn't listening. He was standing there with red star Mao lapel pins in hand, conspiring. Yes, something was brewing in that big, round head of his. "I think this would look good on my uniform, don't you? Right there above my merit ribbons?"

He was contemplating taking dissension to a new level and that made me a little nervous. "You know... if the Shore Patrol sees you with that pin on your uniform, you could be busted and hauled off to the brig."

Willing to disbelieve, he waved me off, "The Shore Patrol monkeys aren't smart enough to recognize a Mao button. And, neither..." He paused while his eyes lit up, "neither is the Master-at-Arms!"

"The Master-at-Arms?" That's when I realized that my bud was planning to return to the ship, salute and ask the Boatswain-on-duty for permission to come aboard, while wearing his red star Mao pin. "Holy shit, big guy! Your ass is gonna be grass!"

He just gave me his trademark sly fox smile and said two words: "Watch me."

So we returned to the ship with our Commie loot and I'll be damned if he didn't pull it off. I came aboard first so I could turn around and watch. Ern was standing there saluting – proud as could be with his red star glaring on his chest. "Permission to come aboard, sir."

"Permission granted."

The Boatswain's Mate didn't notice a thing.

We laughed and chattered all the way up to the shop and proceeded to stow our day's treasure in our sea chests. Hedge came in and asked, "What you two up to now?"

"Oh, nothing, Harry! Just having a good time. Just having a good time."

25 December 1967 ... 192st day - Christmas Day.
In Port - British Crown Colony of Hong Kong.

Merry Christmas, MacLennon! Yesterday, I received a holiday package from my folks. In it was a small 5-inch reel tape with recorded personal greetings from Dad, Mom, sister Jeris and little brother, Jeff. Grandma Florence and other family members provided messages as well. The package included a holiday card, some magazines of interest and a Nebraskaland pictorial calendar but the tape was the best Christmas gift of all. It's good to hear the voices of home.

Sweet old Chief O'Brian allowed the crew to sleep in until 0900 this morning. I guess that was his Christmas gift. After we were up, he put us to work saying that no one in duty section one could take liberty until we had washed aircraft 601. I ducked out of duty and hid in Photo Intelligence with Chapin until 1400. Both of us looked through a civilian employment manual. I came to the unnerving realization that I have no idea what I want to do when I return to the U.S. of A.

At 1545, I reported to Flight Deck control in my dress blues. We are wearing our wool uniform because it's chilly here – daytime temps in the 40s. I was ordered to stand Fly One Aircraft Integrity Watch but after a half hour of walking around on an empty deck the intelligentsia determined that because there were no planes to guard I didn't need to stand watch. That's the Navy in a nutshell – nut being the operative word.

Ernest returned this evening from his day ashore and related his frustrating day to me. Big Ern didn't have a very positive opinion of the tourist action. With camera in tote, he visited world-famous Tiger Balm Gardens this morning. Built by the founder of the Tiger Balm salve industry, the beautifully-landscaped park displays traditional Chinese art and sculpture. Instead of having a rewarding cultural experience, Ern was mobbed by peddlers and beggars. He said that when he tried to take photos of statues, little Chinese men would stand in front of his camera lens, holding up plastic sheets of transparencies, saying, "Take pictures, no good. You buy slides." They kept getting in his way so he finally gave in and bought some of their slides just to appease them.

"The slides were dirty, poorly exposed and too damned expensive," he lamented.

Not much later, a crowd of dirty, Chinese urchins ganged up on Ern hounding him for money. "They were climbing all over me," he said, "literally hanging on me. They wrapped themselves around my leg and I couldn't even kick them off. One kid draped himself on my camera bag."

Ern said he finally took a few Hong Kong Dollar coins from his pocket and threw them in one direction; and while they ran and fought over the money, Ern swiftly departed in the other direction.

And so this was Christmas 1967. No gifts around the tree. No tree. No Christmas music. No Santa. None of the trappings I've come to expect back home every year. Maybe it's just as well.

Last night, Christmas Eve, the ship's Chaplain conducted a worship service in the Hangar Bay for the Christians. I didn't go. I know Mom would be disappointed with me but the irony of celebrating the birth of the Jesus onboard one of the world's most lethal weapons of war just doesn't seem appropriate.

26 December 1967 ... 193st day.
In Port - British Crown Colony of Hong Kong.

Ropes tied to the catwalks suspend 2-by-10 inch planks down to about twenty-five feet from the surface of the water. On each plank balance two Chinese men with very long-handled roller brushes painting the exposed hull of the Oriskany. Men and women on small house boats supply the paint while trimming the ship along the water line. At the same time in the scullery, women collect leftover food scraps from returned trays. On the fantail, Chinese women are given the opportunity to sift through the garbage, collecting anything they deem useable or resalable. The salvaged items are then lowered in a net over the side to eager women and children in boats below.

This is Hong Kong and the storied side painters that work all day for food scraps and garbage. This venture, I'm told, began in post-World War I days by a legendary Chinese businesswoman named Fat Mary. Because of her various business enterprises with the American and British military, she had at one time, prior to World War II, amassed a small fortune but it was all confiscated by Japanese occupation forces. Old Salts onboard know about her. Some have personally met her. Apparently she's still alive although very old.

Pulling on my blues, a rowdy crowd of sailors and I descended to the liberty launch this chilly December morning. Transported to Fenwick Pier on Victoria Island, we headed first to the money changers exchanging our American greenbacks for Hong Kong dollars. Walking solo a block to the harbor front, I entered the four-story China Fleet Club, a large complex of retail stores, bars and night clubs catering to the U.S. and British Royal Navy. In the drinking establishments, Brits and Yanks were already working on their daily binges. I shopped a little and left. I decided to take the Star Ferry over to Kowloon and, once there, was surprised to find more Brits on Kowloon than Victoria. And hot damn! British women! What a treat for a homesick sailor who has been accustomed to seeing only almond eyes in his ports of call. But there they were: beautiful, young, round-eyes with blonde and brunette hair wearing tight sweaters and mini-skirts speaking with that charming English accent. I tried a little flirting but most of these chicks don't have the time of day for sailors.

Out of curiosity, I decided to investigate a little tavern named simply "The Pub". What a great find! Entering through the large oak door was like stepping out of Hong Kong into jolly old England: stacked beer barrels, a Union Jack on the wall, dart boards and best of all, Caucasian barmaids. A lovely New Zealander, probably about 21 years old, named Marilyn waited on me. Blond hair with a face resembling Barbra Streisand, she told me she was slowly working her way to England. I asked her for a libation suggestion and she recommended a German beer called Lowenbrau. New to me, I said, "Sure, why not." It turned out to be one of the best beers I've ever tasted. I visited with Marilyn and a couple of civilian Brits at the bar, just small talk but good conversation nonetheless. I fantasized that Marilyn would eventually get around to saying, "Hey Yank! Why don't I knock off for a couple of hours, take you up to my flat and fuck your brains out?"

Alas, it was merely a three pints fantasy. Around 1800, I bid her farewell and good luck on her journey.

Getting hungry, I ferried over to Victoria and headed for the Hong Kong Hilton. Along the way, I ran into Bart Gordon and invited him to come along with me for dinner. He gladly accepted. Taking the elevator – the lift, as the Brits call it – to the top of the ten story hotel, we entered The Eagle's Nest restaurant, a very high-class white folk's place. Even the staff was non-Asian. As the only people in uniform, we felt a bit out of place amongst the suits and evening gowns but... What the hell? With their very attentive, friendly service, the waiters made us feel welcome and not at all peculiar. Every time I took out a cigarette, a young man was immediately at my side with a lighter flicked and ready. That was a novelty I've never experienced, not even in the States. A dish of chicken fried rice, a beer and a slice of baked Alaska cost me 24 Hong Kong dollars – conversion rate is 4 Hong Kong dollars for every American buck. I left a generous tip.

27 December 1967 ... 194st day.
In Port - British Crown Colony of Hong Kong

We're performing a minimum of aircraft work this in-port period. It's strictly an R&R stop. Bart, Walt Lehmann and I did some custom-tailored clothes shopping in Kowloon. Later, nearing sunset, we crossed to Victoria and taxied to the tram station where we were transported on small rails to Victoria Peak, a rise of 1,305 feet in ten minutes. Each with our dutiful cameras, we snapped photos of one another with the splendid panorama of Victoria, Kowloon and the New Territories behind us. As night fell, city lights, looking very much like stars in the new moon heaven, created a breath-taking display of shimmering color. We took time exposures. From the mountaintop you can't see the poverty, the 10-by-20 foot houseboats serving as home to families of 5 to 10 people, you can't see the shanty towns with dwelling places built with scraps of wood and corrugated metal sheets but you can see the hastily-built concrete high-rise complexes where three generations of one family are packed together in single room apartments sharing bath and toilet facilities with hundreds of other people.

It was very windy atop the peak, and cold – probably in the 30s. I wore my wool jersey under my dress blue top but the other boys were not as foresighted. They were wearing only t-shirts and gabardine blues so we had to cut short the stay because the poor babies were, in their words, "freezing to death."

28 December 1967 ... 195st day. Ibid.

Section Two Duty day again and it seems even colder than yesterday. The Brits on the radio give the temperature in centigrade: "The Royal Observatory currently reports 10 degrees Celsius" – whatever the hell that is. I set out to do my duty to God and my country painting Yosemite Sam on both sides of the tail of 602. This makes the 15th and 16th goddamn time I've painted the little bastard. And the last!

After completing the task, I descended to P.I. for a warm-up cup of coffee. I walked in and damned if there weren't four gorgeous chicks in there. Paul Duncan and Jerry Calloway had scored some round-eye girls out there in the colony and talked them into coming onboard the ship for a tour. They were sharing small talk but I was dumbfounded. I hope they didn't notice me drooling. They were all British with either blonde or chestnut hair, wearing mini-skirts, false eyelashes; flashing their cute little smiles around the room. Two of them couldn't be much older than 16; the other two about 18. They looked like the Go-Go Girls on Shindig! There was a boy with them named Keith with hair hanging in his eyes and over his shoulders but he didn't pique my interest. My raging hormone fantasy already had the girls undressed and in my rack. I think Paul and Jerry just wanted to brag a bit; you know, torture the rest of us unlucky bastards.

If that wasn't enough to give me a 24-hour hard-on, this afternoon British nurses came onboard requesting blood donations for the British Red Cross of Hong Kong. This, I'm told, is an ongoing event for every major U.S. ship that pulls in. At first, these beautiful creatures just wander freely around the ship chit-chatting with the personnel, asking them if they're interested in donating.

The usual follow-up question from the squid is: "Will you be there?"

After the nurse gives her affirmative, the sailor signs up, just for the opportunity to be with her for a half hour. I didn't have to be asked. I hunted down the cutest nurse I could find and said, "Hey, I want to give! Please!"

So, this afternoon, I was lying on the cot in the medical ward with a needle in my arm losing a pint of my life fluid but feeling no pain because about a dozen shapely, young cuties in short, white skirts and high-heeled white shoes kept walking by me. I continued to watch as they bent over their patients. The Ordnanceman in the cot next to me called out to a nurse, "I'm getting lightheaded. I think I'm gonna faint!"

A sweet little brunette came to his side, "You're almost finished, Yank. Don't pass out on me."

She left momentarily and returned with a small washcloth soaked in ice water. She bent over him, placing it on his forehead, speaking a few comforting words. Her bosom was only inches from his face and, from my vantage point, I watched her shapely legs and cute, little ass as her skirt slid higher and higher almost revealing the promised land.

"There you are," she said to him. "Better now?"

"Oh, yeah," he replied.

"Oh, yeah!" I replied.

She turned about and looked at me. She knew what I meant but instead of getting upset, she just smiled, gave me a wink and proceeded to other donors. These prick-teasers know exactly what they are doing. The Ordnanceman looked over at me, "Sweet Jesus, Mary and Joseph. I think I've died and gone to heaven."

"I know what you mean."

All the arousal must have accelerated my circulation because I lost the entire pint in about 15 minutes. Damn! It was over too quickly and I was doomed to return to P.I. and Chapin's not-as-pretty face. But, in the good news department, Old Lady Five Fingers and I have another date tonight.

29 December 1967 ... 196st day. Ibid.

Spread out in my bunk this morning, I scanned through a Hong Kong travel brochure. Damn! Kowloon is only 3-and-a-quarter square miles in size with over two million people living there. Talk about being packed together like sardines! The whole state of Nebraska has only about one million. Over 100,000 Chinese live on houseboats. Ninety-nine percent of the entire colony's inhabitants are Chinese; the remaining 50,000 are mostly Brits with a smattering of Americans, Portuguese and Japanese. The Victoria District is known for its commerce, Kowloon for its industry and the New Territories – 365 square miles – for its agriculture. The duty-free port of Hong Kong was leased to the British in 1898 for a period of 99 years. In the year 1997, it will be given back to China. I wonder what the Commies will do with it once they take control. You can bet your ass there won't be any more U.S. ships anchoring here. They'll probably kick out the Brits, too.

Today, Bart and I joined thirteen other sailors on a guided bus tour of the New Territories. The bus was poorly heated and temperatures in the high country must have been close to freezing. Traveling north from the Kowloon peninsula, all presence of English influence vanishes. Along the Kowloon and New Territories border, on the mountain slopes, lined up like grey and orange concrete dominos-on-edge are dozens of high rise apartment buildings built by the government for resettlement of the colony's poor people. One settlement we passed, the Tsuen Wan estate, houses 175,000 residents. A few more miles down the road, we entered a region of rugged mountains. Boulders and weather-worn pines reminded me of Colorado. The New Territories are a weird composite of terrain. One moment you're in a Rocky Mountain setting and moments later you've descended into a flat, fertile valley where farmers are guiding plows through rice paddies pulled by water buffalo. Crops range from barley and wheat to sugar cane; from peach and apple orchards to banana groves. The semi-tropical climate allows for such diversity.

The end of the trail brought us up to a high spot along the Red China border and the Lok Ma Chau police station, a small building housing two Chinese men in British uniform. Debussing and walking up to the border fence, I brought out my telephoto zoom lens and snapped off photos of villages and rice paddies in the valley below. A People's Liberation Army truck, positioned next to a farmer's hut, pumped out propaganda from two gigantic speakers attached to the top of the cab. We couldn't understand it, of course, but I'd guess it was singing the praises of Chairman Mao and his Cultural Revolution. I'm sure the farmer living in that hut really appreciates the racket but what can he do? Complain? Sure, if he wants to spend the rest of his life in a 3-by-3 foot cell.

As I turned from the fence, I was greeted by a jolly, little Chinese man wearing a straw coolie hat. Flashing a mouth full of rotten teeth, he spoke to me in broken English, probably the only English he knows, "You take picture me. One dollar. Yes?"

He was a perfect subject: shaggy, white Ho Chi Minh beard, deeply-etched weathered face, probably about 80-years-old. Shivering from the cold air, the poor little man wore only a very thin overcoat. Soft hearted Mac took a couple of photos and gave him five Hong Kong dollars. He shook my hand, rattled off a few paragraphs in Chinese and extended me a series of bows to show his gratitude. I returned the bows and returned to the bus. I'll bet thousands of tourists from countries around the globe have a picture of that little guy.

The tour ended around 2100. We dined this evening in the Victoria Central District at a high-class restaurant called The Parisian Grill, our one last good meal before we return to Navy chow. You know, kind of like the last meal before execution. For 25 Hong Kong Dollars each, we enjoyed brandy, a flaming chateaubriand entree and flaming baked Alaska for dessert. Again we were treated like royalty.

Bart wanted to do some last minute shopping so we parted company and I hopped the Star Ferry over to Kowloon where I sought out The Pub one more time. Sitting at the bar, sipping Lowenbrau, I chummed up with a couple of male Brits probably about 25 years old who referred to me only as Yank. I had brought some pre-stamped Hong Kong folding letter forms with me to pen messages to my folks and some friends in the States. I had an extra so I asked Nigel and Paul if they knew any girls in England who might welcome a letter from a Yank sailor. They gave me the name of one

Susan Lees in Shaw Lanes, England. She's 21 years old and, according to my Limey buddies, "well-educated, fine looking with a captivating sense of humor." There's no telling if they're playing a practical joke on me or not. She could very well be a cow. Nevertheless, after the two finished their pints and bid me 'Cheerio,' I sat alone until nearly midnight downing beer after beer and writing. Weaving back to the Navy launch pier, I shouted a loud farewell to the colony: "God save the Queen!"

Yes, I was definitely drunk but I fit right in. The mobs of sailors surrounding me were in the same inebriated state, some of them even too drunk to stand up.

30 December 1967 ... 197st day.
U.S.S. Oriskany underway

Well, Anchors Aweigh! and all that shit. The Mighty Zero and its crew departed Hong Kong this morning weaving slowly through the outlying islands of the colony. There are probably a hundred small, uninhabited islands except for the very last. It had a tall, white lighthouse with caretaker living quarters attached. Now, that would be a cool job: having my own island with plenty of time to read, write, paint and work on correspondence courses toward earning my degree. As soon as we passed the lighthouse and entered open sea, Heavy Weather Condition Three was set and our iron bucket began rocking and a-rolling as we turned south for the Gulf of Tonkin.

We compared our Hong Kong experiences this morning over coffee in the shop. I learned that many of the Air Wing pilots paid big bucks to have their wives and children flown over to Hong Kong during the in-port period. Staying in Central Victoria District hotels, they enjoyed R&R as complete families. It must be nice to have that kind of money. None of the squids or Airdales that I know had their wives or girlfriends fly across the Pacific Ocean.

Hedge said he had talked on the Flight Deck with a very apprehensive Fighter Squadron 111 pilot. Most Officers aren't so open with their emotions, especially to an Enlisted Man. The Lieutenant had confessed to Harry: "I have a bad feeling about this thirteen day line period. I'm so damned close to going home. I had a wonderful time with my wife and two little boys in Hong Kong. I brought them over because I may never see them again. I didn't tell them that but that's the reason. Thirteen is an unlucky number. We shouldn't be going back to Nam. God, I hope I make it home."

Throughout most of this cruise, I haven't had much to say about the Navy Pilots on a personal level, just a lot of criticism. I must admit that my selfish whining is just born out of envy. These men are at the top of their game. Most have come from well-to-do families with strong paternal support. They've had the privilege of earning college or academy degrees; they've gone through grueling flight training and now, in combat, they've truly earned their wings. Some may make a career of the Navy. Others will separate when their hitch is up and find good civilian jobs flying passenger aircraft or some related field. Mister Sampson told me he has his eyes on working in the U.S. Space Program at NASA. Yes, I must admit that I not only envy them, I admire them and wish I was one of them.

CHAPTER XXXIV
LAST CHANCE TO DIE

31 December 1967 ... 198st day.
Gulf of Tonkin, North Vietnam.

We arrived at Yankee Station early this morning, this New Year's Eve Day, and the brass gods were chomping at the bit to get back to business but Mother Nature once again thwarted their desire to kill, maim and destroy with a heavy cloud cover and rain. All three Photo Birds flew missions today but took no pics due to overcast conditions.

This evening, Walt Lehmann, Paul Duncan and I were pooling our creative energy trying to think of a way to bring in the New Year sans booze, sans parties. Walt had his Teac tape recorder set up in Photo Intelligence so we put on a virgin 7-inch tape and made a party on tape by utilizing his sound-on-sound feature. I played the role of the announcer in New York City's Times Square describing the crowd and doing the countdown to midnight. The three of us created then recorded crowd cheers complete with horns blowing, whistles and banging on empty film canisters. We over-dubbed the improvised crowd ten times until it sounded like thousands of people raising hell. At 2340, we transported the recorder, amp and speakers down to our shop and set it up, placing the speakers in the passageway. As midnight approached, we turned on the tape and cranked up the speakers full blast.

"Welcome everyone to our New Year's Eve countdown!" my recorded voice resonated through the 02 level. "We must have thousands of people here with us tonight in Times Square as we wait for the ball to drop signifying the arrival of the year 1968! We're glad you could join us in this celebration especially the men onboard the U.S.S. Oriskany over there in the Gulf of Tonkin. It's party time here in New York and we want to share it with our servicemen in Vietnam. So, we're nearing the magic moment. Count it down with us!"

Dozens of Airdales appeared in the passageway, many of them in their skivvies because they had already hit the sack. The initial consensus was: "What the fuck is going on?"

It didn't take them long however, once they realized the nature of the game, to assume a party mood. They joined in the recorded countdown. "Yes, Ladies and Gentlemen, we have fifteen seconds until the New Year! The ball is lit and about to descend. Join with us now as we bring in 1968! Ten! Nine! Eight! Seven! Six! Five!"

All the men in the passageways were counting with the recording.

"Four! Three! Two! One! Happy New Year!"

The men danced little jigs in the hallway and slapped each other on the back. No kissing or hugging. Our little New Year's Eve party lasted for about five minutes. The men of the other squadrons thanked us for our effort to bring a little cheer into their hearts then retired for the night. I'm glad we did it. So, it's 1968. I sure hope it's a hell of a lot better than 1967. Maybe this will be the year the Vietnam debacle ends.

1 January 1968 ... 199st day. Gulf of Tonkin, Vietnam.

Lyndon Baines Johnson's prayers were answered this morning. The cloud cover over North Vietnam is gone and the sun shines bright. Just one glitch however, someone in the military high command has decreed that all the U.S. Armed Forces in Vietnam will cease hostilities in honor of New Year's Day. So what did our Air Wing do? We flew Alpha Strikes over Nam but didn't drop bombs, just to see if our pilots could get their asses shot down. Fucking brilliant! Our squadron was scheduled for a record six hops in one day. We flew five and did take targeting photos, so many in fact that the Photo Intelligence boys were working until well after midnight. The North Vietnamese had no stand down. Their New Year's Day – they call it Tet – is in late January. One of their artillery shells struck an A-4 from Attack Squadron 164. The pilot managed to maneuver the mortally-wounded Skyhawk out over the Gulf where he punched the ejection seat, ditching the plane in the briny blue. More American tax dollars in the drink. Within minutes, Lieutenant Michael Goldberg, at the controls of Angel-3, was hovering overhead dropping a life line. Shaken but uninjured, the fighter pilot was flown back to the Oriskany.

2 January 1968 ... 200th day. Gulf of Tonkin, Vietnam.

I was nauseated all day. Maybe it's real, maybe it's my mind playing tricks on my body. I am just sick of this whole fucking mess and want to get out of the Navy. Forty-four days and a wake up.

Our three Photo Birds made one hop each today. The war is heating up again. David Beam, flying 602, and his fighter escort came under heavy AAA fire today. The escort was hit and as with the incident yesterday, he made it back to the Gulf waters, ejected and was plucked by Angel-1. Burt Shepherd, Commander of the Air Group – and brother to Alan, the first American in Outer Space – was flying his tactical F-8 Crusader when suddenly it was struck by an artillery shell. It ripped a 10-inch hole through his right wing but he managed to maneuver the crippled aircraft back to the ship and made a perfect Flight Deck landing. Reckon that's why he's Top Dog.

CHAPTER XXXV
LIEUTENANT GOLDBERG'S OMEN

3 January 1968 ... 201th day. Ibid.

Major Alpha Strikes were flown today from all carriers on line. Our Air Group alone launched 127 sorties. Our Det flew two hops. And, I still feel like shit. Even so, I wandered up to the canoe tonight about 2200, a couple of hours after Flight Quarters had secured. Someone was already sitting there. As I got closer, I realized it was Lieutenant Goldberg.

"Michael! I haven't seen you in four months. I mean, not here. I've seen you with your helicopter combat support crew but hey! It's good to see you alone once again!"

"Hi, Mac. How ya doin'?" His return greeting was less than enthusiastic.

"Well, I'm sure glad this cruise is almost over. Aren't you?" I asked.

"Sit down, my friend. I'm glad you're here. I was praying that I could have someone to talk to tonight. And you are my answer." I could tell that he had changed in four months; something was getting him down.

"Well, I've never been an answer to prayer before, Michael. I hope I live up to your expectations."

"No expectation, Mac. I just need an ear. Do you mind if I unload on you?"

"No, of course not. You're one of the best friends I have on this old rust bucket."

"Nice of you to say. Listen, Mac, I think I'm going to die."

"Sure, we all are, eventually."

"No!" he raised his voice. "I'm not going to make it home. I didn't tell you before but I have a lovely wife named Rivkah and two beautiful children, ages four and seven. I love them very much."

Michael began weeping quietly. I wasn't sure how to comfort him or what to say but I had to ask, "What makes you so sure you're going to die? I mean, did God give you a direct message or something? None of us, except for prisoners on death row, knows when his time is coming."

"I had a dream last night, Mac. I saw my deceased zayde, my grandfather for whom I was named. It was very real to me. He was holding out his hand to me, just like he did every Friday night before Shabbos when I was a boy. I was back there again, in the streets of Brooklyn playing stick ball and he came up to me and said, 'Michael, it's time to go home now.' And I walked with him, hand in hand, and we went up the stoop into my house. And when he opened the door, a flood of light overwhelmed us, light so bright it burned my eyes. It was almost liquid. And I felt myself swimming in the light and calling out for help. Next thing I knew I was floating in the sky above my house, looking down, and I saw Rivkah and the children sitting in our parlor, all of them dressed in black and all shedding tears. And, all saying my name in its Hebrew pronunciation. And then I heard zayde above me somewhere reciting the Shema. At that point, a body appeared – stretched out on a table in the middle of the room. As I stared intently the fuzzy image came into focus... and I saw myself lying there. Dead. Ashen white face."

He paused for half a minute with head down. And then continued, "I couldn't bear to see any more. I woke up out of the dream trembling. Trembling all over my body."

I was speechless for a minute. It did sound like an omen but I didn't want to say so. He graciously spared me from having to say anything. "You know, Mac, I'm not afraid of dying. I know there's a better world waiting; a place with no war, no suffering, no pain. But damn it! I hate to leave my family behind. I know they'll be heartbroken and they'll suffer, they will suffer because I am gone."

"Well, if it's true, Michael..." I finally worked up the courage. "If it really is written that this is your time to go, sure, your family will grieve. That's only natural but time will pass and the hurt will heal and they'll get on with their lives. And you'll always be a blessed memory for them. Always. And someday, you'll be reunited with all three of them. You said that yourself, that love is the only thing that's transcendent."

"Maybe Ha Shem will allow me to visit them in the spirit."

"I believe that. And if it is your will, Michael, to be with them, to comfort them in their time of loss, I really believe God... er, Ha Shem will make it happen."

He laughed and wiped his nose with a handkerchief.

"That's funny?" I asked.

"Yes, you saying Ha Shem, and the image of me as Michael the Friendly Ghost."

"Yeah. Why not?"

At that point, I did something I haven't done for a long time. I offered to say a prayer.

He declined. "I've already said the Shema about a dozen times."

"What is that?"

"It's the Jewish anthem, so to speak. "Shema Yisrael, Ha Shem Eloheynu, Ha Shem Echad – Hear, O Israel, Ha Shem is our God. Ha Shem is One."

Before I could utter another word, Michael stood up. "Thanks, Mac. Thanks for listening. There's really nothing I can do. It's out of my hands. I may as well keep going through the motions, right? And just accept it."

"It could be just a dream, you know." Again I tried to offer some reassurance. "I mean, you're combat support and rescue, not combat."

"Could be but I don't think so." He bent over and extended his hand to me, "Thank you, my friend, my brother. And God go with you wherever you travel in this life."

We shook hands but that wasn't good enough. I jumped to my feet and slapped a bear hug on him. "Let's not say goodbye, Michael, just see you later. Okay?"

"Sure, it's a deal. See you later, Mac."

4 January 1968 ... 202nd day. Ibid.

The weather these past two days has been perfect for operations: plenty of sunshine and not a cloud in the sky. Too bad. Everyone was hoping that we'd just be stuck in monsoon rain until time to go home. The U.S. War Machine is taking advantage of the favorable conditions by launching Alpha Strike after Alpha Strike. Yesterday, a major boat repair facility on the Red River was demolished by our bombs. Today strategic targets in and around Thanh Hoa were destroyed.

The thirteen day curse became real today for a pilot from Fighter Squadron 162. His Crusader took a direct hit from a surface-to-air missile. The plane exploded into a thousand pieces before he had time to eject. He was killed instantly. I hope he had time with his family in Hong Kong. They won't even have a body to bury because he is now charred pieces on hostile turf. Our Photo Birds flew only two hops today. Surprisingly enough, we had no camera discrepancies. Our pilots are nervous. Virtually every detachment of Photo Recon Squadron 63 loses at least one pilot per cruise. So far, we've been lucky. The incident today with Fighter Squadron 162 sent a shudder through the hearts of the Air Wing personnel. All of us. We're so damned close to going home and the grim reaper harvested a soul. Every mission is a macabre game of Russian roulette. The pilots arrive on deck, personally pre-flight their aircraft and climb into the cockpit. They taxi and launch from the catapult not knowing if the gun pointed at their head is set on an empty chamber or if it's the one live round that will blow their brains out.

The ship went on shower hours today, the first time since 5 November. Somewhere on this old rusty tub there's a leak or a valve mistakenly turned on... again. It's draining our fresh water supply, and the XO is blaming it on the Enlisted Men again, saying that we're not taking regulation Navy showers. He didn't mention the top brass. They probably have gigantic bath tubs with whirlpools up there in Officer's Country with Filipino stewards giving them massages and blow jobs. Well... maybe not the latter.

5 January 1968 ... 203th day. Ibid.

This morning I reported to the Medical Department for my release from active duty physical. About fifteen other black shoes and Airdales were going through the same process. We were herded like sheep from one Corpsman to the next: dental check, eye exam, blood pressure. We had blood drawn out, then had to piss in a bottle for the boys. The last stop was the real doctor. He felt my belly, back, balls and took a peak up my asshole. I wonder if he enjoyed the view. Next step is having the Navy declare me fit to return to civilian status. I sign the medical release and I'm ready for freedom!

[written later in the day]

This afternoon, Michael's premonition came true. I don't know how to deal with it. I'm spooked. I'm pissed off at God. I'm a fucked-up mess right now. And, poor Michael is dead. Shit! I guess it happened around 1500. One of the A-4s from Attack Squadron 163 was on sortie over Nam when his plane was grazed by a surface-to-air missile. It was crippled and losing fuel so the pilot quickly unloaded his bombs on an empty field and gunned the Skyhawk to the coastline trying to make it out over the Gulf before he flamed out. He succeeded but just barely. He actually lost power over land and glided about a mile out beyond the shoreline where he pulled the ejection cord, rocketed out and parachuted into the drink.

Sent to rescue the pilot, Michael and his crew were there within ten minutes flying Angel-3. Unfortunately, so were three gunboats from a nearby North Vietnamese village. They were bearing down on the floating pilot and the hovering chopper. They began firing. Angel-3 apparently took a direct hit to its fuel tank, veered off, then exploded in a ball of flames. Apparently the force of the explosion blew the crewmen out of the chopper, dropping them in the water below. The pilot of Angel-2, not far behind, observed most of what happened and called in air strikes on the NVA gunboats. Fighter Squadron 111 responded with three fighter jets. They literally blew those motherfuckin' gunboats and their crews into a million pieces. Sent them straight to hell where they belong. Angel-2 retrieved survivors and bodies, bringing them back to the ship.

From our shop, I heard passageway chatter but couldn't make it out. Still, I raced up to the Flight Deck when Angel-2 touched down. I didn't know at that time, of course, that Michael's dead body was inside one of those two black bags they offloaded. Survivors were tied on to litters and I couldn't see their faces from my vantage point. I was praying to God that Michael survived but my worst fear was realized this evening at 2100 when Captain Billy came on the squawk box and gave us the details. I forgot the name of the fighter pilot; he was mentioned first. Then I heard: "Lieutenant Michael Goldberg, pilot of Angel-3, will be remembered for his heroism. In the face of hostile enemy fire, he carried out his duty with valor..." And blah, blah, blah. Bullshit!

The ship's Chaplain followed on the 1MC, delivering a prayer for all of them and their families. Tonight, as I sit here writing, I am not crying for Michael. Like I said, I just feel empty, depressed and angry at God, fate, whatever you want to call it. It's one thing to sit on the canoe and talk about death but when the Reaper actually takes his harvest, you don't welcome the son-of-a-bitch. You hate everything he stands for.

6 January 1968 ... 204th day. Ibid.

I didn't sleep last night. I was just lying in my bunk eyes wide open with a thousand random thoughts racing through my head all night. At 0600, I rolled out on to the deck and hit the showers. I'd been sweating like a stuck hog. I skipped breakfast, not hungry. I shuffled up to the shop. Koppler, Hedge and Danko were there, talking about something and smiling. I didn't catch the drift of it.

"Hey, MacLennon!" Danko looked up and hollered at me. "Did you hear about the Jew helo pilot that got shot down yesterday? Goldberg I think it was?"

I didn't answer. I didn't need to hear this. I knew what was coming. I braced myself.

"Hey," Danko continued with a shit-eating grin on his face, "I heard they took his body down to the reefers in the galley. And, get this! For dessert tonight, we're having Angel Food Kike!" He broke out laughing like a fuckin' hyena.

I don't know how it happened. There's a gap in my memory but the next thing I recall was Danko flat on the deck with me straddling him, repeatedly punching that big fuckin' mouth of his. Danko was yelling, "What the hell, MacLennon? Get off me!"

Harry came up from behind, grabbed one of my arms, jerked me to my feet and threw me on to the steel deck on the other side of the shop. I was lying there face down. I began sobbing uncontrollably. I was finally letting it out. I couldn't hold it back.

I could hear Danko, or maybe it was Hedge, shouting, "What the fuck is the matter with you, MacLennon?"

I began pounding the deck with my fists. "Danko, you asshole! Goldberg was my friend.. He's was not a kike. He was Jewish and he was a better human being than you'll ever hope to be, you bigoted son of a bitch!"

"God, I'm sorry, Mac." I couldn't believe it. Danko was apologizing. I figured he'd go put me on report and have me confined to the brig but the jerk was actually apologizing. "I didn't know he was a friend of yours," Danko said. "He was an officer, and, ah... well, I'm sorry, Mac. I don't blame you for being pissed."

I was still face down on the deck, tears flowing.

I heard Hedge say to Danko, "I think it's better if you just leave. I'll handle this."

"Yeah, okay, Harry. See you later."

I heard Danko and Koppler leave and then Harry got down on his haunches and in a very stern voice, told me: "You're damned lucky that Danko is a good guy. Assaulting a superior Petty Officer could land you in the brig for a good long time, pal. You'd be saying adios to that February release date. Think about that, MacLennon!"

Still lying on the floor, face huddled within my forearms, I asked Hedge: "Why do you put up with Danko's remarks, Harry? I know you're not like that."

"No, Mac. I'm not. I don't hold a man's race, color or religion against him. Listen, MacLennon, you're in no position to be passing judgments after that shit you pulled with Arlington. Ray heard about it too and just kinda shook his head. You didn't make any friends doing that. Arlington's punishment for you was mild. Very mild. Do you know I've gone to your defense several times on this cruise? D'you know that?"

He paused and waited for my answer. I forced out the word, "No."

"I can't hear you, Mac!" he shouted at me. "Say it again!"

I raised my voice looking up at him, "No, Harry, I wasn't aware of that. Thanks."

He brushed off my weak apology and continued, "I've stood up for you guys time and again and I haven't got any thanks, no hints of gratitude. It's mainly you, pal, and Levitt. I know the shit you two pulled in Hong Kong, going off limits and going into a commie bookstore. That stunt could of got you some serious brig time!"

"Really?"

"Yeah really! And that bullshit with Mister Sonniksen getting a Mao Tse Tung poster in his mail. Same. I knew Levitt had done that. Why? Because nobody else but Levitt would do such a stupid thing. The Old Man wanted me to find the culprit and write him up for a Captain's Mast. D'you know about that? Didja?"

Again, starting to feel ashamed, I said, "No Harry. I didn't know. For what it's worth. Thanks again."

He changed the subject, "And about this diary you're keeping. I've read some of it because you leave it on the work bench. Y'know, you come across as one superior motherfucker, MacLennon! Very high and mighty like you're just a little better than all the rest of us... even the officers. That shit just don't fly, son!"

"I didn't realize..."

He cut me off, "You don't know a lot of shit, Mac! I've put up with all your childish crap because you're a good worker. I put up with Danko's crazy remarks because he's a damned good First Class Petty Officer and he's under one hell of a lot of pressure. D'ya know that?"

"No." I muttered.

"No, of course not. Danko's got to keep our planes up and running all the time. The Chief and the pilots are always on his ass to get something fixed on 601, or 602, or whatever. And they always want it done yesterday. That's a lot of grief for one man.

"And as for his anti-Semitic remarks, no it wasn't right. But you know what? He's not really that way either. He's not. Y'see, I just kinda go along with him... and you... and others because we have bigger dragons to slay. Y'know what I mean? Do you?"

"Yeah I do, Harry,"

"All of us get wound tight here on the line and all of us just need to loosen up and laugh once in a while – no matter at whose expense. Sure, you were offended by Danko's words, MacLennon, but that didn't give you the right to fly off the handle! Like I said... you're no fuckin' angel either, Mac. Ray's got you pegged now for a racist. And Arlington. And others."

That opened my eyes wide. "Oh, shit. I didn't know that. I'm really not like that, Harry. I support the Civil Rights Movement and..."

"Shut up! I'm not done."

I clammed up. My body was trembling.

Hedge continued. "And in that fuckin' diary of yours, you keep talking about how you're getting out of the Navy. Getting out of the Navy. Over and over. Well, you know what? I say 'good riddance.' The U.S. Navy doesn't need or want children like you, MacLennon! Not unless you can grow up real fast, act like a man, and develop some esprit de corps. It's about all of us pitching in for one another. Esprit de corps... do you know what that is, Mac?"

"I've heard it but no. Not really." I had to admit I was ignorant.

"I didn't think so. Look it up. And study it. And do it. You'll get along much better in life if you apply it to any work situation. Just in case you hadn't noticed, we're in a fuckin' war, MacLennon. And, nobody needs to be spreading hate and discontent among the troops. That goes for you especially. You and Levitt... and sometimes Aden, too."

I was beginning to feel lower than scum. "Is there any way I can make up for it, Harry?"

"Just keep your pie hole shut, MacLennon! Keep that judgmental attitude of yours in check. And stop writing that whiny shit! Keep your opinions to yourself. And maybe, just maybe... eat some humble pie once in a while. Look around you, pal. There's the big battle and then there's all the little battles. Everyone is fighting a personal battle of one sort or another. Everyone! So, it would just behoove you to walk in the other man's shoes once in a while. Think you can do that?"

I moved to get up. "Yes I can... and yes I will. I'll try real hard, Harry."

He snapped at me: "Don't try, MacLennon! Just fuckin' do it!"

I got to my feet, left the shop, walked down to the head, washed and dried my face and returned to duty hoping to God that Danko didn't have a change of heart and write me up. I tried to will myself invisible for the rest of the day but that was impossible.

Some sort of strikes were flown today; not sure what was bombed. Don't really care. Charlie Rudd took the last photo hop of the day. Returning at 1600, it was immediately evident that Charlie was bent out of shape. With a pout on his face, he said nothing to any of the Flight Deck crew. When Chief O'Brian approached Rudd for systems debriefing, Charlie ducked under the wing and stomped off to the superstructure. Later in P.I., Ray Hines heard Mister Rudd chewing out the Chief: "This goddamned SAM was fired at me and I didn't even know it until my escort told me! The fuckin' ALQ gear didn't work! I could be dead right now!"

The Chief apologized profusely and reassured Rudd it wouldn't happen again. Charlie popped back, "It sure as hell better not! I want to go home just as much as you guys... and not in a freakin' body bag."

So the ass chewing chain-of-command was implemented. O'Brian chewed out the First Class Mechanic who in turn chewed the butts of the grunt mechanics. The poor airman at the bottom of the chain, all he could do was go kick the bulkhead. As for Mister Rudd... I thank God I didn't lose two Officer friends in two days' time.

CHAPTER XXXVI
THE LAST WEEK OF WAR

7 January 1968 ... 205th day.
Yankee Station, Gulf of Tonkin, North Vietnam.

Reading the Stars and Stripes this morning, I see the temperatures back in the states are plummeting. It's below zero in the northern states. Nebraska has received snow in some areas. Here in Vietnam it's sunny and around 70-degrees every day. I'd rather be home in the snow.

We had three photo hops today. Everything worked fine. No near-death incidents to report. No loss of pilots or aircraft from the Big Zero. Michael is still heavy on my mind. I'm not quite sure how to take it. Life is just going on as if he never existed. That's the way it would be if I walked into a spinning propeller. The Flight Deck crew would pick up the pieces and send the mush home to my folks... and life would just go on as if I never existed. Yes, my family would grieve for a few months but outside of them, no one really gives a flying fuck.

This evening the fine, young Officers approached me with art projects. Lieutenant Merkin Muffley and Mister Beamer want me to begin the final Cruise Report cover, completing it by the 13th of January. I sketched a few rough layouts but wasn't up for it yet. Then Harry Sampson actually asked me, he didn't order me, if I would design a special patch for the pilots of the squadron who have completed one-hundred combat missions. He was exceptionally nice about it so I agreed to sit with him and come up with a design. It is round, about 3-inches in diameter showing an RF-8G aircraft in flight with our motto, Eyes of the Fleet, at the top and "100 Combat Missions" on the bottom. Together we chose a color scheme and brought it to finish around 0300 in the morning. We must have polished off 3 or 4 pots of coffee just to remain alert. He was very pleased with the final product. So was I. And because he was in a grateful mood, I thought I'd take the opportunity to ask him if he could cumshaw a leather flight jacket for me. Surprisingly, he said he'd do his best. That would be cool.

8 January 1968 ... 206th day. Ibid.

Reveille P.O. Morgan was nudging me at 0630 this morning. "Get up Mac!"

"Look, Morgan, I was up until 3 A.M. working on a project for Lieutenant Sam! I ain't gettin' up."

"But Chief O'Brian..."

I cut him off. "If Chief O'Brian doesn't like me sleeping in, tell the old fart to stick it up his ass."

"Can I quote you on that?"

"Damned right." I rolled my back to him and pulled the covers over my head. I slept in until 1100 and received no flak for doing so.

It's a Stand Down Day for the Air Wing. After all the damned Alpha Strikes lately, everyone deserves a day of rest. I doubt if the gods were actually feeling compassionate. Closer to the truth is the fact that the skies have clouded over again and rain feels imminent. This afternoon at 1600 I began the final pen-and-ink art for the Cruise Report cover. The project lasted into the evening hours. I was working on it in P.I. so I had plenty of coffee, smokes, good music, and Paul for conversation. I ended up working through the night...

9 January 1968 ... 207th day. Ibid.

...until 1000 this morning – twenty-three hours non-stop except for piss breaks.

There were no flights again today because of the cloud cover. I slept from 1100 to 1600, awoke and returned to the Cruise Cover working again through the night...

10 January 1968 ... 208th day. Ibid.

...until 0730. After devoting about 30 hours to the project, it was finished: a drawn-to-scale map of North Vietnam on the top third, a scale drawing of Aircraft 601 in the middle, Yosemite Sam on the bottom left, a vertical strip along the left margin reading Cruise Report. My hand lettering is not as perfect as printer's type but it will have to do.

Comments were all positive. "Hey, MacLennon, that's really good!"

"Good job, Mac!"

"Excellent!"

The praise made it all worthwhile. Maybe that's what I'll do as a civilian: be a commercial artist. Who knows?

I think we had a couple of sorties today but I slept through them. The weather must have cleared. I didn't notice. We're so close to the end now that most of the Air Wing pilots, including the atheists, are praying for more rain and cloud cover, all except Mr. Beam. He needs only one more carrier landing to complete combat mission number one-hundred.

He has two more days.

11 January 1968 ... 209th day. Ibid.

If the weather broke, we were scheduled for a few hops today but it didn't. This was the Oriskany's last day for potential strikes against North Vietnam, no more death this cruise. Sorry, Mister Beam, you won't get that patch this time around.

The bombs are being retired. Ordnancemen worked throughout the day hauling the weaponry out of the ship's storage magazines and breaking them down, removing stabilizing fins and the fuse housing. When we reach Subic Bay in three days, an ammo working party will unload all of the ship's ordnance at the Naval Magazine which is heavily guarded by Jarheads. It will be stored until needed by another war ship.

The Cruise Report cover came back from the printing shop today. They did a good job on it. I spent most of the day duplicating other people's music on to my own reel tapes. This evening in P.I., Charlie Rudd, Big Ern and I had a discussion about Marxist-Leninism and the Bolshevik Revolution. Before heading to the bunk, I watched an episode of *Gunsmoke* on the closed circuit television.

Yes, I know that shipboard life in Vietnam lacks the drama of those poor Doggies and Marines slogging through the marshes in South Vietnam dodging bullets, mortar rounds and land mines. Yes, it's pretty damned cushy compared to that soldier who tonight is bivouacked in the jungle unsure if he'll make it through another day alive. My heart goes out to the poor bastards. We have our share of hazards out here working the Flight Deck, as the Forrestal disaster proved, but it's nothing close to the terror of hand-to-hand combat. When this is all over, I'll probably be proud to say that I'm a Vietnam Veteran but I won't even dare compare myself to the grunts in the heat of battle witnessing death and carnage on a daily basis. I wonder how many of those men will be able to adapt to civilian life. How do you take a trained killer and make him passive again? A lot of boys who are now in uniform are going to return to the world and not fit in. Their wives, friends and relatives will expect them to just pick up where they left off before they joined the military but that won't be possible. War changes people. It destroys any vestige of innocence that may have remained from childhood. And the folks at home won't understand; they just won't get it. No one will understand except fellow veterans.

Maybe I'm just hypersensitive but I believe what I've experienced out here on one Vietnam Cruise will probably stick with me for the rest of my life. No, I didn't have a buddy shot dead right next to me but I saw a lot of fine men, some of America's best, climb into cockpits and catapult off this carrier never to return. My friends, LT Michael Goldberg and LTJG Zissu died. Enlisted Men died onboard because of senseless accidents. Pilots and Airdales like me were incinerated on the U.S.S. Forrestal. And, how can I ever forget the wounded men I tended in Sickbay that horrible day? I already feel a sort of guilt about making it home when so many had their lives cut short fighting a war, and not even a just war, in my opinion. What the fuck do the politicians and military leaders hope to accomplish in Vietnam? It just seems like one big, tragic mistake. And, that pisses me off royally.

12 January 1968 ... 210th day. Gulf of Tonkin, North Vietnam.

It's my last day in the war zone but there will be thousands of other Swabbies and Airdales to carry on when I'm gone. Harry woke up with channel fever this morning. He's so eager to get home he ordered us to start packing all the Photo Shop equipment. We still have nineteen days to go before we see the Golden Gate Bridge. I don't know why he's in such a goddamned hurry but he's the boss. So all of us Photo Mates, Hines, Dick Aden, Big Ern, Harry and I, turned-to and stowed test panels, cable, camera mounts, brackets, cameras and components placing them in their large, metal, transporting cases.

* * * * * * *

About 1500 today, I heard the Cod Flight land topside. I took a break from my work to go up and watch her. She didn't shut down her props but just sat there amidships as her cargo, including mail from the Fleet Post Office, was unloaded. Then I noticed the two black body bags over by the superstructure ready for onloading. A First Class was crouched next to them. It must have been Michael's body and one of his crew. I wanted to pay my respects before he was flown out to Clark Air Base in the Philippines, and then back to the States. So I walked over.

The noise of the prop engines made it hard to communicate. I hunkered down next to the First Class and hollered: "Is one of these Lieutenant Goldberg?"

He looked at me with an ice-cold stare and yelled back: "Move along, sailor!"

He didn't know that Michael was a friend of mine. He obviously thought I was just a morbid curiosity seeker.

I tried to explain, "But we were..."

He reached out, grabbed the neck of my shirt, and yelled in my face, "I said move along, sailor, or you're going on report! You understand?"

I was pissed but what could I do? I followed orders, stood up and walked back across the Flight Deck and down to the shop. Goddamned Navy!

* * * * * * *

The Oriskany left the line tonight as unassumingly as when she first arrived. Our little aviation photo group is taking a collective sigh of relief enjoying the satisfaction of a job well done. We made it! In the shop this evening, I was thinking aloud: "I suppose when I look back on this experience many years from now, I'll speak proudly of it. I'll say things the old vets say, like: I wish I could do it again for old time's sake.

"Yup," Ern agreed with me and then pontificated: "The old men talk about the glory of it. The politicians talk about the need for it. The sailors and soldiers? They just want to go home."

Dick Aden chimed in, "Yeah! And, by God, we're going home!"

Sitting out on the canoe tonight, watching the indigo waters of the South China Sea, I noticed the waxing moon calculating that maybe by the time it is full we'll be back in the U.S. of A. I shed a few tears for Michael again. I was hoping his ghost would materialize just to let me know there actually is a spiritual realm but no such luck. It was just me, alone. It's so bizarre. He was here and now... he's gone. That's the way it is. We are... and then, we are no more. Two or three loved ones keep our memory alive... and then, they are no more. And we all fade into that massive vapor cloud of forgotten souls. Why were we even here in the first place?

I began to stand up. That's when I saw it. It entered the night sky from the west and streaked to the east, forming a brilliant but thin arc of flame. A shooting star. A meteorite. Was that my confirmation? I would like to think so.

CHAPTER XXXVII
FAREWELL TO PEPÉ

14 January 1968 ... 212th day. In Port Subic Bay; Naval Air Station Cubi Point, Republic of the Philippines.

No muster this morning. The ship moored at Leyte Pier at 0800. Liberty call came at 0900 and I was off the ship at 0901 along with Bart Gordon and Walt Lehmann. We wore our dungarees but carried civilian clothes in one parachute bag. Atop Cubi hill, at good old Barracks 22 we changed clothes. Pepé was there waiting for me. He usually doesn't work on Sunday mornings but he knew our ship was coming in. I had planned on doing some Navy Exchange shopping but Mr. Gonzales had different plans for me.

"Hi Mac!" He gave me a big hug. Bart and Walt looked at each other with raised eyebrows.

Then turning me away from the other two, he whispered, "I want to invite you to my house. Leenda has made a big meal for you but I don't have enough for dem, too."

"That's cool," I reassured him. "They want to go to the nightclubs anyway."

"Okay!" His smile beamed from ear to ear. "Let's go then."

Taking the base taxi to the front gate, we caught a jeepney on the Olongapo side and ordered the driver to Pepé's house in the Bajac Bajac neighborhood. Linda, her big brown eyes sparkling, welcomed me with graciousness, "Hello, Mock, welcome to our house again. We are very happy to have you as our guest."

What a sweet lady she is! Her English was much improved. The Gonzales kids tugged at my pant legs with excitement, "Hey, Mock, Mock! You have candy?"

Pepé, raising his voice in anger, scolded the children in Tagalog and they immediately scurried off into the back yard not to reappear until an hour or so later. Taking seats in his veranda under the shade of two palm trees, Pepé, Linda and I feasted on grilled pork chops, fried rice and an assortment of vegetables grown in their own garden. Most poor class Filipinos have one meat course a week, sometimes two. I felt privileged to be a part of their meat course dinner. Of course the meal would not have been complete without a couple of San Miguel beers. Linda abstained. She doesn't drink.

About an hour later, Pepé looked at his watch, winked at Linda, and proclaimed: "Now, Mac, we are going downtown to see a movie! My treat."

"Really?" I was curious. "Is it a special movie?"

"It's Beach Red!"

My mouth dropped. "You mean... our Beach Red?"

"Yes, our Beach Red!"

The flick had special significance for Pepé and me. Directed by Cornell Wilde, it was a World War II story that was filmed entirely on the Luzon coast one-hundred miles north of Subic Bay back in 1966 when I was stationed here at FIC PAC FAC. Several of our Photo Mate and P.I. friends had signed on as extras in the film. As tempting as it was, I didn't do it because I wanted to use my leave time for when I was home with my family. The film was great fun for Pepé and me. Linda endured it... and us. We laughed like hyenas as Rod Mier was shot in the head. Steve Szczecina always seemed to be in the front line of the troops no matter which division. Joe Rooney had one spoken line: "Yes sir, I'm okay." And, Richard Eisler's dead body was used as a shield against Japanese machine gun fire. My old buddy, Bob Andrise, was somewhere in that celluloid mob of troops but Pepé and I couldn't find him. It was supposed to be a serious war drama and I'm sure we disturbed the hell out of the audience around us. They didn't understand our morbid sense of humor. It's rather surrealistic to come directly from an actual war and find myself amused by a make-believe war. So often, it seems, life is a mind fuck but I just try to accept the ambivalence of it all.

Mr. and Mrs. Gonzales wanted to get home after the movie and relieve grandma of her babysitting duties. I shook Pepé's hand. "Thanks for taking me to *Beach Red*. I probably would have never seen it back in the States. I'll see you tomorrow, Pepé. And, thank you, Linda, for a wonderful dinner! It was delicious!"

She smiled sheepishly. "You welcome, Mock."

They flagged down a jeepney. I headed back to the ship.

15 January 1968 ... 213th day. Ibid.

One month from today, as Dylan sings, "I shall be released." Yes, Harry, I'm excited about it. What am I going to do when I get out? I've made no plans. I have no savings. I'll probably be penniless by the time I get home to Nebraska and will have to live with my folks until I get on my feet financially but I'm sure they'll be glad to accommodate me for a few months.

It was duty day so I had to stay on the Big Zero. There was nothing to do so I duplicated some more music from other people's tapes. I lay on my tatami mat on the shop's deck, blowing smoke rings and listening through stereo headphones. I just bought the headphones yesterday at the Exchange. It's a new thing for me. You can close your eyes and imagine you're right there in the middle of the recording session. Even weirder was falling asleep with headphones. I was listening to Jim Morrison and The Doors and would doze off. I dreamt music but it wasn't the music playing in my ears. *Light My Fire* would be coming through the headphones but my mind was listening to Tchaikovsky's *1812 Overture*. Psychedelic, man!

Someone told me the other day – I think it was Lehmann – that Jim Morrison's father is a Navy Admiral. Can you believe that? What a difference in lifestyles. I'll bet Admiral Morrison sits at his desk every night, wringing his hands and asking himself: "Where did I go wrong?"

16 January 1968 ... 214th day. Ibid.

Late this afternoon with Nikon camera and tripod in tote, I met up with Pepé and went over to his house again. Linda prepared a traditional Filipino supper for us – all personal favorites. The family and I feasted on pancit and fried rice. She does it so much better than those downtown restaurants. She cooks love into the food.

After the dishes were cleared, I set up for shooting portraits in the veranda. I snapped Pepé and Linda; then the two of them with their kids, then some of the neighbors and finally self-timer shots of just Pepé and me. For the rest of the evening, my Filipino brother and I enjoyed San Magoo and talked of the future. If he can't enlist in the United States Navy, Pepé's alternative plan is to receive a law degree at Columbian College in Olongapo and eventually enter politics, a dangerous game in the Philippines, but he's got the balls to do it and do it well. He's endured the humiliation for too many years of being a houseboy for the U.S. Navy. It's a servant's job but he earns more money than most Filipinos. Whatever he chooses to do with the rest of his life I want to be there to encourage and assist him even if it's long distance.

17 January 1968 ... 215th day. Ibid.

It may be the last day I ever set foot on the soil of my beloved Las Filipinas. If I ever walk this land again, it will be as a civilian and probably many, many years from now. Until then I must live my life in the nation of rampant materialism and status seekers. This morning I took a solo hike on the Cubi Point Jungle Trail. A base taxi dropped me at the trail head around 1000. With water canteen over one shoulder and camera draped over the other, I entered into the wilderness area that covers the hills on the southeastern side of Subic Bay. The dangers that had previously given me pause: the pythons, bamboo snakes, wild boars and giant apes no longer bothered me. After all what could they do? Kill me? I've survived the air war and many didn't. If God wants to take me now, I won't object. If he wants me to live, I'll do my best to make up for those who weren't as fortunate.

What a magnificent and mysterious world! As the minutes passed, the overgrowth became thicker and the sunlight more subdued. I passed through bamboo forests and walked through groves of one-hundred foot banyan trees. The ground cover was a natural garden of vines and ferns, brightly colored wild flowers and, in the occasional open areas, thick stands of wild grasses towering over my head. The animals were all around but they hid their faces from me. I could hear the monitor lizards – they can grow up to four feet in length – scurrying through the undergrowth; the chattering of alarmed monkeys in the tree tops; the cackle of wild chickens and the melodic songs of the birds of paradise. All that was missing was a rushing stream among craggy rocks with a nude Filipina beauty bathing her body in the crystal clear water. Yes, my fantasy... again. After two hours of hiking, I stopped and sat on a fallen Banyan trunk crossing my legs, meditating, and listening to the God that speaks to me through His creation. Even though it was afternoon, I sang "Morning Has Broken" and the hidden birds answered with their own chorus. "Praise with elation, praise ev'ry morning, God's re-creation of the new day."

I didn't want to go back to the trail head but I knew sunset would be approaching in a couple of hours. So I did; back to mankind's profane little world. And... I was scheduled to participate in it.

Pepé and I, along with Bart and Walt, planned to make our last night in the Philippines a drunken bar hop. Hypocritical? Most definitely, but that's the way I've been constructed. I speak to life with antinomy; the very same way it speaks to me.

We began with dinner and four beers each at the Admiral Midtown restaurant. Well-primed, our foursome took a jeepney down Magsaysay Avenue to the Sphinx Club, a sleazy little joint with not much to offer in the way of bar girls. After one beer each, Pepé suggested we try the Top 3 Club down in the Filipino section of the strip. "Good looking girls. Cheap ladies' drinks. Cheap San Miguel," he said.

It wasn't much to look at from the outside; just another little night club in a row of night clubs. The 'C' was burned out on the neon sign so that it read: Top 3 lub.

"Thanks, Pepé, old buddy for bringing us to the lub," I said. "After all, we're all land lubbers at heart." He didn't get it. He's accustomed to hearing a lot of stuff from his American friends that he doesn't understand. He just grinned and said: "Put your billfold in front pockets. Some girls here pickpockets."

We already had our wallets in our front pockets, a necessary precaution for the wise in Olongapo, all except Bart.

"Bart," Walt noticed. "You dumb shit! Haven't you learned anything after seven months in Southeast Asia?"

"I've learned that that hole in your face is just the right size for my cock." Bart was drunk already. "Would ya like me to whip it out right here?"

Walt, laughing, came back: "That must be your asshole speaking. Your mouth knows better."

"If it was my asshole, my breath wouldn't smell so sweet." Bart paused, then added, "Hey Walt, if I wash my dick with soap and water will you suck it?"

Walt, in his alcoholic stupor knew he was being set up but he took the bait and said, "No."

"So, then, that makes you a dirty cocksucker!"

Pepé broke out laughing. He was beginning to feel his beer, too.

Walt got in Bart's face: "Fuck you! You overgrown piece of Texas shit!"

"Okay, c'mon baby. You wanna fuck me? Try it."

It was starting to get out of control.

"Hey, you two lovers!" I jumped between them. "Let's just go in and have some fun."

"Yeah, Bart, let's have some fun!" echoed Walt.

"Yeah, Walt!" retorted Bart, adding under his breath, "dirty cocksucker."

"What?" Walt shouted.

I jumped in as forcefully as possible, "Never mind, assholes!"

Leave it up to Pepé to put things in perspective. He raised his voice: "Hey, you guys. You all my friends and this is our last night before you go home to America. No fighting, please."

"Yeah," I agreed.

"And," Pepé continued with his intoxicated grin, "if you want fucking, you find plenty of buto inside."

Mr. Gonzales was the wisest of us all. Of course, he's about ten years older than any of us. He was right about making our last night a happy one. And he was right about plenty of pussy inside the Top 3 Lub. As usual, we stepped inside the entryway and a flock of hostesses rushed over to greet us, about seven of them. Most of them were cute. They all wore tight dresses with hemlines just below their twats, spiked heels, gaudy makeup and again that long, beautiful, black hair that I love.

They spoke the same old lingo: "Hey, Joe! You come seet with me, yes?"

"Hey sailor boy, you buy me ladies' drink. We have good time."

One spoke directly to me, "Hey guapo, you think me pretty? We seet together, yes?"

I'm sure going to miss this in civilian life. The four of us guys were like kids in a candy factory. After a couple minutes of deliberation, we chose our sweets and sat them down with us at a large table for eight. Pepé chose a girl named Gloria who just happened to be his old girlfriend before he met Linda and married. I don't know if it was a coincidence or if he had premeditated the rendezvous. Walt had a sweet, little thing in an orange and yellow striped dress. Bart, being consistent with his lack of taste, chose a chubby bitch who looked like she was about six months pregnant. I don't know if she was. Maybe it was fat. She said her name was Connie. I'm sure that's not her real name. It was obvious that

Connie was either very drunk or blitzed on Red Devils, or both. Not fifteen minutes had passed before she stood up on her chair and performed a striptease dance for us going all the way. Her tits were large for a Filipina albeit somewhat droopy, the thick black hair on her pussy crept down her inner thighs and her little pot belly had stretch marks on both sides. She was already a mother. Connie in the nude was not a very arousing display of female anatomy but we applauded her pitiful efforts just the same. What the hell.

The girl I had chosen wasn't actually a girl anymore. I'd estimate she was in her mid to late thirties. I like the older ones, more experienced. She said her name was Brenda. She had a sultry, sexy look about her, similar to Lauren Bacall. Her black, full-length dress hugged her body emphasizing every subtle curve. What I hadn't noticed, until she sat down on my lap, was her breath. When she closed in on me face to face and began talking I realized the odor was semen.

"What your name, sailor?" she asked, her eyes half open.

"Mac."

"Mock?"

The beer had made me short tempered, "No! Goddamnit! Not Mock. Mac."

She tried but couldn't change the pronunciation, "M-m-m-mock?"

Frustrated, I gave her an alternative. "Okay, my name back home with my family is Gerry. Can you say Gerry?

"Ah, yes," she smiled. "Tjerry."

That was close enough, "Yeah, sure, Tjerry."

"Hey, Tjerry, me think you cherry boy? Huh?"

Trying to back away from her breath, I stated matter-of-factly: "No, Brenda, I'm not a virgin." Of course, I knew what was coming next.

"Cherry lover boy, you want Brenda give you blow job?"

That was enough. I pushed her up off my lap making her stumble to her feet. "No, I don't want a blow job. Bye, bye, Brenda. Go find another chump."

She turned around, flipped me the bird and then wandered off.

The guys asked me what had happened. I told them. They laughed. Bart mimicked her in falsetto voice, "Whatsa matter, Cherry Boy, you no want dickie suckie? You queer boy maybe?"

I shot back at him, "Sure, Bart, you can suck my dick!"

Pepé didn't intervene this time. He was having an agitated conversation with Gloria. They were speaking Tagalog to each another. I picked up a few words here and there: Navy, Oriskany, America, José. She was addressing him by his real name. I thought they were talking about Walt, Bart and me but then they captured our undivided attention, and that of the people around us, when the conversation became loud and angry. Gloria suddenly burst out in tears. A few more words were exchanged and then she stood up, grabbed Pepé by his hair with both of her hands and shook his head furiously.

She screamed at him, "Go to hell!" And ran away.

Pepé was dazed.

"Damn, José!" I exclaimed from across the table. "What the fuck did you say to her?"

His hair tousled, he flashed a smile and then began giggling. I had never seen Pepé this drunk before. He was funny.

"She said she want me to be her boyfriend again," he explained, "but I said I cannot be her boyfriend because now I am Steward in the U.S. Navy on the Oriskany."

"Boy, what a line of shit!" Bart interrupted.

I tell her "I'm leaving tomorrow for America and will never see her again."

"That's why she was angry?" Walt asked.

"No, that why she was crying."

"So," I queried, "What pissed her off?"

"I tell her I have a very rich wife in San Diego and don't need a fucking whore for a girlfriend."

"Yup, that would do it!" We all agreed.

Bart raised his glass, "Here's to Pepé Gonzales! King of the bullshitters!"

"Here's to Pepé!" we chimed in clinking our bottles together, sloshing beer on to the table top.

Walt seemed to have the only sane girl. She was a cute, little thing probably around 18, soft-spoken and shy. We lost her, too, thanks to Pepé. I don't know how many beers he had downed but he was in rare form. When Walt's girl asked him to buy her a ladies' drink, Pepé butted in and asked her, "How much?"

She hesitated, then said, "Eight Pesos!"

"Eight Pesos?" Pepé hollered. Then he began cussing her out in Tagalog for trying to bilk his shipmate. This one burst out in tears, too, and ran off.

"Thanks, Pepé," said Walt, sarcastically. "Now all we have is crazy Connie."

"Hey!" Connie yelled back at him. "I not crazy. I show you good time. How bout we go short time, boys?"

Bart liked the proposal. "You'll take on all of us?"

"You betcha!" she came back. "All four can fuck Connie all night for 100 pesos!"

That was the wrong thing to say. Pepé started arguing with her too, telling her she wasn't worth over 25 pesos even for a gang bang. So, we lost crazy Connie. And then there was just the four of us: Bart, Walt, Mac and our new shipmate, Pepé.

It didn't matter. We were having the time of our lives. The whores had already found new suckers at other tables. We drank and told jokes for about another hour. When Pepé fell off his chair, we knew it was time to go. Poor José, as soon as we walked out of the club, he puked in the gutter. We had to guide him on to the Jeepney that took us back to the Shit River Bridge. And then... it was time to say goodbye, maybe forever.

Offloading, Walt and Bart staggered on toward the Main Gate. I stayed behind with my beloved friend. "I hope we can be together again someday, Pepé."

The realization that this may be the final farewell penetrated through Pepé's inebriated brain. He began to weep. "You write to me from the States. Okay, Mac?"

"Yes, I promise. I'll keep in touch."

He crawled out of the Jeepney, threw his arms around my neck, embracing me and crying like a baby. Sailors and Jarheads were walking by smirking and pointing but I didn't care. Pepé was too blitzed to notice but as he hugged me, I stuffed an envelope into his back pocket containing enough money to get that certification that he is a native-born citizen of the Philippines. With the proper paperwork, he still has a running chance of being chosen for induction into the U.S. Navy.

I was misty-eyed, too. "Live a good life, my friend. I hope all your dreams come true."

"Thank you, Mac, for being like a brother to me," he replied.

I was too choked up to say any more. I helped Pepé back on the Jeepney, handed the driver enough money to transport him home and watched while the Jeepney pulled out, turned and headed down a side street. I waved until he had disappeared into the grey dust. Drunk and dreadfully sad, I made my way back to my floating pig iron city.

18 January 1968 ... 216th day. Ibid.

While the other duty sections enjoyed their last brief taste of liberty, I remained onboard ship working. Our duty section was slated to muster at 1500 in Hangar Bay three. Dick, Ernest and I were in the shop concentrating on our respective activities. We lost track of the time. When six bells sounded on the 1MC, we knew we were in trouble. Bursting through the hatch, we ran through the passageway and scampered down the ladders but it was too late.

Old man O'Brian leered at us as we quickly fell into formation: "Nice you could join us, boys!"

Harry Hedge was standing next to the Chief. They're bosom buddies now. O'Brian looked down at his roster board for a minute, exchanged a few words with Hedge, and then addressed us by name: "MacLennon, Aden, Levitt! You three will be working on corrosion control from now until we tie up at Alameda."

"But, Chief..." Ern started to protest.

"And you, Levitt, better keep your mouth shut! You're on my shit list already. Maybe you'd like to go down to the mess deck and wash pots and pans for the rest of the cruise, huh?"

Big Ern straightened up. "No, sir... Chief."

"And don't call me sir. You know goddamned well I work for a living!"

"Yes, Chief."

Harry just stood there with a smile on his face. He was enjoying the whole scene.

Later in the day, after the three of us sanded and primed our planes for about four hours, we were all back in the shop. Harry was reading a book on Navy regulations. He'll probably put in thirty years instead of twenty. Ernest was visibly pissed. I don't see him that way very often. I knew he was going to tussle with Hedge and it wasn't long before they were in a heated argument back in the shop.

"What's happened to you, Harry?" Ernest asked. "You used to stand up for us. You used to be one of us. And now you're just a whore!"

"What do you mean by that?" Hedge shot back.

"Just what I said! You're getting paid to screw us. And you're getting paid, just like a whore, to fuck Ho Chi Minh and the North Vietnamese!"

"That's bordering on treason, pal!" Harry yelled. "And, you know what?"

"If I'm a whore, then so are you, Levitt... and MacLennon, and Aden, and everyone on this ship, and every swinging dick that's fighting this war!"

"Yeah, I know, we all are!" Ern admitted. "And if I had it to do all over again, I never would have joined the stupid Navy. But, you know, Hedge, the difference between me and you is: I'm getting the hell out as soon as I can; but you, PH1 Harry Hedge, you love being a goddamned whore so much that you want to make a career out of it!"

"Do you remember what the Chief said at muster, Levitt?"

"Yeah, I remember!"

"Well, that goes for me, too. I'll send you to the scullery in a heartbeat and if you don't shut your pie hole right now, you're headed to a Captain's Mast."

The threat of disciplinary action didn't faze Big Ern in the least. He bowed his head for a brief moment, then threw up his hands in a gesture of frustration: "Damnit, Harry, you've just become All-Navy. Shipped-over, started going to the First Class Lounge, and now, your All-Navy! Can't you see what you're doing with your life?

"Yes, I can! Quite clearly! Your brain is too screwed up by your college hippie pals for you to understand all the benefits of a military career. And there are many! A hell of a lot more than civilian life! You're just too fuckin' brainwashed by Pinkos to see the truth!"

Harry was so incensed his entire head had flushed a bright red. "And here's something for you to remember..." he looked around at the three of us. "All of you! You may try to fuck the Navy but when you fuck the Navy, you're fucking with me because I am the fuckin' Navy!"

Good Lord, I thought to myself, now there's a classic quote that will have to go into my book. I've given some thought to Big Ern's analogy even though I think he was over the top. Are we just prostitutes for the military-industrial complex of the United States? Is LBJ our pimp? We would like to think that we're doing something noble, something patriotic by engaging in warfare with the communists in Vietnam. Thousands of men have died and will continue to die for the ideal of freedom and democracy but is it worth the price? I don't know. Young Americans are sacrificing their lives in a war that we could end up losing. Michael Goldberg sacrificed his life.

At 1700, the 1MC crackled to life: "Ship is underway! Shift colors!" The tugs were pulling us out of Subic Bay back to deep water, open sea and home. Paalam, Las Filipinas.

CHAPTER XXXVIII
HOMEBOUND

19 January 1968 ... 217th day. U.S.S. Oriskany Underway.

 I was lying in my rack this morning thinking about Harry yesterday and the word: fuck. It's used to excess in the Navy. Someone once told me that it comes from the Puritan days in early America. A person convicted of the sexual sins of fornication or adultery was placed in public stocks with the letters F-U-C-K written on a plaque above their heads. It meant: For Unscriptural Carnal Knowledge. If that's the case, the word has been around for over three-hundred years but it has always been considered the most crude of obscenities. People don't use it much in civilian life, only when provoked to the max. It is socially taboo amongst common, decent people. As teenage boys, my neighborhood gang and I would use the word occasionally when we were cruising and carousing just to validate how bad we thought we were but we never said "fuck" in front of girls, adults or at social events. It's a guy word that you only use when you're with other guys. Self-respecting girls and women don't say it. Those who do, especially in the presence of males, are automatically pegged as sluts. It's their way of letting you know that they are sexually available. So yeah, I'll be glad to return to civility and civilized language.

    * * * * * * *

 We're at sea now, not sure where. I think we're still off the coast of northern Luzon although I can't see land. We three bad boy Photo Mates are working corrosion control every day. Citations for Meritorious Conduct are being doled out now to motivate men to re-enlist for another four years. Paul Duncan of Photo Intelligence received one. Ray Hines received one.

 Lieutenant Rudd approached me in Photo Intelligence today and told me in a roundabout way that I stand a good chance of making 2nd Class within six months if I re-enlist instead of separating. I just looked him in the eyes, smiled and said, "Thank you for the offer, sir, but I really don't think the military and I are destined to be long-term lovers."

 He laughed.

20 January 1968 ... 218th day. Western Pacific Ocean.

There are riots in Japan. In his first address to the crew over the 1MC since we left Subic, Captain Billy informed us today that the Navy's first nuclear-powered Aircraft Carrier, the U.S.S. Enterprise was met at the Sasebo pier by a mob of irate Japanese college students, the number of demonstrators estimated to be around 50,000. Due to the hostile circumstances, the crew has remained onboard. No liberty. Meanwhile, 82 Japanese have been hospitalized because of injuries sustained as police fought to control the angry crowd. I don't know what their problem is. Maybe they think that a nuclear reactor on a ship can explode just like the bombs did over Hiroshima and Nagasaki. If that's the case they're just ignorant. Controlled nuclear fission is the wave of the future. Yes, it can be used to destroy but it can also help to preserve the earth's natural resources as a most viable energy alternative. Who goads these impressionable students?

We encountered heavy seas today. Forecasts predict fifteen foot swells for the next 48 hours. And it's raining non-stop.

21 January 1968 ... 219th day. Western Pacific Ocean.

The incident with Harry, Danko and I seems to have been swept under the rug. Harry hasn't mentioned it anymore. Neither has Danko. I'm glad.

A letter arrived today from my family back in Nebraska. They're eagerly awaiting my arrival home. I'm nervous about it. I don't think they have any idea how much I've changed in the past seven months.

There was another letter today. The return address was the U.S. Naval Institute, Annapolis, Maryland. I opened it and found a check along with the following letter:

> *Dear Mr. MacLennon:*
>
> *Congratulations! Your photograph of two destroyers underway in open sea has been selected as one of the Ten Best Naval and Maritime Photographs of 1968, and it is with pleasure that I enclose the Naval Institute's check for $100. The prize-winning picture, selected from nearly 1,200 entries, will appear with the other nine winners in the March 1968 Proceedings magazine.*
>
> *Sincerely, Roger C. Taylor, Editorial Director*

What an incredible surprise! Of course, I couldn't keep such good news to myself. Within two hours after I received the letter and check, everybody in the Det who counts knew about it. Even Harry was proud of me. Aware that the Ship's Company Photo Mates don't consider us Airdales real photographers, he wanted to be the first person to inform the arrogant snobs – several who had also entered photos in the contest – that a Flight Deck photo recon tech had just whipped their butts in the Navy-wide competition. Ah, sweet revenge!

24 January 1968 ... 222nd day.
Western Pacific nearing the International Date Line.

The Carrier Air Group has been on alert ever since we entered open sea for another Russian Bear flyover but so far, no Bears. Danko began wearing his Chief uniform today. At 28, he's arrived. Now he can just stand there and shout out orders while toting an ever-present cup of coffee in his hand. After a chat with Hedge, we were ordered to chip paint and sand down the rust on the passageway deck in front of the Photo Shop, one hell of an undertaking for two men and one uncoordinated gorilla but we kept at it for seven hours, our iron scrappers and pick hammers creating the most god-awful noise. Wham! Wham! Wham! It reverberated throughout the compartments and passageways in our sector.

Airdales kept sticking their heads out of their shops along the passageway yelling, "When are you going to quit that fuckin' pounding?"

Dick would shout back: "As soon as we're fuckin' done!"

By 1530, my hands were so blistered, I had to stop. I had an Aircraft Integrity Watch at 1600 anyway; four hours of sitting in Hangar Bay One on the tail of an F-8 Crusader making sure no one tries to steal it. I made the time worthwhile by reading my new paperback, A Nation of *Sheep*, written by William Lederer, co-author of *The Ugly American*.

25 January 1968 ... 223rd day.
Somewhere in the western Pacific Ocean.

Aden and Levitt worked on that damned passageway all morning. At 1300, I took a power sander to it and ground the remaining paint down to bare metal. It was pretty. Then the rain came. The mighty Pacific was churning. Enormous swells were causing our old tub to pitch and roll almost as bad as when we were on the edge of the typhoon. Strong, rain-laden winds whipped across the bow. And once again water began to seep down into the 02 level. Plastic sheets were once again suspended from the overhead in P.I. The passageway next to ours filled with about three inches of dirty water that had seeped down through the Flight Deck timbers. Sailors and Officers were stomping through the water then tracking the mess on to our bare metal deck. We were cussing them but nobody seemed to give a shit.

"Set Red Bear Condition Two!" the squawk box immediately diverted our attention. The Russians were coming. Two minutes passed as we returned to the shop and listened for the next alert. "Set Red Bear Condition One! Flight Quarters! Flight Quarters! All personnel concerned, man your flight quarter stations!"

That was us. We scrambled because we knew that Lieutenant Sampson and Lieutenant Commander Sonniksen wanted to get airborne and photograph the Russians. No screw ups. No missing out this time.

"General Quarters! General Quarters! All hands man your battle stations!"

Pulling on my head gear while double-timing up to the blustery Flight Deck, I was thinking to myself, These two pilots must be crazy for wanting to make carrier take-offs and landings on a day like today. But I guess it's all protocol. The fighter jets and the photo recon aircraft are required to meet the Russians in the air every time they come near us just to let them know that we know they're there and that they'd better be on their best behavior. As the Mighty-O was turning into the wind for launch, the 1MC brought all the hustle to a halt by announcing: "Secure from General Quarters! Secure from Flight Quarters! IFF has responded as friendly!"

The air boss ordered a reversal of operations as we peons on the Flight Deck carried out our duties in the driving rain. Aircraft 601 had to be rolled back from the cats, shut down, chocked and chained. IFF is an "Identification Friend or Foe" radio signal. Because an approaching airborne had not responded to the IFF, it had to be hostile but apparently it finally did mark itself as friendly. So much for the Russian threat.

Ironically, we learned today of another Communist threat, North Korea. Today's front page story in the Musket read: "The Pentagon has announced that a United States patrol boat was surrounded by North Korean patrol boats and captured in international waters in the Sea of Japan late yesterday."

It went on to say: The U.S.S. Pueblo, a Navy intelligence auxiliary ship, was boarded by an armed party some 25 miles from the mainland of North Korea. There were 83 men, including 6 Officers, 75 Enlisted Men, and 2 civilians aboard."

This evening, the men of the Oriskany and its Air Group are edgy. What this could mean for us is a change of orders. Instead of returning home, we could be steaming toward the Sea of Japan to engage in yet another police action.

"Immediate steps have been taken in Washington to gain release of the Pueblo. The North Koreans have charged the United States with 'imperialist aggression' by invading what they say are their territorial waters."

25 January 1968 ... 224rd day. Pacific Ocean.

It's January 25th again. Two days for the price of one. We crossed the International Date Line sometime during the night.

When I awoke this morning, ATAN Thompson was walking through the berthing compartment telling anyone who would listen, "We're on our way back to the line! The Enterprise was sent to North Korea and at 0330 this morning we turned around to go back to Vietnam."

"You're shittin me, right?" I asked, still half asleep.

"Ain't no shit, sunshine! I heard it from good sources."

I flopped back into the rack and yelled: "Ohhhhhhhh, fuck! No! No! No!"

Duncan was no more encouraging when I walked into P.I. an hour later. The first words out of his mouth were: "We're in a world of shit, Mac."

"Whaddya mean?"

"Just that! Who knows what's going to happen in Korea? Maybe another war."

I hated to ask but I did. "Thompson said we've turned back to the line. Is that true?"

"No we haven't. Not yet."

That was a relief. Still, according to Stars & Stripes, there remain many unanswered questions about the incident. Why did the Pueblo wait until the North Koreans were boarding before requesting help? Why didn't the Pueblo crew resist the takeover? She was armed with three 50-caliber machine guns. Assuming Pueblo didn't seek aid, why didn't higher authorities perceive a serious situation and scramble some of the supersonic F4 Phantom fighter jets from Osan or Kunsan, South Korea when the ship reported being accosted by the four North Korean patrol boats? Why didn't the skipper of the boat request instructions after four North Korean sea vessels overwhelmed him? Why didn't the Pentagon or the Pacific Command in Hawaii offer the Pueblo any advice?

I guess I'm looking on the whole mess with a self-serving attitude, praying: Oh, sweet Lord, please just let me go home. I want to be on the outside looking in. It may sound unpatriotic even cowardly but I'm ready for some unwinding. There was a hell of a lot of modern electronic surveillance equipment on the Pueblo. The crew may have succeeded in scuttling some of it but I'm sure much of it is now in Commie hands. The North Koreans have indicated that they will eventually return the crew but they're keeping the boat. Great! The Associated Press disclosed today that the Enterprise will reach waters off the North Korean port city of Wonsan by late Wednesday to add pressure for release of the Pueblo and its crew. All I can say is: they'd better not fuck with the Enterprise if they know what's good for them.

Our leaky, old rust-bucket of a ship just isn't ready to turn around and go back. The materiel condition is lousy. Most of the aircraft are in check. The majority of the pilots have already flown off to Naval Air Station Atsugi, Japan although I've come to learn that they've been placed on hold and cannot return to the States yet. Meanwhile back in the USA, 13,000 military reservists have been placed on alert for possible call up.

26 January 1968 ... 225th day. Pacific Ocean.

Duncan told me today that the ship has not altered course. We're somewhere south of Hawaii and still heading east. That's good news. Preparation for homecoming continues. The crew received ship-wide zone inspections at 1300. Dick and I finally received permission to seal off our section of passageway to all foot traffic so we could finish sanding and painting it. Most everything belonging to us Airdale Photo Mates, job-related and personal, is packed up in boxes, chests, metal crates and stacked to the overhead in our shop. It's totally congested.

Dick and I loaded flares and ejectors into Aircraft 602 and pulled the cameras out of 603. Big Ern skated out on us for three hours avoiding work but as soon as he reappeared, Arlington nabbed him and ordered him up to the Flight Deck to help the plane captain's scrub down our planes. He bitched and whined all the way up.

Rain threatened this evening as the wind increased. Angry ocean swells clapped together in eruptions of white froth. King Neptune is having an orgasm. It's yet another roller-coaster ride on the Big Zero.

27 January 1968 ... 226th day.
Pacific Ocean - position 28-41N, 157-34W.

We're 1,865 miles from the Golden Gate Bridge. The heavy weather remains. Our two destroyer escorts are having one hell of a time keeping up so the skipper has slowed our speed. At 0930, all the men of Photo Recon Squadron 63 Detachment 34 were ordered to Ready Room 3 in dress uniforms for an Attaboy Speech by Lieutenant Commander Sonniksen who was promoted to Commander only last night and is already sporting his new silver oak leaf with scrambled eggs on the bill of his cap. He looked sharp. Once again, as before, he assumed his John Wayne position and spoke: "You men have done a damned good job on this cruise! Our Det lost no planes and, more important... we lost no pilots. We thank God for that but we also thank all of you who worked your tails off to make sure our aircraft were in top flight condition on every hop."

Ron was tugging at my heart strings. Not a bad speech, I was thinking to myself, he even invoked the name of God.

He continued, "As I've said all along, this isn't my Det; it's yours. You guys deserve all the credit. Thanks for giving us, the pilots, outstanding aircraft availability. We're headed home..."

He was interrupted by a spontaneous cheer from all the men. He smiled. "And for heaven's sake, don't kill yourself on those California highways!"

The group laughed.

"Good luck to all of you and... God bless you."

The only time I'd heard Sonniksen speak the name of God prior to this meeting was when he was beseeching the Deity to condemn something or someone to the flames of hell. A Photo Mate from Ship's Company was supposed to take our official Det group photo following the meeting but the weather topside was too inclement and the dumb shit said there wasn't enough light on the Hangar Bay to get a good exposure. Of course, all of us Airdale Photo Mates were thinking, You fucking idiot, haven't you ever heard of photo floods and tripods?

Oh well. We went back to our berthing compartment, changed back to working dungarees and continued to do whatever needed to be done. Thank goodness, corrosion control is all finished. Chief O'Brian promised us we'd be doing it all the way back to Alameda. He must have decided that Dick, Ern and I have been punished enough.

January 28, 1968 ... 227th day. Eastern Pacific Ocean.

After battling insomnia for half the night, I finally fell asleep at about 0400 this morning. When I settle into the rack now, I have thousands of thoughts racing through my head concerning things to do at Miramar prior to discharge and what I'll be doing when I return home as a civilian. I'm both excited and scared. At 21, I'll be a war veteran and still have my whole life before me. Even with my fertile imagination, I have no inkling of what destiny has in store.

The Navy Reservists on the ship are pissed. They learned today that the Navy has placed a freeze on all applications for release from active duty because of the ongoing Pueblo affair. Too bad boys, why don't you just become regular Navy? According to the Morning Musket: "In addition to the freeze, some six-hundred Naval Air Reservists have been called to active duty from civilian life along with 1,400 from the Air Force and Air National Guard units across the country."

They'd better not involuntarily extend us regular Navy short-timers, especially those with only 18 days until the freedom gates open.

29 January 1968... 228th day. Ibid.

Today I asked Harry for an hour of his time, alone, so I could offer another apology for the day I slugged Danko and... to make sure there weren't any residual hard feelings about the whole thing. His response was terse: "There's nothing to talk about, Mac... at least, not right now. We'll be working together back at Miramar. Danko too. We still have time to smooth out any differences... if there are any."

"Sure thing, Harry," I agreed.

He continued: "So, let's just enjoy the fact that we will be home. A little down time will disarm all the guns; all the bullshit we've gone through."

"Amen."

30 January 1968 ... 229th day.
Eastern Pacific Ocean - Home Tomorrow.

Damn, the States must be cold. I was huddled under two wool blankets in my rack through the nocturnal hours and still I was shivering. This morning in the shop, Sea Daddy told us, "You'd better get some extra sleep before noon because we'll probably be awake all night. And, there will be no slacking on anything. No skating, MacLennon!"

So we crapped out on the deck and counter tops until The Big Fly-Off that was scheduled to commence at 1400. The mood was festive; all of our pilots were in great spirits. They were flying home to Miramar Naval Air Station and would all be dicky dunkin' with mama under the covers tonight. Commander of the Air Group and Photo Recon Squadron 63, the Eyes of the Fleet, were granted the first launches by the powers in the tower. One by one, all four Photo Birds taxied up to the cats. CAG Commander Burt Shepard was at the controls of 600 on the left catapult. Commander Sonniksen piloted 601 on the right catapult. The steam billowed up. The two Commanders saluted their respective plane captains and one another. Shepard was first off, followed 15 seconds later by Ron. It was quite impressive, I must admit. It looked like the closing scene of a Hollywood war movie. Someday when I'm an old man I suppose I'll remember scenes like this and think to myself how glorious it was but that's why I'm writing this diary... because I want to remember all the bullshit, too.

The Fly-Off continued with all the other squadrons following suit. By 1700, the Flight Deck and Hangar Bay were barren except for the choppers and a couple of severely crippled birds that will have to be offloaded by crane at Alameda Pier. With the Officers gone, it was time for the Enlisted Airdales to begin moving out of their shops. Everything, and I mean everything, had to be taken to the Hangar Bay. The Avionics shop dumbwaiter carried down most of our Photo Shop and personal shit from the 02 level but first we had to lug them over several knee-knockers in the 02 passageways. By 2200, our shop for seven months was stripped naked. Heading up to the berthing compartment, I turned-to packing my sea bag and other personal items until 0100 then dragging it all down the ladders to our squadron's sector of the Hangar Bay. By 0200, the entire bay was full of Air Wing gear piled high and ready for offloading later the same day.

31 January 1968 ... 230th day. The Last Day.
San Francisco Bay and Alameda.

The night of the 30th extended into the 31st, the final day of our Vietnam cruise. At 0200, I began helping Richard clean up the Photo Shop. Harry the Immaculate wanted it to be in primo condition when we turned it back over to the Ship's Company Photo Lab later in the day. So there we were, in the middle of the night, on our hands and knees with scrub brushes, steel wool, sponges, scouring powder and buckets of water making the old shop look spic and span. We secured from the task at 0400. I should have gone to bed but instead went up topside and out to the canoe, the sacred spot where Michael and I had sat together contemplating the whys of life. I was saying farewell in my own way. I wanted to experience the Oriskany for the last time on the high seas. It was still dark – the dark that comes just before dawn. Hanging low, about to plunge into the western horizon was a blood red full moon. The night air was crisp; the eastern sky a lighter shade of black with pinpoints of stars shimmering through the earth's canopy. Above me was the endless universe; below me, the deep mystical sea. Large undulating swells gently rocked the ship like a babe in its mother's arms. Mother Earth. Father Sky. Sister Moon.

I meditated upon this new life that I am now obliged to live. I thought about youth. I thought about old age. Apparently bad memories fade away with time and only the moments of goodness and joy remain. Those who are nearing the end of their lives revel in the bliss of yesterday but we the young have this day and tomorrow to contend with. Today, we see the world naked, exposed before our eyes. We see hatred, misery and pain. We find it difficult to live for today. Only the desires for tomorrow's better world can alleviate the suffering that is today. Only tomorrow can offer us hope that glimmering moments will again materialize. So we continue to exist for a dream, a wish that tomorrow we can say: "This is a day worth living."

Dawn and 0700 rolled around. Muster was called on the Hangar Bay. Chief O'Brian had departed in a COD flight overnight, along with Lieutenant Muffley, Harry, Calloway and Hines... so Chief Danko was senior man of the squadron for a day. And boy! Did he ever love playing the part! Everyone is so darned excited about getting home... he does his damnedest to spoil the euphoria.

"Listen up, you men!" He was standing with his hands on his hips. "I've heard some scuttlebutt and I hope to God that it's only scuttlebutt that some of you are going to hide today during the offloading. Well, I'm here to say: God help the man I find fucking off because I'll personally see to it that he is court-martialed! You understand?"

A few said, "Uh-huh." The rest of us just looked on with disdain.

"I want every man to be here on this spot one hour after the voice on the 1MC says, 'Ship is moored. Shift colors.'"

Danko looked each one of us in the eyes before dismissing us. Yes, I think old Danko is going to be another 30-year-lifer. He loves being a bad ass Chief. We had about four-and-a-half hours to wait. The ship was supposed to tie up around 1045. I laid down on one of the stripped racks still wearing my dungaree shirt, wool jersey and working jacket because of the cold, damp penetrating air and fell into a deep sleep instantly.

"Ship is moored! Shift colors!"

I was jolted awake by the squawk box and was immediately aware that I had missed the Golden Gate Bridge, the suspended signs, cheers, entering San Francisco Bay, the adoration of two-thousand people waiting for us on the pier. All of it.

It was 1030. Foggy-eyed, I stumbled out to the gun tub and beheld the cities of Oakland, Alameda and San Francisco – the hills, the Bay Bridge, the beautiful California sun. I scampered down to the Hangar Bay and found it jam-packed with mothers, fathers, sisters, brothers, sons, daughters, sweethearts, friends and other relatives of those lucky enough to have people living in the Bay area. Some had driven or flown up from San Diego. It took a while to grasp the fact that I was back in the United States of America, my country, my home.

The unloading process didn't take long – about a half hour. Onboard ship, a few remaining squadrons were still busting ass. Most of the civilians had departed with their sailors. The Old Risky was beginning to look like a ghost ship. I walked up to the Photo Shop for the last time to retrieve my Nikon and case but the damned hatch was locked. Ship's Company Photo Mates had already taken over. So I had to go down, beg them for the key, walk back up, get my camera, and return the key. It's a very strange feeling. I was a living, breathing entity on this big, pig-iron city for seven months and within a matter of hours I'm treated like I don't belong here anymore. The permanent crew just spits out the Air Wing like a plug of tobacco. Fuck 'em! They can have their Mighty-O right up until the day she's cut apart into scrap metal.

In the berthing compartment at 1500, only seven guys from the Det remained; the rest had already taken off for the air terminal. I showered, shined my shoes and packed my douche bag and dungarees into my AWOL bag. I donned my dress blue uniform with my new hero medals: the Vietnam Campaign Medals – one from our government, one from the government of South Vietnam. Yes, I was there, and I have medals to prove it. Thompson, Miley, Dalton, Jackson, Walt Lehmann, Big Ern and I were the last to leave. The Gunner's Mates were scrounging through the berthing compartment preparing to take it over even before we were out the door. Goddamned vultures! With camera case and AWOL bag in tote, I led the way down the ladder and across the Hangar Bay to the after brow.

Laughlin was standing duty.

Smiling, I raised my hand in a salute: "Request permission to go ashore... forever!"

"So long!" he replied, returning the smile. "Good luck."

We walked down the ladder, up the pier to the waiting taxis that would shuttle us to the air terminal. I looked back at the ship:

the Aircraft Carrier that I had called home for seven-and-a-half months; the ominous weapon of war that had unleashed death and destruction on the North Vietnamese people; the ship that held three thousand five hundred sweating bodies, working, sleeping, laughing, bitching – the U.S.S. Oriskany, CVA-34.

I flipped her the bird, smiled and got into the taxi.

EPILOGUE

REMEMBERING OUR HONORED DEAD, MIA & PRISONERS OF WAR

KILLED IN ACTION (KIA)
CDR Herbert Perry Hunter
LCDR John Frederick Barr
LCDR Richard Clark Perry
LCDR David Vance Davis
LT David Lawton Hodges
LT Edwin Ward Van Orden
LTJG W. Armstrong
LTJG Fredric Woodrow Knapp
LTJG Norman Lee Roggow
LTJG Donald Findling Wolfe
LTJG Andrew Gilbert Zissu
Ensign Bruce Merle Patterson
CPO Robert Roland Pineau
PO 2c Charles David Hardie
PO 2c Dale Allen Lash
PO 3c R.M. Ywoynarski
JO SN Raul Antonio Guerra

MISSING IN ACTION (MIA) or PRISONER OF WAR (POW)
LCDR R.D. Hartman
LCDR John S. McCain III
LCDR H.A. Stafford
LT J.M. Krommenhoek
LTJG R.C. Bisz
LTJG D.J. Carey
LTJG J.E. Dooley
LTJG R.E. Foulks
LTJG R.W. Minnich
LTJG C.D. Rice
LTJG C.P. Zuhoski
LTJG D.P. Matheny

FRIENDS MIA PRESUMED DEAD

Lieutenant JG Andrew Gilbert Zissu, Lieutenant JG Donald Findling Wolfe and Journalist Seaman Raul Antonio Guerra were officially MIA at the end of the cruise. Their Early Warning Aircraft, known as a Willie Fudd, launched from the USS Oriskany on 8 October 1967 on a non-combative mission to South Vietnam. In the mountainous, heavily-forested region near Quang Nam their radio went dead. Search aircraft have spotted wreckage but it's in a very remote, hard to reach area. The name *Raul Antonio Guerra* would have been *Gerald MacLennon* if I had not changed my mind about accepting Lieutenant Zissu's invitation to fly along. I cannot in all good conscience say "Thank you, God, for sparing me." because to do so would be thanking the Deity for taking Guerra's life. And... I don't wish that on anybody. Sometimes you just accept fate for what it is... diabolically random.

ORISKANY'S CARRIER AIR GROUP RECORD

President Lyndon Baines Johnson commenced the Vietnam Air War – code name: OPERATION ROLLING THUNDER – in 1965. By the time he brought it to a halt in 1968, no other Aircraft Carrier on Yankee Station saw more action or tallied more losses than those on the U.S.S. Oriskany. Thirty-eight pilots were either dead, missing in action or confirmed prisoners of war. A total of sixty aircraft were lost.

Lieutenant Commander John McCain's squadron, VA-163, had the highest casualty rate. During our 1967 cruise alone, one-third of the squadron's pilots were captured or killed. Miraculously, during that cruise, my squadron, Photo Recon Squadron 63, was the only one to be spared death, injury or loss of an aircraft.

It is estimated that during OPERATION ROLLING THUNDER (1965-1968) U.S. bombs killed over 100,000 North Vietnamese men, women and children. Pilots took great care to hit only the targeted areas but, as in all wars, collateral damage is unavoidable.

RELEASE OF PRISONERS

Through ongoing negotiations, all American Prisoners of War in Hanoi were eventually set free. Following six years and seven months of cruel captivity, Lieutenant Commander John McCain of VA-163 was released by the North Vietnamese government on

March 15, 1973. An extended period of hospitalization and rehabilitation ensued. Nonetheless, McCain continued his Naval career retiring as a Captain in 1981. As a Republican candidate from Arizona, he successfully ran for and won his first U.S. congressional seat in 1982. An influential and respected voice on Capitol Hill, John McCain was an early contender for the United States Presidential race in the year 2000. He withdrew following his defeats in the primaries but remained highly active in the United States Senate. In 2008, Mr. McCain became the Republican Party's top candidate for the Presidency running against Democrat Party candidate, Barack Hussein Obama. It was a hard-fought battle for the aging McCain.

After all the votes were counted, he came up short and conceded the Commander-in-Chief honor to the victor, a man with no military experience whatsoever.

The crew of the U.S.S. Pueblo was released by the North Koreans on December 23, 1968. Their ship was not returned. The release was negotiated. No hostile action was required by the U.S. Armed Forces.

THE TET OFFENSIVE

At 0300 on the morning of January 31st, 1968 – 3 pm, January 30th in California – the North Vietnamese Army and Vietcong guerillas launched a wave of simultaneous attacks on South Vietnamese and American forces in major cities, towns and military bases throughout the South. It came as a complete surprise. In years prior, both sides – North and South – had always called a cease-fire on Tet, the Chinese Lunar New Year. There was no indication that '68 would be any different. But it was.

What an irony! The U.S.S. Oriskany steamed into San Francisco Bay on the very day the Tet Offensive began in South Vietnam… the very day we came home from our WestPac cruise in 'Nam. Had we been on Yankee Station – who knows? Our cruise might have been extended until Admirals and Generals determined if we were needed for combat air support in South Vietnam. Fortunately, the Oriskany was already at her home port.

LIEUTENANT RUDD KILLED IN MANEUVERS - 1971

In 2009 I learned of the death of Mister Rudd on 3 December 1971, thanks to the Internet. After all these decades, learning his fate still hit me like a kick in the guts. He was such a nice guy. God, why him? Why him, God? Apparently he and other pilots were doing touch-and-goes – practice landings and take offs – on the U.S.S. Hancock (CVA-19). The ship had steamed a few miles out of San Diego into the Pacific for the training missions... and something went wrong. Charlie's plane hit the rear of the ship. He either died instantly or later in a hospital. His name did not go on The Wall, the Vietnam War Memorial in D.C. On the Internet I learned that someone who loved Lieutenant Rudd had written the following below his posted obituary, "Although he probably doesn't count in the official books as a Vietnam War hero, he counts in mine." Yes, Amen, mine too... mine, too.

UNCLE BILL KILLED IN SOUTH VIETNAM – 1971

My uncle, William Leon Logan attained the Enlisted ranking of Utilityman Chief (UTC) around 1970. Well-liked by the men he led, he served more than one tour of duty in South Vietnam. His last was at the U.S. Naval Construction Battalion Maintenance Unit 302 in Bien Hoa.

On August 10, 1971 while on detail near Binh Thuy, the jeep that Bill was riding triggered a concealed land mine in the road. The force of the explosion overturned the vehicle and killed its passengers. Bill was dead at age 34. In memory of their fallen Chief, the Seabees of his battalion renamed their unit, Camp William L. Logan. Bill's parents, sisters and brothers, including my old man, attended his funeral in California. His Japanese-American wife still lives in California.

THE RAPE & BEATING OF CONNIE FRANCIS - 1974

Tragically, the life of Connie Francis changed forever on the night of November 8, 1974, when she was in her Howard Johnson's Lodge room after performing at the Westbury Music Fair on Long Island, New York. A man broke into her room. He beat and raped her for hours while threatening her with a knife. He disappeared and was never caught. Connie was ashamed, terrified and unable to perform on stage in further concerts.

"I had never been afraid of anything," she said a decade later in a TV interview, "but after that happened I was constantly afraid and had nightmares for so many years – you wouldn't believe how many. It just wouldn't go away." She became reclusive. Her marriage deteriorated and ended in divorce.

The year after the rape, she discovered that Howard Johnson's hadn't even fixed the lock on the door after she'd been assaulted in their room, so she sued them for negligence and won $2.5 million – at the time the largest personal-injury settlement in judicial history. She also brought charges against hotel security.

In the 1980s, she began to speak publicly on the subject of violence and rape. She also made several public-service announcements for airing on radio and television.

Such a horrible violation of one's body and mind should not happen to anyone, especially not to a woman who was sweet enough to brave "spiders and snakes," carrier landings and take-offs just to bring a couple hours of happy diversion to thousands of homesick soldiers and sailors in the war zones of Vietnam.

Someday, maybe I'll meet her in person and let her know just how much it meant to all of us lonely sailors to see her beautiful face and listen to her soulful voice as she sang one of my favorite love ballads, "My Happiness."

THE DEATH OF BIG ERN – 1978

Big Ern committed suicide at his family's backwoods cottage near Shawano, Wisconsin where he had gone to stay for the summer. A history teacher at an inner-city high school in K4ansas City, Missouri, Ernest had dedicated himself to bringing a better level of education to disenfranchised youth who too often slip through the cracks of American society. According to his father, Calvin Levitt, the stress had taken a heavy toll on Ernest. He had psychological symptoms similar to battle fatigue. Big Ern killed himself leaving no message.

He had visited my family and me several times when I was working at a radio station in Waupun, Wisconsin and then again after I returned to Lincoln in 1973. He loved Woodstock, our 120-pound Saint Bernard dog. I lost contact with him around 1976. The last time we spoke, he telephoned me from Oshkosh, Wisconsin with the good news that he was engaged to be married to a woman

I will call Jane Doe. He was so very happy because up to that point he had never had much luck with the ladies. That was the last time we spoke. When I telephoned his father ten years later to learn his whereabouts, I was told the sad news of his suicide.

Goodbye, old friend. I'm sorry I wasn't there to help you when you needed me. I was too wrapped up in my own life to hear your distress call. Hasta que otre vez en El Cielo, Amigo.

JOSE "PEPÉ" GONZALES, MY FILIPINO BROTHER

Pepé and I corresponded after I entered civilian life. As first it was about once a month but as time passed, we wrote less often until around mid-1969. I wrote a short note to him and he no longer responded. I think we just ran out of things to say. His life had not changed. He was still a houseboy for FIC PAC FAC. Yet, it has always been my hope that Pepé eventually did qualify for enlistment in the U.S. Navy and that he made a career of it. I'd like to envision him and Linda today somewhere in southern California, retired, drawing his retired Master Chief's pension, and very content with life.

DISSIPATION & ABANDONMENT

My drunken, enraged father attempted to strangle my mother to death in 1971. If not for the intervention of my little brother, Dad would have succeeded. The next day, the Old Man packed his camper pick-up truck and fled to somewhere in Iowa. He never returned. Mom did not press charges against him. He died in 1984, at the age of 55, from heart, lung and liver disease caused by excessive smoking and drinking and in my opinion, severe depression. You were an asshole but I loved you, Dad. And, even though I deeply respect my Step-Dad, no man has really been able to step in and fill the fatherly void that you left in my life.

VIETNAM

The Vietnam War officially ended April 30, 1975. We lost.

Distinguished Flying Cross (DFC) for Heroism at Thanh Hoa Bridge, October 1967

by CDR Harry B. Sampson, USN-ret

After our return to the States, in early 1968 I was awarded the Distinguished Flying Cross for action at Thanh Hoa bridge. LCDR Bob Pearl, my escort, was also awarded the DFC. The award was presented for heroism above and beyond the call of duty, for completing our mission under extreme Triple A and Surface to Air missile threats. As a result of my photographs, the Admiral and CAG had confirmation Thanh Hoa bridge was severely damaged and as result, no further strike groups had to return for the remainder of the cruise.

Recounting the day in my own words:

On 14 October 1967, flying an F8 Photographic Aircraft off the USS Oriskany. I was assigned as the Pre-Strike and Post-Strike pilot to take BDA (battle damage assessment) photographs of strike group actions against the Than Hoa Bridge in North Vietnam.

Thanh Hoa bridge lies on the major supply route on the Western Border of North Vietnam. During the heaviest combat in North Vietnam, supplies were being shipped into NV from Thailand and Cambodia; and then shipped North to Hanoi, and North and East to Haiphong. This supply route was the main route; as well; South, to other combat areas in both NV and South Vietnam.

The Strike Group was led by the Carrier Air Wing Commander. Strike Groups at the time included 20-25 strike aircraft with 3 aircraft flights of A4's, A7's, A6's, A3's and F8's to act as fighter support.

One F8 Photographic Aircraft was assigned with an F8 Fighter escort. I was assigned as the Photo Pilot on this particular flight with LCDR Pearl as my escort. LCDR Pearl was the Operations Officer in Fighter Squadron VF-111 and I was one of the four Photo Pilots in the Photo Detachment aboard the USS Oriskany (CVA-34).

The Strike Group was briefed on all possible threats of Triple A guns and possible Surface-to-Air (SAM) missiles. Triple A guns were 14.7 Millimeter (MM), 37MM, 57MM, and the very large 85MM, with numerous smaller arms. The specific triple A guns were effective at all altitudes from the surface to 30,000 feet. The SAM's were effective from 3000 feet to 40,000 feet.

One of the basic tactics that the Vietnamese learned to do was to radar track as well as, visually track the aircraft with Triple A and radar track with SAM's. Then, when it got busy, they would pick an altitude that they guessed the aircraft would use, they barrage fired all their guns to explode at the guessed altitude and fill the sky with FLAK hoping the aircraft would fly into the FLAK. It was a very successful strategy and would cause quite a bit of distraction in each of the specific 3 aircraft flights within the Strike Group. Then, as they got Lock-on's with their SAM's, they would launch several of them simultaneously. Very, very hectic and very successful during the entire campaign.

I briefed LCDR Pearl on our mission which was to fly into North Vietnam, South of Nam Dihn, go North and West towards the Than Hoa Bridge. We were to launch first, rendezvous and proceed the Strike Group to the target and take pre-strike photo's, pull off the target and away from the target about 10-15 miles. Wait until the Strike Group completed their bombing mission and then go back over the target for pictures of strike damage.

As I crossed the beach into North Vietnam I was getting a considerable amount of electronic noise from the big Triple A and tracking SAM sites. The large Triple A guns were capable of radar tracking as well as barrage fire dependent on how experienced the gunners were. We were descending from 20,000 feet while increasing our speed to 600 knots. I was navigating by looking and following the terrain (dead reckoning) as what was necessary for all our targets and flying over the country without any NAVAIDS, watching for Triple A or SAMs and keeping track of my escort.

We were "jinking" (moving the aircraft in high g turns through different altitudes and directions to decrease the radar and visual tracking capability of the guns and SAMs) as we proceeded towards the target. We were well ahead of the Strike Group which was part of the plan for the first part of my flight as I didn't want to get the enemy gun and SAM sites up and tracking if it could be helped; 20-25 aircraft, flying relatively in the same airspace would awaken every gun and SAM site controller as the Group started over the beach.

We made it just South of Nam Dihn (about 50 miles inland and about 100 miles from the target) when the sky filled with black and red explosions at our altitude and dead ahead. The North Vietnamese obviously saw us coming, probably picked up the Strike Group approaching the beach behind us. From that point during the flight the FLAK looked like pictures of flights that I had seen of missions over Germany during World War II. The Triple A shells were exploding at our altitude which was now about 8000-9000 feet. The Vietnamese had guessed our exact altitude and now in front of me the sky was absolutely black and red with large explosions. I knew that I would probably take hits because I could not see how I would avoid hitting something. Traveling at 600 knots and being hit by anything might shorten our trip as we were heading for our target.

I'm still not sure how we managed to get through our "welcome" but we happily did. Along with the FLAK was the constant electronic signals and noise which I was picking up on my countermeasures equipment. The Vietnamese were sending launch signals to their sites which indicated that they were definitely tracking us as we approached the target. Different frequencies on our system might tell us if and when they might launch and where the missile might come from if they launched. Launch of the SAMs could be in track mode with a "Lock-On" or launched without "Lock-On". Therefore, all the signals or noise that we were hearing were important to monitor while I was trying to visually find the target, watch for FLAK and SAMs , and keep track of my wingman.

I visually picked up the main highway leading into and from the Than Hoa bridge and knew that we were now close to the initial run-in spot when I received a rapid rise in frequency from my gear. I saw an indication of missile launch on my equipment which indicated that the missile was coming at me from approximately my 2:00 O'Clock position. Fortunately, I had seen several missiles fired in previous flights over the North and knew what it was as it was streaking towards me. It takes a short time to visually pick up the missile when it is head-on but caught sight and called it out to my wingman. It looks like a flaming telephone pole, moving fast towards our flight but I waited a few seconds when it looked like it was about 2000 feet away from me; pulled hard with my nose up and right to "roll around" the missile hoping that the missile would overshoot. I continued my roll and looked for my wingman as I watched the missile below me and at my 8:00 O'Clock position as it exploded. Now I was awake, I now knew that the Vietnamese were aware of our presence and the flight was going to get exciting.

Following the flight de-brief and talking to my wingman later, he indicated that he saw two (2) missiles and figured that one (1) was probably tracking and "Locked-On" and the other was just fired towards us. It didn't take too long to get back to the task at hand, trying to re-figure where we were and where should the target be after our slight detour. I picked up the road to the target and wanted to make a run "up the highway" for about 5 or 6 miles taking pictures as I crossed the target and about 5 additional miles.

As a Photo Pilot, I knew that it was going to be critical to be "Right On" altitude and airspeed to get good, clear pictures of the target now and on my next run. I had previously programmed the camera for me to be flying at 4500 feet and at 600 knots straight and level wings. I knew that I was not interested in making more runs than absolutely necessary. One Pre-Strike now and the important run after the Strike Group hit their targets.

It was well known that our Air Wing and Carrier had previously tried to "drop" the bridge and was not successful. Other Carrier Airwings had also tried. The Vietnamese knew what our goal had been for a long time and obviously knew the importance to them and they had invested several gun and SAM sites around the bridge.

Now I was approaching my run-in heading and rapidly descending to 4500 feet trying to be about 5 miles on-speed and at altitude. Flying "straight and level" over anyplace in North Vietnam was always a concern and especially over the Than Hoa bridge but "Here we were'. I put my head in the cockpit, started the cameras, checked airspeed and altitude, picked up the highway in my viewfinder and watched as the bridge passed below my aircraft. I turned the camera off, plugged the afterburner in and pulled the aircraft hard and to the left, climbing to 15,000 feet to stay in Vietnam and get out of the way of the strike group.

I pulled off the target and went 10-15 miles south to wait and watch for bombs being dropped. It was obvious as the Strike Group approached the target. The frequencies of signals, the chatter from the flights (although very disciplined) increased as the flight leaders and individual pilots were calling SAM launches and Triple A. The sky was filled with large red and black bursts of Triple A as numerous missiles were fired at the flights. As the individual flights of three (3) called "OFF Target" I was counting and watching the bombs explode and the numerous air bursts going off and waiting for my opportunity to get into the area and get home. With continuous electronic signals and calls from the aircraft which have been hit or nearly hit, it always sounds like mass confusion and impossible to hear as all the individual aircraft try to find their leaders or wingmen as they leave their targets.

Reality is that all this apparent confusion is very disciplined and important to rapidly assimilate among flights what is going on with your aircraft as well as your wingman or flights to get everyone back together. As I watched and listened on strike frequency, I was getting a little nervous having to wait and knowing that we would have these gunners really excited as well as probably a little angry as we would have to go back over the target. I was sure that the Vietnamese knew that after the Strike Group left, a single aircraft would be showing up to get pictures. I needed to wait for a short time to make sure that the target would be clear of smoke and debris or maybe something burning to get good pictures. It seemed like an eternity so I re-figured my fuel state and fuel that I needed to get back to the ship. The ship was about 150 miles from the coast and I was about 100 miles inland. I still needed to use afterburner to get back up to speed to do my mission and climb out from the target after the mission. I did pull my throttles back a little to conserve fuel and was doing about 400 knots in this area because it was a little calmer and less of a threat. Pulling the throttle back and slowing a little always made it a little more comfortable in the cockpit. At low altitude and high speed (over 600 knots) it gets extremely warm and uncomfortable. Especially in North Vietnam with high humidity and high temperature. I checked to find my wingman and saw him high and right about 4000 feet and at the 3:00 O'Clock position. Perfect.

After about 15 minutes and it appeared that the bombs had exploded and the Strike Group was far enough away, I told LCDR Pearl "Let's GO!". I selected afterburner, turned back north and descended towards 4500 feet. My parameters were the same as before, 4500 feet and 600 knots, straight and level wings. Run the same direction for about 5 miles to the target, hit the target and continue for 5 more miles then hard right heading 120 degrees towards the beach as I was climbing to altitude.

We learned, after many aircraft had been lost during my first cruise, we should not stay at low altitude (below about 4000 feet) or climb above 20,000 feet on ingress and egress. Small caliber weapons were a threat at low altitude and SAMs were a definite threat above 20,000 feet Unfortunately, during the earlier cruise aboard the Oriskany, and several other carriers losses, Strike Groups were flying with individual 3 aircraft flights close formation during Ingress or egress. SAMs were being fired at these 3 aircraft flights and if one aircraft took a hit, we were losing all three and potentially all three pilots. The aircraft could not maneuver independently with the aircraft flying on the "Leader's" wing and their head out of the cockpit; not checking their ECM gear.

LCDR John McCain was shot down flying an A4 during one of these earlier missions in this configuration. He was flying off a sister carrier during the 1965-1966 cruise. Following these close formation strategies, the strategy was to fly in these same 3 aircraft formations but with 2000 feet of separation between other 3 aircraft flights within the Strike Group.

As I visually located the road, I started to see small flashes of light from the ground. I figured that the gunners were firing at me with their small Triple A guns (14.7 MM) and maybe even rifles hoping to hit us with a round. Rapidly descending and increasing by speed to 600 knots and leveling at 4500 feet I put my head in the cockpit and turned the camera on. With my head in the cockpit, I found the target in my viewfinder, took 5-7 miles of film, passed the target, turned the cameras off and turned hard right climbing for some altitude. Following a Photo run several thoughts were always on your mind and it didn't matter that by the time I made this run I had been over the beach over 200 times previously. "Don't lose your wingman" turn hard and climb watching for SAM's and Triple A. Head for the coast as fast as the F8 would go. Check for LCDR Pearl (my wingman) and make sure he had me in sight. I think that the gunners had fired every SAM and bullet that they had because the large caliber FLAK was pretty light in comparison to the ingress. I was still receiving several electronic signals of SAM tracking but saw no SAM launches. The beach always seemed like a long way off even though I was flying just under supersonic speed, thought about slowing a little but decided against that. In my head, I was figuring fuel requirements because I knew we had quite a few miles to go after we got "feet wet."

The coast at last. Climb to 30,000 feet, conserve fuel, join up with my wingman to check him for bullet holes and he for me, check for hydraulic or fuel leaks, check his fuel state. Everything was fine with the exception of being very low on fuel. Turn towards what I thought was a good guess for a heading to the ship and turn my NAVAIDS on. We changed to ships approach frequency and I asked for a Tanker status. On a typical Strike Group mission the ship usually launched and had 2 tankers airborne for the returning aircraft.

This particular Strike had several aircraft which had been hit and were struggling to get back. An A4 recovered with a 4 foot hole through his wing. He had been losing fuel since he left the target and had to get plugged into a tanker at the coast for his return to the ship. The A4 had its fuel stored in the wing. The ship advised us that we need to "conserve" because they had no more gas available and they couldn't launch anymore aircraft because they were still recovering the strike aircraft. We would be last to recover on the ship. My wingman had a little more gas than me but we were both in a critical condition unless we could get "aboard" on the first; maybe second attempt. 150 miles at sea; no fuel, and hope that some aircraft in a crippled condition wouldn't hit the ramp or wouldn't foul the flight deck, options for the airborne aircraft become very limited.

We were now about 50 miles from the ship and told that we would have a "ready" deck. The next call that I received was from the "Boss" – the Air Boss controlled the sequence of landing and take-off of all aircraft on-board and was like a "god" to young pilots on the carrier. He was always a seasoned airman, a Commander with several carrier landings himself. The Boss very calmly said, "We have only 1 wire."

"What?" I said, "Bob, did you hear that?" and he acknowledged our situation very quietly. The Oriskany had only 3 arresting wires because of the small 27C flight deck. Most carrier have 4 arresting wires with the 3rd wire the "target" wire.

Oriskany's target was the 2nd wire and the only wire left was the number one (1). The two wires had been fouled with all the damaged aircraft which had landed earlier. Having only the number 1 wire was not too much concern on most carriers, but it was on the Oriskany.

The "Hook to Ramp" clearance for the F8 on our small carrier was about 10 feet if aiming for the number 2 target wire. The F8 was a little over 55 feet long and at an angle with the hook deployed another 3 feet lower and the number 1 wire closer to the ramp we had about 5 feet to miss hitting the back of the ship. In addition, we are landing at 135-140 knots. Because of all these critical parameters, the F8 aircraft was well known as "The Ensign Killer". Normally, if conditions were at all normal, the LSO (Landing Signal Officer) and Air Boss would have a long discussion with the pilot, after landing, if a pilot was continuously catching the 1 wire. In the past several pilots have been killed trying to "get aboard" aircraft carriers and usually when conditions are not ideal.

Okay, that's what we had to go with. I found out much later, after the Strike and landing de-briefs, that we had quite an audience during our landings. It wasn't uncommon following a large strike flight into a very "hot" area of North Vietnam that previous flight crews and sailors would watch the closed circuit TV and actual deck recoveries for damaged aircraft.

Both LCDR Pearl and I landed on the first try, came aboard with a grade of Number 1—OK. OK never happens under normal conditions.

The pictures turned out great. The Admiral and Air Group Commander thought they were perfect pictures and showed that the Strike Group had "dropped" the bridge. We slowed transport of supplies to North Vietnam a little. Unfortunately, the Thanh Hoa Bridge had been knocked down before and re-built several times.

The period of 1969-1971 was a cease fire initiated by Washington. It allowed North Vietnam an opportunity to re-build and re-stock all their weapons storage several times over. I deployed in 1971 as a fighter pilot on the USS Midway and found that North Vietnam had more and better weapons from 1971 through the end of the war in late 1974. As a result, more aircraft were shot down and pilots lost or captured during 1971 through 1974 as compared to 1964-1969.

[I note with pride, fellow pilot and friend, LT David Beam, was also awarded the DFC for valor during our 1967 cruise.]

* * * * * * *

Remembering the USS Oriskany Fire, 26 October 1966 On Yankee Station, Tonkin Gulf, North Vietnam.

by CDR Harry B. Sampson, USN-ret

Forty-six men killed in an explosion and fire aboard the USS Oriskany, CVA-34. Air Wing 16 was aboard the Oriskany in waters off North Vietnam in Late June and early July 1966 supporting other carriers and Airforce assets out of Thailand in strikes against North Vietnam. Air Wing 16 Commander Burt Shepherd was in command of the Air Wing aviation assets of F8 Fighter Squadrons VF111 and VF162, VA163 and VA164 Attack Squadrons, and detachments of A3 heavy tankers, A6 ECM support, F8 VFP Photographic aircraft along with a detachment of Helos.

On the early morning of October 26, 1966 the Oriskany was finishing up a normal weapons on-load from a replenish-ment ship. For normal combat flights and during a normal 12 Hour cycle time of operations in Vietnam the Oriskany could keep about 2 days' supply of bombs and missiles on board without having to reload. The ship was just starting Air Wing briefs in spaces on the 2nd Deck above the Flight Deck for operations to begin a routine 0630 strike mission. On this particular day, I was assigned as the Photo Pilot for the strike and was up at about 0430 getting dressed, eating breakfast and sitting in the briefing room about 0530 for final intelligence briefs. At the end of the replenishment, the weapons Department would receive the Magnesium Flares which were for the aircraft during night operations by high line from the replenishment ship to Oriskany's Hangar Deck. The Flare locker was forward on the starboard side of the ship, just before going into the spaces designated as "Officer Country". There were airmen receiving the pallets of Flares, removing them from the pallet and passing them to a line of sailors as they stacked each flare; individually, into the small Flare locker. The flares were Magnesium flares 3 or 4 inches in diameter and 14-16 inches long with a safety pin on the top of the flare. Magnesium flares are highly flammable and will burn very hot and continuously until burned out of fuel even if in water. As the later investigation revealed, a young sailor accidently pulled the pin on a flare and threw the lit flare into the flare locker and "dogged" down the hatch. Obviously, a better option would have been to go to the open elevator door and throw the flare into the water; but, as usual he probably didn't sleep much during the cruise because it was very early (about 0500). As the flare burned down it set the other flares off inside the locker and created a very large explosion up and forward on the same level as the Officer spaces. The explosion was intense and strong enough to damage the starboard catapult, destroy all staterooms on that deck forward of the locker and One (1) deck above. The explosion was felt all the way to midships and 2 decks above the flight deck to where we were being briefed by the intelligence officers for our strike flight. Smoke was transferred throughout the ship through the ventilation system and into our briefing area. Being on 2 decks above the hangar deck we were one (1) deck below the flight deck. The Captain immediately announced on the 1MC system that we had a fire forward and that all personnel should go "AFT" and "OUT" to the flight deck as he turned the ship to let the smoke go across the flight deck in a 90 degree direction. I was in the briefing room which was midships and 1 deck below the flight deck down a long hallway about 100 feet and then up to the flight deck. The smoke was pouring into the room, although initially we thought we were very safe in this location. Things changed very rapidly and was IFR within a minute or 2. As I got out into the passageway, the smoke had made everything dark and was very strong and burning my eyes. As I walked and partially ran through the passage way I tripped over two people who had fallen down, choking from the smoke so I stopped to help them get up and the three of us finally got to the flight deck. Once on the flight deck we were out of the smoke because the Captain had turned the ship and the smoke was rapidly crossing the deck.

 The cruise would end, the trip home was depressing and sad. We lost a lot of very good men, performed a burial at sea as requested by some of our shipmates and tried to be comfortable without access to our rooms and slept for two weeks in the ready room in our flight suits. However lucky; maybe, that you think you are in control while getting shot at flying but realizing it could have been far worse in an environment that you always classified as

"Home." From then until back to the states there were not many shipmates getting any real sleep. Always responding to every fire alert or strange and different noise. My stateroom was a few short feet away from the explosion on the same deck and; as such, I would not have survived from the fire.

Thirty Three (33) Pilots were lost in the 1966 Fire and 6 MIA's Pilots were shot down during the 1966 cruise. As an aside; between the July 1967 cruise and the end of that cruise in January 1968, Oriskany Air Wing 16 lost 37 Aircraft and 26 Pilots. Comparing that with the normal manning level of 70 Pilots and 60 Combat Aircraft on an Oriskany-sized Carrier, the odds get rather grim. An Air Wing 16 pilot's probability of surviving both the 1966 and 1967 cruises was less than 50%. Although never a good war to all here at home during the time in the late 60's a lot of super professionals (both sailors and airmen) lost their lives doing what was asked of them to the best of their abilities.

NAVY LINGO GLOSSARY

1MC .... ship's crew electronic address system
Aft .... back section of a ship
Airdale .... the Enlisted Men of Naval Aviation
All hands .... all personnel
Amidships .... middle section of a ship
AWOL .... Absent Without Leave
BDA .... Bomb Damage Assessment
Blackshoes .... regular U.S. Navy personnel (non-aviation)
Boatswain .... (pronounced: BO-sen) a foreman of protocol, I think.
Boom-boom .... sexual intercourse in Southeast Asian slang
Bow .... front end of a ship
Brig .... a ship's jail
Bulkhead .... wall
Buto .... vagina (in Tagalog slang)
CAG .... Carrier Air Group – all squadrons temporarily assigned to an aircraft carrier
Cat track .... the slot in the catapult where the shuttle attaches to the belly of an aircraft
Catapult .... a steam-powered mechanical devise on the fore section of a carrier that attaches to the belly of an aircraft by chain and, when released, pulls the plane down a straight track and off the flight deck into the air at about 60 miles per hour – if all parts function as they are designed
Catwalk .... recessed metal walkway around the perimeter of a flight deck
Channel Fever .... being so close to home, one cannot relax
Chocks .... wooden blocks for securing aircraft wheels to prevent the plane from rolling
Chopper .... helicopter
CINCPAC .... Commander-in-Chief of U.S. Naval Operations for the Pacific
CO .... Commanding Officer – on a ship, the Captain
Cold cat shot .... not enough steam pressure in the catapult, sometimes pulling the aircraft to the bow of the ship and dumping it overboard into the ocean
Compartments .... rooms
Corpsman .... an Enlisted Man specializing in medical care
Cumshaw .... pilfered items, stealing from the Navy for personal use
Deck .... floor

Fantail	rear end of a ship
FICPAC	Fleet Intelligence Center, Pacific – located in Pearl Harbor, Hawaii
FIC PAC FAC	Fleet Intelligence Center, Pacific Facility – located in Subic Bay, Philippines
Forecastle	(FOKE-sal) the upper, forward section of a ship
Gripes	anything and everything malfunctioning on an aircraft – usually post-mission
Gung Ho	Chinese for "Can Do," devoted, loyal, tenacious, indomitable
Hatches	steel doorways, each capable of sealing water-tight
Head cal	going to the toilet
Head	a ship's toilet
Helo	helicopter
Hot pump	a forced, swift fill-up of an aircraft fuel tank
Honcho	head man, leader, boss – a Japanese word meaning "squad leader"
Hostess	Filipina bar girl – most of them also available as prostitutes
Island	on a carrier, the command superstructure that rises above the flight deck
J.D.	Juvenile Delinquent
Joe	any American military man (according to Filipinos)
KIA	Killed in Action
Ladder	a ship's staircase
Level	Decks, floors. The top deck is the 01 level with numbers increasing with each descending level.
Liberty	leisure and playtime off the ship
Mess hall	a ship's cafeteria (also referred to as just The Mess)
MIA	Missing in Action
Muster	roll call in formation
NVA	North Vietnamese Army
NX	Navy Exchange, the U.S. Navy chain of on-base retail stores
Overhead	ceiling
P.I.	Photographic Intelligenceman or Philippine Islands
Paalam	In Tagalog (language of Philippines), "Goodbye"
Poontang	sexual slang for vulva, vagina, pussy, cunt, et al.
Port	left side of a ship; also where a ship docks or drops anchor
Props	propeller-driven aircraft

Pud	simple, bland, easy
Pull bar	a steel bar that attaches to the front aircraft wheel structure for towing by a tractor vehicle (NC-3 Mule); can also be pulled by hand.
Rack	a ship's bed
Round Eye	Caucasian girl
NAVSUX	An Enlisted Man's way of saying "The Navy sucks!"
S&R	Search and Rescue
Sayonara	In Japanese, "Goodbye"
Scuttlebutt	misinformation, half-truths, white lies, gossip, bullshit
Scuttled	cancelled, trashed
Secure	finish, complete, quit, to make safe
Shore Patrol	Navy Police
Shuttle	the steel block and pull device in the cat track and on which a chain is attached to an aircraft belly
Sickbay	a ship's medical facility
Skate	(v.) to shirk one's duty; (n.) a man who does everything in his power to avoid work
Skipper	Captain of the ship
Spot	to park an aircraft
Starboard	right side of a ship
Stokes	Litter medical transport stretchers characterized by woven metallic-netting
Tagalog	(pronounced: tah-GAH-log) the official language of the Philippines, spoken on the main island of Luzon – a mixture of a Malaysian dialect and Spanish
Tail hook	the steel rod with metal hook under the rear belly of the aircraft that is lowered, prior to a carrier landing, to catch the wire (arresting cables)
Titi	penis (in Tagalog slang)
Turn-to	hurry, move quickly
VC	Viet Cong communist insurgents
Westpac	Western Pacific
XO	Executive Officer – on a ship, the second in command
Zoomies	U.S. Air Force pilots

CREDITS:

Eternal Father, Strong to Save. (The Navy Hymn) Original words written as a poem in 1860 by William Whiting of Winchester, England. The melody, published in 1861, was composed by Englishman, Rev. John Bacchus Dykes, Episcopaleon.

Morning Has Broken, (1931 Christian Hymn of Praise) Lyrics by Eleanor Farjeon, United Kingdom. Traditional Scottish Melody, "Bunessan"

Referral only: **The Great Mandella** (The Wheel of Life) from ALBUM 1700. Copyright 1967, Peter Yarrow, Warner Bros. Records, Inc.

Referral only: **Masters of War** from Bob Dylan's Greatest Hits Copyright 1963 - Columbia Records/CBS Records, Inc.

CHECK OUT OTHER BOOKS by GERALD MacLENNON:

Available in Paperback or Kindle eBook at:
Amazon, Barnes & Noble, Kindle, Createspace, Walmart
& other book retailers in the USA, Europe, Ireland, U.K. & Japan

Muffet & the Dust Storm: Story of an Iowa Farm Girl during the Drought and Depression of the 1930's – by Norma Hilding

Wrestling with Angels: An Anthology of Prose & Poetry 1962 thru 2017 also inside: **God, Peace, Love & Music,** a sequel

GOD ✪ BOMBS & VIET NAM
Based on the Diary of a 20-Year-Old Navy Enlisted Man in the Vietnam Air War - 1967

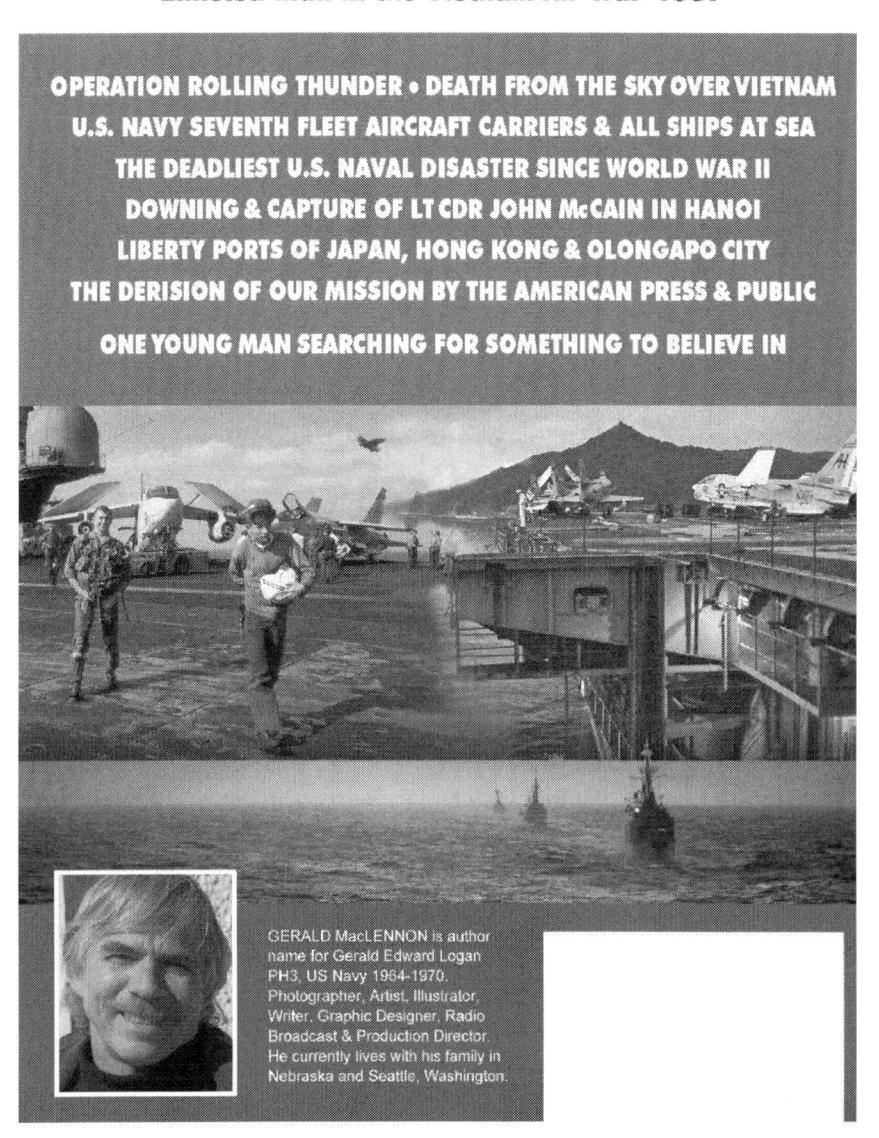

OPERATION ROLLING THUNDER • DEATH FROM THE SKY OVER VIETNAM
U.S. NAVY SEVENTH FLEET AIRCRAFT CARRIERS & ALL SHIPS AT SEA
THE DEADLIEST U.S. NAVAL DISASTER SINCE WORLD WAR II
DOWNING & CAPTURE OF LT CDR JOHN McCAIN IN HANOI
LIBERTY PORTS OF JAPAN, HONG KONG & OLONGAPO CITY
THE DERISION OF OUR MISSION BY THE AMERICAN PRESS & PUBLIC

ONE YOUNG MAN SEARCHING FOR SOMETHING TO BELIEVE IN

GERALD MacLENNON is author name for Gerald Edward Logan PH3, US Navy 1964-1970. Photographer, Artist, Illustrator, Writer, Graphic Designer, Radio Broadcast & Production Director. He currently lives with his family in Nebraska and Seattle, Washington.

Made in the USA
Columbia, SC
23 February 2018